RENOVATING YOUR OWN HOME

A Step-by-Step Guide

David Caldwell

Stoddart

Published in 1996 by
Stoddart Publishing Co. Limited
34 Lesmill Road
Toronto, Canada
M3B 2T6
Tel. (416) 445-3333
Fax (416) 445-5967

Stoddart Books are available for bulk purchase for sales promotions, premiums, fundraising, and seminars. For details, contact the Special Sales Department at the above address.

Canadian Cataloguing in Publication Data

Caldwell, David, 1950–
Renovating your own home: a step-by-step guide

Includes index.
ISBN 0-7737-5802-X

1. Dwellings – Remodeling – Amateurs' manuals.
I. Title

TH4816.C35 1996   643'.7   C95-933305-3

The author and publisher take no responsibility for the use of any materials or methods described in this book, nor for the products thereof.

Cover design: the boy 100 & Tannice Goddard
Cover photograph: Peter Paterson

Printed and bound in Canada

Stoddart Publishing gratefully acknowledges the support of the Canada Council and the Ontario Arts Council in the development of writing and publishing in Canada.

To My Wife

for her patience and understanding during the years
of research and writing involved in this book,
and her continued trust, patience, and persistence, which
provided me with the incentive to continue,

and

to all the families who accept the many challenges
placed on them during the planning, demolition, and
construction phases of a renovation project.

Contents

PART II: WHO SHOULD BUILD FOR YOU?

PART III: PLANNING THE RENOVATION DESIGN

PART V: AFTER THE RENOVATION

PART VI: OTHER OPTIONS

INTRODUCTION

A house grows old so gradually that we seldom notice the small signs of age. Pollution and climatic changes speed the aging process of the structure; poor ventilation strategies in older homes lack the basic energy-efficient products of today, creating many common problems such as window condensation, rotting wood, mildewed walls, and peeling paint.

When family lifestyles and needs change, and home owners realize that portions of the home have fallen into disrepair, their initial plan may be to sell. As housing costs have increased dramatically throughout North America, the thought of selling the present house and purchasing a new energy-efficient home seems to be a financial stretch for more and more young couples. They are now likely to reassess and renovate the existing home. Too often these experiences end up with disastrous results for the consumer.

Where does one start? Renovating an existing home differs significantly from the new home construction model in several areas. The owners must consider many factors, including existing bug, water, and structural problems and the need to hire an inspection service. Specific questions for potential renovators include: Will a renovation result in overbuilding for the area? Can the expansion go to the front, back, and/or sides? Is a second story addition a possibility, and will the existing structure support this expansion? Should they just upgrade by adding a bay window or replacing part or all of the old, inoperable windows with energy-efficient units? Should they replace the roof? Should they remodel the kitchen or just update the drawer and door faces?

It is the intent of this book to provide the average person with answers to these questions and more. By providing basic building information, this book will guide potential lay contractors through the various stages of construction scheduling with problem resolutions to save the money usually paid to the builder or contract managers as supervising costs and profit. For those who do not wish to take on the full responsibility, and plan to have a contractor renovate the home, a step-by-step guide would assist them to follow, understand, and supervise the contractor's work.

In this book I have placed special emphasis on clearly presenting the material so that people with little or no previous building experience will understand it. In order to successfully supervise and/or organize a renovation project, the layman would require an up-to-date manual carefully supplemented with illustrations to clarify the text, and detailed examples of the construction process, descriptions of the work needed, specifications, and checklists. All information needed is presented in a practical, easy-to-follow, step-by-step format.

Renovating a house can be both a demanding and time-intensive task; however, by using a common-sense application of construction knowledge you will experience a new sense of confidence and gratification. You *can* expect to build a home to fit your own personal needs and suit *your* lifestyle.

PART I: RENOVATION CONCEPTS

CHAPTER 1

◆ WHY RENOVATE?

• Three Types of Renovation

Inevitably, during the life of a house, the question of whether to upgrade the house's exterior and/or interior appearance will arise. This usually happens after the effects of normal wear and tear, weathering, and family lifestyle changes require you to maintain, upgrade or alter the house's appearance. Your need could be as simple and inexpensive as painting the window trim, or as expensive as adding a second floor or extending portions of the main floor.

Before deciding to take on the task of financing any type of renovation, first determine that you have a good reason for this course of action. It might be that your family has grown out of the existing house, but you live in a desirable area, you have many friends there, you are located close to work, or shopping is convenient. All these concerns and more must be carefully addressed before proceeding with the thought of renovating. Only one of these might provide sufficient reason to renovate, but all avenues should be investigated to ensure this decision is the correct one.

Depending upon the extent of work proposed, the renovation can be classified into one of three basic categories: maintaining, upgrading, or remodeling.

- Maintaining the house is an essential activity. It serves to safeguard your investment by protecting the exterior structure of the house against the deteriorating effects of the winter winds and summer sun and correcting the normal wear-and-tear abuses that occur inside the home. Maintaining includes everything from simple caulking or painting the siding or interior walls, to installing new maintenance-free gutters or replacing a weathered roof or damaged carpet. These simple renovations are fairly inexpensive, but serve to retain the structural integrity and streetscape appearance of the home.

- Upgrading is usually required when the exterior and interior of the house are starting to significantly show its age, or when the lifestyle of the family changes. This type of renovation brings the existing interior and exterior appearance, and functional workability of the house up-to-date with family needs. As the family grows and changes, the requirements of the individual family members will also change. You may need to develop the basement to provide for bedrooms, bathrooms, study, games room, or family room which will add more practical living space for the growing family. The replacement of inadequate, old-fashioned, inefficient kitchen cabinets and appliances is usually done during this renovation stage, and may include, as well, the removal of the old steel bathtubs in favor of a modern whirlpool tub or shower enclosure. As the house ages the materials used during the initial construction will become outdated. More options are now available for upgrading, and many families choose to replace the high-maintenance wood finishes with low or zero maintenance products such as aluminum or vinyl sidings, gutters, soffits and windows. These types of renovations will obviously cost more, and may require a short-term bank loan.

- Remodeling the existing house goes beyond the general maintenance and upgrading of the structure. It usually involves any one or all of the following: tearing down the existing structure, adding a main or upper floor area to the house, upgrading the insulation factor of walls and roof, upgrading or adding new electrical wiring and/or new heating systems, and/or replacing an extensive amount of old cabinets, appliances, and fixtures. These decisions should be made only after full investigation of the property's potential assets and limitations.

Since this type of renovation will require substantial capital to complete, it is essential that you know the home's present weaknesses and strengths, the future needs of your family, how the renovation will affect the family, and if it can be done within your current financial budget. Some of the answers to the first question can be found by contacting the building inspector of the development department at your area's city hall. That person will inform you of the legal limitations imposed on the property. Additionally, a detailed report can be obtained by hiring a service specializing in home and property inspections. Such inspectors are qualified to inspect the existing structure, listen to your ideas, and then recommend if all, part, or none of your renovation ideas can be successfully completed within your budget and according to the local building code. Their report will provide an objective assessment of your home's present strengths and weaknesses. With this knowledge you will be better able to decide if you wish to proceed with renovating, or consider another alternative such as upgrading or selling.

Naturally, the information that you must provide to the inspection service will have to be detailed enough for them to make an accurate and professional assessment of your house, property, and family's present and future needs. Their recommendations should reflect the length of time your growing family would be able to live in the house, the extent of optimal renovation, and the advantages/disadvantages of the location of the existing property. If the renovation is expensive, when the time comes to sell you may not recoup the investment because you have overbuilt for the area, a significant consideration. Depending upon the existing resale market within your area, you may find it financially more acceptable and wise to make some minor repairs, and sell the existing house and property in order to purchase a larger, more workable home within the same area, or build a new home in another subdivision.

- **Is the Renovation Feasible?**

Prior to purchasing your present home you drove through many neighborhoods before making the decision to purchase. What was it that impressed you about the area and the house? Was it the location of the development, access to amenities, treed boulevards and parks, and style and upkeep of the homes? Reflect back to your initial visual impression of the neighborhood. Have the characteristics of the streetscape significantly changed over the years?

A maintained, positive impression of the existing neighborhood will have a great effect on the future value of the individual homes. A subdivision that has owner-occupied homes usually means greater effort has been taken in maintaining a pleasant appearance and promoting quality renovations that will sustain the subdivision's appeal. Based on prior building styles, lot sizes, and budgets, many of the older subdivisions have gradually developed unique characteristics. Neighbors, in the absence of architectural controls, have usually had advance, casual discussion with other neighbors and unconsciously set their own design standards. When this discussion forum does not exist, no control or subdivision standard setting exists either. This may be very obvious in some residential areas where neighbors are not obliged to inform others of the extent and design of their proposed renovations.

Many city development departments now require that all parties who will be affected by a renovation building permit application be informed of this application so that everyone has the opportunity to address their concerns to the development officer for consideration. If the renovation does not conform to the city's set standards of house-to-lot coverage, structure, design, visual appearance, and the neighbors' concerns, the application will probably be rejected. The renovator will then have the option to appeal and present his argument to a development appeal board. The board members will listen to all parties and provide a verbal judgment followed by one in writing to all parties affected. They will approve the application as is, approve it with changes, reject the application, or request another application with a new design. Because the involved re-application and appeal process can consume a great deal of time, it is strongly recommended that when researching your design requirements, you check with the local city development officer or engineering department to confirm the site coverage, property setbacks, design, structure, and application requirements before going to a designer.

Zoning restrictions in older neighborhoods are usually set by the city, and sometimes developers will request a zoning change especially if adjacent residential or commercial structures suffer from poor maintenance and upkeep. The city may then approve a rezoning request by the developer to change an area from a single-family, low density development to a high density, multi-family, row housing complex. Therefore, when checking municipal building guidelines, also ask for information on the existing and proposed by-law changes to the subdivision to reduce the potential for undesirable development of the neighboring properties. Make sure that all adjacent properties to your home and the subdivision are zoned to your benefit and not subject to change based on the city's known expansion and redevelopment plans.

Another very important factor that many people fail to consider when first thinking about renovating an existing home is the impact the renovation will have on the property taxes. Will the taxes increase so dramatically that the family's budget will be harmed? Taxes are based not only on the size or frontage of the lot, but also rated according to the size or square footage of the home and the home's special features, e.g., skylights, roof finish, whirlpool or hot tub, deck size, tile floors, fireplaces, and other items that the city tax department would consider an upgrade.

- **Proper Drainage**

Have you had any problems with poor drainage such as wet or damp basement floors, pooling of water on the property, or a musty smell in the basement? Any of these occurrences may signal a water table problem, failure of the weeping tiles, cracks in the foundation, or poor property drainage. Weeping tile failure resulting in basement leakage is a significant financial addition to the renovation budget. After a 20-year life the weeping tile system is usually defunct and may require replacement. Foundation settling and subsequent cracks may also result in wet basement floors. Have these problem areas thoroughly inspected prior to any extensive basement development. (See Inspection Checklist, page 30.)

Drainage problems commonly exist in older areas as the soil around the house goes through its settling cycle and gradually reverses the drainage direction toward the home. You can confirm this by checking the slope of any sidewalks in close proximity to the home's foundation wall or whether the flower beds need a yearly addition of soil to bring them back up to the sidewalk level. When these factors are present, consider budgeting for the landscaping of the affected property.

The first 7 to 10 feet of earth surrounding the house perimeter should slope away from the foundation with a minimum 5 to 6 inch drop. The landscaping should allow the water collected by the eavestrough gutters and basement sump pump to naturally drain away from the house toward the street or some other drainage area that will not adversely affect neighboring properties. Overall, including the driveway and sidewalks, there should be a minimum of one to two feet of grade slope from the finished grade of the house to the lowest finished grade at the property line. Sump pits in older areas were allowed to drain directly into the storm sewer; however, because of the concern about water and sewer backup, many cities now require new home

construction and renovation projects to provide a hose
connection from the sump to the city gutter. Inside the
house a plastic pipe system will direct the water to the
outside of the house from which point a flexible hose
directs the water to the front of the property and the
city gutter. People who feel the flexible hose is an
eyesore will choose to install a gravel bed with a

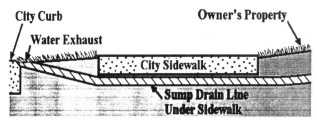

Figure 1-1. Sump drain line under city sidewalk.

three-inch rigid pipe sunk about six inches under the finished grade. Given the property's natural slope to
drain, the pipe will become visible only at the city curb yet allow the water to flow by gravity (see Figure 1-1).

When driving through the newer subdivisions located on flat land, you will notice that sometimes the
developer during the rough grading has placed a continuous earth burm at the rear of the lots to direct the
groundwater or runoff to the front of the lot, hence providing proper drainage. These back-to-front sloping lots
were usually not provided for in the older subdivisions. If you feel that doing this would eliminate any water
problems, have the landscape designer include in his estimate a detailed drawing of strategic earth burming of
the finished grades for permit approval.

To achieve the proper drainage requirements some rural lots will need a culvert pipe at the end of the
property line where the driveway and city street connect. In order to ensure proper installation, some
developers and city inspectors will require the department of highways to install this pipe, with the cost paid
back over a period of time via property taxes. Check with the local city/county engineering department or
development officer for the required culvert size and installation requirements.

Note: Always keep in mind a maintenance-free aspect when having your property landscaped. Doing so
will make it more enjoyable and place fewer work demands on your weekend and holiday time.

- **Sewer Problems**

Many older areas are subject to sewer backups which are usually due to overgrown tree roots blocking the
flow in the older clay tile drains from the home to the city's sewer line. If this has been a problem, or another
bathroom or a garbage compactor is planned in the renovation, the home inspection will indicate if the sewer
pipe is the proper size, in good repair, and clear of any roots or other objects that will impede flow. These
problems will not occur in newer homes as the sewer lines are now manufactured of plastic which will not
corrode or allow the tree roots to enter and create blockages. If the renovation includes an addition or an
updating of washroom facilities, it would be a good idea to have the old tile replaced with the new plastic
maintenance-free lines. Should you decide to leave the old tiles in place, sometime in the future they will get
blocked or possibly crushed by the home's natural settling. Chances of this happening will increase if you have
trees or add shrubs to the landscaping plan as the tree/shrub roots will naturally grow toward concentrations of
water in the sewage lines. When this happens, the home owner, not the city, must pay for service or replace the
blocked pipes on the property. In some cities if the roots of the trees on your property block the sewer system
that is between the property line and the main city sewer, it is the city who will have to remove the blockage.
However, because the blockage was caused by *your* trees, the city will invoice you for the service call and any
repairs required to that portion of the sewer. This is why many home owners elect to remove and replace the
older sewer lines.

Contact the city's engineering department for a copy of the subdivision's utility plan that will show the
depth of the current sewer and water lines (see Figure 1-2), and where they connect to the main lines. The city
inspector or designated land surveyor will then be able to tell you where the proposed footings will need to be

in conjunction with the sewer line, and ensure that the city's sewer connection will be lower than the bottom of the proposed renovation footings. If new sewer and water lines are required, you will save money if the two lines can be trenched at the same time when tying in these utilities to the house. Refer to Chapter 12, pages 124-26 for more information.

Figure 1-2. Location of sewer line for proper slope.

After determining the sewer line is the correct depth and size, it would also be a good idea to contact the city's sanitation department to request a scope of both the sewer and water lines from the house to the city's main. Scoping allows the sanitation worker to view inside the lines to see if there are any line separations, tree roots or other blockages which might cause a future problem years after renovating. In most areas this municipal service is free, but it is always wise to ask about charges.

If you are living in a rural area where the water supply is from a well and the sewage is distributed by a septic system, make sure that these two pipes are separated to eliminate any contamination of the drinking water. A friend of mine told a story of a potential disaster that occurred in a 40-year-old farm home she purchased in a small acreage subdivision. The previous owner was a handyman and jack of all trades, and based on his many talents, he chose to build and contract all the construction work himself. He however lacked the capital to do a proper job, and the county at that time did not have sanitation regulations for septic systems. To meet his budget requirements he excavated a single trench to contain both the water and sewer lines. The new owner was not informed of this shortcut at the time of purchase. She knew that the house would need some upgrades in the next few years, but she felt that they would be minor and within her budget.

Three months after moving in she encountered some problems with the water pressure and called in a plumber. After a preliminary inspection he informed her that everything inside the house structure was OK; however, in order for the water pressure to drop so drastically there must be a leak in the outside line. He indicated he could hear running water just outside the foundation wall, and questioned the location of the water line as it entered the house in the same area as the septic system line.

The plumber returned the next day with a backhoe to excavate the area around the suspected leak, and found the water line had cracked. He also found the sewer line was directly under the water line. He told the owner that had she not noticed the water pressure drop, the trench which holds the water and sewer line could have filled with water, and if a leak developed in the sewer line, her water would have been contaminated. He also informed her that because the new building codes require the water and sewer lines to be separated, he would have to inform the county inspector of the problem who then would require her to move either the water or the sewer line at her expense. She called her lawyer to see if legal action could be taken to have the previous owner pay for this expense, but was informed that he could not be held responsible: when he installed the water and sewer lines no regulation required him to separate the lines. In addition, he had no obligation to inform her, especially if he was not informed of the change in the building code, and she had no way of proving that he knew of the change. Once she accepted ownership of the home any repairs under the new building code became her responsibility. Before buying the home she should have hired an inspection service to check the home top to bottom. This service would have saved her thousands because she could have deducted this expense from the offer to purchase, or required the owner to have the service work done to code at his expense prior to possession.

Note: If you have to provide new water and sewer lines to the home, consider locating the city water-service valve, which regulates the amount of water pressure going into the house, in an area where it can be easily accessed yet out of the way when cutting your grass or digging a garden. Its usual location is in the driveway pad.

- **Maintaining the Streetscape**

Houses on a residential street should be seen as a group and not as isolated buildings. The streetscape of a subdivision depends on the collective appearance of all the houses, with each contributing to a common pleasing blending of roof types, house styles, and features which benefits neighboring houses (see Figure 1-3). A controlled streetscape projects a restful and harmonious quality when the features of houses of similar architectural styles are blended with one another. Since the most functional and effective renovations are those that are simple in shape with clean lines, when contemplating a renovation, think first of the general shape and proportion in simple lines rather than in detail. For example, consider first the completed home's length to its height and width as these proportions can be tastefully accented with well-designed entrances and window features.

Figure 1-3. Streetscape showing houses with visual balance.

You will have noted that architectural styles like fashions in clothes change over time. Admired original creations are usually imitated and perpetuated in styles such as Tudor, Cape Cod, Georgian, Western Ranch, Colonial, and Californian. If you have a creative designer, these established architectural styles, roof-lines, and features can be used effectively to capture a unique quality that will allow the house renovation to look different from the neighbors' homes. Remember for resale that the finished value of the renovated home will depend on its distinct curb appeal. Details such as colors and finishes for the trim, roof, exterior cladding, fence and ornamentation can then be chosen as the blending agents with the adjacent styles.

Be wary of listening to a builder or designer for your renovation who drives through your subdivision to gather ideas, and suggests that imitating another renovation house style will create a balance within the subdivision. This is frequently done if the shape and features of the house are visually attractive and cheap to construct, but this does not prioritize your needs and preferences, and is not very professional practice. When several reproductions of a trendy style have been constructed on the same street, the effect is not one of quality but of mediocrity and monotony. Remember, fads do not usually remain around very long. A good designer or contractor will not choose to simply reproduce other creative house styles, but will use effective roof-lines, walkways, entry designs, and other individualized finishing features. Beware of tradespeople who are often only profit driven. They will potentially overcharge when dressing up a house front with, for example, bay windows, garden windows, or adding a false roof-line. A copy cat effect is not the best way to maintain a unique and quality streetscape. When planning even a minor renovation project, request the builder/designer to be imaginative in design, and direct them to create a renovation streetscape that will complement the area by introducing a new look with proper balance between new and old.

CHAPTER 2

◆ USING THE SUN'S HEAT

● Window Locations

There has long been a demand for energy and the sun has consistently been considered the primary long term source. Recognizing the potential to harness and utilize the sun's heat has sent environmentalists scurrying to gain information on how to construct solar devices. Some options are simple and inexpensive while others require major structural and financial investments.

Local and regional differences exist

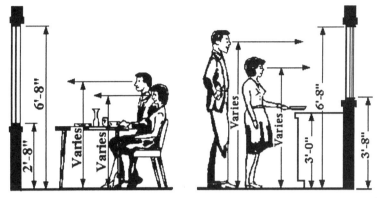

Figure 2-1. Good window sizes/locations for dinette and kitchen.

across North America, yet contemporary window styles even with updated design changes have certain basic characteristics. Almost every home possesses some sort of passive solar window effect. Consider the addition or renovation project as an opportunity to incorporate energy-saving features that were not considered or available when the house was built. Large windows, always very fashionable, can be incorporated into the design at surprisingly little cost, and made more attractive by efficient heating systems and window designs. There are definite dos and don'ts to the proper size and location of windows (see Figures 2-1 and 2-2).

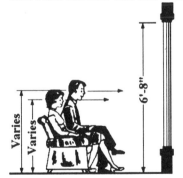

Figure 2-2. A good living and family area view.

1) Do locate and position the windows to take maximum advantage of the sun's radiant heat.

2) Do locate windows for security purposes away from a main street view into the house.

3) Do take advantage of garden views as this will bring the outdoors into the house.

4) Do not have glass areas facing north unless unavoidable. Then consider using triple-glazed or reflective windows to keep the heating costs down in the winter.

Windows located on the east, south and west exposures will assist with heating the house during the winter and are considered a significant form of passive solar heating. The resultant fuel savings can be as much as 30 percent (see Figure 2-3). When planning room locations for the renovation, remember the ideal position for large glass areas is on the south or southeast side of the house. Windows facing east and south get virtually the same amount of sunlight as those facing west, but during the early part of the day the sun's rays are cooler and the ultraviolet rays are not as strong. This is very important during the summer months. At sundown the windows that

Figure 2-3. Location of the winter sun.

face west admit the sun's hotter rays into a room on an angle which causes the overheating known as the greenhouse effect (see Figure 2-4). There is now available a very good selection of solar-backed vertical and venetian blinds, so that windows can face southwest and west without concern for overheating. Window manufacturers have solar-reflecting glass which has become very popular for south and west facing glassed areas. This reflective glass will virtually eliminate the summer greenhouse effect in your home, but expect to pay from 25 to 40 percent more on the window order for this luxury. But the glass will pay for itself within a few years by sometimes eliminating the need for home air-conditioning, and acting as an insulator during the colder months.

Figure 2-4. Location of the summer sun.

Having resided in the home you will be familiar with the prevailing wind patterns. Avoid placing large glassed areas on sides of the house which face north or face the winter winds, or plan to block the wind's force with strategic tree planting. Unless you install triple glazing and/or additional insulation, the windows will frost and heating bills will rise considerably.

- **Passive or Active Solar?**

There are two types of solar heat and energy collecting systems: passive and active.

Passive systems include design features such as strategically located windows, skylights, and solarium rooms which work in combination with heat-absorbing materials to store the heat until it can be used. Natural and man-made materials, such as masonry and stone, collect and retain heat, and when incorporated into the house design as walls or floors, they will gradually radiate heat into the home long after the sun has set. Some of these passive solar-collecting materials, when combined with a thick plastic, water-storage containment tank, will have a greater holding capacity and longer duration over which they release the heat into the house.

Active systems are more expensive and feature more technically advanced methods of storing and distributing the collected energy. Active solar products are more recognized by markets that have government-assisted energy programs or are in the southern climate zones where winter heating requirements are reduced to weeks. When traveling through these areas, you will recognize rectangular solar collectors strategically positioned on roofs or walls in order to collect the greatest amount of solar heat. Heat from the sun is drawn from the panels into the tubing which heats and circulates air or liquid to heat a hot water tank, Alternatively, the heat may be transferred to a storage device and then mechanically distributed throughout the building using air ducts or piping. Active systems, such as photovoltaic cells, though very expensive, will directly convert the sun's energy to electricity which, in turn, will provide sufficient power for some mechanical devices to heat small areas for short periods of time, or supply power for other needs.

- **Selecting Your Windows**

Windows are a necessary and important part of your home. They are essential to allow light and air into your home, but they are also an important part of the architectural design. Excessive window spans, common in older homes, should be avoided in the addition area especially if there is direct exposure to cold winter winds. As much as twice the amount of heat is lost through large expanses of windows as an equivalent area of insulated wall. Generally, a total glass area equal to 12 percent of the floor area of the house is adequate. In living areas, the glass area should be about 12 percent of the floor area; in bedroom areas, this can be reduced to about 5 percent, but at least one bedroom window should have an opener for air exchange, and be adequately sized for an emergency exit.

Because of cheap fuel costs many windows of older homes were manufactured with single-or double-pane glass and products with no consideration for energy efficiency. They were installed using simple foam seals, putty, and metal frames which over the years have failed or deteriorated. The wood frames fail due to condensation on the aluminum sliding-window sections which causes them to corrode, leaving the window inoperable. These units should be replaced with maintenance-free and energy-efficient product. Picture windows with large areas of exposed glass should also be replaced with energy-efficient, triple-pane windows, or protruding multi-pane bow, box or bay windows, or variations of multiple flat window designs. Installing a bay or bow window in these areas will also provide a three-dimensional streetscape to the home and give the appearance of added width and space to the interior of the room.

Energy-conscious home builders must be aware of what to look for when choosing replacement windows. Homes have much better insulation than in the past, and people think that windows have kept up with this technology. However, this is not always the case. Glass is still a poor insulator. People who never had condensation before the installation of energy-efficient windows and extra insulation in the roof area are now experiencing that problem. Since the insulation standards have been upgraded for the addition and other parts of the existing house, the warm, moist air is retained in the home, and then deposited on the windows. If the house is unable to breathe or not receiving a sufficient exchange of air during the cold months, condensation and sometimes frost will form on the inside of the window; frost will melt and then run down onto the sill and into the walls causing water damage. This potential problem can be eliminated with effective air circulation by leaving the furnace fans on during the colder winter months, or adding an air exchanger to the furnace duct system.

In response to the ever-changing energy standards required by the construction industry, window manufacturers have adapted their window units to easily fit the older window rough-opening sizes which allows upgrading of the old, inefficient wood or aluminum windows. They provide both standard and custom window sizes as a window "retrofit" for the home renovator. Provide them with an existing rough-opening size or the dimensions of the proposed space to be filled, and they will build a new window unit to fit.

Note: If you are able to work within their standard window sizes you will be able to save between 10 and 25 percent as opposed to ordering and paying for a custom window size. When it comes time to choose new windows, these three things should come to mind: the efficiency and practicality of the window, delivery schedule, and of course, the price. Unfortunately, the best windows are usually the most expensive which usually follows with practically anything we purchase.

Never has there been a greater variety of windows from which to choose. They come in all shapes, sizes and designs with different types of window materials, glazing and weatherstripping. How do you select the window that is right for you? Consider several criteria: your budget, the proposed architectural style of your home, and your needs. Does the window give you the light, ventilation, or view that you want? Is the window well insulated and weatherproofed? Will it be easy to operate and maintain?

In order to knowledgeably choose energy-efficient windows, visit several suppliers as all the brands and types available will be displayed in their show rooms. At first glance the windows may look very different because of the variety of sizes, shapes and different mechanical opening methods. However, they will fall into the three basic categories of casement, fixed, or awning. Once you have completed your window shopping, base the final decision about whom to ask for estimates on your own research.

Note: Before placing your order, discuss with the sales representative the policy for late delivery and back ordering because of overbooking or broken windows while in transit. Will they repair and install the windows, or will they pay for the framer (who will have to return after he has completed his contract) to install the windows? Most manufacturers have their own service people; therefore have them include this service in their estimate so that you will not have to pay extra for something that is no fault of your own.

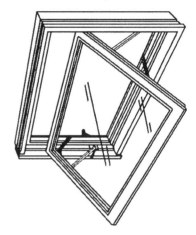

Window styles:

For efficient venting, window styles such as casement or awning are chosen. **Casement windows** hinge on one side, either left or right, and open with a lever or crank to be held in place with a locking hinge lever. This window type can be opened just a fraction of an inch, or completely perpendicular to the house wall depending on your ventilation or cleaning requirements (see Figure 2-5). Because of their method of operation, casement windows are ideal for counters and hard-to-reach areas, and can be cleaned from inside the house. By installing a casement unit on either

Figure 2-5. Casement window.

side of a fixed, center picture unit, direct and/or indirect ventilation of the room can be accomplished. When the wind is blowing from the left to the right, the left casement unit is opened, causing air to be blown directly into the room; if the right casement unit is opened, the exterior wind acts as a vacuum pulling the interior air outside. Having both windows open allows for almost 100 percent exchange of room air. Even during storms a casement window can be open to allow for ventilation without letting in water.

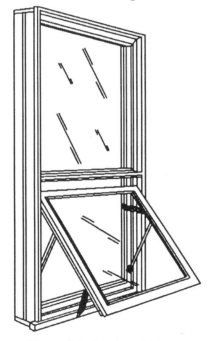

Awning windows are very similar to casement except the hinge is on the top, and they open from the bottom much like an awning, hence the name. Since top-hinged windows direct air downward, they are best placed high in the wall, and are particularly suitable for basements. In areas receiving a lot of rain this style of window can be left open without fear of rain entering the home, which allows continual air ventilation depending on the sash opening. Depending on the angle of the sash, an awning can also direct air upward into a room (see Figure 2-6). Because it opens upward the open sash is exposed to the elements and requires more frequent washings than any other type of operating unit.

A disadvantage to both the casement and awning windows is the screens which are fastened to the inside and hinder fast exits during an emergency. Also the window units open out. Consequently, if the window is opening above a sidewalk or onto a balcony, it presents an obstruction to people walking by, or if on a second story, it could cause a problem for cleaning if someone has a fear of heights. These disadvantages are minimized by the advantages of having good ventilation, excellent weather seal, pleasing architectural appearance, and simplicity of opening.

Figure 2-6. Awning window.

Window materials:

Windows should outlast your home if they are constructed and installed properly from good quality materials. They may be constructed of wood, aluminum, steel, vinyl, or for improved weathering and insulation, a combination of several of these materials. Though windows with better weather protection are more expensive, they can pay off in energy savings.

- *Wood* windows are warm, traditional, aesthetically pleasing, and in themselves a good insulator. They are also considered the least expensive. When combined with vinyl or aluminum they are the best insulated, and rated moderate maintenance.
- *Aluminum* windows, being more durable than wood, are also thinner, lighter, and easier to handle. When properly insulated they are energy efficient and virtually maintenance-free.
- *Vinyl* windows, being the most durable of all the window materials, are lightweight, and considered the most maintenance-free of all finishes. However, with all these benefits they are the most expensive.

Window technology:

Windows, usually the weakest link in the energy system of any house, have seen dramatic increases in performance thanks to space age technology. Research that has been conducted with window coatings has shown that a reflective film when applied to the inside glass can radically improve window efficiency. The reflective film filters sunlight of which only 50 percent is visible to the human eye, and blocks infra-red and ultraviolet radiation, both of which are invisible to humans. Radiant heat, or infra-red radiation, is the heat felt if you hold your hand near a hot object. The reflective film prevents its leaving the house in winter.

It not only chops heat loss in half, but also creates additional comfort for home owners. When the interior glass panes are significantly warmer, there are no cold convection currents of air that produce cold drafts and condensation. By using reflective windows, not only the rate of heat loss is reduced, but the reverse is true. Because this film blocks heat from coming into the house in summer, it reduces heat buildup, and consequently the size of cooling equipment required. Therefore, significant savings on mechanical equipment can be realized. By blocking ultraviolet light which causes furniture, fabrics, and upholstery to fade, the home owner's investments are further protected.

Note: During construction to further reduce heat loss have the framer put a bead of flexible silicone around the perimeter of the tar paper before the window frame is nailed to the exterior wall.

- **Sliding Patio Doors**

Patio or sliding doors have been installed in homes because of their ability to allow more light into the house, enlarge the appearance of a small room, and provide a convenient door access to a deck, balcony, or garden terrace. The operable portion also has a sliding screen section which when open allows for a flood of air into the room. Because this type of door slides to one side, it does not require any clearance for the opening either in the room or outside. Also, the door can be in any position from closed to fully open, and it will not move in a gust of wind.

When selecting a patio door for your renovation, consider airtightness, and check to ensure the opening portion of the door is on the outside of the fixed panel. This will create a thermal-insulating quality because the pressure of the wind seals the panel tightly against the weatherstripping. For security purposes, check the locking mechanism of the vertical adjustments to eliminate the up-or-down movement of the door, and most important, look for a secure locking device. Many burglaries occur through patio doors because of their ease of access by jimmying the lock or lifting the door off the track (see security in Chapter 12, pages 179-80).

Some patio doors come with three or four panels which allows two of the panels to move to one side, or in opposite directions which provides a wider opening for moving furniture or allowing two people to pass each other in the doorway.

- **Renovating with Skylights**

Skylights, or roof windows, can help transform the appearance of a hallway, bedroom, office, or working area. Adding them is a very practical way to brighten normally dark and dingy areas of the home, and bring the outdoors indoors yet retain privacy. Older homes look more modern and appealing which can only add to their house value and marketability.

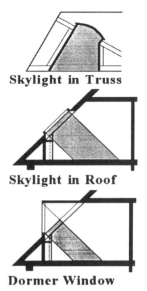

Skylight in Truss

Skylight in Roof

Dormer Window

Figure 2-7. Natural light entering rooms.

The primary function of skylights, which are sealed or roof windows which can open, is to provide maximum natural light into an area that would normally be dark and unattractive. Because skylights are aligned with the angle of the roof they allow more than four times more light into that living space than vertical windows, eg., a dormer window (see Figure 2-7). In homes with skylights, plants seem to grow faster no matter where they are placed in the room. Many of the roof windows are designed to open, permitting more flexibility in the design and placement of the rooms in the renovation project. These units, commonly used to ventilate bathrooms, kitchens, or any area with potential heat collection, will require a pole or mechanical motor to open and close them. When combined with a few open windows, an open skylight will allow heat and moisture to escape, thus cooling down the house and eliminating the cost for mechanical air conditioning.

Skylights offer a practical method of energy efficiency. They can be installed by a carpenter, roofer, or skilled do-it-yourselfer who can open the roof in the morning and have it closed in and weatherproofed by that evening. After the installation you will notice some temperature change in the room as the skylights can act as a solar collector to let in the sun's light and heat during the winter, and slow the loss of heat at night. When

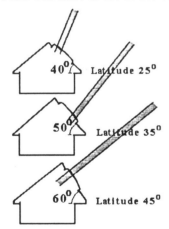

Figure 2-8. Orientation of skylight to proper latitude angles.

skylights, like windows, are oriented south or within 20^0 east or west of true south, they admit the maximum amount of the sun's heat in winter. For optimum solar gain, tilt the skylight toward the south at an angle of the area's latitude plus 15^0 (see Figure 2-8). This can be accomplished easily if you have a pitched roof, but if the roof is flat, mount a reflector on the north side of the installation so the low-angled sun is reflected back through the skylight.

Skylights come with clear or tinted glazing in colors including solar bronze, white, or translucent, and with single, double, or triple glazing. The bronze or gray tinted glazing produces less glare and heat than a clear unit; clear glazing admits the maximum amount of light and heat into a room. Clarity of the view and solar benefit will mean nothing if you place the skylight under a tree since dirt and debris will collect on it, presenting a never-ending cleaning problem. If the skylight is sizable you may wish to shade it with solar blinds on the inside or choose translucent glazing to reduce unwanted solar overheating in summer. However, an added bonus for many U.S. home owners is that a south-facing skylight with clear glazing is considered a passive solar device, and tax credits are allowed by some local government agencies for its installation.

Installing skylights onto existing roofs will require a light shaft, and the space between the roof and the ceiling and the roof slope will determine whether a straight, angled, or splayed

Figure 2-9. Different light shaft configurations for a sloped roof.

shaft is needed (see Figure 2-9). In a straight light shaft the skylight sits directly above the ceiling opening, in an angled light shaft the skylight is positioned off to one side of the ceiling opening, and in a splayed light shaft the ceiling opening can be installed larger than the roof opening. In the latter the skylight will sit above or to the side of the opening which will allow more natural light to enter the room.

The most economical and usually the most reliable choice of skylight is a prefabricated unit. Manufacturers offer skylights in a variety of shapes, sizes, and glazing with fixed and opening designs. Shapes vary from square to circular. Product may be glass or plastic for a flat unit, however domed or pyramidal shapes are usually plastic because that material molds easily to complex shapes, and can be manufactured in sizes from one small enough to fit between two trusses to one large enough to roof a small room. Several skylights can be combined to form one larger unit in appearance. Avoid flat skylights in areas where it will snow; domed and pyramidal shapes are better for supporting snowloads especially if the roof slope is the typical 4 in 12.

- **Solarium and Greenhouse Additions**

Sunrooms, atriums, greenhouses or rooftop gardens go as far back as Roman times. The modern lifestyle with more leisure time catapulted the sunroom and atrium into widespread popularity because they lend themselves well to either renovation or new home construction. With a sunny location, such a room is a winter heat source, and with proper ventilation it becomes a summer out-of-doors porch without the need for mosquito or bug repellants.

The design flexibility of manufactured sunrooms allows them to be incorporated into almost any renovation project. Glass features give a sense of spaciousness to the home, and allow spectacular views of the stars, garden or terrace all year round. Sunrooms are also private protected places for dining out, winding down, doing hobbies, exercising, or just lounging around (see Figure 2-10).

This type of indoor/outdoor living area can be incorporated or retrofitted into the shell of the existing building to create a new living environment without additional square footage. The renovation project could be as simple as a wall of windows, or more extensive, such as

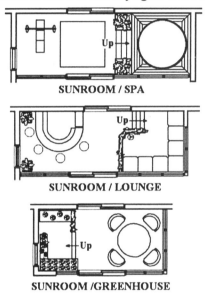

SUNROOM / SPA

SUNROOM / LOUNGE

SUNROOM /GREENHOUSE

SUNROOM /PARLOR

Figure 2-10. Drawings showing different sunroom floor layouts.

removing a portion of the existing roof and installing sheets of roof/wall glass, or excavating a new foundation and adding several hundred square feet to the living area. When the room is built as an addition or requires the removal of part of the roof structure, it requires a permit, and must conform to your local building codes. Make sure that the designer works with the local city engineering department to ensure the solarium, atrium, sunroom, or greenhouse meets the design codes for your local climates.

For maximum efficiency the room should be separated from the main living environment by a 100 percent thermal break during the winter which, when properly designed, will separate the outside cold surfaces from the warm inside surfaces of the structure. The thermal break is achieved by sealing the wood frame and glass with silicone caulking to make sure the walls and ceiling are protected against any unwanted air infiltration. Special, operable thermal roof windows or interior ventilating fans directed to the attic with sealing dampers should be installed to reduce summer heat buildup and ventilate chemicals or water vapor from plant boxes or hot tub/spa. Because the roof and walls are primarily made of glass, it is necessary during the winter months to provide sufficient heat and air circulation to this area. This means that a solarium or atrium requires 2-1/2 times as many floor ducts to provide adequate air movement, and must have its own return-air vent to reduce the chance of winter condensation and freezing.

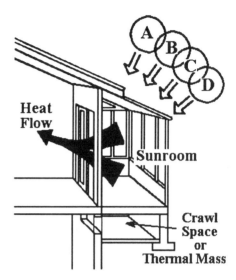

Figure 2-11. Sunroom addition showing seasonal heating and air flow.

(A) Summer, (B) Fall, (C) Spring, (D)Winter.

A sunroom or atrium design can be an extension to a kitchen or living area, or a room with its own entrance.

Sliding glass doors or insulated metal French doors leading to the house can be opened or closed to balance the heat distribution between the solarium and the living environment during different seasons (see Figure 2-11). In the summer the ventilating windows can be opened to help keep the room cool, and supplementary heating and air conditioning working with the shades and blinds can maintain constant temperatures in any weather.

A greenhouse, on the other hand, is primarily for growing plants, and is more likely to be self-enclosed without direct access from the main living environment. It is thermally glazed but not completely thermally broken, and automatic roof ventilation to exchange the inside air is very important for growing purposes. A solarium or greenhouse which has been specifically designed for passive solar energy should have a south or southwest orientation, and will store heat during the day and release it into the house at night. The principles of passive solar energy are simple. The main purpose of the structure will be to collect and store the sun's warmth, and then be capable of distributing this collected heat upon demand to other areas of the house. Heat-storing materials include water, cement, rock, and brick, and therefore the structure can be constructed with a thermal mass of rock, brick, or sand under a concrete slab and masonry floor to help store solar heat. Energy-efficient double or triple glazing with an R-20 wall insulation, along with operable solar shades or reflective blinds, are essential to control the temperature in the summer and winter.

CHAPTER 3

◆ GENERAL RENOVATION CONCEPTS

● Expansion Limitations

North, south, east or west? The direction the house can expand and the direction you want the renovation to face may not always match. A house situated on a rectangular lot usually has the side boundaries situated directly on the city's sideyard requirements and thus will not allow an extension (see Figure 3-1). The options then are to add on to the front, or the back, or go upward, all of which is still limited by the distance from the existing property line to the house and controlled by the city's zoning or land use requirements.

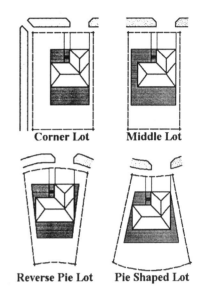

Corner Lot   Middle Lot

Reverse Pie Lot   Pie Shaped Lot

Figure 3-1. Lot configurations showing directions of expansion.

A wide triangular, or pie shaped, lot with the street to the north or east is still considered the most desirable scenario but rectangular lots will also provide areas of the house with a south/east or south/west exposure so that the renovated portions are able to take advantage of the sun. This concept of conserving/utilizing energy was usually not considered when homes were being built between the 1940s and the mid 1970s.

When contemplating the renovation design, remember to limit any large glass areas facing north, consider shady areas created by large trees or the neighbor's house (an item usually missed), and finally, identify the direction of the winter winds and accumulation sites for snow or falling leaves. The latter should be considered when planning an addition as the new structure could change the direction of the wind pattern, and hence snow or leaf collection zones, causing an undesired accumulation at an entrance or access area. Considering the above factors could save considerable dollars on heating bills, and reduce or eliminate potential cold drafts, window condensation, and areas of high maintenance.

If the proposed renovation includes an attached garage which requires the removal of any existing out-buildings, or construction of a new garage on the property, there are a few items to consider. The location will determine the incline of the driveway: remember that more than a 12 percent slope from a horizontal grade

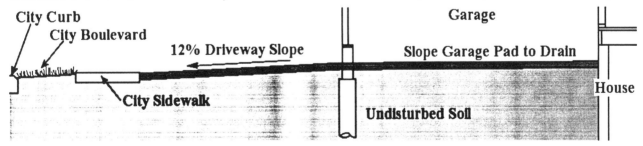

City Curb
City Boulevard
12% Driveway Slope
City Sidewalk
Undisturbed Soil
Garage
Slope Garage Pad to Drain
House

Figure 3-2. A proper 12 percent driveway slope.

could be too much for winter access in icy conditions (see Figure 3-2). Have the designer contact the surveyor to find the best garage location with the easiest, allowable driveway slope in order to incorporate that slope in the working blueprints. Place the driveway as close as possible to the road or lane as allowed by the building code as paving costs are directly proportional to the length of the driveway. Try not to reduce the landscape potential of the lot by planning a driveway down one length to reach a garage placed at the back of the lot. If the plan includes a wide garage, make sure the lot is wide enough for the proposed renovation and garage, leaving the sideyard space required by city zoning.

Consider the proposed renovation in conjunction with the adjoining properties. Will the new windows be looking directly at a neighbor's garage or RV pad? Will their windows look directly into one of yours, or a spot in the backyard chosen as a private area? To maintain happy relations, assess whether the design and placement of the renovation will be aesthetically pleasing and compatible with your neighbors' homes: will the proposed renovation protrude to block a view of a park or central boulevard, shade a once-sunny flower bed, or cause a potential security problem by reducing the light from a street or lane light standard? These considerations reflect good manners of design (see Figure 3-3). Request the designer to do an on-site inspection of these architectural features to be sure that these problem areas will be discussed prior to the design presentation.

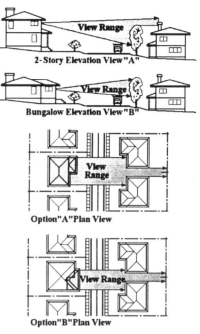

Figure 3-3. Addition "A" showing good view. Addition "B" showing poor view.

As discussed previously, the shape of the lot determines the size, visual presentation, location and sometimes the type of renovation, i.e., split level, bungalow, 2-story, possible. Before committing yourself, have an impartial appraisal made by either an inspector, the selected designer, or a mortgage lender. If possible provide them with photocopies of the original building pocket of the lot and house blueprints, as this will provide them with all the pertinent information in order to make a fair assessment. Check with the city to verify that all local improvement taxes have been paid and estimate the amount they might increase after the renovation. Finally, to safeguard your interests consult a lawyer who is experienced with real estate and building contracts, and familiar with your mortgage holder or bank. Your banker can provide you with an approved list of lawyers. If you cover all these bases your renovation investment will be protected.

● **Understanding Your Lot**

Knowing approximately the additional space required and the budget allocated, try to visualize the entire building on your lot, and not just a detailed sketch of the proposed addition. First select the style that will fit the lot location and restrictions, i.e., bungalow, split level or 2-story (refer to page 21). Then depict the living

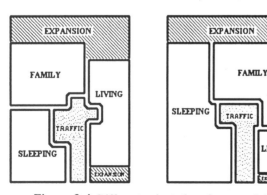

Figure 3-4. Different orientations for potential expansion of the living environment.

spaces as several boxes which can be moved around to adapt to the shape and exposure of the lot. This is an opportunity to play with new and existing components of the house (see Figure 3-4), and better understand the total workability and needs of the family's lifestyle, traffic patterns, yard utilization, etc. The arrangement of the addition components can then be adjusted to the orientation of the lot and compass direction. Allow for several configurations that will fit within the city's setbacks, then select the floor plan that most naturally falls into place.

Because there are so many variables to consider, visualizing all the living areas of the house as several boxes can avoid costly mistakes during the design stage of the renovation project. The general ideas introduced when designing a new home also pertain to renovations. Consider having the family areas on the south or sunny side, and to the rear away from high traffic or easy visual exposure. Try to orient these areas to overlook a visually enjoyable direction, such as the garden or terraced area of the yard. Place the kitchen, laundry, and service entrance near the east or front of the house for ease of access. Stairs should be easily accessible from all areas of the house, and are best located with a northern exposure. Bedrooms and work areas service the house better if located to the north or northwest. Will any of these ideas fit the existing house structure, future plans, and budget? Your designer will be able to answer your concerns and assist you in these problem areas.

If the lot has variable, steep side-slopes for grades, the type and direction of the renovation could require the installation of retaining walls to keep earth from falling onto neighboring property. If left, the sloping property might also direct ground-water onto the neighbor's property, causing basement flooding (see Figure 3-5).

Figure 3-5. Side-sloping grades requiring retaining walls to hold back earth and water.

The front street will generally be noisier, dirtier, and less safe than the fenced backyard of the lot. Cars and friends will frequently park on the front street or driveway causing visual obstructions. The front view may become secondary to the more pleasing and private landscaped backyard, and should be windowed and landscaped with this in mind. This is why so many newer homes are locating the living environment to the rear of the house, and a smaller more formal sitting room to the front.

When renovating it is almost impossible for every room in the finished house to have the perfect location; however, observing a few simple suggestions will help avoid your worst nightmares. Although your subdivision may not have had design controls in place, some external components of the house have already been established, eg., the existing garage or driveway location. Follow these simple guidelines when designing your new renovation plan:

1) Locate the proposed/existing garage and driveway accesses.
2) Locate the new service accesses for garbage, meter reader, milkman and newspaper deliveries.
3) Locate an entrance with a mud area or washroom to limit dirt trackage through the house.
4) Identify how friends and visitors will approach the house, and locate the main and service doors.
5) Locate new windows for view or security, keeping in mind the direction of the summer/winter sun and prevailing winds.

● **Finishing Touches**

Any house looks best on the lot when it appears to hug the ground, so the main floor level should be kept as close as possible to the finished grade of the property. It is also important to maintain the correct slope or grade away from the addition for proper drainage. All this requires a careful calculation of how much material will be removed for the renovation/addition, and how much of it can be re-used for backfill and regrading around the new and old structure (see Figure 3-6).

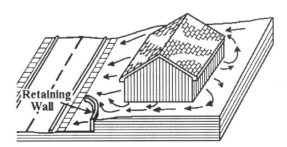

Figure 3-6. Proper grade slopes must be provided around perimeter of structure.

The surveyor can calculate the depth of the addition's excavation, and the contractor excavating the basement will usually be able to determine in his estimate (within two truckloads) how much earth he should leave to achieve the proper finished grade. This is particularly important in cases of small renovations, narrow lots, and zero lot-line construction where there is inadequate space to stockpile this soil. If not calculated correctly in the estimate for these construction scenarios, any dirt will have to be removed or hauled in at a later date at additional cost to the owner. In addition, it is important to discuss whether you want to maintain the existing *eight*-foot (plus or minus) basement height, or opt for the more expensive but functional *nine*-foot height. This choice will affect the designer's working drawings, the surveyor's grade staking, and soil excavation calculations.

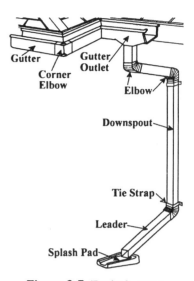

Figure 3-7. Typical gutter, downspout, and leader arm.

Most cities now require eavestrough downspouts to drain away from the property rather than to the storm sewer as in the past. This new by-law might require you during upgrading or renovating to remove the existing gutters and downspouts, patch the access to the storm sewer, and redirect the new downspouts onto the property with an extension arm (see Figure 3-7).

Cost of maintenance should be a primary consideration when choosing the new exterior cladding materials. Depending on the selected finish, the exterior cladding installed onto the new and existing outside walls should require little or no maintenance during the first seven to ten years of its life. Exposure to weather over a period of time for any material will require some maintenance, and during the life of a house this will have an impact on the overall value of the property. Renovating presents an opportunity to protect your new and older investments by choosing from today's more durable materials that are more resistant to sun, moisture, and ice damage. These include aluminum/vinyl siding, brick veneer, and some stucco finishes.

There is an excellent selection of durable, quality exterior finishes on today's market, and a good designer or builder can advise you about the durability of new and existing products. Exterior finishes fall into two categories: those needing maintenance in the form of paint or stain every five to eight years, and those which need little or no upkeep.

Products needing maintenance:

        Cedar siding   - horizontal or vertical

                              - painted wood windows

                              - plywood wood trims

      Asphalt shingles - on south/west exposures

Products needing little maintenance:

        Stucco (colored) - on weathered exposures (usually only washing required)

        Aluminum, vinyl siding - on direct south/west exposures

        Pine shakes - on weathered exposures

Products needing no maintenance:

        Brick or stone faces

        Stucco

        Concrete roof tiles

        Cedar shakes/shingles

For wood frame construction, most mortgage companies agree on a 30 to 35 year life expectancy for a house. During the renovation process, the existing wood frame structure should also be carefully inspected and repaired if necessary to guarantee that it, along with the renovated portion, will last beyond a lifetime.

Limit the number of exterior finishes used on a house when renovating. Avoid trying to match the older existing cladding for the addition unless the material is only a few years old and still readily available. The attempt to match the older, weathered exterior materials may not only be time consuming, but not as cost effective as imagined. The finished house could look like a patchwork quilt where nothing matches which will substantially reduce the curb appeal and the home's resale value. To avoid the end product looking like an addition and not part of the house as intended, it is important to have the designer incorporate the principles of symmetry when merging new and old products together on one elevation view. It is a common design practice to use one continuous product type other than trim and brick features over a large area as this is usually more pleasing to the eye.

- **Colors**

The use of different colors has different effects, i.e., light colors make objects look larger, and dark colors do the reverse. Bright colors used over large surfaces will make an object stand out from the surrounding surface, sometimes to the extreme. Bright colors and different textures should therefore be used only to emphasize or enhance features to which you wish to draw attention. For example, firehalls, hospitals, and government buildings usually have brightly textured stone, brick, steel or marble entrances so they will stand out. In smaller residential structures, the window trim, gutters, soffits and fascia in white or a color darker than the exterior wall color by two color tones will enhance the house's features.

Figure 3-8. House with horizontal lines.

Color, texture, or their combination can be used to fool or misdirect the eye. Horizontal lines suggest width (see Figure 3-8), and vertical lines give the impression of height (see Figure 3-9). If the renovated appearance at the streetscape level of the house is small, the use of one color on the walls will give the illusion of greater size. Use a dark color over a light color to reduce the height of the lighter color, i.e., a dark roof on a white house will connect the house to the ground. When planning your renovation and finished streetscape colors, there are two principal areas to consider: the roof and the walls. The colors on these two areas must not conflict. Colored shingles or tiles will limit the selection of color for the walls; grey or earth tone colors on a roof will not dominate or detract from any other colors planned for the walls. The colors most commonly used are the simple, down-to-earth colors, i.e., greys, beiges, tans, and whites. Save those bright, dramatic, and unusual colors for your interior decorating.

The local climate, and the number and size of tree and plant selections for the proposed landscaping, will also affect the selection of color and texture to be used. In areas where there are many rainy and overcast days, use white surfaces with light cheerful color as this will offset the depressed feelings created by this type of weather. Where you are able to preserve existing trees to give color and

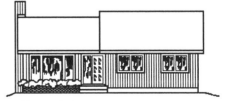

Figure 3-9. House with vertical lines.

texture, simple white surfaces provide contrast. Where few trees grow, the use of bright colors and different textures will make a significant difference.

NOTES:

CHAPTER 4

◆ SELECTING THE RENOVATION STYLE

● Determining the Final Cost

There are in reality only four basic house styles: bungalow, 1-1/2 story, 2 story, and split level. Other styles are modifications of the original models to accommodate building and zoning requirements. Each has its advantages and disadvantages. Your choice for the renovation will be determined by budget, existing house type, lot size, and personal preference.

No matter who is supervising the project the main consideration should be "What will be the final cost?" How does one determine which completed house type would work best when added to the existing home, and whether it is affordable? One method limited to the newly constructed portion of the renovation is the basic cost per square foot, but depending on the status of the existing house structure the cost per square foot of the total renovation may differ drastically. As an example: If after inspecting your home it is found that the foundation wall or main floor structure requires reinforcement to support a second story and the property will not allow you to expand horizontally, the expenditure to reinforce the existing structure could be prohibitive. You might then reconsider building a new home or purchasing an existing home better suited for your needs.

A few phone calls or better yet a visit to some show homes of several well-established builders will provide you with a general cost per square foot *per renovation style*. Once you have that information, multiply the approximate cost per square foot of the proposed addition times the floor area required, and for a margin of error add 5 percent of that total to give you the new construction cost. For the existing home renovation, multiply that floor area of the house by 50 percent of the appropriate cost per square foot and for a contingency factor add 10 percent of the grand total cost excluding any landscaping and outbuildings, i.e., garages or sheds. This should fall within your renovation budget. A good renovation contractor should have the experience and knowledge to renovate your home within that set budget, and meet the detailed standards and quality specifications you have discussed and included in the builder's contract. If the quote falls within your budget, and you plan to subcontract the house, you have between an 8 to 20 percent safety margin in your favor. (Refer to the building cost sheets in Chapter 11, pages 113-18.)

How does one determine which house style can feasibly be added to the existing home?

● The Bungalow

The bungalow has the advantage of providing the owner with the greatest selection of house style additions. Lot providing, if you are able to renovate without the addition of a second floor, the main bonus remains that there are no stairs to climb, other than those leading to the basement, and the occupant continues to have easy access to all areas of the house. Living in a bungalow is therefore less fatiguing, and potentially fewer accidents occur especially where children are concerned. If the intent is to enlarge the existing rooms of your home, it is often cheaper to add to a bungalow. The value of the home will increase regardless of the square footage added as more people reaching retirement move out of the multi-level house style and into a bungalow. On the other hand, if you are planning a major

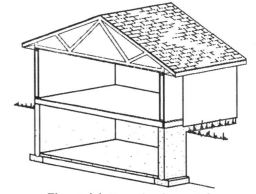

Figure 4-1. Bungalow house style.

addition rather than a simple renovation, this can be the most expensive house type to build onto. In general a bungalow requires twice as much roof, foundation, footing and basement floor as a 2-story house for the same floor area, and if not properly designed, heating and plumbing installation problems may be encountered. Therefore, if the existing main floor living space will be increased by more than 600 square foot, additional living space can be provided more economically by adding a second floor.

The construction costs to convert a bungalow to a 1-1/2 story home are considerably less than the expansion of the full main floor area. The existing structure of a bungalow is usually sufficient to carry the added weight of a partial upper floor; however, if a full upper bath is planned, a main floor wall needs to be widened to accommodate the new sewer lines to the basement. Although the insulation requirements for the 1-1/2 story house are usually more expensive due to increased wall and roof surface areas, the added living space that this house style provides makes it a very economical design with the least initial capital outlay. The stairs required to access the upper level are usually built over the existing stairs to the basement which limits excessive loss of main floor living area. If you require more than three bedrooms and one bath in the proposed renovation project, it would be more economical to consider a 2-story or split level house.

Although this individual house style will not be discussed, depending on the lot and existing floor layout, a bi-level style addition could be an alternative if the bungalow style renovation costs are too high, or a grade variation exists from one side of the property to the other. It creates a split level component that allows you to develop the basement with less effort and cost. Because the footings of the bi-level design are at the local frost level, usually a four to five foot depth, larger basement windows are possible than for most house types. The lowest level may consist of a four foot crawl space which is cheap for excavation, but still requires footings below the frost line. A further expansion on this theme is the full split-level addition which provides an additional level of increased living space. The full excavation costs relatively little more and increases resale value since it will contain more usable square footage. The major drawback to both styles is the addition of a stairwell to access the new upper/lower floor living areas which introduces climbing as a daily activity. If the existing floor plan allows and the designer is given some freedom for design, it might be possible to eliminate the original set of stairs and allow that stairwell to be filled in, providing more room expansion on the existing floor plan. However, note that the amount of space required to accommodate stair access to the different levels is usually twice that required by a 1-1/2 or 2-story home.

Advantages of bungalow additions	*Disadvantages of bungalow additions*
✓ Horizontal floor plans are easy to construct.	✗ There is privacy with only walls as sound buffers.
✓ Bungalows offer the greatest convenience for indoor/outdoor traffic patterns.	✗ Bungalow additions cost more per square foot to construct.
✓ Heating/cooling/plumbing systems do not have to negotiate additional floors and ceilings.	✗ Bungalows require wide lots, and take up space that might be used for outdoor leisure activities.
✓ All major rooms are located on one level, i.e., no stairs required.	✗ Heating/cooling installation costs tend to be higher.
✓ The full-height basement provides an option for additional future development.	✗ For reasons of privacy/security some people do not feel comfortable sleeping on a main floor.
✓ Retrofitting mechanical equipment after construction is completed is easiest.	✗ 1-1/2 story and 2-story additions require stairs that reduce main floor space.
✓ Bungalows are easy to inspect and maintain due to their proximity to the ground.	

• The 1-1/2 Story Style

The 1-1/2 storymain floor usually contains a finished living area and provides an undeveloped second floor as a future sleeping area with washroom facilities. Check if during the initial construction the owner/builder planned for future expansion of the upper floor by locating wider plumbing and heating walls on the main floor with the roughed-in ducts and plumbing stacks already in place. This is an important consideration when developing the upper floor as the alignment of the upper floor plumbing wall to the main floor wall will determine the major expenses for the renovation project. The more directly the heating, waste, and water lines are situated over each other, the less the main floor ceiling demolition required. Completing the development of the 1-1/2 story house requires less external structural changes, yet realizes less than the full development potential of the

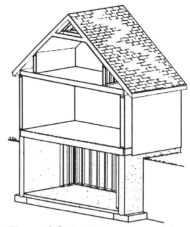

Figure 4-2. 1-1/2 story house style.

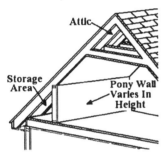

Figure 4-3. A pony wall with storage area.

upper floor area because of the sloping exterior walls. Compared to 100 percent utilization of a 2-story addition, the 1-1/2 story development will allow for about a 35 to 60 percent increase in the total living floor area. Additional expenses incurred will be insulating the steeply angled roof rafters of the upper floor and framing in vertical pony walls for electrical outlets and furniture placement. The building code allows this style to have shorter, usually non-structural pony walls in order to gain as much living area as possible for the upper floor. These pony walls are usually 36 to 72 inches in height, and set away from the intersection of the roof rafters and main floor ceiling-joist area, creating an unlivable triangular area generally used for storage (see Figure 4-3). The addition of shed or dormer attachments (see Figure 8-4) adds attractive roof-line features and allows for some nice interior decoration concepts such as window seats, but they do add to framing and roofing costs. An alternative renovation idea for this area is placing operable skylights in the roof rafters, or installing large attractive operating windows in the gable ends to bring in more light (see Figure 4-4). This means that the main floor area needs only minimal renovation work or can remain as is without adding square footage.

Figure 4-4. Operable skylight or large window unit for 1-1/2 story.

The undeveloped second floor may in itself comprise the renovation project without the need for external structural expansion of the main floor area. However, when main floor expansion is necessary or a full second-story addition is required, the 1-1/2 story and the bungalow style considerations are the same.

Advantages of 1-1/2 story development	*Disadvantages of 1-1/2 story development*
✓ It is fairly easy to maintain.	✗ Dormers and sloped ceilings cause oddly shaped and sized rooms.
✓ Due to its efficient shape it has low heating/ cooling costs per square foot.	✗ There is no additional basement area for development if further expansion is required.
✓ It provides more privacy with two distinct living levels.	✗ Upper floor rooms under the roof area, when not properly insulated, tend to be cold in winter and hot in summer.
✓ This style is the most economical to renovate with a low cost per square foot if the upper floor is left to be developed later.	✗ Stairs to the upper level take away developable main floor space.

- **The 2-Story Style**

The 2-story stylebuilt on narrow lots in older subdivisions has insufficient width to accommodate expansion to the sides which limits the direction of potential development. If this applies to you, consider developing to the front, back, or even up. If the main floor and basement structure will allow for the added weight, there are many cost-effective advantages for building a third-story renovation/addition especially if there are no height restrictions set by the city. For those areas restricting upward development and depending on the roof slope for proper head room, you might consider the addition of dormers to stay within approved roof-height limits (see Figure 8-2). Construction costs for narrow-lot homes can be reduced by simply stacking the third floor structural walls on the same interior main and second floor walls. These walls are then readily accessible for the plumbing and heating lines to the third-floor addition/renovation, and

Figure 4-5. 2-story house style.

the bathrooms can be designed on top of each other thus sharing the same piping. The stair access to the third floor can usually be built on top of the existing stairs. Too often the addition of a third floor to an already narrow house has the tendency to make the visual streetscape look even boxier because the house will be more than twice as high as it is wide. This problem requires careful attention by the designer, but can usually be overcome by emphasizing horizontal lines or the attachment of decorative features on the sides, i.e., cantilevered bay, bow, box, or garden windows which will give the illusion of greater width (see Figure 8-8). When you see the homes in your area being renovated, you could work with your neighbors on the streetscape to eliminate hedges or fences which act as dividers between the properties. Grouping the landscaping of lots can also create a park-like setting which will give visual width to narrow home styles.

Main floor outward additions such as family rooms or room expansions can become very expensive: a full basement structure is usually required, and the walls of the existing home will require some form of demolition and reconstruction for the new room patterns and structural changes to work properly with the existing floor plan. The cost to add a 2-story structure might be worthwhile considering because the structural groundwork for the main floor addition is in place and the extra construction costs will be for the additional floors and walls. Unexpected costs are usually incurred when the home's existing plumbing, electrical, carpet, wall, and interior/exterior finishing materials have not been maintained. These problems will occasionally force the owner to upgrade the existing two floors to match the newer products selected for the renovation project. Owners of 2-story homes frequently choose not to renovate and prefer to sell and purchase a new home because the total projected cost is often too expensive to justify.

Advantages of a 2-story development	*Disadvantages of a 2-story development*
✓ More privacy exists between sleeping/living spaces.	✗ Stairs make housekeeping less timely and tougher.
✓ It is cheaper to construct, requiring half as much roof and foundation area as a horizontal expansion of the same square footage.	✗ The upper floor of the house tends to be hot during the summer.
✓ The stacking of the levels makes it cheaper to heat and cool.	✗ The upper floor limits direct access to the outdoors for young children, and in the event of a fire.
✓ The exercise from walking up/down stairs keeps you physically fit.	✗ Maintaining the exterior of the upper story level is more difficult.
✓ Due to its compactness on many lots there is usually more room for outward expansion.	✗ It requires more hall space, therefore reducing the room sizes.
✓ It is adaptable for small-sized lots.	

• The Split Level Style

This style is often a choice of first-time home buyers as it may demand less capital outlay, provides the most extensive selection for expansion styles, and allows for the simplest renovation planning over time. Interior renovations of four-level splits are the most common when solving problems of family expansion. By redesigning the existing third-level family room area into bedrooms, the lower fourth-level (or basement) of the split becomes the displaced family/recreation room. A three-level style also provides the options for an inexpensive upper fourth-level expansion over the main floor

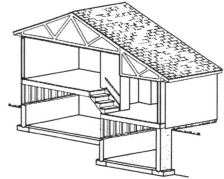

Figure 4-6. Split level house style.

level of the home (see Figure 4-7). This maintains an easy flow from floor to floor with only four to eight steps between levels. The actual number of stairs to the new floor level depends on the depth of the existing finished floor requirement. Note that the main floor living area has to have a full foundation beneath it in order to structurally support the addition of another level above (see Figure 4-6).

A split has a significant drawback when the existing structure has already utilized a good portion of the lot to the sides or the back. Check with the city development department to ensure that the lot is large enough to accommodate a horizontal addition. The multi-level design also makes it more difficult to select and define the

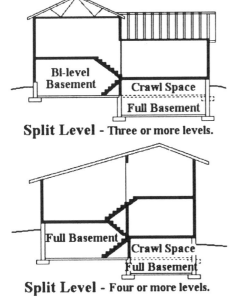

Split Level - Three or more levels.

Split Level - Four or more levels.

Figure 4-7. Optional floor levels of a split.

area that will be excavated for a partial or full basement. For example, if you wish to develop to the back and full width of the house, you will have to contend with two or possibly more levels. The question will be, do you mirror the existing foundation levels or excavate across for a full basement? Remember that all excavations require the footings to reach below the frost line, and the piles to reach undisturbed soil or be sunk a minimum of ten feet below the finished grade. By following the existing foundation levels of the full basement footing, you will be able to expand the existing living areas; however, the partial foundation cost for a crawl space under the upper level of the addition which will most likely be used for storage may seem a wasted expense. The cost to excavate the additional three or four feet to a full basement depth for the addition will be more cost effective over the long term (see Figure 4-7).

Your budget however may not justify additional excavation, labor, and concrete costs for the full basement development. Depending on the design and location of the floor levels, the cost to excavate a four-foot crawl space with footings will be cheaper than placing a concrete grade beam and pile system to support the same structure.

The goals and intended budget of a renovation are least effectively met by extending the split level style laterally. Based on many cost-related decisions this is the least recommended house style on which to attempt a major renovation.

Advantages of a split level development	*Disadvantages of a split level development*
✓ Short stairways provide easy access between levels.	✗ Too many roof-lines can make the overall appearance cluttered and disorganized.

Advantages continued:

✓ Multi-level zoning provides privacy between levels.

✓ It provides options for larger windows at the lower level development.

✓ It works well on side-sloping or hill lots.

✓ Stair climbing is considered a bonus by the health conscious.

✓ Split levels can allow access to the outside from two or even three levels.

✓ Multi-level designs provide a visual transition if attached to a bungalow or 2-story home.

Disadvantages continued:

✗ Room arrangements and traffic patterns can seem disjointed because of stair climbing between levels.

✗ Heating/cooling installation and maintenance costs can be very expensive.

✗ Staggered levels result in higher construction costs.

✗ Retaining walls, if required, become very expensive.

✗ Maintenance is high as a result of the many levels and staggered roof-lines.

✗ Multiple, short stairways utilize greater square footage than simple, full flights.

✗ Restrictions on the location of the addition may increase the amount of renovation work required in the existing home.

CHAPTER 5

♦ THE HOME INSPECTION

• Assessing Your Home

The following list should be completed and provided to the people who will be inspecting your home. If you are unable to answer all the questions, have the person who is inspecting the home complete it for you. This list will allow you to understand, and better prepare you and the family as to the extent and effect the proposed renovation might have on your family's lifestyle.

House Design	Desirable	Undesirable	House Location to	Desirable	Undesirable
Interior			Church	☐	☐
Electrical	☐	☐	Friends	☐	☐
Lighting	☐	☐	Schools	☐	☐
Plumbing	☐	☐	Shopping	☐	☐
Furnace	☐	☐	Parks	☐	☐
Hot water	☐	☐	Play areas	☐	☐
Humidity	☐	☐	Transit	☐	☐
Painting	☐	☐	Work	☐	☐
Insulation					
Basement	☐	☐	**Maintenance**	**Required**	**Not required**
Roof	☐	☐			
Walls	☐	☐	Electrical upgrades		
Bedrooms			Ceiling fixtures	☐	☐
Master	☐	☐	Wall outlets	☐	☐
Secondary	☐	☐	Panel upgrade	☐	☐
Bathrooms			Plumbing upgrades		
Main	☐	☐	Water line	☐	☐
Master	☐	☐	Sewer line	☐	☐
Secondary	☐	☐	Fixture upgrades		
Windows/Doors	☐	☐	Kitchen	☐	☐
Recreation	☐	☐	Bathrooms	☐	☐
Storage	☐	☐	Flooring	☐	☐
Security	☐	☐	Interior		
Privacy			Ceilings	☐	☐
Children	☐	☐	Walls	☐	☐
Parents	☐	☐	Replacing		
Exterior			Furnace	☐	☐
Drainage	☐	☐	Hot water tank	☐	☐
Driveway/Pad	☐	☐	Humidifier	☐	☐
Eavestroughing	☐	☐	Painting	☐	☐

House Design continued:	Desirable	Undesirable	Maintenance continued:	Required	Not required
Garage	☐	☐	Eavestroughs	☐	☐
Fascia	☐	☐	Siding	☐	☐
Roofing	☐	☐	Soffit	☐	☐
Sidewalks	☐	☐	Roofing	☐	☐
Soffit	☐	☐	Fence	☐	☐
Wall finish	☐	☐	Sidewalks	☐	☐
Landscaping	☐	☐	Snow shoveling	☐	☐
Fence	☐	☐	Tree pruning/Removal	☐	☐

• Inspection Services

A detailed inspection of the house is an important aspect of the renovation process, and a valuable tool for the home owner, contractor, and financial institution. Such reports will not guarantee the identification of all the problems involved with renovating the existing house, but will assist in evaluating the overall condition of the building structure. In most cases, the inspectors are registered engineers who are impartial, familiar with past residential construction methods, and hired to accurately locate and identify potential or existing problems. It is often suggested that the home owner attend the inspection to gain a better visual understanding of the problematic areas. Doing this will also eliminate the need for a detailed and illustrated report which usually results when the client is unable to attend, and can double or triple the cost of the inspection. A typical inspection will cost about $200 with the more detailed inspections ranging from $300 to $800 dollars. The inspection will determine how the various existing components, i.e., structure, plumbing, heating, electrical, etc., will interact with the proposed addition or renovation. It will identify potential problem areas that will need to be addressed, and will provide advance warning of work required prior to the construction start. You want no surprises after construction begins.

A typical inspection and report will not address the presence of harmful contaminants such as radon gas, lead paint, asbestos, urea formaldehyde, toxic or flammable substances, groundwater, and airborne hazards. Also excluded in typical inspections are reports on the workability of mechanical equipment for swimming pools, wells, septic systems, security systems, central vacuum systems, water softeners, sprinkler systems, fire and safety equipment, and the presence or absence of rodents, termites and other insects. If a more detailed inspection is required for these specific items, electricians, plumbers, mechanical contractors, etc., will be called in to test the equipment and view the property with the inspector to determine mechanical fitness or level of infestation. Be prepared to pay for these additional services.

A further safeguard after the inspection and during the renovation is to either have the selected contractor do a backup inspection to verify the report's content, or have each of the suppliers and subcontractors inspect those same areas for mechanical fitness. Because these trades will be working on your project, use them only to confirm the inspector's report. They might not be impartial and might see an opportunity of obtaining more work and cash flow. The equipment might not be as defective as they say. The detailed inspection report can also be used by the owner to ensure everything relevant gets included in the subcontractor's estimate. It will specify the work to be done, locate the cause of these problem areas, assess how the existing structure will affect the renovation, and finally suggest solutions for these potentially costly problem areas.

An inspection service will provide an unbiased opinion of the current conditions of the house and site. The on-site inspection will provide a clearer understanding of the proposed renovation project, but more importantly it will produce an accurate assessment of the house's structure which will affect the final cost projection for the work. The condition of the existing structure and materials used will determine the quality of material and workmanship required. The final cost of the renovation can be greatly influenced by trying to match existing wall thicknesses and material types with the newer styles and more energy-efficient products. Depending on the age of the house, you might find behind the drywall and wood panelling old, corroding pipes, wiring below existing code requirements, rotting structural studs, or other unknowns that will affect the final renovation direction and cost. These problems can be fixed by replacing the old, worn-out materials with newer, noncorrosive, and up-to-code materials, but it is best to find these costly problem areas before starting the design and renovation work. Knowing this, you can then more confidently select the direction and size of renovation that will better suit the house and the needs of the family.

The inspection service will also review any existing blueprints, plot plans, and mechanical service records which may determine how they complete their own checklist, and when combined with your list will reduce the possibility of any items being overlooked on a single list. If these documents are not available, the inspection service may have their designer measure the property and existing house, and provide a detailed set of working drawings consisting of a surveyed plot plan, detailed floor plans, sectional drawings through the house, elevation drawings, and a detailed specification sheet.

A thorough inspection checklist usually begins with the substructure of the building, continues to the living areas, the attic/roof area, the exterior of the house, and ends with the property report. Upon completion and review of the checklist, the inspection service will provide a report to the home owners, giving the inspector's assessment and renovation recommendations. This report is not designed to indicate the type of renovation required, but rather to detail the problem areas of the existing structure and the impact the renovation will have on the property, existing services, basement sub-structure, outbuildings, and lifestyle of the family during and after the construction period. It may also identify other structural and design problem areas in the existing house. Feel free to ask for an opinion on the effect the two structures will have on each other. For example, the new structure will have to go through a settling and adjustment period which the existing has already completed: how can any side effects be minimized?

If you live in an older part of the city where the homes have special features or historical backgrounds, the inspector, while doing his research at the city hall, might find the house registered as a heritage house. If so any renovation work will be restricted to and controlled by the province, state, or city guidelines. Any extensive, exterior renovation or addition is subject to their pre-approval which will include the restoration of existing historical features to maintain the house's visual and historical importance. These controls usually apply to houses built prior to the 1930s, or to the residence of a person of some historical prominence.

The following pages provide a more extensive house checklist used by many professional home inspectors. You are encouraged to use it yourself as a learning tool. Once the inspection checklist and drawings of the existing home have been completed, this information is taken to the surveyor who can then confirm the building pocket's accuracy. This current building pocket will show the true location of the house on the lot, and how much space is available for expansion based on present city by-laws.

Inspection Checklist

Name: _____ Address: _____ City: _____

Legal Description: Lot: _____   Block: _____   Plan: _____ - _____

Date: _____ ____, 19 ___.   Phone No. Residence: (___) ____ - _____

SUB-STRUCTURES

Foundation Walls

■ **Construction**
☐ Can't See ☐ Poured Concrete ☐ Concrete Block ☐ Treated Wood Foundation ☐ Other _____

Condition
☐ Can't See ☐ Good ☐ Fair ☐ Poor
Description: _____
_____

Structural cracks, Movement
 ☐ Can't see ☐ Major ☐ Minor ☐ None
 Description and location: _____
_____

■ **Water Leakage**_____
☐ Major ☐ Minor ☐ None
Location: _____
_____

Moisture content, Condensation
 ☐ Damp   ☐ Efflorescence   ☐ None
 Description and location: _____
_____

■ **Insulation Value**
Exterior Joists R- _____
Exterior Walls R- _____
☐ Fiberglass ☐ Loose Fill ☐ Foam   R._____
Description: _____
_____

Vapor Barrier
 ☐ Good   ☐ Fair   ☐ Poor   ☐ None
 Exterior Joist Level ☐ Yes ☐ No ___ Mil
 Exterior Walls   ☐ Yes ☐ No ___ Mil
 Description: _____
_____

Air Infiltration
☐ High   ☐ Low   ☐ None
Location: _____
_____

Possible Frost Heaving
 ☐ Likely   ☐ Unlikely
 Location: _____
_____

Basement Floor

■ **Construction**
☐ Poured Concrete   ☐ Undisturbed Soil   ☐ Fill Sand   Covered with: _____   Other: _____

■ **Condition**
☐ Can't See   ☐ Good   ☐ Fair   ☐ Poor
Description: _____
_____

Structural cracks, Movement
 ☐ Can't See ☐ Major ☐ Minor ☐ None
 Description and location:_____
_____

■ **Water Leakage**
☐ Major   ☐ Minor   ☐ None
Location: _____
_____

Moisture content, Condensation
☐ Damp   ☐ Efflorescence   ☐ None
Description and location: _____
_____

■ **Floor Drainage**
☐ Sump Pump   ☐ Floor Drain   ☐ None   Drains to: ☐ Sewer   ☐ Natural Drain   ☐ Other _____
Location: _____
_____

Structural Floor Supports

■ **Structural Beam**
☐ Can't See ☐ Wood ☐ Steel ☐ None ☐ Other
Material: _____   Size: _____

Condition
☐ Can't See   ☐ Good   ☐ Fair   ☐ Poor
Description: _____
_____

■ **Structural Posts**
☐ Can't See ☐ Good ☐ Fair ☐ Poor ☐ None
Material: _____   Size: _____
Condition: _____

Floor Joists
☐ Can't See ☐ Wood ☐ Other
Material: _____ Size: _____ Spacing: _____
Condition: _____

■ **Subfloor**
☐ Can't See   ☐ Tongue and Groove (T&G) Plywood   ☐ Plank   ☐ Other
Condition: _____
_____

■ **Cross Bridging**
☐ Can't See   ☐ Solid Blocking   ☐ 2 x 2 Wood   ☐ Other
Condition: _____
_____

Heating System

■ **Type**
☐ Gas   ☐ Oil   ☐ Electrical   ☐ Other: _____
☐ Forced Air   ☐ Boiler   ☐ Baseboard

Heating Capacity
____,000 B.T.U. output No. of Furnaces: ___
Furnace set on: ☐ Floor ☐ Joists ☐ Other __

■ **Condition**
☐ Good   ☐ Fair   ☐ Poor
Description: _____
_____
Date last inspected: _____

Combustion Air
☐ Exterior Supply ☐ Interior Supply ☐ None
Sufficient Return Air: ☐ Yes ☐ No
Description: _____

■ **Accessories**
☐ Humidifier   Type: _____   ☐ Air Cleaner   ☐ Heat Pump   ☐ Air Conditioner   ☐ Heat Exchanger
Problems: _____

Hot Water Tank

■ Type

☐ Gas   ☐ Oil   ☐ Electrical   ☐ Other _____   Water Softener: ☐ Yes ☐ No

Problems: _____

Make: _____ ☐ Owned ☐ Rented_____

Water Service

■ Condition

☐ Good   ☐ Fair   ☐ Poor   ☐ Needs Service

Problems: _____

_____

Leaks

☐ Yes ☐ No   Pressure: ☐ Good ☐ Restricted

Problems: _____

_____

Plumbing Service

■ Type

☐ Cast Iron   ☐ Copper   ☐ Plastic   ☐ Combined

Condition: _____

_____

Shut-off Valves

Main: ☐ Yes   ☐ No   Other: ☐ Yes   ☐ No

Condition: _____

_____

■ Insulated

At Joists: ☐ Yes   ☐ No   Around Pipe: ☐ Yes   ☐ No   Possible Freezing: ☐ Yes   ☐No

Problems: _____

Septic System

■ Condition

☐ Good   ☐ Fair   ☐ Poor   ☐ Needs Service

Problems: _____

_____

Leaks

☐ Yes ☐ No   Pressure: ☐ Good ☐ Restricted

Problems: _____

_____

■ Plumbing Drainage

☐ Cast Iron   ☐ Plastic   No. of Stacks: ____   Main Location: _____   Secondary Location: _____

Problems: _____

Plumbing Fixtures

■ Condition

☐ Good   ☐ Fair   ☐ Poor   ☐ Needs Service

Problems: _____

_____

Leaks

☐ Yes ☐ No   Pressure: ☐ Good ☐ Restricted

Problems: _____

_____

Electrical Service

■ Type

☐ Overhead   ☐ Underground

Meter Location: ☐ Front   ☐ Back   ☐ Side

Capacity

☐ 60 amp   ☐ 100 amp   ☐ 150 amp

Panel Location: ☐ Basement ☐ Other: _____

■ Wiring

☐ Aluminum   ☐ Copper

Problems: _____

Condition

☐ Good   ☐ Fair   ☐ Poor

Problems: _____

Electrical Fixtures

■ Type
☐ Grounded   ☐ Not Grounded

■ Exhaust Fans
☐ Kitchen   ☐ Bathrooms   ☐ None
Problems: _____

No. of Fixtures per Circuit
☐ Per Code ☐ Not Per Code ☐ Needs New Panel

Efficiency: ☐ Good   ☐ Fair   ☐ Poor
Service required:_____

FLOOR LEVELS - MAIN/UPPER

Exterior Wall

■ Construction
☐ 2" x 6"   ☐ 2" x 4"   ☐ Other: _____
☐ Standard   ☐ Other: _____
Problems: _____

Insulation
☐ Can't See ☐ Fiberglass ☐ None ☐ Other:____
Value: R- _____
Problems: _____

■ Maintained
☐ Well   ☐ Fair   ☐ Poor   ☐ None
Problems: _____

■ Wall Finish
☐ Plaster ☐ Drywall ☐ Paneling ☐ Combined
☐ Painted   ☐ Wallpaper   ☐ Other: _____
Problems: _____

Cracks
☐ Major   ☐ Minor   ☐ None   ☐ Other: _____
Location: _____
_____

■ Moisture/Condensation
☐ Major   ☐ Minor   ☐ None   Location: _____

Interior Wall

■ Construction
☐ 2" x 6"   ☐ 2" x 4"   ☐ Combined_____
Problems: _____
_____

Cracks
☐ Major ☐ Minor ☐ None   ☐ Other: _____
Location: _____
_____

■ Wall Finish
☐ Plaster ☐ Drywall ☐ Paneling ☐ Combined
☐ Painted   ☐ Wallpaper   ☐ Other: _____
Problems: _____

Maintained
☐ Well   ☐ Fair   ☐ Poor   ☐ None
Problems: _____

■ Moisture/Condensation
☐ Major   ☐ Minor   ☐ None   Location: _____

Ceilings

■ Finish
☐ Plaster   ☐ Drywall   ☐ Wood   ☐ Combined
☐ Textured ☐ Painted ☐ Other: _____
Problems: _____

Cracks
☐ Major ☐ Minor ☐ None ☐ Other: _____
Location: _____

Floors

■ **Finish**
□ Carpet □ Lino □ Tile □ Wood □ Ceramic
Underlay: □ New □ Old Type:_____
Problems: _____

Level Problems
Noticeable: □ Extremely □ Fairly □ None
□Foundation Movement □Post Movement
Correctable: _____

■ **Leveling Required**
□ 1 x 2 Nailers □ Wood Shims □ Other Location: _____

Windows

■ **Type**
□ Sealed □ Awning □ Casement □ Sliders
□ Wood □ Aluminum □ Vinyl □ Combined
Weatherstripping □ Yes □ No Type: _____

Glazing
□ Single □ Double □ Storm Windows
□ Crank Locks □ Lever Locks

■ **Condition**
□ Good   □ Fair □ Poor
Problems: _____

Seal
□ Good   □ Fair   □ Poor
Problems: _____

■ **Sill/Brick Molding Condition**
□ Good   □ Fair   □ Poor   □ Paint Peeling   □ Caulking Damaged   □ Moisture Damage   □ Rot
Location: _____

Fireplace

■ **Type**
□ Doors   □ Open   □ None
□ Masonry □ Zero Clearance □ Stove_____

Flue Condition
□ Good □ Dirty Damper Condition:_____
Problems: _____

■ **Combustion Air**
□ Supplied   □ Not Supplied
Problems: _____

Evidence of Damage
□ Yes   □ No
Problems: _____

ATTIC/CEILING AREA

■ **Ceiling Type**
□ Flat □ Sloped □ Peaked
□ Drywall □ Plaster □ Textured □ Other: ___

Structure
□ Can't See □ Trusses □ Rafters □ Joists
Spacing: □ 16" o.c. □ 24" o.c. □ Other: _____

■ **Condition**
□ Good □ Fair □ Poor □ Dryrot □ Damaged
Problems:

Roof Sheathing
□Plywood □Plank □Pressboard □Other:
Problems: _____

■ **Insulation**
□ Fiberglass □ Cellulose □ Other:_____
Problems: _____

Moisture/Condensation
□ Major □ Minor □ None □ Other: _____
Location: _____

■ Ventilation
□ Can't See □ Soffits □ Peak □ Gable
□ Adequate   □ Inadequate
Problems: _____
_____

■ Attic Access
□ Yes   □ No   Insulated □ Yes   □ No
Location: _____
Problems: _____

Air Infiltration
□Wall Plates □Attic Hatch □Electrical Plugs
Location: _____
Repairable: □ Yes □ No □ Caulking
□ Vapor Barrier □ 2 Mil □ 4 Mil □ 6 Mil

□ Interior Hatch   □ Exterior Hatch

EXTERIOR

Foundation

■ Condition
□ Good   □ Fair   □ Poor
Problems: _____

Cracks
□ Major □ Minor □ None □ Other: _____
Location: _____

Exterior Walls

■ Cladding Type
□ Stucco □ Siding □ Brick □ Other: _____
□ Full Wall Height □ Half Wall Height □ Other
Location:_____

■ Wall Structure Damage
□ Can't See   □ Major   □ Minor   □ None
Wall Type: □ Wood   □ Metal   □ Other
Problems: _____
_____

Cladding Damage
□ Major □ Minor □ None □ Other: _____
Location: _____
_____

Moisture/Condensation
□ Major □ Minor □ None □ Other: _____
□ Discoloration □ Moisture Damage □ Rot
Correctable: _____
_____

Roofing

■ Type
□Asphalt □Wood □Tile □Built-up □Other: ___
Problems: _____

■ Expected Life
□ 1 year □ 5 years □ 10 years □ Longer ____
Repair Required: □ Major   □ Minor □ None
Problems: _____
_____

■ Eavestrough
□ Good   □ Fair   □ Poor   □ Other: _____
Problems: _____

Roof Drainage
□ Good   □ Fair   □ Poor   □ Other:_____
Problems: _____

Overhangs
□ 12" □ 18" □ 24" □ Other: _____
Damage: □Can't See □Major □Minor □None
Problems: _____
_____

■ **Flashing**

☐ Good   ☐ Fair   ☐ Poor   ☐ Other: _____

Problems: _____

■ **Chimney Flue**

Fireplace: ☐ Good ☐ Fair ☐ Poor   Furnace: ☐ Good ☐ Fair ☐ Poor   Caulking: ☐ Good ☐ Fair ☐ Poor

Problems: _____

RENOVATION PLANNING

Utility Costs (per annum)

■ **Heat** _____   **Electrical** _____   **Water** _____

Expected Changes: *Heat:* ☐ Higher ☐ Lower   *Electrical:* ☐ Higher ☐ Lower   *Water:* ☐ Higher ☐ Lower

On-Site Services

■ **During Construction**

Power: ☐Yes ☐N/A   *Water*: ☐Yes ☐N/A   *Gas:* ☐Yes ☐N/A   *Heat:* ☐Yes ☐N/A   *Telephone:* ☐Yes ☐N/A

■ **Site Access**   ■ **Portable Toilet Required**

☐ Good   ☐ Difficult   ☐ Yes   ☐ N/A   Location: _____

Construction Requirements

■ **Permits Provided**

☐ Building   ☐ Electrical   ☐ Plumbing   ☐ For All Services   ☐ Other: _____

Notes: _____

■ **Inspections**

☐ Building   ☐ Electrical   ☐ Plumbing   ☐ City   ☐ Other: _____

Notes: _____

■ **Existing Plans Available**

☐ Plot Plan   ☐ Floor Plans   ☐ Elevations   ☐ Real Property Report   Drawings Required: ☐Yes ☐No

Notes: _____

■ **New Drawing Requirements**

☐ Plot Plan   ☐ Basement/Main Floor Plans   ☐ Elevations   ☐ Sections   ☐ Stair Details   ☐ Kitchen

Details: _____

Notes: _____

Areas Requiring Demolition

■ **Exterior Walls**   **Interior Walls**

☐ N   ☐ S   ☐ E   ☐ W   ☐ All ☐ Part   ☐Kitchen ☐Bath ☐Bedrooms ☐Dining ☐Hall

Details: _____   ☐ Entrance ☐ Living ☐ Family ☐ Other: ____

_____   Details: _____

■ Outbuildings, etc.

☐ Garage   ☐ Shed   ☐ Sunroom   ☐ Deck   ☐ Patio   ☐ BBQ   ☐ Fence   ☐ Driveway   ☐ Sidewalk
☐ Trees   ☐ Shrubs   ☐ Poles   ☐ Other: _____

■ Items to be Removed

☐ Overhead wires   ☐ Poles   ☐ Fences   ☐ Trees   ☐ Shrubs   ☐ Driveway   ☐ Sidewalks
☐ Planters ☐ Gas Lines ☐ Underground Electrical Line ☐ Sewer Line ☐ Utility Box ☐ Water Line ☐ Other: ____
Notes: _____

■ Items to be Replaced

☐ Overhead Wires   ☐ Poles   ☐ Fences   ☐ Trees   ☐ Shrubs   ☐ Driveway   ☐ Sidewalks
☐ Planters   ☐ Gas Lines   ☐ Underground Electrical Line   ☐ Sewer   ☐ Water Line   ☐ Utility Box
☐ Other: _____
Notes: _____

Plot Plan

■ Showing

☐ Existing house location _____   ☐ Material storage area _____
☐ Existing garage location _____   ☐ Equipment access _____
☐ Existing outbuildings _____   ☐ Top soil storage _____
☐ Existing trees & shrubs _____   ☐ Excavated earth storage _____
☐ Existing property dimensions _____   ☐ Gas meter & line location _____
☐ Existing house dimensions _____   ☐ Electrical meter & line location _____
☐ Existing driveway _____   ☐ Water service line location _____
☐ Existing sidewalks _____   ☐ Sewer line location _____
☐ Existing planters _____   ☐ Utility service pole location _____
☐ Septic system _____   ☐ Telephone service box & line location _____
☐ Water well _____   ☐ Other _____
☐ Other _____   ☐ Other _____

■ Soil Conditions

☐ Good   ☐ Fair   ☐ Poor   ☐ Clay   ☐ Sand   ☐ Silt   ☐ Gravel   ☐ Mixed   ☐ Other: _____
Concerns: _____

■ Groundwater

☐ High   ☐ Low   ☐ None
Concerns: _____

■ Grade Drainage/Slope

☐ Good   ☐ Fair   ☐ Poor   ☐ Needs to be Raised   ☐ Needs to be Dropped
Notes: _____

Family Information

Total Persons: _____   Daytime Occupancy: _____   Pets: ____
Male: Ages: _____   _____   _____   _____   _____   _____
Female: Ages: _____   _____   _____   _____   _____   _____
Will be required to move out during construction: ☐ Yes   ☐ No

You might not be very happy after reading the inspection report to find what needs to be serviced, repaired, or replaced. After years of service much of the mechanical equipment such as furnaces, humidifiers, air filters, and heat exchangers fall into disrepair and require replacement. Many inspection services will provide you with approximate costs for repairing and replacing the equipment, and these prices will vary depending upon the location, labor costs, quality of materials, and local economic conditions. The following list is an example of repairs and guesstimated replacement costs. You should however get actual price quotes from local suppliers and subcontractors to ensure correct pricing.

Item	Price	Estimated Cost ($)
Ground fault circuit in bathroom	Each	50.00 - 125.00
Add one switch/plug	Each	35.00 - 150.00
One 40 gal. gas hot-water heater	Each	300.00 - 600.00
Heat pump	Each	1,400.00 - 2,500.00
Energy-efficient gas furnace	Each	2,000.00 - 4,000.00
Furnace air cleaner	Each	375.00 - 700.00
Drum humidifier	Each	200.00 - 350.00
Increase overhead house power to 150 amps	Each	800.00 - 1,200.00
Install compressor in air conditioner	Each	1,000.00 - 2,000.00
Service air-conditioning/heating system	Each	100.00 - 200.00
Clean furnace ducts and flue	Each	3.50 - 5.00
Install new plastic hot/cold water lines	All	800.00 - 2,200.00
Add a separate service line for an appliance	Each	150.00 - 250.00
Auger house main sewer line	Each	100.00 - 250.00
Remove and patch 3 sq. ft. of stucco/parging	Each	150.00 - 350.00
Remove asbestos around pipes	All	2,000.00 - 4,500.00
Sump pit/pump installation with drain/fill lines	Each	2,500.00 - 6,000.00
Remove and replace 100 sq. ft. concrete	Sq. ft.	5.00 - 8.00
Add R-20 insulation at floor joists or attic	Sq. ft.	.90 - 1.40
Add insulation behind existing walls	Sq. ft.	2.50 - 4.00
Repair foundation or basement floor cracks	All	200.00 - 700.00
Install weeping tile system	All	400.00 - 1,500.00
Install attic turbine vent	Each	200.00 - 375.00
Install fan and vent to soffit for bathroom	Each	150.00 - 200.00
Remodel kitchen cabinets (upper and lower)	Lin. ft.	300.00 - 600.00
Remodel fixtures for a four-piece bath	All	3,000.00 - 7,000.00
Remove and replace asphalt shingles	Sq. ft.	1.20 - 2.50
Replace gutters and downspouts	Lin. ft.	3.50 - 7.00
Replace 3' x 5' window with aluminum/vinyl	Each	250.00 - 400.00
Install insulated metal storm door	Each	250.00 - 500.00
Install one deadbolt lock in exterior door	Each	75.00 - 150.00

CHAPTER 6

◆ FINAL PREPARATIONS

Now is the time to prepare for a reality check with the banker. Knowing your budget limitations will help you decide on the best renovation house style for your family. Take the plot plan, inspection report and your budget to the selected drafting service for discussion and preparation of the initial renovation presentations. As mentioned in Chapter 10, it is a good idea to have several presentation drawings printed for distribution to the suppliers and subcontractors for pricing. The completed presentation should consist of floor plans and at least two elevations showing sufficient details and dimensions for the tradespeople to provide a price quote within 10 percent of the cost. These prices, however rough, will show the banker that you are  prepared to complete the necessary legwork which will provide them with an accurate, complete cost for the renovation project. Before making the final decision to print several presentation drawings for pricing, and proceeding with the working drawings, here are a few thoughts.

Consider the quality or standard of living your family wants to enjoy on a day-to-day basis over the length of time you will be living in the house. Will the members of your family be able to adapt themselves to the way of life that will be determined largely by the new room layout of the house? Does the flow and layout of the house fit the way you like to live? Will it be large enough and suited to meet future needs, i.e., 10 to 15 years into the future? Will it be able to accommodate present furniture in the desired room layout, or will there be the added expense of purchasing new furniture, and/or storing or selling the old? If the plan is to sell the furniture, the proceeds from the sale will minimally assist in reducing the purchase cost of the new; however, expect to recoup only a small portion (20 to 40 percent) of the estimated value. Will the completed home be a pleasant place to live in during cold, snowy, or wet months without having to change or add mechanical devices, i.e., dehumidifiers, furnace air filter, and heat exchanger, to make the house more comfortable? There should be no doubt or compromise by the family as to the practical usability of your chosen house style. This will also guarantee its value and habitability for future owners should you decide to sell. Finally, will the proposed addition/renovation be visually pleasing with the desired streetscape without it looking like an addition or after thought?

If you have answered yes to all questions, then complete your working blueprints, but if you have any nos or not too sures reassess the house presentation. Your family's future well-being is at stake. Remember, you will be spending a substantial amount of money for the working blueprints, and making changes on presentations is much cheaper than redrawing whole working drawings. Spending the extra time and money for good working drawings will save you many sleepless nights and thousands of dollars during construction.

- **Seeing the Banker**

The best scenario for the renovation process is, of course, to go to a designer, explain what you want, have him redesign your home, move your family out of the construction mess, and then proceed to build. Unless you have won the lottery, this is usually not feasible.

Whether you intend to supervise and/or renovate yourself, or hire a general contractor to renovate for you, before spending time and money looking for a contractor or a designer, see your banker about pre-approved *first* or *second* mortgages and construction financing. If not satisfied with what your bank has to offer, do some shopping around. There are many banks and trust companies willing to barter for your business, and sometimes at better rates. Determining the maximum qualifying mortgage or loan can place the reality of renovation costs into the correct perspective. The size of mortgage you will receive depends on many factors: the bank's appraised value of the existing house and proposed renovation (usually done by an independent appraiser), total income and net worth, prevailing interest rates, and available cash for start-up payments and interim financing. With the assistance of the bank's loans officer, a calculation of available interim financing will be determined. If applicable, these funds must be able to carry the construction process prior to receipt of the scheduled mortgage draws. Of course, the more cash available for start-up costs, the more likely the bank is to approve the mortgage.

When completing the applications for interim financing and mortgage approval with the selected bank, be sure you understand clearly the implication. It is common practice in mortgage or interim financing arrangements for a lender to require clear title on the property prior to any construction start. Having the mortgage/loan registered against the title eliminates any claim someone else might have on the property and house, and also provides the bank with its collateral. This means that if the bank's mortgage is registered on title, and you or your selected contractor fail to complete the renovation for any reason, 100 percent of your debt to the bank will be paid in full through the sale of the property.

The next step is to hire a designer and have the presentation and working drawings initiated. The process of requesting prices from the building contractor, suppliers, and subtrades can begin on receipt of the presentation blueprints, and on the basis of these drawings and estimates you can make the mortgage/loan application.

The following pages are typical application and loan information sheets that must be completed and approved before the final mortgage/loan approval will be given by the bank. This detailed process for approval consists of providing the bank with two sets of blueprints in working drawing form and two plot plans completed by your selected surveyor, and completing the bank's building, structural and finishing specification sheets shown on pages 45 to 47. First, the bank will require a standard application fee for an independent appraisal using your presentation blueprints and completed cost projection sheet (see page 43). Once the bank has this appraisal, the legal mortgage/loan documents can be initiated by the bank and made ready for your signature. During the presentation and working drawing stage of the renovation plans, maintain close contact with the mortgage officer to make sure that the mortgage/loan application is being processed without any delays.

Many banks may not provide construction mortgages to self-builders unless you can verify that you have sufficient equity in a savings account and in the house, and have or are willing to take some construction courses through a local college or postsecondary school. Upon completion of these courses you will be able to provide the bank with a letter of introduction and intent which should be included in your mortgage/loan application. This letter will show the bank that you are determined in your objective to complete the renovation of your home, and have the necessary knowledge of residential house construction to complete the project. The following is a sample letter of introduction and intent to a financial institution for residential mortgage/loan application.

- **Sample Mortgage/Loan Application**

Date of Letter

Name of Bank
Street Address
State/Province
Zip Code/Postal Code

Re: HOME RENOVATION FOR MR. & MRS. APPLICANT

Dear Sirs:

The reason for my wife and I acting as our own general contractor are varied and numerous. From your perspective, the most important may be my previous construction experience in which my father, brother and I completely renovated the family bungalow, adding approximately 1,200 square feet. All the work from mixing the cement for the piles to the finished trim was done by ourselves. It is my intent on this project to limit our contributions to organizing, scheduling, and occasionally sweeping up. Through courses my wife and I have taken, along with several books studied, we have developed a comprehensive three-part building system. (See enclosure for list of courses taken and list of books researched.)

The first part is a proposed 75 working-day construction schedule which outlines the responsibilities required to keep the project moving along on time. We will be using a three to seven day advance notice/confirmation call system to ensure punctuality from the suppliers and subtrades. As 75 working days translates into less than four months, I am projecting August 22 as the scheduled occupancy date (a one month allowance for delays, no shows, rain...) as April 23 is the ground-breaking day.

The second part of the system is a bound diary and daily *Things to Do* checklist where I keep notes of key meetings and discussions with suppliers and subtrades each day. This will help avoid the "misunderstandings" normally associated with the subtrades and suppliers during the construction period. The diary and daily *Things to Do* checklist are also used to assist in scheduling the various stages of the project.

The third and final part of the system is the supplier/subtrade index where I keep copies of the signed quotations and contracts from the suppliers and subtrades. I will require a minimum of three quotations per supplier/subtrade for proper pricing of the proposed renovation project.

Along with our system come the organizational skills and dedication of my wife and me. We both have commerce degrees and college business diplomas and my wife also has an arts degree. Obtaining these academic designations stems from our organizational ability and our determination to complete what we start.

Having both of us involved in this project is a great benefit as the potential for marital tension is lower than if only one spouse were to undertake the project. Also, not having children is certainly advantageous given the amount of evenings and weekends that will be consumed.

Probably one of our biggest reasons for acting as our own general contractor is financial. In our 4-1/2 years of marriage, we have done OK financially, comparatively speaking. We are very aware of the cost savings in renovating our own home, so much so that we have already thought about some day taking on the responsibility of contracting a new home.

In reference to my job with _____, fortunately my boss has agreed that during the renovation period I can time-share with another part-time employee so that I can be on-site during the day when needed. I have been with this firm for almost 4-1/2 years now, and my boss, Mr. _____, is fully aware of my intentions.

My father, who has built two homes of his own and a cottage, will be assisting me with some of the day-to-day supervision of the suppliers and subtrades. He will also be making himself available to open and lock up the house every day for the workers when I am not on-site.

In summary, we are confident in our ability to successfully organize the renovation of our home, and we look forward to the next opportunity to use your services again.

Sincerely,

Mr. Applicant
Attached: Addendum;
copy of quote

ADDENDUM

COURSES ATTENDED:

Building Your Own Home, Faculty of Extension,
University of _____ , ... Fall 1994.

How to be Your Own General Contractor, Continuing Education,
_____ College, ... Winter 1995.

The Legal Aspects of Building a House, Mr. _____, Lawyer,
Continuing Education, _____ College, ... February 1994.

BOOKS RESEARCHED:

1) The Complete Guide to Contracting Your Home, A Step by Step Method for Home Construction, by Author / Publisher.
2) The Layman's Guide to Renovating Your Own Home, A Complete Step-by-Step Guide, by Author / Publisher.
3) How to Be Your Own Contractor, by Author / Publisher.
4) Do It Yourself Contracting, Building Your Own Home, by Author / Publisher.
5) Be Your Own Contractor, by Author / Publisher.
6) Renovating Your Own Home, by Author / Publisher.

(NAME OF YOUR FINANCIAL INSTITUTION)

COST PROJECTION FOR HOME RENOVATION
****

Branch ....

Date ....

NAME: .... **APPLICATION NO.** ....

LEGAL DESCRIPTION: ....

CIVIC ADDRESS: ....

DEMOLITION COST	$ _____
BASEMENT (Forms, Footing, Concrete, Weeping Tile, Dampproofing, etc.,)..........	$ _____
BASEMENT FLOOR (Concrete and Labor, etc.)	$ _____
HOME PACKAGE AND/OR MATERIALS (Lumber, Nails, Siding, etc.,)	$ _____
PLUMBING	$ _____
HEATING	$ _____
ELECTRICAL WIRING AND FIXTURES (Including Installations).........................	$ _____
INSULATION	$ _____
DRYWALL, TAPING, TEXTURING..	$ _____
EAVESTROUGHING	$ _____
SIDING/STUCCO..	$ _____
PARGING	$ _____
PAINTING	$ _____
KITCHEN CABINETS AND VANITIES	$ _____
FLOOR COVERINGS	$ _____
CERAMIC TILES, MIRRORS, TOWEL BARS, etc.,.	$ _____
DRIVEWAY, STEPS AND SIDEWALK	$ _____
OUTBUILDINGS	$ _____
LABOR (Give estimate of labor costs exceeding $1,000 not included above.)	$ _____
PROJECTED CONSTRUCTION COSTS	$ _____
5% CONTINGENCY FACTOR	$ _____
TOTAL PROJECTED CONSTRUCTION COSTS	$ _____
CONFIRMED LAND VALUE	$ _____
PLANS AND PERMITS	$ _____
SURVEY AND ENGINEERING	$ _____
LEGAL COSTS	$ _____
PROJECTED TOTAL COSTS	$ _____

- **FINANCIAL STATEMENT AND LOAN REPORT**   FILE NO. _____

  BRANCH _____   DATE _____

□ M □ F	Last Name		First Name		Middle	Age	Birth Date

Address		City	State/Province	Zip/Postal Code	Yrs at Present Address	Phone No.

Previous Address if less than 2 Years	Yrs.	□ Married □ Single □ Widowed □ Separated □ Divorced	No. of Dependents Excluding Spouse

Name and Address of Present Employer	Yrs.	Occupation	Phone No.
Previous Employer and Address	Yrs.	Occupation	Phone No.

Spouse's Name	Occupation	Age	Name and Address of Spouse's Employer	Yrs.

Bank	Address of Branch	Type of Account — Number

Automobiles — Year Make		Value	Other: Trailers, Boats, Motors, Snowmobiles, etc.	Value

Real Estate Owned	Address or Legal Description	Value	Mortgaged To	Amount

Have you ever declared bankruptcy? □ Yes □ No If yes, are you a discharged bankrupt? □ No □ Yes — Date _____ .	Customer since: Date _____

Social Insurance Number	Driver's Licence Number	Are you a Gold Card Holder? □ Yes □ No	Indirect Liabilities

ASSETS	Omit Cents	LIABILITIES						
		Instalment and Charge A/C's Bank and/or Finance Co.'s	Date Opened	High Amount	Date of Last Payment	Monthly Payment	Balance	X If We Are to Pay
Bank a/c								
Bonds and Stocks								
Life Ins.								
Mtge. & A/S Held								
Automobiles								
Real Estate								
Other								
		Mortgages and/or Rent Under Monthly Payment						
						Sub Total		
						Surplus		
						TOTAL		

MONTHLY INCOME AND REPAYMENT (must be completed)		**RELATIVES/CLOSE FRIENDS** Name / Address / Relationship	**MONTHLY BUDGET** Complete where monthly credit obligations exceed 30% of monthly take home pay.
Gross Employment Income	$ _____	1. _____ 1._____	
Spouse's Income $ _____ (%)	$ _____	2. _____	Utilities $ _____
Other (Include Family Allowance.)	$ _____	3. _____	Groceries $ _____
Total Gross Monthly Income	$ _____	4. _____ 2._____	Clothing $ _____
Less Deductions at Source	$ _____	5. _____	Auto Expenses $ _____
Take-Home Pay	$ _____	6. _____	Insurance (Auto, Life, Fire) $ _____
Deduct monthly payments before loan (See above.)	$ _____	Sub. _____ 3._____	Medical and Dental $ _____
Disposable Income	$ _____	7. _____	Entertainment and Vacation $ _____
Total Debt Service Ratio	$ _____ %	Total _____	Sundry $ _____
			Savings $ _____
			Total Monthly Expenses $ _____
			Instalment Loans Payment $ _____
			Other Monthly Payments $ _____
			Total Monthly Outlay $ _____
			Take-Home Pay $ _____
			Surplus/Shortage $ _____

The foregoing information is furnished for the purpose of obtaining advances from (   ) and is hereby certified to be true and correct. I authorize and consent to the receipt and exchange of credit information with any credit reporting agency, credit bureau, or person or corporation with whom I have financial dealings, and agree that information so received may be retained by you.

_____   _____
            WITNESS   SIGNATURE

• HOUSE BUILDING OUTLINE SPECIFICATION SHEET

NOTE: Starred items * must also be included on plans.

BRANCH _____

MORTGAGE APPLICATION NO. _____

Applicant(s):	Legal Description:	Civic Address:

EXCAVATION: Soil Type _____ Depth from Finished Grade to Footing Bearing _____

FOUNDATION: Material _____ Walls _____ Footing Size _____

CONCRETE: Type _____ Strength _____ PSI at 28 days: Reinforced: □ Yes   □ No

SERVICES: □ Mun. Water   □ Well   □ Mun. Sewer   □ Septic System

□ Waterproofing   **OR**   □ Dampproofing Material _____

TILE DRAINS: _____   □ Perimeter   □ Underfloor   □ Sump Pump

EXTERIOR WALLS: _____   □ Solid Masonry   □ Frame   □ Other _____

EXTERIOR FINISH: Brick Type _____   □ Stucco   □ Wood   □ Other * _____

CHIMNEYS: _____   □ Masonry   □ Prefabricated   Size _____

FIREPLACE: * _____   □ Wood or Coal   □ Electric □ Gas   Flue or Vent Size _____

MEMBER	SPAN	SPACING	SIZE/THICKNESS	MATERIAL AND GRADE
BEARING PARTITIONS *				
OTHER PARTITIONS *				
BASEMENT COLUMNS *				
FLOOR JOISTS *				
FLOOR JOISTS OTHER *				
CEILING JOISTS *				
ROOF RAFTERS *				
ROOF TRUSSES *				
STRUCTURAL BEAMS *				
ROOF SHEATHING				
WALL SHEATHING				
SUBFLOORING				
G1S UNDERLAYMENT				

WINDOWS: Type of Frames _____   Type of Sash _____

SPECIAL GLAZING: _____   □ Storm Sash   □ Fly Screens

DOORS: Type of Frames _____   Exterior Doors - Size and Type _____

     Interior Doors - Size and Type _____   Storm Doors - Size and Type _____

KITCHEN CUPBOARDS: _____   □ Wood   □ Metal   □ With Doors   Countertop Finish _____

INTERIOR FINISH: _____   □ Plaster   DRYWALL   Type _____   Thickness _____

AREA	FLOOR COVERING	WALLS AND CEILINGS	DECORATION
LIVING ROOM			
DINING ROOM			
KITCHEN			
FOYER			
BEDROOMS			
BATHROOMS			
FAMILY ROOM			
OTHER			

OUTLINE SPECIFICATION SHEET CONTINUED

INSULATION: Type and Thickness: Exterior Walls _____

Basement Space: Walls _____ Ceilings _____

Roof _____ Floor _____ Slab _____

ROOFING: Type _____ Grade or Weight _____ Eavestrough ☐ Yes ☐ No

PLUMBING: _____ ☐ Three - Piece ☐ Shower over Bath ☐ Shower Cabinet ☐ Laundry Tubs ☐ Other

EXTRA PLUMBING: _____

DOMESTIC HOT WATER: Method of Heating _____ Capacity of Heater (Wattage) _____

Type of Tank _____ Capacity of Tank _____ Conditioner ☐ Yes ☐ No

HEATING SYSTEM: Type of Fuel _____ Type of System _____ Details_____

_____

ELECTRICAL SERVICE: No. of Amperes _____ No. of Circuits _____ Special Wiring _____

Special Equipment __ _____

OWNERSHIP: List of all equipment subject to Conditional Sales Contract or Rental _____

_____

SPECIAL FEATURES: _____

_____

_____

TYPES OF SURFACES ＊ Walks _____ Driveway _____ Parking Pad _____ Other _____

PARKING ＊ _____ ☐ Garage: No. of Cars _____ ☐ Carport ☐ Parking Pad

LANDSCAPING: Sodding _____ Sq. Yds. Seeding _____ Sq. Yds. ☐ Shrubs ☐ Trees

• FINISHING SPECIFICATION SHEET

PRODUCTS and MATERIALS	DETAILS	COST ALLOWANCE
1. Kitchen/Bathroom Cabinets		
2. Flooring		
3. Doors		
4. Windows and Trim		
5. Light Fixtures		
6. Appliances (Built-in)		
7. Fireplace(s): Zero Clearance or Masonry		
8. Extras		
9. Garage: Finish (Insulation/Drywall) Door Door Opener		

10. Landscaping: Concrete Drive: Double $ _____   Single $ _____

Concrete Walks: $ _____

Sodding: Front $ _____   Rear $ _____

Fencing: $ _____

Deck: $ _____   Size: _____

11. Size of Home: _____ sq. ft. _____ sq. m

I certify that the house(s) will be built in accordance with this Outline Specification and the accompanying plans and with the residential standards of the local building code for the area. "Notice to Borrowers" below has been noted and will be followed.

Date	Applicant's Signature

- ♦ **THE BORROWER** is responsible for ensuring that the house is built in accordance with approved plans and specifications.

- ♦ No changes are to be made without the approval of (Your Financial Institution).

- ♦ **THE BORROWER** must ensure that construction conforms at least to standards of design and construction prescribed by the Residential Standards of The National Building Code. These Standards are available at any government department of housing.

- ♦ One approved copy of the plans and outline specification must be available on the site during construction.

- ♦ **FAILURE TO COMPLY WITH THE ABOVE MAY RESULT IN DELAYS OR IN THE REDUCTION OR CANCELLATION OF THE LOAN.**

- ♦ A home owner or purchaser should have a written agreement with his contractor or subcontractors to ensure that the house conforms with the specifications. As this outline specification is for your financial institution purposes only, agreements should include a more detailed specification of the proposed house.

    NOTE:
    Two copies of this outline specification and of the plans must be submitted with each application. Borrowers should include details of special or other features that may be pertinent for appraisal purposes. Additional sheets may be used where necessary. One copy will be retained by your financial institution and one approved copy will be returned to the applicant.

- **Mortgage/Loan Payments**

The lender will inform you of interim interest charges on the mortgage advances which will be deducted from your final advance. It is calculated from the date the first advance was made to the date the first actual mortgage payment is due, usually the first of a specific month. The interest rate for this period is based on the mortgage rate negotiated between you and the bank, and is usually much better than a personal loan rate. If this is a first or second mortgage the solicitor will have been instructed to pull the title to the property, and identify the lender as mortgage holder on the property. Monthly mortgage payments of principal and interest include monthly property taxes, or the lender may give you the option of paying them personally monthly or as a lump sum payment when the taxes are due.

If you made a personal loan for the renovation project, the bank has already registered your personal guarantee or their interest on the property title. The interest will be payable as per their payment schedule and the agreed upon interest rate.

- **Inspections**

As the renovation progresses, inspections will be required by the city and mortgage holder. The purpose of the inspections is to ensure that the construction conforms with the approved plans and specifications, and local building standards. These inspections must be done as the lender requires information on the progress of construction in order to advise the solicitor of dates and amounts of mortgage/loan money to be advanced. For major renovation projects at least three inspections will be required by the city, but your lender might require more (see inspections below). If the renovation project requires the removal of existing structural walls and supports, an inspection should be requested to ensure both the city and lender's inspectors approve completion of this portion of the renovation. If your lender require more inspections, or their inspector feels that you have not completed all the required work and suggests an additional inspection, be prepared to pay a fee for the additional inspection(s).

Advances post-inspection can be arranged with some flexibility to satisfy both parties. You may request that the advances be paid directly to yourself, and you in turn pay the subtrades or contractor according to the agreed upon payment schedule or building contract.

When the final inspection is requested the home renovation should be completed and ready for occupancy. At this time the lender will advance the final payment. The solicitor usually deducts his fees for services from this amount, and forwards the remainder to the home owner or builder less the required lien holdback. This holdback is held in a trust account until the lien period passes, usually about 45 days depending on the State or Province.

Here is a sample of the stages at which inspections are usually required:

INSPECTION NO. 1	INSPECTION NO. 2	INSPECTION NO. 3
Ready for construction	Basement ready for backfill	Interior ready for drywall
☐ Excavation	☐ Excavation	☐ Roof complete
☐ Foundation footing	☐ Foundation	☐ Rough plumbing
☐ Temporary supports in place	☐ Weeping tile	☐ Rough wiring
☐ Additional supports required	☐ Waterproofing	☐ Framing, sheathing
☐ Existing structure to code	☐ Backfill	☐ Exterior doors, windows
☐ Insulation, vapor barrier required	☐ Floor framing	☐ Roughed in heating
	☐ Subfloor	☐ Basement floor poured
	☐ Insulation, Vapor barrier	

INSPECTION NO. 4
House complete - Ready for occupancy

☐ Drywall and taping complete
☐ Heating equipment installed

INSPECTION NO. 5
House ready for painting/finishing

☐ Interior doors hung
☐ Floors finished
☐ Exterior complete
☐ Kitchen cupboards installed
☐ Plumbing complete (fixtures installed)
☐ Electrical complete (fixtures installed)
☐ Baseboard, trim, etc.
☐ Site improvements

- **Mortgage Inspector**

Mortgage/loan inspectors control the amount of monies advanced to the lawyer at completion of certain construction phases. These inspections are done when an inspection request card has been completed and mailed, or the request phoned into the inspection department or mortgage/loan officer. Be sure to display prominently the address card supplied by the bank at the front of the lot, and check that you have complied with all the construction phases noted on the card before requesting any inspection(s).

Mortgage/loan inspectors differ from the city inspectors in that they approve the completion of specific construction stages and certain building requirements, eg., frost insulation under garage grade beam, basement frost walls, rough plumbing/heating/electrical completion, drywall, painting and finishing completion. Building code compliance is left to the city building inspectors.

The larger financial institutions have their own inspectors whereas some smaller banks, trust companies, and credit unions will hire independent inspectors. Either way, make sure that you fully understand when the inspections are required, the length of time between contact and inspection, and who is responsible for initiating the inspection process and construction draws.

- **City Inspector**

City inspectors can be either your best asset or your worst enemy; therefore, before starting the renovation project, review your documents from the city to understand their requirements. Know when to request inspections, and schedule meetings with the inspector placed in charge of reviewing your house plans. He can inform you of any unforeseen problems such as city property, sidewalk, street or lane upgrade requirements, or soil conditions which will require an engineer's report. Being aware of these potential problems will save you time and money.

Utilize a city inspector's knowledge and expertise. The inspector will review your house and plot plans making sure that the materials are correct and structural requirements are satisfied. As an independent observer he will inspect the workmanship of the individual subcontractors, and make sure the heating, plumbing, electrical, insulation, house structure, grading, etc., have been done correctly, and according to the local building code.

When you pay for your building permit at the city hall these inspection services are included. If you have any questions or concerns during construction, request an inspection. The inspector is usually more than pleased to help, and will inform you of any deficiencies that can be more easily corrected at that time than later at great expense.

NOTES:_____

PART II: WHO SHOULD BUILD FOR YOU?

CHAPTER 7

◆ WHICH WAY TO BUILD?

• Contracting Yourself

If you are planning on being your own contractor, you must do your homework. When going for a loan you need to have all the facts available and at your fingertips when any questions are asked. The mortgage/loan officer may or may not grant a loan depending on his estimation of your ability, financial and otherwise, to complete the construction satisfactorily. You must be able to convince the officer that you have the necessary knowledge and time to collect estimates, and supervise the construction correctly as required by the local building code. Being your own contractor takes a lot of hard work, time, organizing ability, and a knowledge of construction not possessed by the average lay person. This is why many home owners choose to pay project management fees to general contractors and let them do the work.

If you are prepared for the experience of a lifetime as your own contractor you will be required to:

1) collect estimates, and select and hire subcontractors for concrete, framing, electrical, plumbing, heating, etc.;

2) make arrangements to purchase and have delivered at the times required the correct quantities of building materials needed for every step of the renovation;

3) schedule the various stages of construction, and oversee their correct completion on time and on budget.

If your existing utilities need repair, replacement or relocation due to the renovation, you will also have to make application for the connection of the sewer, water, power and/or gas lines, and determine their new connection locations on the house and street service lines.

When collecting or reviewing estimates, check to see that the suppliers and subtrades are registered with the local Workers' Compensation Board. For subtrades that are not registered or have misrepresented their position to you, make sure you understand your responsibilities as a lay contractor by contacting the local Workers' Compensation Board and getting the necessary insurance against any mishap.

Even though the renovation project is a size you think you can contract yourself, and the family can save some money, think twice about living in a house under construction and having to put up with periods of no heat, no water, daily drywall dust and dirt, no cooking facilities, and no privacy. Depending on the extent of the renovation, this reality may lead to daily family fights followed by an unnecessary divorce. All kidding aside, here is a personal story which happened during a renovation project.

I thought that being a home designer and working in the construction industry daily gave me the advantage of knowing what potential problems might occur during a renovation project and that I could eliminate or reduce them considerably. Not true! My wife and I had just made an offer on a house which needed a little work and a small addition to the rear to make it more open and create a more energy-efficient home. My wife, however, obviously knowing something more than I, said, "Spring weather has not always been such a great time of the year for renovating so I would prefer to go on holidays for the first month of the renovation." I thought that it was a great idea because, as a construction jock, I would be in my element, and on my own with no "little woman" looking over my shoulder asking me to explain every construction detail.

Our offer was approved with a 30-day possession which allowed time for designing the renovation, getting the permit from the city, collecting all the estimates, getting a construction loan, and scheduling workers for the second week of occupancy. I thought this was going to be so much fun! The 30 days flew by and we moved in, making sure the movers placed only essential supplies and furniture on the main floor during the renovation, i.e., pots and pans, some food, sofa bed, television, etc., with the remainder going into the basement to be locked up.

I had the excavator dig the hole in the backyard and the cribber pour the foundation, ready for the framer to lay the joists a few days before my wife was to leave town. On the Wednesday morning, as I was driving her to the airport, the city was at the house to turn off the water and sewer; the subcontractor was to extend and reconnect the lines by the time I returned. On my return the sewer and water lines were just being completed ready for connection, and I proceeded to contact the city water and sanitation department to request a reconnect.

Mistake No. 1: When I called, the department said that I should have booked the reconnect at the time the disconnect was requested. They were booking for the Friday of the following week. Explaining the situation I requested a reconnect the following Friday or as soon as possible. I told my tale to the contractor working on the water and sewer. He laughed and said that this was not the first time he had heard of this happening. He did not have the authority to reconnect the main water line until it was inspected and a meter installed, but he could install a tap to the main line so I could connect a hose to get water that way. He indicated the sewer line was working, and I could fill the tub and the toilet tank with the hose. You can imagine how much fun I had over the next nine days dragging a 75-foot hose behind me to wash, bathe, and wash dishes in cold water, as well as make sure the toilet tank was always filled. Other than that things were moving along. The framer arrived on time and laid the joists and subfloor, and put up the walls and roof before demolishing the existing structure.

Mistake No. 2: During the first week I was so involved with scheduling the framer I forgot to have the windows sent. I anticipated no problem as I knew they could be delivered the next day. When I called the manufacturer they reminded me that it was Friday so the Next Day delivery was first thing Monday morning. OK. No big deal. I had the framer staple some polyethylene to the door and window openings until Monday. Problem solved.

Mistake No. 3: When the framer demolished the wall between the existing house and the addition, I had the electrician remove the meter which disconnected the power to everything including the furnace. He would return the next Tuesday to install the switches and plugs, and reconnect the meter on the wall of the addition. No heat, no problem. I had the framer "poly" off the living room where I slept on the sofa bed, and I would use the wood-burning fireplace to heat the room. Friday night I ate cold leftovers with raw carrots in front of a warm fireplace. Saturday night I decided to celebrate my existence so I brought in enough wood for use till morning and ordered a hot pizza. The bonus for that week was the city had arrived to inspect and install the water meter so I had hot and cold water.

Mistake No. 4: I was so tired from having to keep the logs going on the fire that I decided I would sleep in on Sunday. When renovating in an area with existing houses and snoopy neighbors, you should always remember to make No Trespassing or Do Not Enter signs. Sunday morning at 8:30 I was laying on the sofa bed when I heard voices. Assuming I was hearing neighbors and not knowing where the voices were coming from because polyethylene does not act very well as a sound buffer, I chose to ignore them. Then the voices became so clear they seemed to be in the same room. I opened my eyes and our eyes met. The very embarrassed couple said, "We thought the house was vacant." I angrily answered, "The only way you could have gotten in was to pull the polyethylene off the door frame, and to do that you had to walk by my car. If you are not out of here in 30 seconds I'm calling the police." They apologized several times and promptly left. I smiled thinking to myself "I'm glad I wasn't taking a bath."

Other than those small but irritating inconveniences, there were no *major* mistakes, and the neighbors who woke me up were forgiven. My wife had a great chuckle when she heard about my adventures. On her return we decided to do the interior painting ourselves and spent many late nights painting and talking about the self-contracting experience. It had been gratifying, even with its frustrations. Problems should be taken with a grain of salt and written down in a diary as a story to tell other friends who are considering a renovation.

Many of my clients who hire a project manager also wish to do some of the subcontract work themselves, assuming that they will save on the labor costs, e.g., insulating, painting, etc. Before committing to this undertaking, ask yourself a few questions.

- Do you have the time it takes to do the work?
- Will you slow down the construction schedule by doing this work yourself?
- Will your work look professional enough?
- Are you able to purchase the materials at the same cost as the subcontractor?

Consider too that if you also have to rent some equipment in order to do this job, how much will that add to the cost of the project?

As professionals, the subcontractors will in most cases take less time to complete the same job, and that will save some bank interest charges. As well as having their own tools, they are also able to purchase the materials more cheaply as they get a bulk discount from the supplier. To verify that this is the case, get some personal estimates from some suppliers and subtrades, and compare your prices with the trades'. I think you will be surprised. Maybe it will be to your advantage to stay at work, keep bringing in a salary, and spend your evenings and weekends inspecting and doing the service work required. You will find that the service work included in being your subcontractor's "joe boy" or "gopher" will take up much of your time. You will also hear from some subcontractors "I forgot this," "Could you get that?", "You should have gotten this one instead," or "Supplying this was not in our contract." Be prepared as these are just some of the incidentals attached to being your own contractor.

If you are lucky enough to have a retired family member who is close by, has some knowledge of construction, and is willing to spend a few hours per day at the house to open it in the morning and lock it up in the evening, you have a gold mine. Most suppliers and subcontractors become more conscientious when someone who is representing the builder is around the construction site, not getting in their way, but watching them and asking the occasional question. This person will also be able to keep you informed of the progress when you are not able to be on the job site. Include this person's name and function in your letter of introduction to the bank.

● **Hiring a General Contractor**

Having sufficient information on house construction will give you an edge over consumers who are so trusting that they choose a contractor based on a nice personality. Many home owners when initially speaking to contractors do not know how much of the home will be affected by the renovation, have little or no knowledge of construction, and do not know how much they can participate in the planning and construction. How do average consumers ensure that they have chosen the most honest and experienced contractors for their home renovation projects? Confidence in selection is based on research through contacts, conversations and books that promote a practical, in-depth understanding of construction. Building a home becomes a personal quest to create something specific to your own needs and different from any other house regardless of who builds it. When the home owner, without the direction of the contractor, has taken the time to plan traffic patterns, assist in creating the detailed drawings, and learn the pros and cons of dealing with suppliers and subtrades, the knowledge gained will put him on a more level playing field with a home builder/renovator.

So, in a sense, you have already started your homework. You know what you want, and will learn as you read on how the process of construction works. Choosing the right contractor is a most crucial step to realizing your dreams. As discussed in many chapters, it is critical that you select a minimum of three potential contractors to bid on the project, and then narrow the choice down to one. Since the builder will schedule the project and spend your money, the success or failure depends on the relationship that you and he carefully enter. It should not be based on a casual discussion at some show home, but rather your gut feeling, his final price, and a detailed contract. As in any profession builders will vary in the quality of construction provided. Just as there are good lawyers, skilled surgeons, and reliable builders there are bad, incompetent and dishonest ones.

Established custom builders come in a variety of forms, such as a large company, a family partnership, or even a one-man operation. These builders have an established name within the industry and have been in the business for many years. They are often associated with the more exclusive estate and executive subdivisions which cater to the more expensive custom home or renovation project.

Over the lean years some of these builders have adapted their building services to provide potential clients with graded building "packages." Those people requiring a renovation to their existing home, or families on a budget unable to afford the full executive style, are happy with a revised version or components of one of the builder's conventional model homes. These builders tend to purchase large quantities of similar materials for use in all their middle and lower end homes. This bulk purchase practice allows them to pass on the savings to the potential home owner, and provides the builder with a known construction cost. The home owner can expect to pay a premium price for the services of the established builder; however, you will receive quality products for the price, and a good warranty contract.

Semi-retired custom builders are few and far between; however, if you have the patience to track them down they are out there. Many semi-retired contractors are willing to take on renovation work during their slow times, and some will work in a supervisory capacity for a fixed fee. Know in advance that your construction project will not have a time schedule, but the end result will be pride in a structurally well-built quality home. This type of builder is meticulous. By themselves or with long-term apprentices they methodically demolish and renovate the house stick by stick until finished. During the construction process you will meet such a builder's family, friends, and past clientele who visit bringing him coffee and sandwiches which he will repay with a tour of the home which includes explaining in great detail the use of quality materials and methods used in all his homes. For people who are not in a hurry, who like a lot of individual attention, and who do not mind ending up with a lifelong, almost fatherlike friendship, this would be a good way to go. These contractors are very obliging with clients' requests and will go to any extent to satisfy;

however, always expect additional invoices for services rendered as this is where they make the greatest portion of their profit.

New generation builders are usually ex-framers and tradespeople trying to make a name for themselves on their own. They tend to build only a few homes for the first few years hoping to get recognized as quality builders. They lack the business experience and financial reserves of the established builders to weather the seasonal ups and downs of the construction industry, and the fluctuating economic times. Initially, they depend heavily on word-of-mouth advertising from suppliers and subcontractors that they have worked with in the past. These same subtrades may have constructed their own principal residences, which in turn establishes a credit rating with a financial institution. After proving their abilities with their own homes, close friends and relatives may have them build or renovate homes which can then be used to advertise completed projects. During this initial stage of growth these builders are willing to work for wages in order to get a start, and will provide quality construction to potential clients at a reduced construction cost.

In order to gain respect within the industry, it is usual practice to join one of the local builders' organizations or a chapter of the National Home Building Association. This membership will provide them access to a warranty program for future clients, as well as a connection to the same suppliers and subtrades used by the established home builders. If these new builders survive the lean years, their future clients will be proud to promote their companies because they were provided with great service and well-constructed homes.

Mobile builders are handymen, transient laborers, or jacks-of-all-trades who, after completing several building projects, have gained enough basic knowledge of the construction industry to promote their abilities in the renovation section of a local newspaper.

They usually own a beat-up and rusting half ton truck or van which inevitably breaks down somewhere between jobs, leaving the client waiting at the job site for days without a phone call. When they do finally call, they expect you to feel sorry for them and accept this unfortunate delay. Exhibiting an obvious drive for profit and disregard for customer satisfaction, these contractors always arrive late, never return phone calls once a deposit has been received, provide price quotations on the back of their business cards, are not concerned about quality, will always ask for advances, and will accept a three-week job which will be extended to 10 weeks. The worst scenario is that they will disappear after taking your deposit. As a streetwise purchaser it would be best to deal with these contractors on a pay-as-you-complete basis, with no or as little up front deposit as possible.

Know that the quality of the work will be fair to mediocre and that these builders are best suited for simple painting jobs and small renovation projects. They are usually lacking the necessary building skills, business sense, and reliable reputation found in the established or new builders.

● **Buyer Beware**

If you have had friends who had a general contractor build or renovate their homes, you have likely heard some of the horror stories that occurred during the construction. Word of mouth can be the best or worst form of advertising for a general contractor. There are many ways to protect yourself against unreputable, fly-by-night contractors.

Before selecting a general contractor, see his work. If he is a small builder, get at least three client references who will allow you to ask questions and view their homes. If you plan to work with a larger builder, visit their show homes. This however is not always the best method to assure consistent quality since a show home usually represents their best work. As in the first case, it is fair to ask for three references who have been living in the builder-constructed home for about two years. This will verify that the builder constructs a quality home, and provides an appropriate post-construction maintenance service. Many of the suppliers and subtrades provide some type of a warranty for their work. It is not usually written on their estimate sheets, so you or the selected contractor should have the warranty period and products under warranty listed on the estimate.

A small contractor who builds or better yet renovates three to six homes per year, and has been in business for at least seven years, is usually an efficient operator with a low overhead. Such a contractor will make a greater attempt to satisfy the client and save you money. Any contractor that has specialized in renovations rather than new home construction will have more knowledge of potential problem areas when old and new construction meet. He would have encountered similar construction problems before, and will know how to rectify them. I also believe the contractor who is driving a truck and working on-site with his trades is most likely to give good value. On the other hand, the contractor who drives a mercedes or cadillac, has glossy presentation pictures, or spends much of his time at the office or racquetball court should trigger concerns about where the money is going, and who is supervising the construction project.

It is not necessary to be an expert in the construction industry to come to an informed opinion on how well a house is constructed. Even a professional inspector cannot see what is behind drywall or under carpets. Like you, the inspector can judge only what he can see, and then form an unbiased impression. The clues, eg., the care in which the finishing has been completed, are there. Check the hand railings, door trims, baseboards and kitchen cabinets to see if they have been sanded smooth, and the joints and corners tight or properly sealed with caulking. You can also assess quality through the selection of plumbing appliances, finishing hardware, heating equipment and kitchen cabinets for being well built and intended to stand the test of time. If able to view a renovated home, check the joining seams between old and new sections for cracking, bulges, sloping floors, etc. Ask the inhabitants for their honest opinion on the quality and efficiency of the contractor's work.

- **Builder Contracts**

After selecting the builder, the next step is drawing up a detailed written contract. However, a small builder generally does not have a prepared contract. Many home builders associations, stationery stores, and lawyers have contracts which can be amended for your needs. All standard contracts should include the following: an agreed upon price and method of payment which corresponds with your payment schedule or the bank's construction advances; a specified completion date; working drawings and detailed specifications; and rights and responsibilities of both parties clearly outlined, such as terms of warranties, method of settlement for incomplete or unsatisfactory work, responsibility for fire and liability insurance, coverage for Workers' Compensation, protection of property, and any other details you wish to add. The contract should also include a statement preventing the builder from assigning his responsibilities to others, an arbitration clause in the event of any disputes, and details that constitute the acceptance of occupancy by the owners. This agreement, along with the final plans, drawings, and specifications, will act as a guideline for your relationship with the builder to the completion of the renovation project. It must be signed by both parties before the shovel turns any earth. Once the contract is completed to your satisfaction, you will need the services of a lawyer to review it. It is sometimes best to choose a lawyer who has dealt with your bank, and is knowledgeable about construction mortgages in order to protect your interests above the builders. The lawyer should review each section of the contract with the owner, and question anything that might cause any misunderstandings.

Especially when renovating, the contract should specify in detail the work to be done by the builder. But, remember no contract is perfect, and sometimes surprises will affect the final construction cost. A common but good example of this problem is where the designer does not show the driveway, sidewalk, sidewalk/patio/driveway piles, and concrete patio locations, and the builder, supplier, or subcontractor might not include them in his costs. This error could cost thousands of dollars. If the contractor leaves those items out in his cost projection, his estimate would look cheaper, and later he will be able to charge extra because they had not been included in the blueprint and therefore his contract. He's got you!

When dealing with any contractor, it is a good idea to include signing and marking of the working blueprint when making changes to the renovation project. As an example, the contractor might suggest after reviewing the working blueprints that it would be cheaper to move a window over a few inches which will allow the cabinet maker more room for a built-in pantry unit. Have *the contractor* mark this change on two sets of blueprints and initial the change. Your set of revised and initialled working blueprints should never be used for anything other than forming part of the contract, and becomes vitally important when there is a disagreement.

It is essential that the home owner knows the standard of work and quality of materials that will be going into the renovation/addition project. Most builders have a list of standard construction specifications that they provide to their clients, but be aware that there are different specification sheets for the different categories of quality, i.e., standard, executive, and custom. The quality of materials and selection available for each of these categories is primarily determined by the existing home's finish and client product selection. The more custom the renovation project, the greater the selection *and* cost. See Sample Construction Specifications, pages 58 to 61. These specification sheets are also valuable if you plan on contracting the renovation yourself as they provide the suppliers and subcontractors with a detailed list of the expected custom standards required.

You may use the contractor's design services or your own designer for drawing the detailed plans. If you choose to use the contractor's designer he should treat you as "his" client, and protect your interests over the builder's. He should provide a detailed plan containing all the builder's specifications as well as a detailed list of your own. Hiring your own designer automatically provides the builder with your detailed specifications, and does not hold you to theirs. Once again, make sure your renovation/addition plans have not been compromised.

Almost all builder contracts contain an insurance clause which will be the builder's responsibility to provide. This insurance policy is usually a general coverage policy protecting the property against vandalism, material theft, and contractor errors. If you are going to work with a contractor that has not done any work for you in the past, have his insurance policy reviewed by your insurance company. Having this information, your insurance company will be able to provide additional coverage in areas that are not covered by the contractor's policy, such as accidental damage, additional liability, and possibly a mortgage protection clause.

Finally, before signing the builder's contract, provide the bank with a copy of the contract unsigned, as the bank might require changes; also make sure your mortgage or construction loan is approved *before* you sign the formal building contract. For their files the bank will require a copy of the building contract, builder's specifications, and completed bank's specification sheets (see pages 45-46) along with the blueprints, plot plans and financial application as previously discussed. If you have not already completed these documents, your building contractor or designer will be able to help you. Do not let anyone but the bank see your financial package as that is personal information.

Having completed all of the above, and receiving the approval of the bank and lawyer for the builder's contract and mortgage package, you may start the construction. Some financial institutions will allow you to start the excavation of the foundation up to backfilling stage before signing the mortgage/loan documents provided that you have a signed interim financing agreement in place, you own the property clear title with no encumbrances against it, and have a valid foundation permit from the city engineering department. This is *not* a good practice. If the bank or city inspector requires structural changes to the foundation or house structure after reviewing the floor plans, you might be inviting extra expenses. The worst scenario will require demolition of the existing foundation in order to make the structural changes. There goes your budget and possibly your dream renovation.

Through no fault of your own or the builder's, sometimes materials or products cannot be delivered on schedule, or become out-of-stock items, eg., windows, kitchen cabinets, floor coverings and finishing products. Be prepared to choose a new product which usually means upgrading and purchasing a more expensive line. When walking through the house during the framing, you might feel that a room is too small or you require a wall removed, a window added, a door opening enlarged, or a fireplace added. If this happens, expect the contractor to extra-bill you for the service. Even if you feel this will not happen, have a backup plan with your lender by applying for a pre-approved, personal demand loan. Five percent of the construction cost is a safe figure, and if not used, you owe nothing. During my years of construction experience this backup has come in handy more than once.

SAMPLE CONSTRUCTION SPECIFICATIONS
****

CONSTRUCTION SCHEDULE "A"

For New and Existing Portion of House.
- Demolition of existing home and outbuildings as per plan, and removal of all materials;
- Removal of sinks, toilets, tubs, cabinets, and fixtures with minimal damage and set aside for owner to sell;
- Demolition of fences, driveways, sidewalks, or planters as per plan, and removal of all materials;
- Replacement or construction of any fences, driveways, sidewalks, or planters as per plan;
- Footings to rest on undisturbed soil;
- Two 3/8" or 1/2" dowels top, middle, and bottom of existing foundation to tie into new foundation;
- Three 3/8" or 1/2" dowels at existing footing to tie into new footing;
- 2500 psi (17.5 mpa) concrete type 10 in steel-reinforced concrete walls and footings;
- 2000 psi (15.0 mpa), no air, type 10 basement concrete floor and 6 mil poly vapor barrier over tamped, sand-fill base to top of footing;
- Asphalt dampproofing on exterior and interior concrete walls;
- Continuous 4" diameter weeping tile covered with minimum 6" crushed rock around house draining to a sewer, drainage ditch or dry well;
- Covering of weeping tile around footings and window wells with landscapers' felt;
- Repair, replacement, and/or connection of old weeping tile to the new perimeter tile;
- Minimum grade of lumber to be #2 spruce or better, all fir to be #2 or better;
- 2" x 6" exterior walls with R-20 fiberglass insulation;
- Existing 2" x 4" exterior walls to be strapped on interior to match new wall thickness;

- R-40 ceiling insulation in all main house attic, R-20 ceiling insulation in garage, R-32 in areas where the upper floor of the house extends over the garage area;
- 6 mil poly vapor barrier caulked at all joints;
- Caulking around all existing door and window openings;
- Poly vapor hats around all new electrical outlets on all outside walls and cold ceilings;
- Header joists to be doubled when exceeding 4'-0" in length;
- Trimmer joists to be doubled when header joists exceed 32";
- 2" x 10" fir floor joists @ 16" on center (o.c.) with 2" x 2" cross bridging and strapping;
- Provision of bridging at 7'-0" o.c. or less;
- Double joists under all nonload bearing partitions;
- Hollow steel adjustable columns to be 2-7/8" diameter with 4" x 4" steel top and bottom plates, top plates to be bolted into structural beams with 2" lag bolts;
- Structural wood columns to be a minimum 6" x 6";
- 3/4" sturdywood or plywood tongue and groove subfloor, glued and screwed;
- Existing exposed subfloor to be wedged and rescrewed to existing floor joists;
- 2" x 4" @ 16" o.c. for all frost walls in basement with R-20 insulation, full height;
- Roof trusses are 24" o.c. engineered trusses;
- 1/2" spruce plywood roof sheathing with H-clips;
- Pine or cedar shakes on slopes of 4/12 or greater;
- Asphalt roof shingles #210 - slopes of 4/12 or greater,
                    #235 - slopes of less than 4/12;
- 3/8" sturdywood or plywood wall sheathing with siding; 1/2" with stucco;
- 1/2" drywall throughout and all cold ceilings 5/8" rigid fireboard;
- 3000 psi (20.7 mpa) concrete, exposed aggregate for all walkways and driveway, all reinforced with 1/2" rebar, 20" x 20" grid;
- Stairs: - rise 8" maximum - run 9" - tread width 10-1/4" minimum;
- Headroom clearance 6'-4" minimum - stair width 3'-0" minimum;
- Stairs with more than two risers to have a handrail 2'-6" (minimum) above nosing;
- 2" x 10" fir deck header board attached to house with building paper, flashing and caulking.

EXTERIOR SCHEDULE "B"
- Existing cladding to be removed and finished as per plan;
- California style stucco, siding as per plan;
- Repair, replacement, and/or connection of prefinished metal soffits, fascia and eavestroughs;
- Double-glazed, wood casement window units, as per plan;
- Building paper around all windows, doors and exterior areas;
- Caulking around all new windows, doors and exterior areas;
- Insulated steel exterior doors, as per plan;
- Removal of existing taps and replacement with frost-free units, location as per plan;
- Exterior weatherproof electrical outlets, locations as per plan;
- Lot is rough-graded, slope to drain away from building;
- Deck and piles or rough-in as per plan.

GARAGE SCHEDULE "C"

- Garage floor (where applicable) - 3000 psi (20.7 mpa), no air, type 10 concrete over sand-fill base complete with (c/w) wire mesh and rebar (20" x 20" grid);
- Drive through 13' x 14' concrete garage pad - 3000 psi (20.7 mpa), type 10 concrete over sand-fill base, c/w rebar (20" x 20" grid);
- Attached garage to have reinforced foundation and grade beam, as per plan, with piles or footings, frost void form under grade beam;
- Plug-ins for electrical garage door openers;
- 220 volt power plug in garage;
- One 16' x 7' or two 9' x 7' metal sectional overhead doors, stained/painted/insulated;
- 5/8" drywall fireboard on all common walls;
- 1/2" drywall and insulated garage (R-20 ceilings and R-12 walls);
- Half H.P. garage door openers with two remote controls;
- Frost-free water tap;
- Garage floor drain with backup check valve;
- Stairs to basement from garage.

INTERIOR PLUMBING SPECIFICATIONS SCHEDULE "D"

- Removal and replacement of all existing copper hot and cold water lines with 1/2" flexible lines;
- Removal and replacement of all cast iron drains and replacement with plastic lines;
- Double stainless-steel kitchen sink, c/w sink garbage disposal and vegetable spray;
- Two porcelain water closets;
- American standard bidet or equivalent;
- Custom tile with waterproof tile board in master bath shower unit , c/w glass shower door enclosure (modesty lines);
- Fiberglass one-piece tub and shower units in main bathrooms;
- Fiberglass whirlpool, c/w six jets, 72" x 36";
- Porcelain basins in all bathrooms;
- Ice-maker water line connection for kitchen refrigerator;
- Single-lever brass taps throughout;
- Insulated #50 (40 gallon) hot water tank;
- Supplying and installing of in-ground sump pump, container, and drain lines;
- Roughed-in plumbing for four-piece bath in basement.

GENERAL SPECIFICATIONS SCHEDULE "E"

- Complete vacuum system with power head;
- Complete built-in dishwasher;
- Complete built-in trash compactor;
- Complete built-in microwave;
- 220 volt outlets for cooktop, oven and dryer;
- 100 amp electrical service with copper wiring;
- Two 100,000 B.T.U. mid-efficiency furnaces;
- Smoke detectors as per building code;

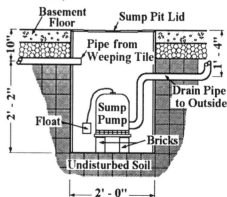

Typical in-ground sump and pit.

- Dryer vent to outside;
- Mirrors over vanity sinks, 36" or by vanity width;
- Weiser or equivalent: black pearl handles in all bathrooms, bedrooms and master bedroom, etc.,
- Weiser or equivalent (locking): black pearl handles in all bathrooms and master bedroom doors;
- Bathroom outlets on ground fault interrupter circuit, as per Electrical Code;
- Ceramic tiles 18" over whirlpool and decking; full height above kitchen countertops; splash row above all vanities, one row around built-in shower unit;
- Paint-grade modular doors (colonial style or equivalent), pine casings and baseboards throughout, mirrored closet doors in master bedroom and foyer; or
- Oak grade modular doors with lacquer finish (colonial style or equivalent), oak casings and baseboards with lacquer finish throughout;
- Garage stair access to basement of house with railing;
- Textured spray ceilings throughout;
- French glass doors in dining room, den, master bath;
- TV outlets and telephone outlets, as required by owner;
- Oak spindle railings and handrails painted to match decor;
- Gas fireplace or "O" clearance metal fireplace, c/w log lighter, glass & brass with remote lighter;
- Custom kitchen, bathroom and laundry cabinets, as per plan by cabinet maker;
- Complete security system with glass break, motion sensors, door pads and window pads;
- Complete intercom system including waterproof bathroom speakers;
- 40 oz. stain protected carpets with 3/8" commercial foam underlay throughout halls, stairs, bedrooms and living areas;
- Candide or equivalent lino in kitchen, mud area, laundry room and main bathrooms;
- Ceramic tile in front entry, master bath en suite;
- Cedar deck approx. 15' x 26' with railings and steps. 5' x 6' concrete pads 3000 psi (20.7 mpa), type 10 concrete over sand-fill base, c/w rebar (20" x 20" grid) to be placed at bottom of deck steps.

- **Alternative Construction Contracts**

If you are also interested in saving some money, and are willing to spend some time researching construction costs, there are alternative building contract forms available at some stationery suppliers. Note that the information for mortgage purposes as well as any of the protection clauses must remain the same.

If you do not feel comfortable taking on the total renovation project yourself, an alternative is to hire a home builder or supervisor on a flat rate or by the hour. These methods can be very flexible with portions of work subcontracted by the do-it-yourselfer, eg., insulating, caulking, painting, or window, carpet and cabinet selection, and the remainder of the renovation work, eg., excavation, framing, plumbing, heating, electrical, handled by a project manager.

Note: Alternative methods of construction can cause problems when the client becomes too free with upgrading the quality of material or fixtures without first confirming the effect these upgrades will have on the cost of the renovation project. When first collecting estimates, discuss in detail with the project manager and suppliers the difference between, eg., a contractor's standard quality of painted pine and a custom upgrade of stained oak.

Cost plus:

This method is favored by some clients who wish to select the quality and price of materials and products resulting in a known final construction cost plus a 10 percent surcharge of the total construction value. The contractor in this instance is guaranteed a profit at the end of the renovation project. The building contract and specification details remain the same as stated in the contract information for mortgage/loan purposes as well as any of the protection clauses, i.e., the work to be done by the builder, a date for completion, the plans and specifications to be followed and completed in a good and workmanlike manner, the price to be paid, and the times at which payments are to be made.

The guaranteed profit allows the builder to declare a profit margin up front so that the client does not have to worry about any hidden or unforeseen costs other than chosen upgrades. This, however, does not let the contractor off the hook. He still must provide up front a total cost for construction, and the client is able to review all estimates received by the contractor and reject or approve those quotes. To this end include in the contract that the contractor supply you with a *minimum* of two estimates for each area of construction, i.e., electrical, framing, plumbing, windows, heating, etc.

In order to protect yourself further, it would be prudent to collect estimates on your own from other contractors for price comparison. The estimate should include a detailed list of required materials and labor. Also, remember that estimates should have a validation date that gives sufficient time for the house to be completed.

Project management:

This method of construction is the happy medium between the do-it-yourselfer and the hiring of a general contractor. As potential home owners become more knowledgeable about construction, the contractors become more innovative in methods of attracting clients. The concept of project management came about when the market became oversaturated with builders. Some of these builders, usually the smaller ones, were unable to survive, and they returned to the work force, sometimes working for other builders as supervisors or contracting out their experience and services to owner-builders.

The project manager's job description does not require him to do the financial bookwork. He is contracted to provide specified services to the home owner. In return for this service he can request construction advances at certain stages or a lump sum payment upon completion of the renovation project. These services may include applying for permits, gathering estimates, ordering materials, scheduling subcontractors for all stages of construction, ordering materials and supervising the construction project on a day-to-day basis. The project manager's building contract and specification details remain the same as stated previously in this chapter as does the inclusion of any of the protection clauses. Once again, it is a good idea to collect estimates on your own for comparison with the project manager's. Remember when collecting or reviewing estimates to check that the suppliers and subtrades are registered with their local Workers' Compensation Board, and if they are not to find out the extent of your responsibilities.

In this business arrangement it is now the responsibility of the home owner to keep a proper accounting of the mortgage/loan advances and payments to the suppliers and subtrades. When the project manager provides you with the invoices, be sure the required lien holdback percentage (15 percent) held back by the solicitor from the mortgage/loan advances is passed on in the payments to the trades. You will be responsible for making or having the proper subtrades make the necessary applications for the connection of sewer, water, power and gas; the project manager will mark the correct locations for the house and street service lines. Your accounting responsibilities include providing adequate theft and liability insurance on the property and house during the renovation project.

Regardless of whether you choose to contract yourself or contract out, if you review Chapter 11 and find that a certain step has not been delegated, before signing any contract clarify who is responsible for its completion. Clients have told me the biggest headache on any construction project is dealing with the subtrades. Complaints that the last subtrade has not completed the work correctly or cleaned up properly will require a judgment call on whether or not to call the subtrade back, do it yourself, or have someone else fix it and charge that cost back to the subtrade's final payment. In all instances it is wise to inform the subcontractor and let him do the repairs or hear the probable consequences.

● **Builders' Warranties**

Any warranty is usually only as good as the builder. However, the home owner can protect his own interests by doing his own supervising and inspections from the very start of the renovation project. As a result, the builder will double-check his work and his workers.

No matter how good or conscientious the builder, small problems will always occur. These include sticking doors, cracks in the drywall, uneven foundation settling, and hairline fractures in the garage or basement floors. Most builders will fix these problems as a courtesy to the customer, and some well beyond the contractual warranty. Some will force the customer to harass or plead for the required repairs, and will finally do them begrudgingly. Others may try to lay the blame on the owner, and suggest that the service call and subsequent repair will be at additional charge, prepaid.

All new homes and large renovation projects carry an "implied warranty of habitability" which forces the builder to repair major structural defects, such as a failing foundation walls, beams or water leakage. Usually any small problems such as nail popping and drywall cracks after the one-year warranty period leave the owners with no alternative but to make the repairs and pay for them themselves. When major structural damage has occurred after the first year, the only recourse for many home owners is to take costly legal action against the builder. In almost all instances this action will exceed the actual cost of the repair. Before you sign a contract, ask the builder to investigate the local private-home warranty programs set up by some insurance companies or a home builders association in the area. For major renovation projects these new home warranties will insure the home for the required first year's service work, major structural defects, and potential failure of the plumbing, heating, cooling, and electrical systems for the first five years of occupancy. They can sometimes be extended to up to ten years of protection. The builder will apply for and pay a one-time insurance premium to the new home warranty program for this coverage. The fee is passed on to the home owner as part of the renovation cost, and any remainder of the warranty can be passed on to new owners if you sell the house within the term of the warranty.

If, for some reason, the builder cannot or does not complete the repairs, the home warranty will cover the expense after a relatively small deductible is paid by the owners. Some builders are too small or have insufficient business experience to apply to the Home Builders Association program; however, many private warranty programs by insurance companies will accept them if they pay a larger premium. If this is a major concern, request the builder to apply to either of these programs and provide proof of a warranty before you sign the contract.

With any type of business deal it is up to the customer as well as the businessman to keep the relationship on a professional level. Here are a few dos and don'ts that should be kept in mind when dealing with any builder during the renovation project.

Dos

✓ Get his home and mobile phone numbers.
✓ Keep communication open and honest.
✓ If you see something wrong do not hesitate to point it out to him.
✓ If you are wrong, admit you made a mistake.
✓ Insist on knowing the construction schedule.
✓ Until the construction is complete, keep the relationship friendly but businesslike.
✓ Try to see things from his point of view, too.
✓ Keep an eye on the work by asking questions.
✓ Keep a diary and Things to Do list.

Don'ts

✘ Do not criticize his work in front of other workers.
✘ Don't try to get free extras from the contractor.
✘ Don't get in his way while he is working.
✘ Do not demand changes. Pose them as questions.
✘ Do not expect major structural changes late in the construction, i.e., walls or doors moved.
✘ Do not make any quick changes without thinking it over and talking to the builder.
✘ Don't ask too many questions on-site. Write them down to be discussed after the working day when no workers are around.

- **Arbitration Clause**

Consumer arbitration is a simple and economical procedure whereby a business and the consumer may submit their dispute to a trained impartial third party for resolution. An arbitration clause in any contract with a builder, supplier, or subcontractor is designed to protect both the consumer and the supplier, and should be looked on by both parties as the best form of protection against any disputes. This clause will provide an alternative and relatively cheap method of correcting an unresolved situation, yet because of the costs involved, it should be an effective deterrent against starting a dispute.

Arbitration is available when all other forms of mediation have failed. Mediation will work only when both parties have agreed to resolve the problem; however, it is not legally binding on any of the parties. When the mediation process has failed and an arbitration process has been agreed to by both parties, one of the parties may initiate a request to the local arbitration society.

The society maintains a list of qualified persons chosen from all segments of the community who have taken and passed the necessary courses to maintain their appointment as a registered arbitrator. A list of potential arbitrators plus their biographies will be sent to both parties. Each party will be given a time period to choose and submit the names of acceptable arbitrators, and one who is believed to be impartial and selected by both parties will be the designated arbitrator. No one can ensure the impartiality of any arbitrator, but with disclosure as a condition of accepting the appointment the process of arbitration will assure optimum objectivity. If no one arbitrator is acceptable to both parties, each will select one arbitrator who in turn will select a third to serve as the chairperson. When this happens, the majority decision of the three arbitrators shall decide the question.

Any of the parties may at their own cost have a lawyer present at the arbitration hearing. The administration costs of the arbitration, including on-site inspections and technical witnesses, will be borne by both parties, or if the arbitrator sees fit will be charged to the losing party. Arbitrations are usually held at a time and place convenient to the parties and arbitrator.

Under most State/Provincial laws an agreement to arbitrate is binding on both parties; however, if one of the parties after signing the contract fails to arbitrate, the other party may bring court action to force them into arbitration. If, after this action, the first party continues to refuse, the arbitration will proceed without them, and the ruling of the arbitration will be binding on both parties. The arbitration award in most states and provinces is enforced by the court which means that a written award by the arbitrator may be taken to court with the damages filed and enforced as if it were a judgment or order of the court, yet without a hearing of the case.

- **Builders' Lien Act**

The building contract should be drafted to protect you against any claims under the Builders' Lien Act of the state or province in which you reside. The Builders' Lien Act may vary depending on the local or federal requirements. In all cases, workers, suppliers of materials, subcontractors, and contractors who have provided materials or labor on the construction of your home are given the right to apply for a lien on your property if they have not been paid. The Act may give them the right to sell the land and to hold back sufficient funds for their unpaid accounts. If your contractor neglects to pay his workers from the draws, you may be required to pay them even though you have already paid the full advance minus the lien holdback to the contractor. Make sure the contract protects you personally against any liability and spells out what makes the contractor personally liable for payment to his suppliers and employees.

Your contract with the builder should also include provisions for the holdback of funds by your lawyer on each draw and that no release of these lien funds will be made until all lien rights on the property have expired, and proof in writing is provided by the the builder that he has paid all outstanding accounts and laborers to the date of the last mortgage/loan draw. The amount of the holdback will vary in different areas, but is usually at least 15 percent which should be held back for 45 days from the completion of the job. As an example: Each subcontractor and supplier, i.e., plumber, electrical, heating, carpet, cabinets, etc., will have a 15 percent holdback from their full contracted price. The 45-day lien holdback date will start on the day that they completed their jobs and will not be required to return to the job site other than for final adjustments or service calls. The holdback payment will be made once you are sure that the job has been 100 percent completed in a workmanlike manner, the subcontractor or supplier has paid his suppliers and employees for your job, an inspection has been completed and an approval given by the district/bank's inspector, and you are fully satisfied with the job. In some cases the mortgage/loan contract with the bank may require the solicitor to retain this holdback from each draw for you as protection. It is a good practice to ask the bank what their policy is, and confirm that the solicitor will not advance any lien monies to the contractor until you are assured your interests are protected.

- **Supplier/Subcontractor Contract**

If self-contracting the renovation project, you might want to adopt a simple, easy-to-understand contract that can be used for all the suppliers and subcontractors. Attach a copy of the contract to the estimate received from each subcontractor. Be sure to review the estimates, and account for all the labor and materials *he* is required to supply for the job. Read the chapters that refer directly to the suppliers' or subcontractors' estimates, and make sure that everything has been included. If not, add an addendum to the appropriate estimate sheet, and have the owner of the company sign it. Make sure that somewhere in the estimate or addendum it states what materials and labor necessary the company is to supply to complete the contract in a good and workmanlike manner.

If the sample contract on the following page plus the subcontractor's estimate is not sufficient for you or the bank, standard contracts can be purchased at most stationery stores.

SUPPLIER / SUBCONTRACTOR AGREEMENT

Date:_____.

SUPPLIER/SUBCONTRACTOR

Name: _____   Estimate Date:_____

Address:_____   Total Estimate: $_____

_____   Workers' Comp. No.:_____

Zip/Postal Code:_____   Expiration Date:_____

Business Phone: _____ - _____ .   Tax ID Number:_____

Cellular Phone: _____ - _____ .

Guarantee or Warranty:_____

JOB ADDRESS/ LOCATION:

LOT: _____ BLOCK:_____ PLAN:_____

LEGAL ADDRESS: _____

PAYMENT SCHEDULE:

Upon Completion of:_____   Amount: $_____

Upon Completion of:_____   Amount: $_____

Final Payment Due:_____   Amount: $_____

Total Payable (less 15% lien holdback) $_____

Completion Date: _____ , _____ .

Lien Holdback of _____ % to be held for 45 days after satisfactory completion.

♦ Additional materials/labor to be included in estimate by Supplier/Subcontractor with no extra charges.

_____

_____

_____**or see attached schedule.**

ARBITRATION CLAUSE:

Any dispute arising out of this Agreement shall be settled by arbitration in the following manner:

Either party may serve upon the other a written notice requiring the matter to be arbitrated and such notice shall set out the name of the arbitrator appointed by the party giving such notice. Within seven (7) days of receipt of such notice, the other party shall appoint its arbitrator and notify the first party of the name of the same. The two arbitrators so appointed shall select a third arbitrator within three days after notice of their appointment, and the arbitrators shall hear the dispute and, by majority decision, make a decision or award. It is agreed that any compensation required by the arbitrators shall be shared equally by the parties thereto regardless of the decision or award made.

CONDITIONS:

All work to be completed in a good and workmanlike manner, in strict accordance with local building regulations and specifications contained in the working blueprints.

_____   _____
Signature of Supplier/Subcontractor   Signature of Builder/Owner

• **Keeping a Diary**

I have found that a good diary or day timer is worth a mint on any construction project. During the renovating and building of my first homes and apartments, I found that my greatest problem was remembering what the suppliers and subtrades said, and when they said it.

The following story highlights the value of a diary. A finishing plumber on one of the house projects said that he was having a problem fitting the water closet onto the subfloor, and the framer should be called back to service the work correctly before he could do anything more. In my diary I wrote down the date, person's name, the time the person spoke to me, and what the discussion was all about. I promptly called the framer who said he was very busy, but would be over late the next day and would call first. I recorded that conversation in my diary. The next day went by and no phone call. I called the framer the next morning who informed me that he was too busy and had not been near a phone, but he would be there that afternoon at 3:00. That sounded reasonable and I let that one go, but once again I wrote all the information down in my diary. This same scenario repeated itself for several days until he finally showed five days later. He inspected his work and said it was OK, but the lino installer had built up the subfloor incorrectly and I should call him to service the work. Once again, I wrote it all down in my diary. I called the lino installer, told him the whole story and asked when could we meet. He said tomorrow at 7:30 a.m. before he had to be on another job site. I was at the house ten minutes early expecting the worst, but to my surprise he showed. He informed me that he had noticed the bump when installing the linoleum, but he did not say anything because he thought that maybe I was going to put in a fixture that needed the bump. I wrote down all that information.

To make a long and frustrating story short, it was *not* the framer's or the lino installer's fault, but that of a junior rough-in plumber who had installed a spacer sized for a quarry tile floor which was too thick for a linoleum floor. I was informed that a different crew than the finishing plumber's crew had installed the spacer. The other workers failed to check with the head office, confirm with the blueprints, or inspect this fellow's work, and it therefore was not caught. It took over ten days with weekends before the finishing plumber arrived and fixed the "bump." Would you believe that it was the same person who said that it was the framer's fault? He said to me, "By the way, for your information, this lump is called a 'gusset' (see Figure 7-1). Thanking him very much, I said, "Now that you have informed me of the proper terminology, I will be able to speak to your boss on his level when I ask him to pay for the damages that you caused."

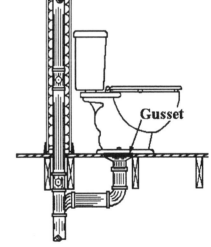

Figure 7-1. Location of toilet gusset.

My diary and Things to Do list for those days were starting to fill up. I was really angry about the time delay as ten days meant ten days more interest paid to the bank. In the morning I called the plumber's boss and told him about my delay and expenses. He informed me that he would have to speak to the plumber who worked on the job, and he would get back to me. Once more I wrote the information in the diary. Several days passed and he had not called, so I called him. He apologized and said he had spoken to the plumber, but he could do nothing about my problem. He even had the gall to say that I should have seen it, and then called him to fix it. That was the last straw. I deducted my time and interest charges from the plumber's last payment with a letter of explanation. This was not the end of it. Over the next few months I received several invoices with interest charges which I ignored. The next month I received a final invoice along with a letter from his lawyer who I promptly contacted, and read the entries from my diary and Things to Do list which explained the whole involved story. He was understanding, but requested photocopies of my diary and Things to Do list. This discussion was also recorded in my diary. Several days later he called me, saying he had received the photocopies, had spoken with the plumber, and under the circumstances the matter would be dropped. I requested a letter from him verifying what he had just said. It was received a few days later, and the matter was closed. I am still using the same plumber, and have not had a problem with service or repair since.

This is just one example of a potentially frustrating and costly problem that can be dealt with successfully by keeping an accurate record of conversations and events. Everything done and said, including names, phone numbers, discussion content, addresses and times of discussions, deliveries, and pickups, is recorded daily. This information has been invaluable in disputes with people who do not keep daily records. I retain my diaries for many years as a sample for my clients to view, and in the event of future problems or incidents arising during the length of a warranty. I have had to refer back to my diary on several occasions to eliminate any doubt as to which subtrade was responsible for repairing some damage.

Other suggestions include taking photographs of the construction site, purchasing a cellular phone as the monthly billing is a record of all the phone calls, and also remembering to record in your diary the weather conditions and verbal discussions with *all* the subcontractors. There have been a few occasions where, if I had recorded the details of a discussion or taken pictures of the site, many sleepless nights and on-site arguments with the subtrades would have been eliminated.

To again illustrate my point, in 1991 I was building a house and everything was going to work out just fine with the scheduling. The weather was cooperating, and the suppliers and subcontractors were timed perfectly. I had completed the foundation, floor joists, city/mortgage inspections, and backfilling prior to pouring the grade beam and piles for the garage. Since surveyors do not stake out the garage and structural pile locations, I requested the cribber to flag these areas with wood stakes so the water and sewer contractor would not run his pipes under any structural piles. I also marked on the foundation with spray paint where the water and sewer lines were located in the basement so the installer would know where to excavate. I then took a picture of the stakes and foundation markings from two views for my records. That evening I called the water/sewer trencher on my cellular to inform him that the site was ready, and the pile auger was scheduled for 12:00 the next morning. I also told him that my cribber had marked where the garage and structural piles were located. He was pleased to hear that I had everything marked with stakes, and one of his best men would be on-site in the morning to excavate and install the water and sewer pipes. I informed him that I would not be on-site until 1:30, but he said that as long as the piles and garage were marked I would not be needed. He said that his worker would be informed, and the job would be completed before 11:00 that morning. All this was recorded in my diary. I contacted the pile contractor to inform him that all would be ready for him to drill the piles at 12:00, that my cribber would be on-site, and that I had the concrete ordered for 1:30. He said everything would be taken care of. Meanwhile, I took my usual quick drive-by the job site in the early morning to make sure that vandals had not moved or broken anything. As an added precaution I took pictures of the stake locations, too.

Regardless of all these precautions, the water and sewer installer pulled the pegs out because they were in his way, and proceeded to trench where the stakes were located because it was the shortest and most direct line for his pipes. When the cribber and the pile auger arrived, the cribber had to remeasure and restake the pile locations. Since the scheduling between the piles being drilled and the concrete arriving to be poured into the pile cavity was very tight, this remeasuring made the cribber very angry. Not knowing what had been done by the trencher, the piles were drilled, and when the auger was pulled out, a loud, gurgling sound was heard followed shortly by water pouring out of the hole. The cribber who had worked for me for years knew what had happened, and he contacted me on my mobile. He suggested that they proceed with the remaining piles as he did not think that he would hit the water or sewer line again because the earth around the next pile stake looked undisturbed. I told him to continue, then contacted the city to have the water turned off, and phoned the water/sewer installer to meet me at the job site immediately.

By the time I arrived at the construction site, the city had turned off the water at the property, and the water/sewer installer was sitting in his truck having a smoke. I suggested to him that he bring the backhoe the next day to re-excavate, repair and/or move the pipes. I also said that he should be prepared to pay for any costs or damages that he might have caused, and that those costs would be deducted from his estimate. The worker became very defensive and said that his boss had not told him about the stakes, and that they were not near the area that he had worked in. I suggested that he change his story, but when he refused, I contacted his boss and described the situation to him. The owner said that the worker had been with him for 12 years, that he had no reason not to believe him, and he would not be held responsible for something I had done wrong. I informed the owner that I keep a diary of all discussions, that the cellular phone bill would show that I contacted him the night before, that the cribber would verify that he correctly marked the area with stakes, and that I had photographs of the stakes from the day before and that morning. I also had the speakerphone on so the worker and the other subcontractors standing near to my car could hear the whole conversation, and, if needed, they would be willing to verify that the owner of the trencher was at fault for all damages and costs.

The owner quickly changed his story, suggesting that maybe his worker was trying to protect his job. He stated that this complication had never happened before and that he would have a serious talk with his employee. He also agreed to pay for any damages that his worker caused, and instructed me to deduct it from his estimate.

If I did not keep a diary, take pictures, and purchase the cellular phone, I believe it would have been the worker's word against mine, and probably my loss. Instead, when all the damages were added up and deducted from the estimate, I owed the water/sewer installer $76.74. What does that tell you?

- **List of Things to Do**

It is also very helpful if you keep a daily list of Things to Do that is separate from your diary (see sample list, page 70). This will provide you with a record and daily checklist with specific dates, phone calls to be made, items to be picked up, and people to be seen. This list is a short form of the diary and should be considered a backup for it. Some days you will find that you were only able to complete the important items on your list. Any of the items missed that day should go onto the list for the next day. Always make your list in the evenings after all your work and phone calls have been completed, and your mind and body have had some time to relax. This list will help organize your day, making the construction schedule more workable and easier to complete. In summary, these suggestions provide a historical record that can remain with the house, and some interesting and funny stories for your friends.

THINGS TO DO TODAY

Date: _____ ____, 19___.

	Phone No.	Who to Call/Speak To	Time	Date	Subject
1.	___ - _____	_____	__:__	_____	_____
2.	___ - _____	_____	__:__	_____	_____
3.	___ - _____	_____	__:__	_____	_____
4.	___ - _____	_____	__:__	_____	_____
5.	___ - _____	_____	__:__	_____	_____
6.	___ - _____	_____	__:__	_____	_____
7.	___ - _____	_____	__:__	_____	_____
8.	___ - _____	_____	__:__	_____	_____
9.	___ - _____	_____	__:__	_____	_____
10.	___ - _____	_____	__:__	_____	_____
11.	___ - _____	_____	__:__	_____	_____
12.	___ - _____	_____	__:__	_____	_____
13.	___ - _____	_____	__:__	_____	_____
14.	___ - _____	_____	__:__	_____	_____
15.	___ - _____	_____	__:__	_____	_____

Notes:_____

_____

_____

_____

_____

_____

_____

PART III: PLANNING THE RENOVATION DESIGN

CHAPTER 8

♦ CREATING THE RENOVATION PLAN

• Key Design Principles

While looking at the existing subdivision and house streetscape, many people may have a mental picture of the proposed renovation/addition based on their identified needs. This chapter will assist you in understanding the basic component elements which created a new floor plan for your family's present and future lifestyles.

There are potentially five elements required in a house: formal/casual living, sleeping, family, working, and garage areas. These must be arranged in relation to each other in order to satisfy the different living habits of the family, and take maximum advantage of the house location on the lot. A successful floor plan will be created by orienting carefully all the component areas which have an impact on the various activities of each family member. In order to satisfy the new requirements of the family members, you may have to consider alternative utilization of the existing elements before you find the most workable arrangement. Regardless of having decided on maintaining a bungalow appearance, or converting the style to a 1-1/2 story, split level or 2 story as the completed visual, try to connect the elements of living, sleeping, family and work areas of the proposed floor plan with a minimal amount of hallway. Some hallway is necessary to allow a smooth transition from one area to another without passing through the elements, creating a high-maintenance traffic area (see Figure 3-4).

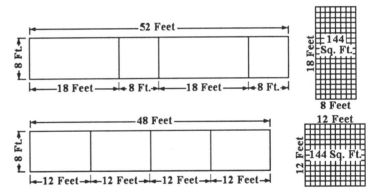

Figure 8-1. A square and a rectangular wall with the same floor areas. The square is more economical.

As the new house plan evolves and begins to function on paper, a common thought is to correlate the renovated room size to the potential arrangement of existing furniture. Some consideration must be given to negotiating around furniture without cramping the space, or constantly bumping into the other family members. However, avoid focusing solely on furniture "fit" during the design phase as furniture can always be moved, changed or stored, but your family lifestyle and renovation budget are less flexible.

There are two basic principles to remember in the design phase.

Principle No. 1: A square has less wall area than any other shape generally used in house planning. The greater the wall area, the higher the construction and maintenance costs. A larger outside wall perimeter will result in increased weather exposure, and therefore increased fuel consumption during cooler winter months. A simple wall shape equals less enclosing wall surface equals cheaper construction costs (see Figure 8-1).

The more corners in the design, the more expense involved regardless of whether they are inside or outside. The new setbacks, courtyards or protrusions of any kind added to the existing house will weather differently than the older portion, and sometimes cause undesired wind swirls, snow drifts or heating problems when exposed to the prevailing winds or the summer sun. These new features, however, when properly considered at the design stage can benefit the efficiency of the house when the renovation is completed. Changes might include replacing older walls which have little or no insulation with the newer 2" x 6" energy-efficient wall structure, resulting in a reduction or no change in current heating/cooling bill even with additional square footage.

The square box style of house is less attractive than the rectangular style with a longer frontage or streetscape. This is especially true of the 2-story salt box styles. Unfortunately, some houses in existing subdivisions are

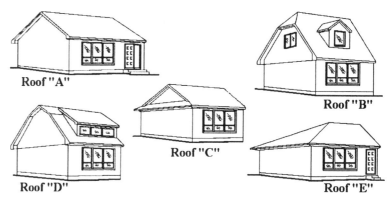

Figure 8-2. (A) Gable roof, (B) Clerestory gable with a bullnose and a gable dormer, (C) Dutch gable roof, (D) Gambrel roof with shed dormer roof, (E) Hip roof.

small in square footage, and in order for them to appear larger, they were built to the maximum width the property boundaries will allow. This reality may limit your proposed home expansion, and some compromise between visual impressions and costs will have to be made in your design.

Principle No. 2: The simpler the roof design, the lower the cost. The roof type with a variety of slopes and angles will add not only to the visual streetscape of the renovation, but also to the cost of the construction.

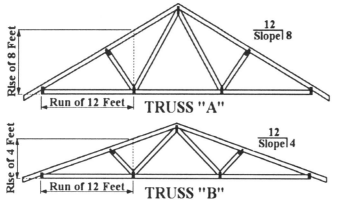

Figure 8-3. (A) 8/12 truss slope. (B) 4/12 truss slope.

Dormers, hips, bay, and garden windows, as well as porches, require additional on-site cutting, framing and flashing. The more complicated roof types over time will require more maintenance and add to long-term expense (see Figure 8-2).

Most builder/contractors in the 1990s are using premanufactured roof trusses which can vary from a high pitch 8/12 roof to a low pitch 2/12 roof. The slope of a roof is the distance the roof rises over a standard 12 inch length, eg., a rise of 4 inches to a typical length of 12 inches equals a 4/12 roof slope (see Figure 8-3). Generally there is not a great difference between cost and efficiency of 2/12 to 5/12 roof slopes; however, when the slope exceeds the 5/12 slope the cost increases drastically.

The potential cost of the roof design needs to be considered at the design stage especially when finishing the exteriors of high-pitched gable ends and dormer windows; these styles take substantially more material to finish the larger surface area of the walls as well as the overhangs. Even though the dormer windows will provide for more living space in those rooms, the cost of the dormer and the finishing of the added floor space will have to be weighed carefully against the increased cost and the final visual streetscape when building the dormer (see Figure 8-4). Can you justify the added expense?

As discussed in Chapter 4, it is possible with the steeper, pitched gable roof of the 1-1/2 story design to use the space under the roof slope for living or storage area. This practical option is not possible with a hipped roof. The latter is also more expensive due to the more

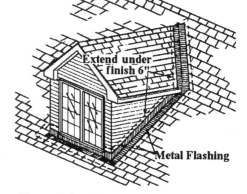

Figure 8-4. A Gable dormer with window.

complicated truss design, the additional labor to lay the shingles, flashings and roof capping at the intersections, and the additional lengths of eavestrough required.

In summary, if you have a limited construction budget, consider very carefully the basic design of your house. Living requirements, house and roof style, building shape, roof and wall balance, roof wall and trim colors, and cohesiveness with the adjacent home styles are some of the more important items to consider when working with the designer.

- **Space Planning**

Living Room: We are all beginning to wonder whether the living room still has a viable place in the house plan. In the older style house plans the living room usually faces the front street, is located away from the common gathering area of kitchen/dinette, and contains the largest square footage. Before deciding to reduce, relocate or eliminate this area in the completed renovation, ask if it will affect the future value of the home. Many clients retain the living room or great room for formal socializing, as a space to display their antique or good furniture, and as an area into which the dining room table can be expanded when the family gathers for special family or group functions. Unless there is a drastic change in public perception of this room, it will remain a requirement for resale; therefore try to keep the room simple in shape, functional in design, and warm and pleasing to the eye.

Dining Room: A separate, formal dining area clearly defined from the living room is desirable; however, in many existing homes this is not always possible because of space requirements. A more informal dining area as an extension of the family room/kitchen is the usual compromise. Its boundaries can be visually defined with a sofa, half wall, cabinetry, lamps, arches, floor finishes, or even window coverings. This room should be large enough to accommodate a table with at least six chairs, and a buffet or china cabinet, and have sufficient circulation space around the table when the chairs have been pulled out even with the edge of the table. Because many existing homes have narrow dining areas many renovation projects include the addition of a bay or bow window to the side of the house. In addition to space, review storage needs and convenience of access to china, linens, etc., within or adjacent to the dining room. Also consider ways to facilitate food service, i.e., improved functional flows between the kitchen and dining areas.

Family Room: A designated family room on the main floor is a relatively recent addition to the house plan scene and reflects a significant lifestyle change. Homes built up to the 1970s allocated development space for rumpus or "rec" rooms in the basement to distance noise and clutter. Today's families wish convenience plus the opportunity to connect casually with other family members in a faster paced lifestyle, hence the main floor family, or great, room.

Of all the rooms in a house, this family area has to be the most adaptable because of its many different uses. As a gathering place for family and friends, or where each family member can pursue their own interests, it has to creatively combine the requirements for entertainment, relaxation, study, and/or children's activities.

Often the focal point of the home, this central living space should be informal, open, and easily accessed from the other areas of the house. It is commonly combined with other connecting rooms in order to expand visually. For example, by adding additional sitting area to the kitchen and breakfast nook or dinette, a very large country style environment is created even in a small house. A major design consideration is the location of the front, back, and side entrance doors. It is undesirable to have an access door opening in the direction of the family area, kitchen, or dining areas because of cold drafts, loss of privacy, and clean-up considerations. Also, try to locate the family area so that it cannot be used as a primary passage from one area of the house to the other. If this is not possible accept only a small corner or area of intrusion.

The length and width of the room may vary, but note that long, narrow rooms are harder to furnish than a square one which is more useful and complementary for different furniture placements. Be sure that the design allows for sufficient unbroken wall area for furniture placement and that walls are not cut up for door openings. The number, height, and width of windows also affect the amount of wall space for furniture. If this room is located at the back of the house, windows and doors can take advantage of the more pleasing view of a landscaped rock garden or terraced deck (see Figure 14-3).

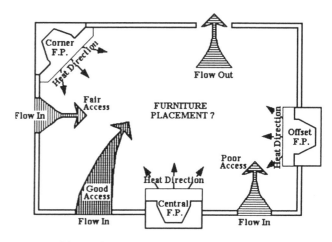

Figure 8-5. Traffic flow around fireplaces.

If the plan includes a main floor or basement fireplace, try to place it away from the normal traffic route, visible from all corners of the room, and preferably on an inside wall. The latter placement will not obstruct an outside view, or permit the conduction of cold air from the outside. Remember that a fireplace will take up a length of five to six feet, and requires at least 42 inches of wall length on either side of the fireplace hearth

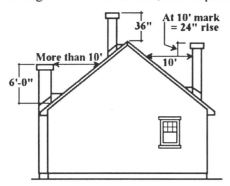

Figure 8-6. Chimney heights for different chase locations.

for comfortable furniture groupings. Locating the fireplace close to a doorway or traffic pattern will complicate furniture placement. Consider the hearth as part of the fireplace, especially if it will be raised, and allow sufficient space for traffic circulation and furniture placement (see Figure 8-5). Adding a fireplace requires consideration of the flue which if not situated properly could protrude through the roof in the front of the house and visually affect the streetscape. The building code states that if a flue or chimney is less than ten feet away from the peak of the house it must protrude a minimum of 24 inches above the location at which the horizontal ten foot line occurs, more than ten feet away from the peak the inside measure-

ment of the chimney chase must be a minumum of six vertical feet (see Figure 8-6). If this occurs in the front of the house it is advisable to provide a framed flue chase to cover the flue's obviously added appearance. Other options include placing the fireplace on an outside wall with a vertical flue and an elbow extending out beyond the main floor exterior wall, or better yet installing an energy-efficient fireplace with a horizontal flue through an outside wall.

Because of limited main floor living or restricted property space the renovation project may have to consider placing the family room in the basement. Suggestions to improve this allocation include selecting the bi-level or split which will allow for the installation of larger windows, or installing an extended foundation wall on a bungalow addition for skylight inserts (see Figure 8-7).

Finally, when renovating make sure that you have or will have sufficient electrical outlets around the room. Think of locating several plugs and the cable TV outlet adjacent to the planned entertainment center. Consider placement of vacuum outlets, intercom units, telephone and stereo speakers in relation to each other when planning the room and potential furniture arrangements.

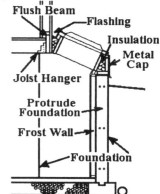

Figure 8-7. Skylights to basement.

Informal Dining: A breakfast nook or dinette area is a common component of the main floor living area. Sometimes separated by railings or half walls, this informal eating area close to the kitchen does not entirely duplicate the function of a formal dining room, but when floor space is limited, this area can serve as the semi-formal dining area.

With both mother and father usually working, the family requires an area allowing visual and verbal communication during the day-to-day activities of cooking, playing, and relaxing. Without this comfortable kitchen atmosphere the family members could become segregated to their own chosen areas with little social interaction. The family activities that occur

Figure 8-8. Garden and bay windows for visual enlargements of the kitchen and dinette.

around an informal dinette or nook should be discussed in great detail as the needs of the family will determine the features, use, and size of this area. For safety there should be easy access or a panoramic view from the kitchen or family room via a large picture window or patio door onto the deck, garden, terrace, or children's play area. Does your family gather for regular meals three times a day? Will friends or guests be welcome to sit in this area while you work in the kitchen? Is the area large enough for a holiday gathering of family and relatives without being crowded? Do the family members use this area as a stopover on the freeway between the refrigerator and the rest of the house? If you have answered yes to any of those questions, you must consider very seriously how the circulation inside, outside and around this area will occur.

In order to add space to a potentially small breakfast nook, many home renovators take advantage of a bay window addition plus or minus the French door option. It will visually expand the eating area, provide additional space for tables and chairs, and also allow a broader view of the backyard play areas. Bay windows also allow more sunlight into the nook, kitchen and family room as a result of the additional glass placed into the three, angled walls of the bay compared to the smaller glass area of a flat wall (see Figure 8-8).

Kitchen: The kitchen is almost certainly the most widely used, and probably the most expensive room in your house. A kitchen that is both attractive and efficient is every homemaker's ideal. But perfect kitchens do not just "happen." They are the result of a well-thought-out plan that considers everything from the size of the family to the location of overhead lighting, and many other important details in between.

Questions to consider in your renovation plans include: Does the existing kitchen space match the new kitchen plan, and if not what has to be done in order to accommodate the kitchen layout desired? How often do I entertain, and is the entertaining formal or informal? Is there more than one cook in the family, and do they work together in the preparation of the meals? How modern do I want the appearance, and how much cleaning do I want to do? Do I design the kitchen primarily for resale, or will we be living in the renovated home long enough to benefit from some extra frills?

A self-appraisal by the cook or cooks is the next step. Is cooking a happy experience, or not? Will it be necessary to have the kitchen work area clean all the time, or do open shelves and hanging utensils create a working environment that you find pleasing? Check out magazine ideas and other peoples' kitchens, and then take a good look at your present kitchen. What do you like, or not like about its appearance and efficiency?

Which appliances do you consider indispensable in your daily work schedule? Have you ever considered a built-in oven, or a cooktop with a barbecue in an island, and will it fit into the existing work space? Are the existing appliances the right color and in good working condition for continued use, or will the budget allow the purchase of new units if required?

The three primary work areas in any kitchen center are the range, refrigerator, and sink. Most of the steps taken during meal preparation will be from one of these work centers to another. The normal work-flow pattern is from food storage (refrigerator) to preparation (sink and adjoining space) to cooking (range) to final serving preparations. After meals, the pattern flows from the clean-up area (sink) to storage (refrigerator).

The first principle in kitchen redesign is to maintain these three primary work centers in a convenient relationship to each other within the space provided. The most satisfactory way of achieving this is to locate them so that their arrangement forms what is commonly called the "work triangle." Within reason, the shorter the distance around the perimeter of the triangle, the fewer the steps required for meal preparation and clean-up. The triangle may be scaled to suit the actual floor area allocated for the kitchen, and ideally the sum total of the sides should not be less than 12 feet and no more than 22 feet. Of all the work stations in the kitchen, ovens are the least active; therefore, built-in ovens and microwaves are often located outside the work triangle.

The shape of the work triangle may be modified according to the available space and your personal requirements. The most compact, equal-sided triangle occurs with the U-shaped kitchen; the most elongated is with the L-shaped or island kitchen. Ideally, and for maximum efficiency, the traffic flow into the kitchen from adjoining rooms, or from other activity centers in the kitchen, should not cross the work triangle (see Chapter 9 for kitchen layouts).

Ensure that there is sufficient design information on the blueprints to relate your exact requirements to the kitchen salesperson. It is the designer's responsibility to show the locations of all the fixtures such as the range, refrigerator, dishwasher, cooktops, microwaves and built-ins that might affect the traffic patterns, and hence the workability of the kitchen. Islands or pantry areas, telephone desks and their electrical plug/switch locations should be drawn or notations made on the working drawings sufficient for the cabinet supplier and installer to understand. This detailed information is required by the cabinet designer to determine the placement and locations of his cabinets in accordance with the owner's appliance and electrical requirements.

Kitchen efficiency is dependent on adequate and conveniently located storage space for the appropriate items required for a specific center. Here is a checklist of items for planning storage spaces near the individual kitchen centers.

Near the sink:

☐ Cleaning supplies
☐ Bottle and can openers
☐ Trash bin and trash bags
☐ Paper towels and cleaning rags
☐ Scouring pads and brushes
☐ Soaps, cleansers, detergents
☐ Wash cloths and hand towels
☐ Cutlery and paring knives
☐ Cutting board
☐ Strainers

Near the oven:

☐ Mixing bowels, serving dishes
☐ Cookie trays, cooling racks
☐ Baking utensils
☐ Hand mixers, food processor, blenders
☐ Casseroles, baking dishes, roasting pans
☐ Carving set, oven mitts, hot pads
☐ Spices, flour, sugar, oils, vinegars, shortening
☐ Packaged/dried fruits and nuts
☐ Pastry board
☐ Rolling pins, sifters, ice-cream scoop, etc.
☐ Mixing bowels, measuring cup

Near the cooktop:

☐ Ladles, scrapers, whisks, etc.

☐ Frying pans and sauce pans

☐ Griddle, sandwich grill

☐ Measuring spoons and cup

☐ Seasonings

☐ Containers of rice, sugars, pastas

☐ Hot pads and oven mitts

Near the refrigerator:

☐ Storage containers, freezer bags

☐ Aluminum foil, plastic wrap, waxed paper

☐ Bread containers, cookie jar

☐ Serving trays

☐ Paper towels, lunch bags, freezer tape, etc.

Kitchen cabinet storage:

☐ Dry/canned goods, cereals, pickles, jams, pop, junk food, etc.

☐ Cook books, recipes

☐ Salad bowls, cheese boards

☐ Silver polish and cleaning supplies, brooms, etc.

☐ Broilers, toasters, juicers, tea kettle, serving pitchers

☐ Everyday coffee mugs, dishes, glassware

☐ Bulk item storage, i.e., napkins, paper towels, flour, sugar, glass jars, etc.

☐ Everyday linen, place mats, napkins

☐ Glass door display area for cups and saucers etc.

☐ Junk drawer for elastics, twist ties, pencils, scotch tape, coupons, etc.

☐ Pet foods

Bedrooms: Remember for renovation purposes that the three-bedroom house remains the most popular for resale value as it provides for a typical family of parents with children of both sexes. An individual may spend more time in the bedroom than any other room in the house; therefore, bedrooms should be designed to suit individual needs, and provide the maximum amount of privacy and comfort for leisure and study periods. Renovating to enlarge bedrooms or add bedrooms in the basement is usually the result of the children growing up and wanting to become more independent. These new adult lifestyles will suggest a self-contained living/bedroom area, and may require the designer to pay special attention to soundproofing. This will ensure that the positive relationship between the family and a growing adult will remain intact yet allow an area of privacy for the teenager with limited supervision and interference from other family members.

A **master bedroom** is no longer considered just another room. Although access to the other bedrooms with small children remains important, electronic visual and listening devices have helped this surveillance aspect. Master suites require attention to self-sufficiency, privacy, and comfort needs, and lend themselves well to a zone design concept, i.e., sleeping, relaxing, dressing, washing, and grooming areas. To address these functions effectively the two adults will each require their own space with as little interference from their mate as possible.

Depending upon the present orientation of the bedroom, a renovation project to increase space may include the repositioning or addition of a window or door to allow a once-dark bedroom to have sunshine and proper cross-ventilation. Consider the new window placement carefully to ensure the windows are not too large, too long, too narrow, or too high off the floor to block a view. Consider door access onto a deck to provide a fire exit. If positioned properly, wall space between the window and door frames will accommodate the placement of furniture. Furniture frequently occupies almost half the square footage of the bedroom with the remainder allocated to traffic flow; a one to three ratio of furniture area to floor area is recommended to allow for better movement flow. Decisions on furniture placement in the room should be considered early in the design to determine the location of electrical, telephone and cable outlets.

The biggest complaint made by couples in existing homes is the lack of closet space provided for two adults sharing a room. With the introduction of manufactured closet organizers, closets can become less cluttered, with each item having its own cubicle. For hanging items a minimum rod and shelf space of five feet should be provided for each adult. Walk-in closets can also be used as private dressing areas when the wake-up schedule differs. If this is the case, try to locate the master bathroom in close proximity to the closet and/or dressing area. In general, a clear floor space of at least 54 inches for dressing should be provided between the closet and the closest piece of furniture. Having this will also allow for an outside closet door swing without cramping the dressing area.

Floor area utilization in the master bedroom is open to change according to need and resale considerations If for convenience a baby is to share the parents' room, the space provided for one owner's relaxation can be easily converted to accommodate a crib, change area and highboy dresser.

Secondary bedrooms should be separated from the master bedroom by a sound barrier. Closets, bathrooms, or 2" x 6" insulated walls will achieve the desired effect. Children very often share bedrooms when young, as this provides a safe and secure sleeping area. You may want to create a bedroom large enough so that there will be sufficient space for bunk beds plus an extended joint play area which will permit better use of space for sleeping, playing and dressing. When the conversion to single beds is indicated, the bedroom must allow sufficient space for arranging the single beds with individual play and closet space as well as privacy (see Figure 8-9). Young children also require storage facilities for clothes, toys, books, play table and writing supplies, which in later years will convert to storage for books and computer software. Long-term planning is essential to obtain two separate, private spaces within one room which will also house two study areas with the proper storage, lighting and outlet placement.

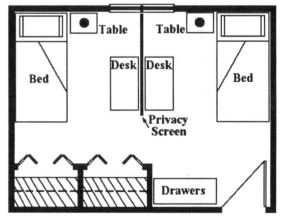

Figure 8-9. Room conversion from a bunk bed to single beds.

Bathrooms: Planning your bathroom renovation must start with an analysis of the family's needs in terms of the following considerations:

Family size. The greater the number of family and friends using a bathroom the larger it should be, or the greater the number of bathrooms required. Achieving this will mean rethinking the use of existing space in other rooms, or adding to the house to provide sufficient floor space for built-in showers, jetted spas, and linen storage. Remember wall space may be required for electrical outlets and perhaps even more fixtures. When existing space is limited and the same bathroom is used by family members of the opposite sex at the same time, compartment designs with doors can increase its utilization and reduce family conflicts (see Figure 8-10).

Family age. The ages of family members will also affect planning needs in a bathroom. Children may dictate the installation of soil-resistant surfaces and storage for step stools, training supplies, and appliances. If the family includes elderly or disabled individuals, adaptions may include doors wider than 30 inches, grab bars, and storage space for appliances and other aids for their safety and convenience.

Family schedule. How many people leave for work or school at the same time? You may need multiple or compartmental baths. Two basins and a privacy toilet will allow a working couple to get ready for work at the same time in the morning. Try to plan facilities that are extensive enough to meet personal preferences and are arranged appropriately to ensure effective utilization of time and space.

Door location. Check that the new door swing direction will not cause inconvenience or injury to persons entering the bath or using a fixture. Consider pocket doors for maximum utilization of bathroom space as they are designed to slide into wall openings thus leaving more standing and working room (see Figure 8-10). They are usually installed where there will be traffic interference or where there is little room to swing a standard hinged door. These space savers can be installed with a door lock, silent plastic rollers, and rubber stops to eliminate any undesired noise. The wall that will contain the pocket door must be specially constructed in order to eliminate the impact of stud warpage which will cause the door to bind. To reduce the possibility of warpage, construct the wall of 2" x 6" wood studs, or better yet metal studs. The disadvantages to pocket doors will also have to be considered. The wall containing the pocket door should not have any electrical wiring, support any cabinetry, or be used as a structural wall.

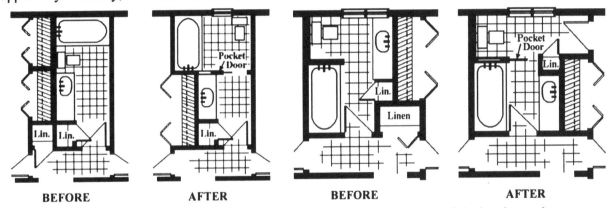

BEFORE   AFTER   BEFORE   AFTER

Figure 8-10. Possible bathroom renovations with pocket doors to suit the family's changing needs.

Heating. No one likes to go from a warm bed or shower to a cold bathroom. Check the standard heating requirements and ensure that a new heating duct one inch larger in diameter than the standard five inch size is installed especially if the bathroom has a window. You may also want supplementary heat via heat lamps as they speed up drying time and keep you warm in the winter when reading your favorite book.

Ventilation. A bathroom generates more moisture than any other room in the house, and adequate ventilation will prevent mildew, musty odors, peeling walls and ceilings, and fogging of mirrors. Specifically, an exhaust fan with sufficient capacity to handle eight air exchanges per hour is needed. The fan can be wired independently or with the light switch. If the planned bathroom or powder room is small and without a window, wire the light and fan together. For the exhaust fan to work properly, provide sufficient intake air by allowing a 3/4-inch space from the finished floor to the underside of the door.

Electrical outlets. Today's bathroom requires many conveniently located electrical outlets for hair dryers, hair curlers, timers for spa pumps and steam showers, shavers and all the other electrical gadgets that abound. Consider the users of the bath and their electrical needs, then install outlets and switches to match. Because of high humidity, be sure the washroom wall outlets are ground faulted with reset buttons located in another washroom to prevent electrical shocks, a very real possibility in bathrooms. Ground fault or reset buttons should also be located at the main electrical panel. Locate all switches so they cannot be reached from the tub or shower area. This not only ensures safety, but is also a requirement of most building codes.

Mirrors. Mirrors strategically located can make a bathroom both beautiful and more functional. Big mirrors can make a small room look larger; small or hinged mirrors properly located can aid in shaving and make-up applications. Mount mirrors so that the upper edge is at least 72 inches above the floor, allowing tall persons to see the tops of their heads. A full-length, door-mounted mirror is very handy for checking pants or skirts.

Fixture upgrades. Many homes built before the 1960s were designed with cast iron fixtures and copper piping which after many years begin to show their age. Chipped porcelain, cracked fixtures, rusted pipes or screws, loosening welds, and normal wear will cause them to look old and the pipes to fail. When renovating or adding to your existing home, replace these fixtures, drains, and pipes with newer and more efficient plastic piping. Out-of-date tubs, sinks, and toilet fixtures can easily be refinished or replaced. If the plans include the addition of a shower or a change from a five-foot steel tub to a six-foot fiberglass jetted spa, the designer must enlarge the bathroom, or relocate some of the fixtures with their new water and drain lines in order for the new spa and/or shower units to fit properly into the space provided. Enlarging the bathroom usually means incorporating it into the new addition, utilizing space taken from adjacent rooms or even relocating the bathroom to a more suitable area of the existing floor area. For renovations of an existing bathroom the plumber must gain access to the pertinent floor joist areas of the basement. If these basement areas have been previously finished the ceiling must be removed for this purpose. Because plumbers are not experienced renovators, to reduce the amount of unnecessary damage to the existing structure, ask the framer during the demolition to remove those areas of the basement ceiling that will need to be accessed by the plumber, electrician, heating contractor, etc.

Laundry: Laundry facilities should be located for convenience. Over the last ten years lifestyles have changed and the most common location for laundry facilities is no longer in the basement. Many home owners have requested a main floor laundry and mud room combination conveniently located by the attached garage access door. Space and equipment considerations include a washer, dryer, counter space for sorting or folding, and upper and lower cabinets for storage. With the return of fabrics requiring wet hanging, a separate closet is an advantage if there is sufficient room. Provide main floor closets for day-to-day outerwear, and a basement closet when exchanging summer clothes for winter. If shelves are needed for detergents, softeners, measuring cups, bleaches, and scrub brushes, consider having the clothes rod extend only three-quarters across the closet (five feet should be sufficient), so one-quarter of the vertical space can be reserved for adjustable shelving. This extra closet storage may also be used for an ironing board and vacuum appliances. It is always wise to have as many wall plugs as possible in this area.

The most convenient location for the laundry/mud room is adjacent to the kitchen, but this is not always complementary to the proposed floor plan. If the design will allow a laundry area close to the kitchen, it will allow you to move from one area to the other with ease and accomplish more work in a shorter timespan. An ironing center in or near the kitchen to maintain surveillance during cooking or entertainment activities with the family is ideal. Convenient built-in boards may be considered, but the price sometimes does not justify the need.

It is also nice to have a window in the laundry room for the daytime sun. If you are unable to incorporate one in the design because of the room layout, ensure the plan includes adequate fluorescent lighting.

If the renovation plans include a second story, check to ensure the new layout includes designated space in a central collection area or in all bedrooms for the temporary storage of dirty linens and clothes. Then ask the designer to suggest a proper location for a laundry chute to simplify the transfer of dirty clothes. This way the clothes will end up in the main floor laundry room itself or in close proximity, perhaps in a closet. If space will allow, think of having a laundry closet or actual room on the upper floor. For the larger family this will greatly reduce constant trackage to a less convenient laundry room on the main or basement levels. A closet space with increased depth is required to house the washer and dryer, and a floor drain with watertight flooring is mandatory. If space is tight, a stacked washer and dryer would allow space for a soaking tub or small sorting counter. A screen or folding lowered doors should be installed to conceal the laundry center when not in use.

Storage: Insufficient storage has always been a major problem in older homes. There never seems to be adequate storage space designed into a contract house plan. The renovation phase is an excellent opportunity to correct this situation by allocating specific storage areas, and closet organizer systems for items to be kept out of the way, in good condition, and yet readily accessible. In addition to everyday clothing, consider the following.

Outdoor clothes, such as jackets, hats, boots, and rainwear, should be kept in the mud room, or at the back or front entrance. Depending on numbers entertained, the front entrance closet should be large enough to contain all visitors' coats and accessories.

Everyday clothes and blankets in most geographical areas are seasonal. It is advisable to have a separate closet moth-proofed and cedar-lined to protect these articles when not in active use.

Linens and toiletries should be stored adjacent to bedrooms and bathrooms with various depths and heights of shelves for the different varieties of items.

Toys which are used most often should be stored in the child's bedroom. A chest, bank of drawers, or shelves can be built in the room or contained in the closet; they should be designed low and easy to open so the child can find and return the toy(s) with minimal effort.

Hobbies and family games can be stored in a general purpose closet or cabinet in or near the family room for easy access. These items, such as photo albums, scrap books, stamp or coin collections, puzzles, board games, cameras, videotapes, cassettes or disks, should be organized according to daily versus occasional use.

Cleaning equipment, such as brooms, mops, dustpan, polishes and cleansers, should be located centrally as they are used frequently in all parts of the house. Provide a storage space for tall items such as an ironing board and vacuums, along with shelf space for the cleaning materials. Under-vanity storage for tub and toilet cleansers and cloths is usually sufficient for the bedroom/bath areas. Portable, rechargeable, wet/dry vacuum units require adjacent wall plugs for recharging, perhaps in closets, under vanities or behind doors.

Sports equipment storage is seasonal and requires easy accessibility and protection from the weather. It should be kept in a dry, clean place where it can be inspected and serviced when needed.

Overflow storage areas for possessions not in use generally consists of a corner in the basement. Items such as luggage, old trunks, Christmas decorations, and odds and ends of sentimental value are better stored off the floor and on shelves in a dry, well-ventilated room. Space requirements will vary depending on the size of the family and the number of residing packrats. Speaking as a reformed packrat, I find it is best to sort through the collection and get rid of unusable items at the dump or a neighborhood garage sale before the renovation starts. Doing this will give you a better idea of space needed.

Garden tools and furniture are usually stored in the basement, the garage, or a portable garden shed which can be locked. A considerable amount of space is required for patio furniture, barbecue equipment, lawnmower, snowblower, weeder, garden hose, shovels or rakes and sometimes children's outdoor play toys.

Also consider ease of access and movement of the larger equipment when needed.

Canned goods and preserves require a cool and sometimes climate-controlled place so they can be kept without spoiling until used. For safe storage of bulk canned goods, preserves, wine, and beer, an insulated closet or room in the basement against an outside wall is sufficient.

Household tools are usually kept in a workshop, or an area of the garage that is well ventilated and heated. Depending on the handyman and the type of projects and hobbies initiated, the space and storage needs will vary. Work benches, shelves, cabinets and peg boards are very useful for storing smaller equipment and supplies. Extra care should be taken for the storage and ventilation of paints, solvents, and any other flammable materials.

Garages: Many women will confirm that if they are unable to find their husbands when the inlaws arrive, dishes need to be washed, women come over to chat, and family members are having a disagreement, chances are they can be found "putzing" in the garage. To some men the size of the garage is directly proportional to the size of the family and number of drivers, however, others base it on their degree of involvement in auto repair or carpentry activities.

People who have never had a garage would most likely say that they had gotten along quite well without one, and that not having one had only been a little inconvenient in bad weather. Then one day they purchase a house with a garage or carport, and after a few months of enjoying the benefits of a garage they say, "I don't know how I ever got along without one." People living in warm southern climates without a garage will also have their complaints, but in reverse. In the hot summer months even at 7:00 a.m. getting into a hot car is like getting into a sauna.

If the renovation includes a garage, know how it will be used in addition to the number of vehicles it will protect. Will it be used as storage space for seasonal items that are not in use for several months of the year, i.e., bicycles, golf bags, lawnmower, summer tires? Will you need additional space for a workshop, for shelving for preserves and canned goods, for a freezer, or even for the children to play in during bad weather? Many home garages are designed to house the furnace, air conditioner, water heater, washer, and dryer. When this is the case, make sure that the garage will be large enough to hold these items with sufficient room to walk around the parked cars.

If you have chosen an attached garage and the climatic conditions are such that you have heavy rain or snow falls, it would be a good idea to have a centrally located floor drain. When the concrete finisher is spreading the concrete for the garage floor, he will slope the concrete to the floor drain so the surface can be properly hosed down to eliminate tracking dirt through the house. The drain should also have silt traps so that the small rocks and dirt can be thrown in the trash rather than possibly clogging the drain or polluting the storm sewer.

The garage floor should conform to the finished floor and grade of the house and lot. If the garage is set too low on the lot, the required number of stairs into the house could take up valuable parking room. Heavy rains could cause water to run into the garage, possibly damaging stored items, and the thawing/freezing cycles of snow will cause the garage door and even car tires to stick to the floor. On the other hand, if the garage floor is set too high on the lot, you might have to truck in sand or fill at extra cost to make sure the perimeter grade beam or footings sit on solid ground. In the colder zones where winter temperatures reach below the freezing point, too much fill might cause the foundation and garage floor to shift and crack. To eliminate these problems, discuss your garage requirements with the surveyor who will provide the designer with the proper finished floor height.

When the garage is attached to the house, the building code will require a fire-rated wall and access door to separate the garage area from the living area in the event of a fire. If you place any equipment having natural gas pilot lights in the garage take precautions to properly vent the garage and provide a safe place to store any flammable liquids, making sure they are a safe distance away from any flame.

Note: As an energy-saving idea, if the renovation design includes a masonry fireplace, let it protrude into the garage, and any heat given off by the fire will heat the masonry and radiate into the garage.

Garage doors come in all heights with many widths, styles, and designs. Sectional overhead garage doors are the most common door sold in the residential marketplace (see Figure 8-11). They are called sectional because they arrive prebuilt in sections, and then each section is hinged to the inside of the door to allow for ease in the vertical roll. The sectional door can be constructed of almost any type of material, but the two most common are wood and metal.

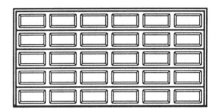

Figure 8-11. Five panel sectional door.

The light metal door is considered almost virtually maintenance-free. Although slightly more expensive, it has become the most common as it is lighter in weight, and better insulated than a wood door. The metal door is usually constructed with two, molded, metal veneer faces, and filled with a polyurethane insulation giving it a very high insulation value. Metal doors can be ordered with a wood grain finish.

The cedar sectional door, although the most expensive of the wood overhead doors, is used mainly by those people who prefer a visible wood finish. The beauty of the cedar grain is realized and protected with a good oil or stain finish which prevents the acceleration of weathering for many years. The construction of the wood door is limited to only a few types of wood as some woods will warp with certain weather conditions. Wood doors can now be purchased with a highly weather-resistant, plastic or paint finish which will make them cheaper than cedar in price, and will provide the home owner with many years of maintenance-free operation. A wood door is much heavier than a metal door, and is insulated as wood acts as its own insulator.

Both metal and wood sectional doors do not swing outward and therefore allow for parking the car adjacent to the garage door itself. Sectional doors are well suited for an electronic door opener: the mechanism will not have to work hard as each section is usually designed with an easy roller at each side. Because of the weight difference metal doors need a less powerful door opener, making them more comparable in price to wood doors.

If you own a van you should consider purchasing a taller door unit. The most common door height for a van is eight feet, although a higher door yet should be used if an air-conditioning unit is mounted on the roof. At the design stage, check with the city permit office and developer's control officer to see if garage door height restrictions apply.

The American and Canadian governments have ranked the top three causes of heat loss via garage doors. The most obvious is leaving the door open while the garage is not in use. Air infiltration between the sections is the next major source of heat loss. This is compounded if the door does not have a proper seal and perimeter weatherstripping . The greatest misconception is that a properly insulated door is the more important factor for an energy-efficient door. Studies show that the door does not have to be thick or well insulated, but rather must have proper sealing or weatherstripping. Ensure that the door purchased is adequately weatherstripped on the bottom and the sides. Vinyl or rubber are most commonly used as they are the most flexible, and tend to withstand the changing weather conditions. The top of the door is usually sealed with a wood or metal stop.

All insulation and weatherstripping should be added to the door unit by a professional installer at the shop prior to installation. This will satisfy your warranty and eliminate any problems that might arise from the do-it-yourself job.

Convenience... Security... Energy savings. These are the major reasons home owners decide to buy an automatic garage door opener, and a good quality opener certainly justifies the investment. Most people think bargain hunting for a garage door opener is a simple matter of saving on the sales cost and installation, and installing the opener in an afternoon. Consider that you will probably have to rebalance the door before installing the opener, and this could cause more loss of time and money than it is worth. Buying items of this type on sale will usually only provide the basics, and things like an extended warranty, service, adjustment, weatherstripping, lubrication, and extra transmitters will often be extras.

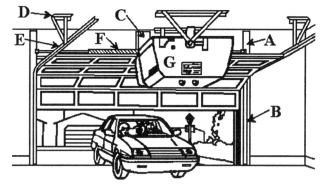

Figure 8-12. Components of an overhead garage door system. (A) 2" x 4" flat stud, (B) Vertical door rail, (C) 2" x 10" face mounted timber, (D) Horizontal rail bracket, (E) Horizontal rail, (F) Counterbalance door spring, (G) Garage door opener.

The garage door-opener unit must be attached securely to the roof truss structure with the roller brackets, center chain and steel carriage bar being attached to the structural wall of the garage. The garage studs and door header are set too far into the wall and are not structurally strong enough to properly hold the brackets and bar when the door is operating. It is the job of the framer to attach flat-mounted 2" x 4" studs to each side of the door and a centrally located face-mounted 2" x 10" timber to the header to which is bolted the bracket and bar units (see Figure 8-12).

Garage doors and children are always a concern. Teach and remind children that garage door openers are not toys and that playing with them could lead to serious injury. Ask for a safety reverse mechanism on the opener, and check it every six months to make sure no one will be trapped under the door.

CHAPTER 9

♦ PLANNING THE KITCHEN IN DETAIL

• Basic Kitchen Layouts

Five basic designs are seen in residential kitchens today. Each of the kitchen floor layouts has both advantages and disadvantages, and all have many variations. For an expanding family, consider choosing a design that will allow good circulation, eg., the U-shaped or L-shaped kitchen which can adapt to become rounded or octagonal. The design selected should suit your budget and family lifestyle.

Note: Renovating a kitchen may require accessing existing pipes in the basement especially to move any main floor plumbing lines. Because some original cast iron and copper pipes are not compatible with the new plastic piping, you will be required to replace all the old existing pipes.

Two wall or corridor kitchen:

They have an efficient floor plan that provides maximum counter and cabinet space in a long, narrow room and eliminates hard-to-reach corner space. The work triangle is compact and efficient with major appliances strategically located on two facing walls. For comfort and safety, the corridor should have a minimum of four feet between the countertops of the base cabinets to minimize congestion when two people are working. Wall-to-wall width should be no more than ten feet and no less than eight feet. This design is extremely functional for the one cook family, or the in-law suite of a proposed addition/basement renovation.

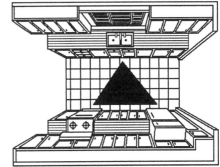

Figure 9-1. Corridor kitchen.

L-shaped kitchen:

Arrange appliances and work space along two perpendicular counters (see Figure 9-2). As the most popular kitchen plan, it adapts to a wide variety of arrangements. Optimal when existing space is limited, the proposed design requires incorporating the informal eating area within the kitchen's work space. Modifications of the L shape may also include a work center, pantry or telephone desk.

Frequently one run or end of the L doubles as a room divider. This plan frees floor space for other uses, and directs traffic away from the cook's work area. With this design, placing the sink and appliances can be challenging. If not thought out or designed properly, this kitchen plan can result in the appliances being located too close together with no counter separation, or at the extreme ends of the L.

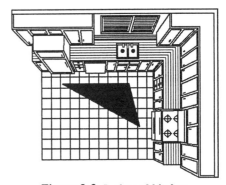

Figure 9-2. L-shaped kitchen.

U-shaped kitchen

These layouts require more space, but are considered by many experts to be the most efficient because of their compact work triangle and the easy separation of the work area from family traffic patterns. This kitchen layout allows for a convenient pass-through which also provides a more open effect between the kitchen and eating area.

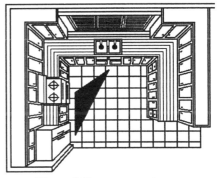

Figure 9-3. U-shaped kitchen.

This floor plan divides appliances and work areas among three connected counters arranged in a U shape, with some or all parts of the U extending into the room without wall support. Generally, the sink is placed at the base of the U, and the range/cooktop and refrigerator on the adjacent sides, resulting in a tight work triangle that eliminates wasted effort. Counter space is continuous, and special angled corner cabinets with lazy Susans are suggested to fully utilize storage space. Problems will arise if the kitchen is narrower than six feet between the two sides.

Island kitchen:

Islands have helped expand and create more interesting styles of kitchen floor layouts in recent years. Usually centrally located and free standing, they can be fixed or portable, adding extra work space wherever needed. If fixed, they may contain a sink, dishwasher or cooktop. They can also provide an eating counter or coffee bar with an overhanging portion of the counter designed to accommodate two to four bar stools/chairs. Besides being extremely adaptable, islands can effectively control traffic, provide a tighter work triangle, create more work space, and add convenient storage/shelf areas. Islands are especially useful in renovation projects with limited kitchen space that require a visual separation other than a wall to divide the kitchen space from the family or other living spaces.

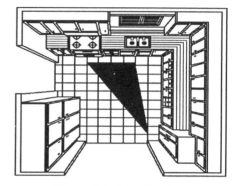

Figure 9-4. Island kitchen.

Peninsula kitchen:

This is another variation of the U-shaped or L-shaped plan. In this arrangement, one side of the U or L is used as a peninsula that provides the convenience of more storage space, and effectively acts as a divider between the kitchen and a formal dining area. The upper and/or lower cabinets may be made accessible from both sides. The peninsula may also function as a breakfast or snack bar. There should be a minimum of six feet between the side work areas with a minimum of five feet between facing work centers to allow two people to easily pass while working. Place the oven and refrigerator where their open doors will not interfere with or stop the cooking process, and at least 24 inches away from each other.

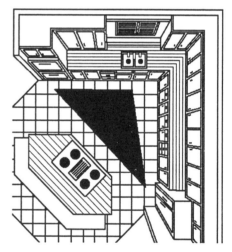

Figure 9-5. Peninsula kitchen.

• Kitchen Centers

Since each kitchen task requires a particular working surface and/or appliance, as well as specialized tools and basic ingredients, it makes sense to organize "centers" by locating the needed equipment, space, and appliances in a convenient work configuration.

The **sink center** handles food washing, trimming, dish clean-up, and garbage disposal. Appliances include the sink, a mechanical garbage disposer, a dishwasher, and sometimes a trash compactor. Counters are recommended on both sides of the sink. A dishwasher is commonly placed to the left of the sink; a left-handed person, though, may prefer to have it on the right side. Provide storage for soap and other cleaning materials and towels near the sink. Locate dishes and flatware storage close to the dishwasher for ease in unloading.

The **refrigerator center** handles the storage of perishable foods. A refrigerator/freezer combination, or a separate freezer unit allows longer storage of many foods with easy accessibility. An infrequently used freezer may be best located in an adjacent utility room or the garage, freeing up valuable kitchen space. A counter on the door latch side of the refrigerator serves as a handling area for groceries. The refrigerator works to dissipate heat and the range works to create heat; therefore, it is inefficient and unwise to put the refrigerator next to the range. When the two are in close contact, heat from the range may interfere with the refrigerator's cooling system.

The **preparation center** is the place for mixing and preparing foods prior to cooking or serving. A primary requirement is a surface for cutting and chopping which may be either built-in or easily accessed. One or more electric outlet for a food processor, mixer, and other small appliances used in food preparation is handy. Sometimes a lower-than-usual counter is installed as a "baking" center. Ample storage in close proximity for dry ingredients, baking pans, casseroles, and utensils needed for measuring and mixing is helpful. Safe knife storage is a must. Storage of small, infrequently used appliances, such as the food processor, juicer, mixer and electric can opener, presents a challenge. Where counter space is limited, an appliance center or pull-out pantry might be the answer. The best place for this center is near the refrigerator and/or sink for easy access to food products and equipment clean-up.

The **cooking center,** once the location of the sink and refrigerator has been been decided, is usually self-evident. Separate wall ovens and microwave ovens can be placed anywhere outside the work triangle that is convenient. Remember to allow adequate heat-resistant counter space next to the range. Ranges and some cooking surfaces require overhead exhaust hoods and ventilation fans to filter grease-laden air and remove cooking odors while some cooktop units vent through the floor. Duct work for exhaust systems can be concealed inside the above-range cabinet and vented through the roof, or installed in the lower cabinet and vented through the floor. Consider some strategic shelving for these areas as both systems involve loss of storage space, especially the lower cabinet ducting. For safety, it is wise to position a gas range away from a window as drafts can extinguish the pilot light or flame, and curtains blowing in the breeze could catch fire.

Counter space is the remaining space available after the major appliances within the work triangle have determined the basic layout of the kitchen. Ensure the layout permits counter surfaces adjacent to the sink, refrigerator and range of sufficient length to support the activities of those centers. The working surfaces are a standard height throughout the kitchen; changing the counter height for personal preference other than for a "baking" center may have an impact on resale at a later date.

• Kitchen Planning Mistakes

Strive not to do the following:

✗ Do not allow traffic patterns to cross the work triangle and interfere with the three primary work centers;

✗ Do not place the sink in a blind corner, too close to a wall, reducing arm movement; in an island with little counter space; or too near the range;

✗ Do not install electrical outlets dangerously near water sources;

✗ Do not place the refrigerator next to the range;

✗ Do not install a built-in oven and range side by side, creating a fire hazard;

✗ Do not place appliances so that they block hot air and return air registers;

✗ Do not plan the aisles narrower than four feet;

✗ Do not allow doors to swing into work areas or against appliances;

✗ Do not place shelves too high, or specify them too narrow for what they will hold;

✗ Do not select hard-to-care-for or non-heat-resistant counter surfaces.

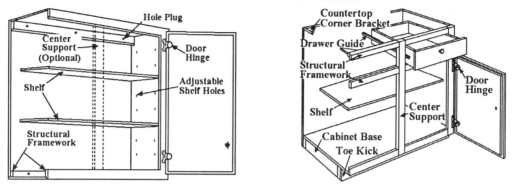

Figure 9-6. Typical upper and lower cabinet assembly with optional center support.

Note: Many cabinets that are premanufactured are constructed of particle board or pressboard, and in order to obtain structural strength they are designed with a center support for cabinet units wider than 32 inches. These supports reduce access to the shelving unit for the storage of larger dishes, cookware, and equipment (see Figure 9-6). If this is the case, check with the kitchen manufacturer and ask if they carry another line that will not require these supports.

● Selecting the Proper Kitchen Cabinet

If there is a room that will maintain or increase the value of a home it is the kitchen. A kitchen is the hub of the household for making meals, eating, relaxing, and socializing. It should be attractive and efficient.

A well-designed and arranged cabinet system with special attention given to the location of the refrigerator, sink, dishwasher, and cooking center will reduce work, and save steps between the different work centers. Here, as in other areas of the house, storage cabinetry should be designed keeping in mind the items to be stored. The house must be measured, and the space carefully divided with drawers, shelves, and work centers correctly proportioned to satisfy the specific needs of each area.

When the kitchen and/or bathroom has become out-of-date, but the budget does not allow for a complete upgrade and replacement of the cabinets, consider a face lift. Do the drawers and cabinet faces look worn, but the storage capacity and the appliance locations are still satisfactory? Changing the face of the doors and cabinets, even when the cabinet frames were made of metal as in many contract homes around the 1950s has become a quick and inexpensive method of upgrade. When retrofitting new cabinet faces onto existing frames, have them measured and inspected by the manufacturer's sales representative. Not all kitchen cabinet suppliers will provide just the cabinet fronts as many are more geared to supplying full cabinet packages for the new home construction market or larger renovation projects. A simple look through the local Yellow Pages under Kitchens and Cabinet Makers should provide you with several sources for estimates. Many of these businesses carry sample door fronts in a show room for viewing and are able to provide a good selection of different finishes, colors, and hardware for the style selected. The size of the rooms, the number of drawers and doors to be replaced, and the quality of hinges and drawer gliders selected will determine the final cost; however, the final price, including the installation, will be only a fraction of the cost to replace all the cabinetry. Cabinet makers can also provide side or under cabinet panels, and toe kicks to match the drawer and door fronts selected. Upgrading the interior of the cabinets may require a few days to complete a small paint job.

For the more extensive renovation the framer or finisher will remove the old floor finish and subfloor and replace it with new products in preparation for the base cabinets. This removal provides the new cabinets with a solid and level floor area. It would be very expensive to match new cabinets to the configuration of the old. Ceramic wall tiles or wall materials that might affect the placement of the upper cabinets must also be removed. People who wish to recycle the wall/floor materials will find it difficult, if not impossible, to find new products that match, and their removal time consuming and expensive especially if done by the suppliers.

For both the complete or face replacement projects there are four basic cabinet types from which to choose: natural unfinished wood cabinets, stained or lacquered wood cabinets, painted wood cabinets, and wood or plastic laminate cabinets.

Unfinished wood cabinets can be purchased at substantial savings when the owner is willing to do some of the home's finishing and painting. This cabinet type has been presanded and with minimal clean-up is ready for staining or painting. The cabinets must be delivered to the house in sufficient time to allow finishing prior to their installation, and the finished appearance can match other woodwork and trims throughout the home.

Stained or lacquered cabinets are made of a higher quality of wood such as oak and usually finished at the cabinet shop in a carefully controlled, dust-free environment that ensures a high standard of uniformity and curing of the finish. This dust-free environment is essential as there are sometimes multiple spraying applications required, and if the cabinets are finished in the house during construction, particles of dust will attach themselves to the finish, resulting in a highly visible flaw. This cabinet style is usually selected because it is relatively low in maintenance.

Painted wood cabinets can reduce the final cost of the cabinets if the wood is of a cheaper quality or a man-made fiberboard and the owners decide to do some of the painting themselves. Painting is relatively easy, and since they can be painted after their installation, and do not require a complete dust-free environment, this is a good way to save some money. Because the painting process will take the same spraying and drying time in the manufacturer's shop they will usually charge as if the cabinets were being stained or lacquered. To verify the actual price difference, compare the paint cost plus the personal labor with the painting contractor's quote and the price charged by the cabinet manufacturer.

Wood and plastic laminate cabinets are usually finished at the cabinet manufacturer's shop. They are constructed of wood or wood fiberboards, and then covered with a factory laminate. Wood and plastic laminates require little maintenance and come in a wide variety of wood grain finishes and colors.

There are three types of cabinetry construction that can be considered depending on style, budget, and design: cabinets built on the site by a carpenter, custom-built units constructed and assembled in a local cabinet or millwork shop, and mass-produced units available from factories that specialize in cabinets. Even when a large part of the cabinets are produced in a shop, the carpenter is responsible for the installation, a job that requires skill and careful attention to detail. The final cost of your cabinets will depend on the materials selected, the shape, number and style of cabinets, and the quality of countertop selected.

In all cases, the house must be measured by the sales representative to determine the size and shape of cabinetry required to fit each area of the house. From working with the blueprints and their on-site measurements, they will draw a detailed sketch of the cabinets for the kitchen, bathrooms, and laundry that will match their modular sizes to your design requirements. Location and size of the appliances must be known by the salesperson in order to configure cabinets with the appliances; each work center must be discussed in detail so that the proper size and type of drawers and cabinet doors can be sized and drawn with the correct

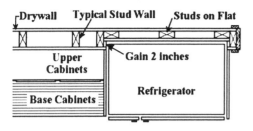

Figure 9-7. A refrigerator set
into typical stud wall.

swing. Most refrigerators and ranges protrude beyond the face of the cabinets. It is possible to have the cabinet and the appliance face flush if the appliance is located on an interior wall and the framer reduces the wall's stud width by two inches at that location, thus allowing those appliances to be set further back into the wall (see Figure 9-7).

Countertops take more abuse than other parts of the house so it is very important to choose the best finish and color for your family's requirements from the selection of plastic laminated, marble, ceramic tile, and man-made plastic. During regular use a selected countertop will be exposed to heat, moisture, scratching/cutting, and staining from all products and appliances, and each product has its unique limitations.

When the drawing is completed, sit down with the representative to discuss and verify in detail the location, type, swing, and size of every drawer, door, shelf, and appliance in each room (see Figure 9-8). If the sales-person gets too busy, he may forget a feature that was discussed, and then assume that you wanted something else, or forget it completely, eg., a certain drawer size, door finish, or cabinet style. If there is no note to call and ask questions it might be missed in the estimate; if not caught before ordering there will be an additional cost to purchasing another cabinet to correct the mistake.

If some or all of the following items are selected, review them twice with the salesperson, at the initial meeting to discuss the design, and at the final meeting with the kitchen drawing and estimate.

Consider these aspects:

- name and style of cabinet face;
- corner cabinet shelves or lazy Susan;
- sizes of cabinets, width and height;
- size and location of appliances;
- doorknob style;
- sizes of kitchen, bathroom, and laundry sinks;
- door swing and hinge location;
- number of shelves in each cabinet;
- style of pull-out for drawers;
- locations for cutlery, hand/dish towels, detergents, pots and pans, plates, drinking cups, containers, canned goods, mops and brooms, food staples, etc;
- refrigerator set into a wall in order to have it flush with the cabinets;
- distances between cabinets for circulation, especially around an island unit;
- dropped counter areas in the kitchen;

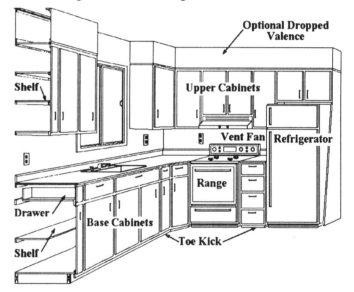

Figure 9-8. Schematic drawing of typical kitchen
cabinet and appliance locations.

- location of the correct number of vanity sinks;
- supply and installation of the sunshine or island fluorescent ceiling unit;
- end panels required to cover the side(s) of the refrigerator;
- valences over the cabinets or open to the ceiling. (If cabinets are open to the ceiling, is there a trim allowed in the price to finish the top of the upper cabinets?);
- corner cabinet for the lazy Susan or shelves is angled or square to the corner;
- drawer locations, sizes and contents, and sectional compartments;
- height placement of all upper cabinets if the wall height is more than the norm;
- island or counter section to fit the cooktop unit selected;
- glass or special cabinet door features;
- special shelves or knickknack areas;
- special spice shelves on the cabinet doors;
- correctly named color, style, and design of the countertop;
- correct distance from the countertop to the underside of the upper cabinet;
- cutting of the countertop for the sinks, cooktop with venting to the basement, and countertop-mounted plugs included in the price;
- linen, pantry or broom closets supplied by the cabinet manufacturer. (Include any pull-out drawers or special shelf units in the price estimate);
- time to service damaged cabinets;
- toe kick finishing material included in the price of the cabinets;
- pull-out cutting boards included in the estimate;
- narrow cabinet area for trays and breadboards.

Note: The templates and measurements for the cutouts of the sinks and countertop appliances are provided by the suppliers. Giving these templates to your installer prior to the cabinets being installed will eliminate the possibility of requesting the carpenter to return to cut the countertops after the cabinets have been completely installed, or having to pay an additional charge to hire someone else.

Once the primer coat of paint and textured ceilings have been completed in the house, the finishing carpenter places the plywood overlay for the finished floor over the subfloor before the cabinets and/or vanities are installed. Doing this will eliminate any additional cutting, planing, or filing of the overlay in order to fit under the cabinet toe kicks, or match odd corners and angles caused by the cabinet shape or design. This will also protect the cabinets from being scratched or gouged by the workers when laying and stapling the overlay. If the overlay is installed after the cabinets, and filler pieces are used, this could result in an uneven floor surface for the finished floor material with the filler seams and staples showing through the lino.

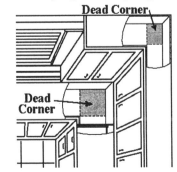

Figure 9-9. Typical dead corner locations.

Premanufactured cabinets are considered the most economical because they are built on an assembly line with standard modular widths and heights. They are usually built using a cheaper wood or pressboard, and laminated with a veneer wood or vacuum plastic finish. The cabinets are assembled by stapling and gluing the wood members together which will limit their durability and therefore their life span.

Show rooms display different kitchen configurations and designs in a wide variety of colors, finishes, faces and hardware styles; however, they are limited to fixed, rectangular, modular sizes which do not always allow the cabinets to effectively fill the space in the design. In order to achieve the appearance of fit, several different widths of spacers may be installed between each modular cabinet to fill the required area. Visually they are attractive from the outside, but once the cabinet doors are opened there is less actual storage space behind. Rectangular and modular configurations create dead corner spaces, and do not fit on angled custom walls (see Figure 9-9).

The cabinets, without the doors attached, are delivered by the carpenter to the job site in a large covered van. The cabinets are numbered in sequence of installation, and placed in the designated rooms to eliminate installation errors. Inspect the cabinets and countertops on delivery for any scratches, dints, discolorations, or questionable markings that will require their return to the manufacturer for servicing. If not caught on the delivery day or shortly after, it will be very hard if not impossible to keep to the overall construction schedule due to the delay resulting from cabinet returns.

The carpenter will first check the floors for level. If the cabinets require leveling, he will attach the base cabinets by securing them together with wood screws to make sure they will not separate, and will slide them into position. Using wood wedges he will adjust the

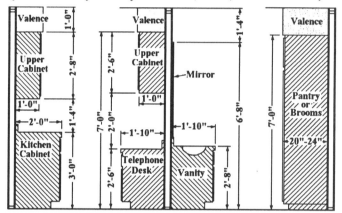

Figure 9-10. Cross section showing sectional view of typical upper/lower cabinet requirements.

height of the cabinets until level, and then locate the wall studs to which he will fasten the cabinets with long wood screws. The screw heads will be covered with plastic plugs for camouflage.

To find correct placements for the upper cabinets, the carpenter must first measure to find the seven-foot wall height, i.e., the top of the cabinet. Once again he will attach the upper cabinets together with wood screws to make sure they will not separate when positioned. Using adjustable supports the upper cabinets are raised into position, the wall studs located, and the cabinets fastened to the wall with long wood screws covered with plastic plugs. Wall heights may vary with the design of the house. If higher than the norm, make sure your cabinet designer and supplier are aware so that they can make the necessary adjustments. They might be required to provide higher upper cabinets so the visual proportion of the cabinets to the rooms will appear in balance (see Figure 9-10).

The countertop supports and the finished countertops are glued and precut to size in the shop except for one end. If adjustments are required, the cabinet length is measured, and the countertop is cut on-site to fit the adjusted length. All perimeter joints, countertop splash backs, and cabinet attachment to the walls will be covered with a bead of caulking that matches the cabinet and countertop colors. Once the countertop is securely fastened to the base cabinet, the carpenter installs the sliding drawers, door faces and hinges onto the correct cabinets. He then adjusts the hinges for a proper door fit, and installs the knobs.

One significant benefit of the modular unit is that the handyman, if willing to spend some time in the evenings and weekends to install the cabinets, can save some money. Most modular cabinet manufacturers provide detailed instructions for installing their product, and these directions should be studied and carefully followed. As previously stated, floors and walls are seldom exactly level and plumb, therefore shims and wedges will be required so the cabinets are not broken or twisted during installation. Doors and drawers cannot be expected to work properly if the cabinet framework is not installed correctly.

These cabinets, somewhat limited by their design, selection, and quality of materials, have found their place in the market based on price advantage. If budget limits are a serious consideration, consider the premanufactured modular units.

Custom built and pre-assembled cabinets have greater selection in color, design and finishing. Because they do not have specific widths and heights, the cabinets can be manufactured to fit the required space with only end spacers required to finish the cabinet face. Every inside inch of space is utilized, dead corner spaces are non-existent, and because they are custom-made the cabinet shape will be able to fit onto any angled custom walls.

The cabinets are all manufactured at the cabinet shop, and delivered to the job site in numbered sequence for installation. The carpenter must follow the same installation procedures as with the premanufactured units by checking for level, fitting wood wedges, and camouflaging the screw heads with plugs.

Most kitchen cabinet manufacturers order prefabricated countertops from companies that specialize in these applications as it is the more economical route for the supplier as well as their clients. The countertop supports are assembled in the shop without the finished countertops installed, and then measured and cut to fit tightly to the wall and side cabinets on-site. Once satisfied of the fit, the arborite/formica sheets are glued to the counter support with contact glue. All rough edges are routered, sanded, and filed for a smooth finish. To complete the job, the base cabinet perimeter joints, countertop splash back, and cabinet attachment to the walls are covered with a bead of caulking that matches the cabinet and countertop colors. The carpenter before leaving will do any required paint touch-ups, and install the drawers, door faces, and hinges on the correct cabinets. He then adjusts the hinges for a proper door fit and installs the doorknobs.

Custom-built and pre-assembled cabinets are not limited by their design; however, they are more expensive than the modular units. Because of their wide range of color and selection, and higher quality of materials, they are usually included in the specifications of custom home builders for the middle and upper end housing market.

Cabinets built on-site are considered the cadillac of all the cabinets. If lucky enough to find a carpenter that is able and willing to custom-build your kitchen, bath and laundry cabinets on-site, you will have quality cabinets that will last a lifetime. The price should be comparable with the custom-built and pre-assembled cabinets. Time factors should be the main consideration when having a carpenter build the

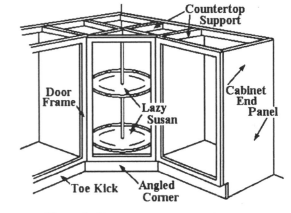

Figure 9-11. Cabinet framework installed.

cabinets on-site. Compared to having them semi-assembled in the shop, and installed on-site which only takes a few days, the carpenter might take a week or two. This time period should be scheduled into the construction time, and adjustments made for the renovation completion date.

A carpenter is not necessarily a salesperson, and he may not be able to provide a detailed drawing; therefore, take sufficient time to thoroughly discuss and draw a sketch of the drawer, storage, and cabinet requirements. An alternative suggestion is to hire the designer to review your cabinet needs, and draw detailed floor plans and elevations of the cabinets for the carpenter. If the original design is not available, provide details of the actual lengths and heights of the walls, taking into consideration the locations of the windows, electrical switches and plugs. The size of the appliances should also be available along with any custom features such as appliances being set into interior walls.

The carpenter will build the cabinets from the bottom up, using plywood or paper templates, and will sketch locations of the appliances and cabinet parts on the floor and walls for correct locations and measurements. The base or toe kick area is constructed first and nailed securely to the floor and back wall after making sure that the floor is level. Once the level has been found, the skeleton, or structural framework of the base and upper cabinets, is constructed and the end panels of the cabinets installed. Once the framework and panels have been secured to the walls, the perimeter face frames, which hold the hinges for the doors and drawer guides in place, are installed, and the shelves measured and cut for installation (see Figure 9-11). Now that the basic structure and rough-opening locations for the drawer and cabinet doors have been determined, the carpenter will measure the size requirements of the drawer frame to be built and installed. The drawers are glued, checked for square, nailed together, and then set to the side.

The counter measurements are taken, and the countertop supports assembled without the finished counter-tops. The counter supports must be measured, and cut to fit tightly to the wall and side cabinets on-site. Once satisfied that the counter support will fit, the carpenter will cut the formica sheets to size, and glue and finish them by following the standard installation process of routering and sanding. When the glue is completely set, the perimeter joints of the formica, countertop splash back and cabinet/walls contact will have a bead of caulking applied. If the owner has selected ceramic tile as the counter's finish, the cabinet installer must cut and fit sheets of 3/4-inch plywood sheathing as the structural base for the top, then glue and screw a top sheet of 1/4-inch good-one-side plywood on which to set the tiles.

The cabinet door and drawer faces can be made by the carpenter; however this will add about a week to the contract time. Many carpenters order the faces from companies that specialize in these prefabricated items, and provide a wide variety of styles, sizes, and finishes, eg., painted or stained. These are delivered to the job site precut to the exact dimensions with edges and hinge holes machined and ready for installation.

The cabinet maker will install the hinges onto the prefinished cabinet doors and mount the door in the opening, making the necessary adjustments to the door for a proper fit. The prefinished doors can then be removed when either you or the painting contractor paints the cabinets, and the carpenter will return to re-install the cabinet doors and mount the hardware.

Note: It is the responsibility of the cabinet installer to sweep, pick up, and remove all his debris from the house, and place that material on your trash pile for pickup.

I have had personal experience with all three types of cabinet installations and preferred the custom-built and pre-assembled units for 90 percent of the houses. The possession date for moving back into the house usually required scheduling the finishing of the house with cabinets, painting, carpets, and so on to a very tight time line; however, I remember the built-on-site units with much satisfaction and pride as all our cabinet needs were considered and installed as per the design. It was a joy to have every square inch used, and all the desired features at our fingertips.

CHAPTER 10

♦ WORKING WITH THE DESIGNER

Note: *At this point, log every date, name, time and discussion in the diary.*

• Choosing a Designer

Word of mouth is usually the best way to find a designer. Check with satisfied friends for the name of the person who designed their renovation project. Chances are you will receive the same service. Ask the friends to allow you to review his set of presentation and working drawing blueprints, as this will provide a complete visual example of the quality of working drawings you might expect. The question you now have to ask is "Will that same service be what I require to renovate my house?"

Another common method of finding a designer is spending some time on the phone, and the local Yellow Pages can help you there. Usually found under Drafting Services or House Plans, these businesses will vary in services provided, selection of plans for viewing, experience, quality of work and, of course, price. The larger, more colorful ads will attract your attention, but do not ignore the smaller ads as large does not always mean the best in quality of design or price.

Designers are unable to do renovation projects without detailed blueprints of the existing house. If these plans are not available, you will need to find a design service willing to measure the home and lot, and provide a new set of working drawings. This cost will be in addition to the renovation design and blueprinting price.

Many designers are now using computers for their design projects. Computer Assisted Design and Drafting (CADD) provides the advantages of a sharper image and faster modifications as the plans do not have to be erased and redrawn on paper. These services will be more expensive however, and the design remains only as good as the designer and the clear communication of your needs. Since the standards and quality of the designer will determine the finished product, it is important for you to contact as many design services as possible, and ask each designer the same questions.

Basic questions:

- What are their hours? Will you have to take time off work to see them?
- How many years have they been in the business of designing homes?
- Do they have a portfolio for you to review that includes renovation projects?
- Do they provide an inspection/design service for the existing structure?
- Will they take on-site measurements of the existing house and what are the charges?
- Will they provide a detailed set of blueprints for the existing house?
- What do they provide as a full set of working drawings?
- How long will the renovation design take from presentation to finished working drawings?

- How much will the completed design service cost with eight sets of blueprints?
- Will they be available to answer any questions during construction?
- Does their service include making an application for a building permit?

You should then shortlist your selection to the best three, contact them again asking more detailed questions (see detailed questions), and finally make an appointment to see them at their offices. This way you will be able to observe their portfolios and "people" skills to know if you will be able to work closely together. If the designer has spent most of his career behind a drafting table and not on the job site, the greater the probability his services will be limited to designing, and not include the other services, such as measuring/inspecting the renovation project. When the economy is booming, many designers who work for architects, builders, and other design services are willing to do designs in the evening, usually out of their houses. Many established design services frown on their employees doing evening work because they get no break from their work schedule, it takes potential jobs away from their business, and many times the clients call the designer during working hours to ask questions. These night workers usually advertise in the classified section of a local newspaper, charge less than the established design services, and work on a cash basis. However, there will not be any guarantee that the working drawings have been checked for errors, or that they will be available for assistance after they have been paid. Based on their answers and your gut feeling, make your final decision.

Detailed questions:

- Will you be dealing with the owner or another designer?
- If, during the presentation, you are not satisfied with their work and do not wish to continue, how much will it cost?
- Does the designer live in a house designed/built by his design service?
- Are they familiar with development controls for subdivisions and local building code requirements/restrictions? What is their liability policy?
- How many contractors do they design for, and will these drawings be used by them in the future?
- Can they provide you with a list of builder renovators and subcontractors for quotations?
- Do they provide an inspection service of the house and detailed structural drawings as part of the working drawing package?
- If required, will they do on-site inspections during the renovation, and is this an additional cost?
- Do they offer any other services, eg., basement planning, landscape drawing?

Note: At the same time that you are working with your designer, spend your Saturdays and weekdays after work driving around subdivisions that have new homes under construction to collect business cards of suppliers and subcontractors. Many of these people can be approached directly if they are still on the job site cleaning up or finishing the day's work. Remember that these workers may have been in the construction business for years, and when they see a novice do-it-yourselfer they will give you a sales job equal to or better than that of a used car salesman. By listening to their responses to the questions that refer to quality of work, price, and warranty after the completed job, you will be assured that you are talking to the right person. When these basic questions are answered directly, without any hesitation or change of subject, you are talking with a subcontractor who has experience with self-contractors and custom-home builders. The subcontractor who brags or jokes around and does not really answer your questions should leave some serious doubt in your mind. If a subcontractor's crews are working within driving distance of your home, they would seriously consider working on your home renovation. Always keep in mind that you will have to get at least three price quotations from each supplier or subcontractor to assure yourself of the best price.

If it is late in the day and there are no workers around, walk through some of the vacant homes under construction. You will find business cards nailed to wall studs or placed on window sills, or advertising signs on completed job sites. *Please keep in mind that you are in someone's house and on private property.* Respect their house as you would have them respect yours. Leave the house the way you found it, remove mud from your shoes before entering, close the doors behind you, obey No Trespassing signs, and most importantly do not smoke while in a house under construction!

- **Initiating the Design Process**

Having chosen a designer that will suit your needs, set up appointments for on-site measuring and then discussion of your rough draft material prior to starting the presentations. Multiple presentations are recommended if your information is in rough form or not to scale, and designers welcome the opportunity to suggest cost-effective or structural changes. *Before* and *after* presentations are valuable for the client to take home for comparison, review and discussion with the family and return with any required changes (see Figure 10-1). During this period the designer should be updating his master drawings and providing you with blueprints of the changes as per the discussions. It may be necessary to have several meetings to ensure all changes are fully understood and agreed upon as they could affect your overall budget, and the final appearance of the home.

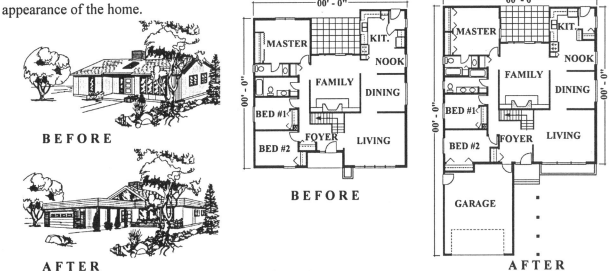

Figure 10-1. Before and after presentation floor plans and renderings.

Take each presentation home to review, and mark on it any changes that you feel are needed. If you do not understand something on the presentation, or have any questions about the construction process, make notes to be asked at the next meeting. Do not assume anything. The more knowledgeable you are at the presentation stage, the easier it will be to understand the final working drawings and the renovation process. The completed presentation blueprints should consist of the floor plans of the existing house plus addition with only overall dimensioning, and a front elevation of the finished renovation for the streetscape visual. These presentation blueprints can then be used to obtain rough estimates of prices from suppliers or subcontractors. Suppliers or subcontractors can also make suggestions that might benefit or assist in keeping construction costs in line; however, it is your money, so consider them carefully. If you believe their suggestions are logical and within your budget, and they can answer questions, such as how it will benefit your renovation project, if the product is energy efficient, and what the payback time will be, then the suggestions should be seriously considered. This step will also tell you if the project is still within your price range and will let you make any last-minute changes before proceeding with the final working drawings.

If at this stage there are only minor changes to the presentation, the designer can then proceed to the working drawings. However, if the suggested changes are substantial enough to change the structure of either the existing house or addition, continue to request as many presentation drawings as necessary until you are totally satisfied with the floor plan(s) and streetscape visual.

- **Checklist Before Working Drawings**

This list is designed to assist you and your family in clarifying questions of habitability and initiating discussion about the presentation. Putting all your trust in a renovation contractor or designer might misdirect you from your final goal. You and you alone should make the decisions about what you like/do not like and what you want/do not want. Review this list again with the designer prior to commencing work on the working drawings.

Exterior streetscape:
- Do you find the house attractive and does it look balanced?
- Are the walls, doors and window areas visually well proportioned with the roof area?
- Will the roof shed snow, or are there valleys where ice can build up causing potential structural damage?
- Will the designer show flashing around the base of the chimney where it meets the roof, or where a wall and a roof meet? This prevents any unwanted water from entering (see Figure 12-82, page 193).
- Will the designer make note of or register sufficient roof ventilation for adequate air exchange in the attic area? Minimum requirements are one vent per 300 square feet.
- Are there more than three steps up to the front entrance? The fewer the better.
- Is the front door entrance eye catching?
- Is the sidewalk and entrance well lit with natural light?
- Is the service door entrance visually exposed, or can it be protected with a gate and motion detector?
- Will the utility meters be located so as not to interfere with proposed sidewalks, and are they easily accessed for servicing?
- Is the driveway to the garage straight and easy to maneuver without hitting a power box or light standard?
- Will there be waterproof wall plugs by the garage and house for the use of electrical equipment or a car block heater?
- Can the driveway, sidewalk, and entrance be well lit for high visibility from the house to see who is approaching?
- Will the plans show hose taps (bibs) at the front of the house for watering the grass, and in or near the garage for washing the car to limit connecting multiple hose extensions?

Front entrance:
- Is the front entry landing protected from the elements with a roof overhang?
- Is the front foyer large enough for three adults to stand comfortably with the front door and entry closet doors open?

- Will the drawings show a peephole, so the occupants can see who is at the door?
- Does the foyer door open directly into a living environment, or is there a partition wall or railing separating the two?
- When the front door opens, imagine a blast of cold air. Could that make you consider changing the door swing?
- Is the front entry closet in close proximity to the entry door?
- If the foyer is sunken, is it possible for someone to trip and hurt themselves? If so, the foyer may be too small, the step(s) too close to the door entrance, or a railing required.
- Will the foyer be well lit with its own light and switch?

Mud/laundry entrance:
- Does it have sufficient counter space for shopping bags and parcels?
- Is the closet large enough to hold bulky winter coats and provide space for boots?
- Will the floor material be easy to maintain on a day-to-day basis?
- Does it have sufficient storage cabinets for your family's needs?
- Are the cabinets over the washer and dryer easy to access?
- Is there a sink for soaking clothes?
- Will the exterior landing be well lit? Will there be glass in the entry door? Will it be safety glass?
- Is there a convenient area outside for the storage of garbage cans? Will it be secured?

Living area:
- Will the room fit your furniture, and allow sufficient circulation space for walking and cleaning without moving the furniture?
- Will there be an opening window close by for the circulation of fresh air?
- Does the window area provide sufficient privacy, yet allow the family members a good view of the entry walkway?
- When not in use, can the room be closed off with French doors to keep dusting and heating to a minimum?

Family area:
- Is there sufficient wall space to fit your existing or planned furniture and entertainment needs?
- Does the fireplace location allow for furniture grouping with sufficient circulating space for the rest of the room?
- Does this room have a large window allowing the family to enjoy a view of a garden or deck area?
- Will there be good access to the front door, patio door and service door yet provide sufficient privacy?
- Is the flooring you selected durable and easy to maintain?
- Will this area require a ceiling fan for air circulation or additional lighting?
- Will there be sufficient electrical plugs for the electronic appliances?

Dining area:
- Is this area easily accessed and serviced from the kitchen?
- Is the room large enough to fit your furniture, and allow sufficient room for expansion during family get-togethers?
- Can it be separated from other rooms of the house to keep its cleaning maintenance down?
- Does it provide sufficient privacy from neighboring windows?
- Will your furniture allow for good traffic circulation when people are seated?

- Will the ceiling fixture be centrally located over the table? Does it remain centrally located when the table is expanded?

Kitchen:
- Is it a workable kitchen when more than one person is moving about? Will they get in each other's way?
- Will it be well lit day and night, and easy to maintain?
- Is there sufficient storage for all appliances and groceries and is it easily organized for quick access?
- Is there sufficient counter space beside each major appliance as well as additional counter space to hold and operate small appliances? Will there be enough, convenient electrical outlets?
- Do you have to purchase new major appliances, or will your existing units fit?
- Has the designer allowed for sufficient pantry and broom storage?
- Will the kitchen have a conveniently located exhaust fan to vent cooking odors?
- Can the children's play area inside and outside be seen from the kitchen?
- Does the kitchen allow for quick, unobstructed access to the telephone?

Hallways:
- Are the hallways too long, taking valuable room space from other parts of the house?
- Will the halls and stairways be well lit with conveniently located three and four way switches? Imagine a night scenario when a family member having a restless sleep needs access to other areas of the house.
- Are the locations of the bedroom and bathroom doors in close proximity to each other, and away from hazardous stairs?
- Will there be any convenient electrical plugs for night lights, etc?

Bathrooms:
- Will the windows and fans provide sufficient air ventilation?
- Is there sufficient elbow room for shaving, brushing, and grooming activities without feeling cramped for space?
- Will the door swings interfere with bathroom space when entering or exiting?
- Will the size of the hot water tank be sufficient when the shower is running and someone turns on a tap or flushes a toilet in another part of the house? This test can be made when the plumber has installed the fixtures. What will the designer register as the proper tank size? If you feel it is inadequate, have him indicate a larger size.
- Has the designer allowed sufficient wall space for towel bars, medicine cabinets, mirrors; storage space for towels, lotions; floor space for laundry hampers, scales, garbage baskets, etc.?
- Will the floors and walls be easily maintained on a day to day basis?
- Will the room be adequately lit and contain a sufficient number of ground fault plugs?

Bedrooms:
- Are the rooms large enough for your furniture with sufficient traffic space around the pieces?
- Will the windows provide sufficient daylight, evening privacy, and adequate ventilation for the room without interfering with furniture placement?
- Will the designer provide enough, conveniently located electrical outlets for your intended furniture arrangement and electronic needs?
- Do the bedrooms have adequate closet space with a generously sized dressing area, and do the closet doors open wide enough for accessing the closet organizers without unusable corners?

Basement:

- Will you be planning to develop a basement under the addition? If so, you might consider a nine-foot basement rather than the standard eight-foot one.
- Will the locations of the structural posts limit the room sizes and locations? Consider moving them using structural wood or steel beams.
- Will the furnaces, hot water tanks, floor drains, or sump pits be located adjacent to or under the stairs where they will not affect future basement development?
- Will the basement have adequate ceiling lights and ventilation, and will the windows provide adequate natural light for the rooms when developed?
- Have provisions been made for a three or four piece bathroom?
- Have you visualized where the storage areas are to be located for easy accessibility without a negative impact on any future development?
- Will the designer note or show proper floor slopes for drainage, eliminating any puddling or basement flooding?

Stairs:

- Is their location central, thus allowing good access from most areas of the house?
- Are they designed wide enough for moving large pieces of furniture?
- Did the designer allow for the required headroom to the basement as per building standards?
- Are they too steep?
- Are the stairs safe for children? Can they be made child-safe by shutting them off with a door or gate?
- Will the vacuum hose reach the full length of the stairs (both up and down)?
- Will there be any electrical plugs for night security lighting?

General questions for all areas of the house:

- Is there sufficient wall space at the front entry landing for a mail box?
- Does the house require a laundry chute?
- Are the storage and closet spaces sufficient for the family's needs?
- Will all electrical outlets be conveniently located for telephones, vacuum hose plugs, intercoms, security system, exterior motion sensors, night light plugs, and those handy rechargeable flashlights and vacuums?
- Has the designer on a separate page from the drawings registered the location of the security system for window pads, glass break, and properly located motion detectors to secure all the floors and stairwells?
- Have you identified wall-switch locations, and considered energy-saving dimmer switches?
- Will the attic access be in a convenient yet out of the way location, eg., in a closet or storage room, and not in a hallway? Is it easily accessible by a step ladder?
- Will the hot-water tank size be adequate for the needs of the family? A two-bedroom house should have a 30 imperial gallon unit, a three-bedroom house a 40 imperial gallon unit or two 30 imperial gallon units, and a four-bedroom house should have two 30 imperial gallon units.
- Did the designer register firewalls and fire-rated doors for the utility room and the party wall separating the garage and house?
- Will the utility meter locations be discussed with your designer, and located on your drawing as per the

building code, i.e., away from all opening windows and doors? Will these meters be easily accessed for reading?

- Is the furnace thermostat(s) sheltered from drafts and sun which can drastically affect its function?

- Is the method of ventilating the rooms with fresh air satisfactory? Do the windows allow the intake of fresh air and the exhaust of stale air without causing blowing, drafty winds? Determine the wind directions, and have the window manufacturer locate the openers for proper venting.

- Will the heat and cold-air return registers affect furniture placement? Can the designer indicate where they should be on the plan?

- Have fire prevention measures been considered? Should you have fire extinguishers? Will the smoke detectors be properly located, and wired directly to the house power with a battery backup?

- Can you visualize the family escape routes if a fire occurs?

- Do bedroom and bathroom door locations allow for privacy from other main traffic areas?

- Is there a closet centrally located for the storage of the vacuum hose and equipment?

- Have you considered any special wall-plug locations, eg., wall lighting for paintings?

● **Working Drawings**

It will be necessary to have several meetings at the working drawing stage, as this is where the structure and details of the renovation project start to emerge. Request a meeting after the working floor plans, sections, and elevations have been drawn, but before the final details, such as dimensions, siding, window sizes, or required details, such as electrical, plumbing, and heating, have been completed. This step will allow you to review and compare the before and after drawings, and the final details of the plans without the confusing measurements, dimension lines and notes. This drawing stage will also allow you to plan the development of the addition's basement by locating any new structural posts and stairwells, furnaces, hot water tanks, sump pits and floor drains. Have the designer discuss with you how the basement can be best divided for your present and future requirements. Once the details have been added, return to page 98 and review the checklist.

Your designer should be visually walking you through the house plans, explaining the differences between the old and new structure, the new door swings, room sizes with the proposed locations and types of switches, and the interior and exterior plugs, light fixtures, and any built-in systems as a finished or rough-in product. If at this time you remember some structural changes which have not been previously discussed at the presentation stage, and you wish to include them in the working drawings expect to pay for the additional work if they require erasing on the original plan. It is still best to catch a problem at this stage and pay the little extra rather than during construction when it could cost thousands to make the change, if even possible. Because of building code changes or just working too quickly, it is possible for even the best designer to make a mistake on the working drawings. Having several people review the presentations should let you, the designer, suppliers, or the subcontractors catch any discrepancies in the house plans.

Assuming you have not missed anything, that all changes have been completed, and you are satisfied with the process, your designer can now complete the working drawings. At the last meeting, once again he will walk you through the house plans, explaining all the final electrical, structural, and general notes, specifications, finishing details, and revisions made to the drawings. If you require any additional notes or minor changes, speak now as this is your last chance for changes before blueprinting.

Every designer has different drawing standards, detail requirements and a personal style when doing working drawings. The designer's education, level of experience, and personal standards of quality will determine the amount of information placed on the finished working drawings. However, the final set of blueprints should address the following: foundation and floor plans, applicable elevations and section through drawings, a perspective rendering (optional), and a plot plan.

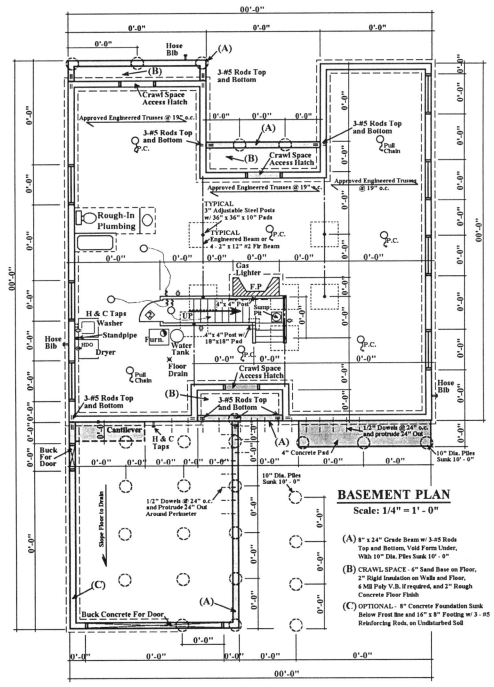

Figure 10-2. Foundation plan working drawings. Extension areas shown as shaded.

The **basement or foundation plan** shows the location of the perimeter footing, concrete/wood structural walls, doors and windows, structural posts, water/gas/sewer lines, floor/sump drains, furnaces, hot water tank, structural information, and all necessary dimensions.

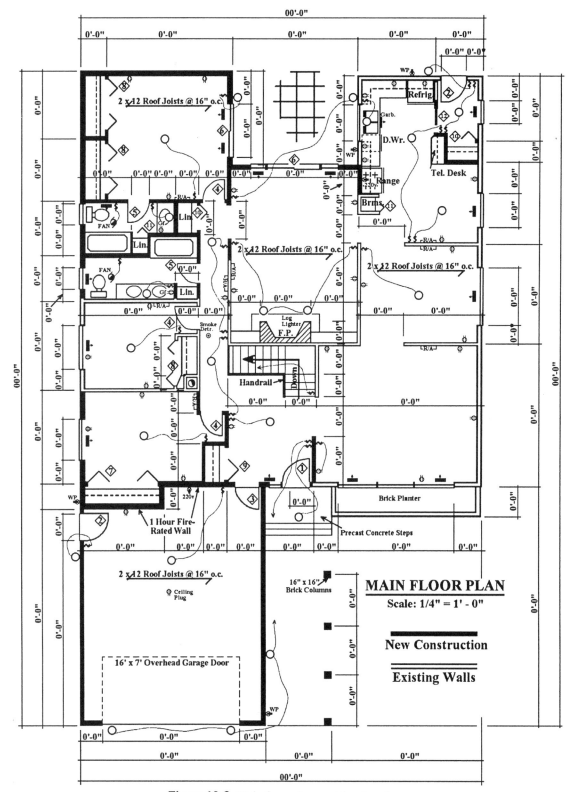

Figure 10-3. Main floor plan working drawings.

A **floor plan** drawing shows the location of all wall partitions, distance between walls, door and window locations, room sizes, door schedule, location of electrical switches, plugs, light fixtures, appliances, plumbing/heating fixtures, structural information, and all necessary dimensions for that floor.

Floor plan door schedule:

1) 36" x 80" Metal-Insulated Door w/ Storm Door

2) 32" x 80" Metal-Insulated Door

3) 32" x 80" Metal Self-Closing Fire-Rated Door

4) 30" x 80" Hollow-Core Door

5) 30" x 80" Hollow-Core Door w/ Privacy Lock

6) 72" x 80" Glass-Sliding Patio Door

7) 84" x 80" Hollow-Core Bi-fold Door

8) 72" x 80" Hollow-Core Bi-fold Door

9) 48" x 80" Hollow-Core Bi-fold Door

10) 36" x 80" Hollow-Core Bi-fold Door

11) 18" x 80" Hollow-Core Door

12) 32" x 80" Hollow-Core Pocket Door

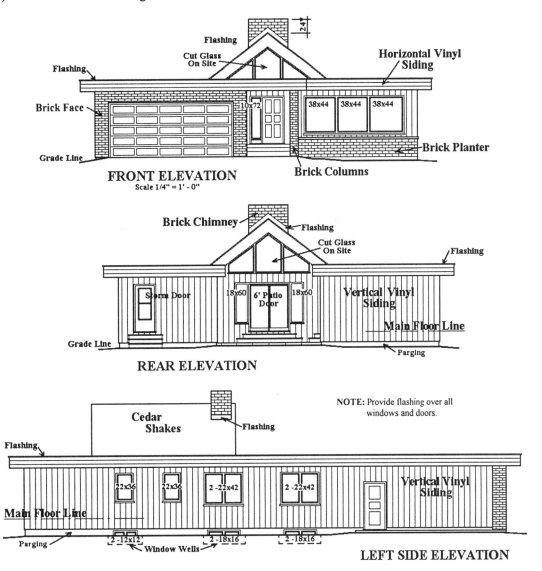

Figure 10-4. Three elevation views affected by the renovation project.

The **elevation drawings** may include all views of the front, rear, left, and right, or depending upon the complexity of the renovation, be as few as two views of the portion of the house which will be visually altered by the addition or renovation project. The elevations provide a flat perspective of the house as if someone is looking at it directly without any visual depth. They will show the window and door placements, exterior material finishes and locations, grade and floor heights, and all necessary dimensions.

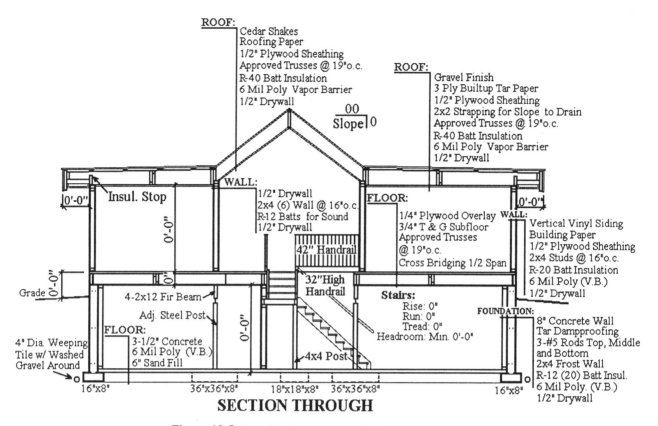

ROOF:
Cedar Shakes
Roofing Paper
1/2" Plywood Sheathing
Approved Trusses @ 19"o.c.
R-40 Batt Insulation
6 Mil Poly Vapor Barrier
1/2" Drywall

ROOF:
Gravel Finish
3 Ply Builtup Tar Paper
1/2" Plywood Sheathing
2x2 Strapping for Slope to Drain
Approved Trusses @ 19"o.c.
R-40 Batt Insulation
6 Mil Poly Vapor Barrier
1/2" Drywall

$\dfrac{00}{\text{Slope} \mid 0}$

Insul. Stop

0'-0"

WALL:
1/2" Drywall
2x4 (6) Wall @ 16"o.c.
R-12 Batts for Sound
1/2" Drywall

FLOOR:
1/4" Plywood Overlay
3/4" T & G Subfloor
Approved Trusses
@ 19"o.c.
Cross Bridging 1/2 Span

0'-0"

WALL:
Vertical Vinyl Siding
Building Paper
1/2" Plywood Sheathing
2x4 Studs @ 16"o.c.
R-20 Batt Insulation
6 Mil Poly (V.B.)
1/2" Drywall

0'-0"

42" Handrail

32"High
Handrail

Stairs:
Rise: 0"
Run: 0"
Tread: 0"
Headroom: Min. 0'-0"

FOUNDATION:

8" Concrete Wall
Tar Dampproofing
3-#5 Rods Top, Middle
and Bottom
2x4 Frost Wall
R-12 (20) Batt Insul.
6 Mil Poly. (V.B.)
1/2" Drywall

Grade 0'-0"

4-2x12 Fir Beam

Adj. Steel Post

0'-0"

FLOOR:
3-1/2" Concrete
6 Mil Poly (V.B.)
6" Sand Fill

4x4 Post

4" Dia. Weeping
Tile w/ Washed
Gravel Around

16"x8"   36"x36"x8"   18"x18"x8"   36"x36"x8"   16"x8"

SECTION THROUGH

Figure 10-5. A section through the building showing the stairs.

It is essential for many of the suppliers and subtrades to view at least one **section through** of the width or the length of the house showing the stair direction, interior heights, and the wall, roof, floor and basement structure of the house. This information will allow them to provide a detailed structural quotation.

Figure 10-7. An ink line perspective rendering.

A perspective drawing or rendering shows in three dimensions how the completed house, including all trees, sidewalks, and house finishes, will look. These drawings are usually done at extra cost by most design services and can be completed in full color or a black ink line on white watercolor board. Nice to have as a memento or on display in the home if you can afford it.

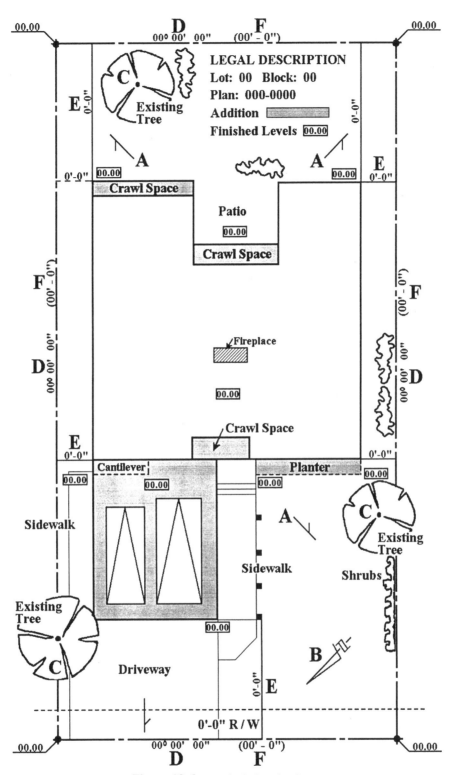

Figure 10-6. A typical plot plan layout.

A **plot plan** shows **(A)** the required slope-to-drain of the lot, **(B)** orientation of the house and addition according to the north compass direction, **(C)** existing trees or shrubs, and driveway, **(D)** perimeter lot indicators showing the North, South, East, and West compass directions in degrees, feet, and inches, **(E)** sideyard measurements of the lot boundary to house, and **(F)** perimeter lot measurements.

At the time of application for a building permit, the city building inspector will also have to review the working drawings before you can start construction. If the inspector finds something wrong with the working drawings, the liability of your designer is usually limited to making the necessary corrections with new sets of blueprints provided to you at no cost. If you have the house designed by an architect, the design cost will usually include a fee for liability insurance. Discuss this potential problem and the company policy before hiring.

Your final meeting with your designer will most likely be the shortest. You will receive the blueprint copies, shake hands and pay the first bill for your design project.

Note: In order to keep your finances in order, I suggest that all payments on invoices come from one bank account, i.e., one specifically set up for all payments for the house renovation project. All payments whether cash (via cheque made payable to yourself) or invoiced should be recorded by means of a cheque. The cheque should note what or who the payment was for, an invoice number, and whether it is a deposit, advance, or final payment made in full.

• Optional Design Services

The designer's primary service is completion of the presentation and all working blueprints for the home renovation. Many design services deal with suppliers and builders daily, and this direct knowledge of the construction industry is beneficial if they can provide you with a list of reputable subtrades for estimates.

Some design services may offer to draw plot plans for minor renovations, coordinate on-site inspections, and provide written reports advising you of any problems arising during construction or informing you about energy-saving options to consider. If the design service has the ability and is interested in providing on-site inspections during important phases of the construction process it would be a good idea to include this in your design contract. Many people not yet sure of their supervisory ability will find this service invaluable especially when the designer is accessible to respond to any concerns and protect your interests with follow-up site inspections. He can be hired on an hourly basis or prenegotiated fee to provide at least seven on-site inspections to verify that the supplier and subcontractors are following the specifications and the working blueprints, as follows:

1) Inspection of the foundation, footings, structural pads, and weeping tiles prior to backfill;
2) Inspection of the floor joists, stair headroom, subfloor, main/upper floor framing including roof prior to installation of the windows, and finished roof materials;
3) Inspection of the rough-in plumbing, heating, electrical, exterior wall, and firestops prior to installation of the wall insulation;
4) Inspection of the wall insulation prior to application of the vapor barrier;
5) Inspection of the vapor barrier and exterior cladding prior to application of the drywall;
6) Inspection of the plywood overlay prior to installation of the finishing package and cabinets;
7) Inspection of the finishing package, including door swings, and cabinet installation prior to installation of the hardware.

With a good set of detailed house plans and a knowledgeable designer, the construction project can be an enjoyable and a less troublesome experience.

PART IV: PROJECT MANAGEMENT

CHAPTER 11

♦ STARTING THE PROCESS

• Shopping for Suppliers and Subcontractors

In order to get the best possible construction price for your home renovation *you should get a minimum of three price estimates* from each of the suppliers and subcontractors required for the completion of the project. See the list below. Sometimes with the more expensive items (marked with an *) four or five estimates may be advisable.

If you deviate from this system and decide that you are getting tired and two estimates are enough, or you are running out of blueprints, this can be a BIG MISTAKE. For the little extra cost, purchase more blueprints from the designer. If you do not, the final construction cost of your home could end up being thousands of dollars too high. I have made that mistake myself, and seen it happen dozens of times. It will be regretted, and can be avoided.

Not all of the suppliers or subcontractors require a full set of blueprints, so divide them up according to their areas of need. Start saving yourself about 100 dollars by dividing the blueprints, then save thousands with the suppliers and subcontractors by shopping smart.

• How to Divide the Blueprints:

Sections = SE	Full Set of Blueprints = FS	Elevations = EL
Plot Plan = PP	Floor Plans = FP	Basement Plan = BP

Blueprint(s) required

Development Control Officer	FS
Bank Mortgage	FS x 2 Will return one set
Surveyor	FS
City Permits	FS x 2 Will return one set
Excavator	PP, BP
Foundation Cribber	FP, PP, SE, BP
* Framer	FS
* Window Supplier	FP, EL
* Electrician	FP, EL, BP
* Plumber	FP, EL, BP
Light Fixture Supplier	FP, BP
Concrete Supplier	FP, SE, BP
Furnace/Heating Installer	FS
* Drywaller/Taper/Insulator/Texture Installer	FS
* Painter	FS
Finisher	FP
* Lumber Supplier	FS
* Kitchen Cabinet Supplier	FP Photocopies

Roofer	EL
Roof Truss Supplier..	FS
* Siding/Stucco Installer..	EL
* Carpet/Lino/Tile Installer	FP Photocopies
Fascia/Soffit/ Eavestrough Installer.........................	EL
Intercom/Security/Vacuum Installer........................	FP Photocopies
Concrete Driveway/Sidewalk/Floor Installer	PP, FP, BP
Fireplace Installer	FP Photocopies

The above suppliers and subcontractors are the companies which account for about 92 percent of the cost of a major renovation project. The remaining costs includes appliances, weeping tile, waterproofing, railings, laminated beams, and garbage removal.

- **Collecting and Receiving Estimates**

This part of the preconstruction process is probably the most time consuming and frustrating. Most of your time will be spent delivering blueprints to suppliers and subcontractors for pricing. To utilize it well, prepare separate information packages for each delivery in advance. Each package should have a label with the supplier's name, address and phone number stapled on their set of blueprints along with a list of your detailed requirements. This list will ensure that they are all pricing similar products, and your final choice will be objective.

Remember, if you are subcontracting the house yourself, you are considered a builder, and should be requesting builder prices from the suppliers and subcontractors. The level of builder pricing you will receive will depend entirely on how much material you purchase, and the number of subsequent referrals the suppliers and subcontractors will potentially receive from your business. Some design services have negotiated special pricing with many of the subtrades you will be dealing with. As an example, many of my clients are able to contact a particular lumberyard, framer, window manufacturer, etc., and receive a class 1 or 2 discount, because over the years a sufficient number of my clients have requested estimates and purchased products from those companies. In return for these referrals I was given a preferred contractor's rating, and my clients subsequently benefited from that purchase power. Ask if your designer offers this service.

Calling and meeting with the suppliers and subcontractors is the second most important task other than the actual construction. This is where you can make or break your budget. Start by keeping your diary or day timer updated hourly with names, times and phone numbers. Doing this will provide you with an accurate record of your discussion, the meeting time, date, and place. During this initial phone contact, suppliers and subcontractors are very receptive to the potential business opportunity, and will be willing to provide you with information not readily given after the construction start. Try to get their home and/or mobile phone numbers at this time. Doing so will ensure that you are able to contact them if you have questions or run into any problems before a scheduled meeting or during the construction period.

The hours spent contacting suppliers and subcontractors to set meetings will raise your blood pressure. If your contacts are busy, some will not show, some will not return your call, or some will show sometime in the next few days usually without calling first. This does not mean that you should strike them off your list. If they have a good reputation, but do not show after the second attempt, be persistent. Call them back. Ask them if they are interested in giving you an estimate as you do not want to waste their time or yours. You might find that continuous pressure will pay off. Human nature especially in the housing industry comes with many variables that change daily.

It is important that you inform the supplier or subcontractor that you are having other estimates done. Doing so is fair business practice and will let them quote competitively. It will also ensure that they will give you their best price.

Before delivering the information packages to the suppliers and subcontractors, get a city map, mark on the map the location of each supplier and subcontractor, and then try to set up initial meetings in their order of proximity to each other. I have found that dividing the city into four sectors will speed and better organize your deliveries. Each sector represents one day to deliver the information packages; divide each sector into two parts which will represent morning and afternoon deliveries. Make a habit of calling them a day in advance of each meeting; set aside about one hour in the morning to confirm same day appointments and at the end of each day to set new appointments for the next day or two.

Allow a fifth or sixth day for repeat deliveries due to the no shows. Try to rebook the no shows early in the morning before they leave the office for the job site. If they do not show or have a good excuse the third time, and their reputation is not exceptional, forget them. If you are unable to connect with them for the basic estimate, you can imagine the potential frustrations when it comes to the actual work or installation. Spend the afternoon of the fifth day to deliver new information packages for meetings set up to replace those that did not show, or to get additional estimates.

During this initial meeting, request that they have the blueprints and estimate completed on a certain date for the next week, and schedule that meeting at the same time as your present delivery if possible. Now that they have the full information package and a date set to pick up the estimate, make sure that you remind them of their meeting. Call them three days, then one day before the pickup is scheduled to jog their memory and ensure that a completed estimate will be ready when you arrive. Doing this also provides them with the opportunity to ask any questions that might have been missed during the first meeting.

The estimate should contain a detailed list similar to yours naming the product(s), materials, and labor they are promising to supply. If they feel they have an item other suppliers do not provide, have them include it in the estimate as an option for your consideration. When this happens, go back to the other subcontractors, and ask them to include that same item in their estimates, or price it as an option. Make sure you know in advance who is responsible for supplying specific items before selecting your final estimate. Prices will vary drastically depending on the material they are expected to supply. Do not be fooled by cheap estimates that give a single, nondetailed, total package price, and especially one that is given on the back of a business card. In the end they might cost more, especially if the supplier or subcontractor has assumed that you will supply and pay for all the materials. (I will repeat this caution several times in the following chapters where it was a significant issue when I was building.) Also discuss with the suppliers and subcontractors the lien holdback that will be required by your financial institution, and their terms of payment. Request that payment coincide with the mortgage draws. This should not surprise them as it is common practice in the building industry.

You will find that many of the estimates you receive will have been calculated on the square footage. Double-check that the designer has correctly calculated the *actual* living area square footage. Some designers may include dead areas such as chimney fireplace chases or basement stairs as part of the square footage. They should not as these areas are not living and usable environments.

Here is a story that might interest you. Several years ago a home builder contracted me to design a home for a very wealthy client of his, and I provided him with several different presentations for his client's approval. Several weeks went by before he returned with an approved, revised presentation requiring some of the rooms to be enlarged, and an additional main floor nanny suite and laundry room. I informed the contractor that these changes would add substantial square footage and construction cost to the home, and his response was "The more square footage they add to the house plan the more profit for me." This of course was true, however, he took me aside and further requested that I "fudge the final square footage of the living area of the house," saying, "You know what I mean." When I firmly refused, he then asked me to leave the house's square footage off the working drawings. Even though I knew what he was planning to do, I complied because my design fee is based on the square footage so the actual square footage would be on my invoice. I hoped that his client's contract would require that the invoices be shown.

I was very uneasy about this situation, and as we progressed through the working drawings it became obvious this builder was trying to put something over on his client. He requested changes that would reduce his cost but not his client's, eg., changing the truss spacing from 16 inches to 24 inches on center. Being distanced from his client, I was unable to ask whether they had approved of these changes. However, I knew I would be able to get that information from the city after the working drawings were completed and the builder applied for the building permit. The land titles office later did a computer search from the address and legal description to give me the owners' names and address.

I then contacted the property owners and when they affirmed they were having a house built by a particular contractor, I explained what the contractor had requested and planned. They thanked me, and said they would get back to me. Two weeks later they phoned to inform me that they had fired the contractor and hired someone else after discovering that he had padded the square footage by 64 square feet and overcharged $12,000 by reducing the specifications. They informed me that they would never have known, and asked me to redraw the plans with their new specifications. Their contract with the second builder now included a third party to inspect his work during the construction. The moral of the story is *buyer beware!* Build in safeguards and know your contract.

It is also possible for each estimate to vary in price because of different name brands supplied, warranties, and after installation services. If you feel more comfortable with a particular company and product, but you prefer someone else's price, tell the preferred company of your predicament. Without giving the price of the lower bid, ask if they can sharpen their pencil. You will often find that they are able to meet and sometimes beat the lower bid. If you are also lucky enough to be in a position to pay cash upon completion rather than the usual 30 days, they will sometimes offer you an additional discount. It never hurts to ask! Make sure you have a good warranty contract and that you know the supplier will still be in business to service their work.

Note: Initially, it will not be necessary to wait for three estimates from *all* the suppliers or subtrades before starting construction. Some trades, eg., painters, finishers, electrician, concrete driveway/sidewalk installers, carpet/tile/lino or stucco and siding installers, are not scheduled until later so one estimate will be sufficient to fix a construction price for the mortgage application. During the initial construction phase you will have time to shop for the additional estimates from these suppliers and subcontractors, so do not panic.

When you have chosen the supplier or subcontractor, verify in a follow-up letter the price, service to be supplied, product to be supplied, payment schedule, holdbacks, service or product warranties, and notification of responsibility for the removal or clean up of any debris resulting from their service or crews. Be sure to keep a copy for your files.

For your convenience, on pages 113 to 118 I have provided sample quotation sheets. I have used this format to record the many estimates received for residential, multi-family and commercial renovation/construction projects. This useful chart serves as a constant reminder of the number of estimates that have to be collected before proceeding with any construction project.

Job Number:_____ Address: _____ City: _____
LEGAL DESCRIPTION: Lot:_____ Block: _____ Plan: _____ - _____
Owner: _____ Phone No: (_____) _____

BUILDING COSTS	DATE		COST ESTIMATE						FINAL NAME & PRICE		
100 - Plans and Design Fee											
101 - Demolition/Building Permit											
102 - Surveyor Building Pocket											
103 - Surveyor Stake-out											
104 - Surveyor Grade Certificate											
ENGINEERING											
105 - Soil Test											
106 - Structural											
107 - Wood Foundation											
UTILITIES											
108 - Water Line & Trenching											
109 - Sewer Line & Trenching											
110 - Gas Line & Trenching											
111 - Temp. Electrical Service											
112 - Electrical Service											
113 - Utility Consumption											
114 - Gas Line Application											
115 - Winter Frost Allowance											
CONSTRUCTION COSTS											
116 - Demolition - Backhoe											
117 - Topsoil Removal											
118 - Demolition - Framer											
119 - Refuse Container Rental											
120 - Portable Toilet Rental											
121 - Excavation & Backfill											
122 - Dirt Fill or Disposal											
123 - Framing Lumber Package											
124 - Wood Foundation Package											
125 - Structural Beams											
126 - Roof Trusses											
127 - Prefabricated Wood Stairs											
128 - Deck Joist Lumber											

BUILDING COSTS	DATE	COST ESTIMATE						FINAL		
129 - Deck Railings										
130 - Deck Floor Material										
131 - Deck Stairs										
132 - Concrete Costs										
133 - Winter Costs										
134 - Concrete Pump										
135 - Footings										
136 - Foundation										
137 - Structural Pads										
138 - Grade Beam										
139 - Pilings										
140 - Foundation Reinf. Rebar										
CONCRETE FINISHER										
141 - Reinf. Rebar & Wire Mesh										
142 - Basement Floor										
143 - Garage Floor										
144 - Driveway Pad										
145 - Sidewalks										
146 - Patio										
147 - Steps										
148 - Precast Concrete Steps										
149 - Concrete Sealer										
FILL SAND/SPREADING										
150 - Basement Sand										
151 - Garage Sand										
152 - Driveway & Sidewalk Sand										
153 - Foundation Waterproofing										
154 - Weeping Tile & Gravel										
155 - Weeping Tile Cloth Cover										
156 - Basement Window Wells										
157 - Sump Pit & Liner										
UPPER STRUCTURE										
158 - Rough Grading										
159 - Finished Grading										
160 - Spreading Black Dirt										
161 - House Framing Labor										
162 - Deck Framing Labor										

BUILDING COSTS	DATE		COST ESTIMATE						FINAL		
163 - Window & Door Caulking											
164 - Roofing Material											
165 - Roofing Labor											
166 - Window Cost											
167 - Exterior Doors											
168 - Storm Doors											
169 - Plumbing											
170 - Heating											
171 - Air Conditioning											
172 - Electrical											
173 - Eavestrough											
174 - Soffits - Fascia - Gutters											
175 - Batt Insulation											
176 - Loose Fill Attic Insulation											
177 - Rigid Insulation											
178 - Vapor Barrier											
179 - Foam & Caulking Sealants											
180 - Drywall Material & Labor											
181 - Masonry Labor											
182 - Masonry Material											
183 - Steel Angle Iron											
184 - Siding and Installation											
185 - Stucco and Application											
186 - Parging and Application											
187 - Painting - Int. & Ext.											
188 - Finishing Labor											
189 - Finishing Materials											
190 - Cabinets											
191 - Carpets and Linoleum											
192 - Marble and Ceramic Tile											
193 - Wood Flooring											
194 - Wood Railings											
195 - Iron Railings											
196 - Wood Paneling											
197 - Mirrors											
198 - Medicine Cabinets											
199 - Bathroom Accessories											

BUILDING COSTS	DATE	COST ESTIMATE						FINAL		
200 - Light Fixtures										
201 - Ceiling Fans										
202 - Wallpapering										
203 - Decorating Cost										
204 - Garage Door										
205 - Garage Door Opener										
206 - Skylights										
207 - Shutters and Louvres, etc.										
208 - Winter Propane Heating										
209 - Fireplace										
210 - Fireplace Mantel and Instal.										
211 - Security System										
212 - Intercom System										
213 - Exterior Security Lighting										
214 - Built-in Vacuum System										
215 - Sprinkler System										
216 - Garage Unit Heater										
217 - Waterproof Membrane										
MISCELLANEOUS										
218 - Supervision										
219 - Travel and Fuel										
220 - Additional Labor										
221 - Cellular Phone										
222 - Phone Bills										
223 - Developer Damage Deposit										
224 - Rental Equipment										
225 - Garbage Removal Fee										
226 - House Cleaning										
227 - Furnace and Duct Cleaning										
228 - Window Cleaning										
229 - Home/Constr. Insurance										
230 - Workers' Compensation										
231 - Cable TV Connection										
232 - Telephone Connection										
233 - Surround Sound System										
234 - Delivery Costs										
235 - House Inspection Service										

BUILDING COSTS	DATE		COST ESTIMATE						FINAL		
LEGAL and MORTGAGES											
236 - Legal Fees											
237 - Bank Interest											
238 - Property Taxes											
239 - Off-site Levies											
240 - Land Cost											
241 - Land Interest											
242 - Mortgage Application Fee											
243 - Bank Appraisal Fee											
244 - Mortgage Insurance Fee											
245 - Mortgage Draw Interest											
246 - Interim Financing Costs											
247 - Selling Costs - Advertising											
APPLIANCES											
248 - Range Hood											
249 - Dishwasher											
250 - Range											
251 - Refrigerator											
252 - Washer & Dryer											
253 - Barbecue											
254 - Cooktop Stove											
255 - Microwave Oven											
256 - Trash Compactor											
257 - Freezer											
EXTRAS											
258 - Drapery											
259 - Venetians											
260 - Fence											
261 - Patio											
262 - Retaining Walls											
263 - Sod, Trees & Shrubs											
264 - 12 Volt Yard Lighting											
265 - Washed Rock, Cedar Chips											
266 - Septic System											
267 - Water Well											
268 - Water Softener											
269 - Driveway Culvert											

BUILDING COSTS	DATE		COST ESTIMATE						FINAL			
270 - Sauna and Heater												
271 - Steam Shower Heater												
272 - Hot Tub or Spa												
273 - House Address Numbers												
274 - Garbage Cans												
275 - Mail Box												
276 - Outdoor Xmas Lighting												
277 - Moving Costs												
278 - Hotel Costs												
279 - New Telephones												
280 - Furnace Air Filters												
281 - Special Humidifiers												
282 - Heat Exchanger												
283 - Water Hoses												
284 - Lawnmower												
285 - Snow Blower												
286 - Storage Shed												
287 - Power Attic Fans												
288 - Garage & House Door Weatherstripping												
289 - Light Bulb Replacements												
290 - Federal Taxes												
291 - 5% Contingency Fee												
DEDUCTIONS												
292 - Federal Tax Rebates												
293 -												
294 -												
295 -												
296 -												
ADDITIONAL COSTS												
297 - Brick Walking Paths												
298 - Flower Plantings												
299 - Gazebo												
300 - Firepit												
301 -												
302 -												
T O T A L S :												

- **Construction Schedules**

The standard start-to-completion contractor's schedule for an extensive renovation is usually 49 to 60 working days depending upon the weather. As a lay builder, and out of consideration for your lender, a minimum 65 to 80 working-day construction schedule will allow for bad weather and other construction delays. When sitting down to review the schedule, remember that the most important part will be the advance phone calls made to the suppliers and subcontractors confirming their on-site start dates. These calls are made to jog their memories, and ensure that their tendency to overbook will not lead to a delay in your work schedule. It will be your job to act as a subtle irritant, and remind them by phone on several occasions and especially several days prior to their start date on your construction project.

The framer is the key subtrade in the construction process, and his accuracy and attention to detail sets the tone for the subsequent trades. If a framer has a five-man crew with some men working with him for many years, his crew will work together as a unit with every man knowing what is to be done and what is expected from the boss. Each worker will have a designated job to do with minimum supervision and without error. This allows the boss to coordinate the demolition, layout of the existing/new structure, and framing of the walls and floors without excessive delays due to questions and on-site miscommunication between inexperienced workers. This framing crew will complete a renovation involving approximately 50 percent of a 1,200 to 1,600 square foot house in about eight to ten working days, give or take one day depending on weather or crew size on any given day. This time frame for a 600 to 1,200 square foot addition includes demolition of the existing house, installation of the floor joists, and roof preparation.

Some items will extend the construction schedule:

1) For angled walls, bay windows, bow windows, fireplace and chase, and different framing methods, add one day to the framing schedule.

2) To match several different walls, roof slopes or valleys, and peaks that require additional stick framing, add one day to the framing schedule.

3) For every 200 square feet over the basic 1,200 square foot addition, add one day to the framing

4) For each worker less than a five-man crew, add half of a working day to the framing schedule. A framing crew of less than three men will take about 15 working days.

5) If building in cold weather or before/after the building season, your schedule will have to adjust.

Construction sites left unattended when the subtrades are not on the job site or during the evening/night hours will experience material thefts and subsequent delays. To avoid replacement delays, place lumber in an area that is well lit and not easily accessible. Other materials, such as wire mesh, nails, caulking, and polyethylene vapor barrier delivered too early, should be stored in a safe place, eg., small items in your vehicle or in the subcontractor's truck for the evening. If this is not possible, hide them in the basement where they cannot be easily seen or accessed by vehicles, or chain heavy items such as wire mesh to a post or a section of the house with a key lock. Do not accept early delivery for items such as tubs, toilets, spas, sinks, and showers. If the subdivision is busy with construction crews the items will very likely be stolen. Instruct suppliers to deliver these items *only* on the day of installation.

Note: Construction insurance covers some of the potential theft or breakage of materials during construction. However, sometimes the deductible to be paid out will not cover the full cost of the item, so you will have to cover the cost out of pocket.

NOTES:

CHAPTER 12

◆ WHAT TO EXPECT FROM SUBCONTRACTORS

This chapter describes what each supplier and subtrade should be expected to provide as a service, what options can be considered, and what you as a consumer should look for when requesting estimates, purchasing materials, and clarifying responsibilities during the construction period. The best protection a purchaser has when dealing with members of the construction industry will be a detailed contract, i.e., one which stipulates what labor and material will be supplied and installed, and what the supplier or subcontractor will not be responsible for.

A smart shopper should know as much as possible about a service or product before purchasing. If you have any questions or doubts about a product, ask the salesperson for a reference address so you can see the work or product as it would look on an existing house. A purchaser should always ask for an arbitration clause, warranties, guarantees, and the retailer's return policies before signing any contract, and should insist that these items be written into the contract (see Contract, pages 65-66).

Every smart shopper must remember the buyer beware slogan. There are too many fly-by-night outfits that prey on people who have limited knowledge of the rights of the consumer, and are not familiar with the rules and regulations set by the consumers and corporate affairs organizations for the area. Always check to see if the company has a business licence, is registered with the Better Business Bureau or builders' organization, and does not have any outstanding legal action registered against them in the state/provincial courts which might affect your renovation project.

• The Surveyor

Surveyors are usually computerized for convenience and accuracy of drawings. They will provide a building pocket of your lot and existing home which will indicate the front, rear, and side yard widths, size of the lot, and the exact location of the house, outbuildings, trees, fences, and city services on the lot. They can also suggest the most suitable orientation for the proposed addition. A building pocket will greatly help your designer, and eliminate any possibility of zoning and subdivision infractions. Request the final survey to locate the proposed addition on the morning of the excavation. Having it marked and staked at that time will prevent vandals from moving the survey pegs, resulting in a resurvey, or worse yet an incorrect excavation.

Ask the surveyor for assistance to change existing grade slopes of the house plot plan, i.e., out of the ground to eliminate any window wells, or to

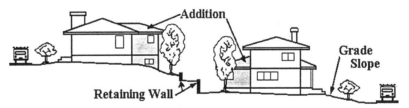

Figure 12-1. Retaining walls required for a renovation project.

assist with planning special landscaping for the future. He will position and adjust the existing grade heights to best suit your needs in relation to existing sewer heights and required lot drainage considering your neighbor's finished grade and house position.

Note: The existing grades on ad-joining properties usually determine the final grade and floor heights for the addition. If your renovation project plans to drastically vary the existing grade, the surveyor will suggest locations for retaining walls to maintain the integrity of the neighboring grades (see Figure 12-1).

All renovation projects require a new plot plan. However, if there are no basement foundation changes/extensions, eg., a bay window or even an extensive upper-story development, the drafting service can provide a revised plot plan. If no existing plot plan is available, they may have to do an on-site measurement of the house and property to provide an accurate plot plan for the building permit office.

If the addition requires a foundation, take the set of renovation blueprints to the surveyor for a detailed plot plan. Make sure you discuss the finished grades for drainage; the number of steps required at the back entrance, garage and front entrance; floor heights from finished grade; existing and new basement ceiling heights; proper driveway slope; depth and location of water and sewer lines; location and direction of the addition on the lot; and finally the driveway length. For your records request about eight copies of the finished plot plan. When the final plot plan is completed, usually in a few days, you will have all the necessary information to return to the bank to secure the mortgage or loan approval. At the same time take a set of blueprints to the city, pay the required fee, and make an application for construction.

Later in the construction, after the house addition and garage foundation and framing are completed and before the foundation has been backfilled, you will request the surveyor to return to verify that the house complies with the plot plan. When this is completed, he will provide you with a Real Property Report. Request at least eight signed copies for distribution. This report is an extra charge and is in addition to the plot plan provided. It is required by financial institutions as a legal document to verify that the house complies with all city setback and sideyard requirements and that it lies within all property boundaries. If the Real Property Report does not comply with the city setback and sideyard requirements, the financial institution will not provide you with any additional loan money or mortgage until you rectify the problem and the house complies with the zoning restrictions.

This Real Property Report is very important if you are planning to sell the house in the future. If it is overlooked and not done during the construction period, and the house for some reason does not comply with the surveyor's plot plan, you might have to pay a very large penalty to the city, or worse yet have to move or demolish the addition. A sale might be blocked because of this noncompliance; you might be living in the house for a long time whether you like it or not. The city engineering department will require a copy of this report for their records; the bank or the lawyer will require a copy for final mortgage registration on the title. This document is also used by the landscapers to confirm that the property contours and grades are complying with the city grading requirements. Failing this, the landscaper will hire and charge back to you a bobcat service to bring the grades to proper height before commencing any landscape work. At your expense the surveyor will be required to resurvey the property, and provide another Real Property Report. As you can see something that seems to be so simple like grade compliance can cause significant financial damage. Hiring a qualified and experienced excavator, foundation contractor, and bobcat service who have worked with plot plans and surveyors on a day-to-day basis will help eliminate this problem.

Note: When this is all completed, request that the surveyor return your set of blueprints so it can be used to collect other price estimates. If he requires a record of your plans have him take photocopies of the blueprints.

- **Permits and Approvals**

In many parts of North America it is a requirement to purchase a building permit from the city or county. The permit will be used to update the property taxes, and ensure that any changes to existing structures, even the minor addition of a bay window, will conform to the zoning by-laws. Any internal structural changes will also require a permit and subsequent inspections by the city engineer or development office. In some federal jurisdictions the city or county may without advance notice initiate an on-site inspection of a house to confirm the accuracy of their tax file on your home and property. They will measure the exterior dimensions of the house and property to see if it conforms to their records, and do a visual inspection of the house to make sure you have not installed, changed, or removed any mechanical or electrical devices that will affect the present by-laws or tax base. Failure to acquire or to question the need of a permit for even the simplest renovation project might result in the issuance of an order to purchase the required permit, and/or pay a penalty. If you take the precaution of asking if a permit will be required, you will find the city is not out to charge you for every project unless it affects the structural integrity of the home, requires a structural foundation, or protrudes into the home's sideyard requirements. The following are a few examples of projects that require or do not require permits in most jurisdictions.

Permits are required for:

✓ Installing electrical and mechanical devices that require an upgrade of the piping/electrical system;

✓ Any changes to the supporting structure of the basement or main floor bearing walls;

✓ Adding fences or retaining walls affecting the natural grade or view of neighboring property;

✓ Adding decks, gazebos, or sheds that require a foundation, are above certain heights from the finished grade, and will interfere with the view of neighboring property.

Permits are not required for:

✗ Replacing existing windows or doing the normal seasonal maintenance projects;

✗ Replacing the existing roof or wall materials of the house with similar materials;

✗ Adding or replacing sidewalks, patios or driveways that do not interfere with utility lines;

✗ Upgrading existing cabinets, floor finishes, wall finishes, electrical/plumbing fixtures, or replacing other items not requiring upgrading of electrical or mechanical systems.

Note: Always check with the city development/engineering department to see what the permit requirements are for your particular renovation project before starting. Many city development departments in addition to the standard building permit require that you make application for a demolition permit if existing structural walls are to be torn down in order to accept the new structure. An inspection may be required by the engineering department to see that all portions of the building are properly and safely braced prior to the bearing wall being demolished.

Regardless of whether you have chosen to supervise the renovation on your own or have selected a builder, if the bank is involved, they will require copies of the building permit in addition to all the forms and information previously discussed in Chapter 6.

If your existing subdivision has design controls, the control officer working for the developer or the city will require one nonreturnable set of blueprints (elevations, cross section, and floor plans) for review. The bank and the city each require two copies of the blueprints and plot plans, one of which is nonreturnable. Once you have received the city's approval, they will each return one set of blueprints and a plot plan with a conditional building permit.

Before you receive the approved blueprints and plot plan from the city, the planning department will tell you the plans are ready to be picked up and indicate that they have been approved, or approved with conditions. You will owe some money for the building permit, the fee usually based on an estimated construction cost. Many city planning departments require that you provide to them a grading certificate upon completion of the foundation backfill to confirm a proper grade slope away from the house structure. The issuance of the construction permit allows you to proceed with the construction on the condition that at foundation backfill you will contact the surveyor to stake out the proper finished grades and hire the bobcat service to comply with those stake markers. Once completed the surveyor will resurvey the property for proper grade and provide the grading certificates to you and the city. The city will then allow you to proceed to completion with the renovation project.

Note: Keep the approved plans returned by the city in a safe place, and do not use them to acquire any estimates. They should become part of the permanent record of the house along with mortgage documents, cancelled cheques, inspection reports, invoices, diary and any other documents pertaining to the house.

- **Foundation Excavation**

Excavation contractors use heavy equipment, such as a caterpillar, backhoe or gradeall, to dig the foundation hole. With the plot plan in hand and survey stakes located properly on the lot, they will excavate for the addition to the foundation depth predetermined by the surveyor. To achieve this the excavator uses a surveyor's transit and a grade marker to confirm the final foundation's footing depth. This depth must also be to undisturbed soil.

Note: Have the excavator protect the existing city road/lane sidewalk and curb by covering them with a burm of compacted soil. The dirt should be spread wide enough to accommodate the width of a dump truck, and thick enough to withstand the weight of the truck when fully loaded. This seemingly unimportant request will limit damage to the road/lane curb and sidewalk, and avert the city service crew repairing the damage and sending you an unexpected and expensive bill.

Prior to moving his equipment on-site the excavator should inspect for power lines or any other obstructions, such as tree limbs, shrubs, and fences, which might interfere with equipment movement. The space available for him to work will determine the size and the maneuverability of his machinery. If power lines need to be moved, ask the utility company and electrician to move the existing lines to a safe position. Tree limbs, shrubs, and fence materials will have to be removed at the owner's expense, either by doing it yourself or hiring someone with experience. Remember to speak to your neighbor about removing any common fences that sit on the property line, or any shrubs which might be destroyed by heavy equipment moving between the buildings. Have them agree in writing that they will allow any equipment or workers to cross that portion of their property adjacent to the construction project, and that you are willing to repair any damage caused. Also include in the letter a few photographs of the area in question taken at different angles prior to any construction start, and have them sign the back. This will protect you both from potential disputes during and after the construction.

It is advisable to check with neighbors and the city development department for any potential groundwater problems in the area. In northern areas such problems can be expensive and some contractors will only excavate when the frost is in the ground during the early spring, or when the groundwater has dried up in the fall. Even if the ground seems to be dry, when having to pour footings or drill for piles, it is advisable to install an interim drainage line. Once the earth has been disturbed by an excavation, or should an unusual seasonal increase in temperature occur, the groundwater around the excavation may thaw, creating a major water problem.

A client of mine with previous renovation experience was interested in expanding the back of his home for a family room. A stickler for details, before he contacted me to design the project, he asked a neighbor and the city engineering department if there was a groundwater problem. The city said that there had been some problems reported, and his neighbor related the following story about their addition experience four years previous. The excavation segment in the early spring did not encounter any water; however, during the summer and early fall they began experiencing water seepage from the perimeter of the basement floor. This effectively halted further inside development of that area. The water was pooling at a low spot so the first year he rented a water pump with a flexible hose in order to apply caulking around the perimeter of the basement. This sounded very practical until he found the water came in as fast as it was being pumped out. He could not afford to rent a pump year round, so he purchased one on sale for $237. After pumping for three years he decided to have an expert assess the problem and provide an estimate. It seems that the perimeter weeping tile had more groundwater than it could handle, and excess water was being forced up the intersection between the house foundation and the basement floor. In order to rectify the problem, the expert recommended the perimeter of the concrete basement floor be saw-cut to install a drainage pipe that would connect to a sump system. This would allow any water accumulating under the floor to drain to the pipe, circulate through the sump system, and flow out to the city curb/sewer system. He concluded the story by saying he was not planning on doing it for a while as it would cost him $4,700. He would have to cut and remove the concrete, install the pipe, place crushed rock around the pipe, install a new vapor barrier, pour new concrete with an adhesive to fill the trenched area, and finally retrowel the area for a smooth finish so a concrete sealant could be applied to the whole basement floor area. He then added remorsefully that his contractor had suggested the same pipe system be installed during construction for $350.

After hearing this, my client decided to pay the additional expense and have weeping tiles installed inside and outside the footings prior to the backfill (see Figure 12-7). I included in the drawings a general note requesting that additional crushed rock be placed around the weeping tile to provide better drainage to the sump, as well as landscapers' felt be placed over the tile and rock to block sand from entering and causing the tile system to fail. To this date he has not had any water problems.

Obtaining adequate space for heavy equipment movement and backfill storage on the site will result in damage to the existing landscape. To reduce the impact on existing trees, shrubs, and plants, determine which items can be moved with minimal damage to the root systems. Many of the large or less hardy will not survive the double move to an interim holding area until the permanent position is found. One option is to have a tree mover provide a quotation and a guarantee of their survival after the move. If he cannot provide a guarantee, contact several local tree farms to determine the replacement cost of plantings that are younger and more hardy. You may be surprised that this cost is less than the tree mover's, and tree farms will usually provide a one-year replacement guarantee for all new plantings.

Excavating for a full basement or crawl space might sound very simple, but it requires a man who operates a machine that removes about four cubic yards of dirt at a time being able to carefully maneuver the bucket to within several inches of the existing foundation wall, and excavate a new and level hole to within 1/2 to 1 inch of its required depth without damaging the existing footings. The unwanted earth from the hole is directly loaded into waiting trucks which transport the dirt to a dump site. The dump site should be located as close as possible to keep the truck transportation costs down. It is a good idea to ask neighbors, the excavator, or local builders if they know of any current sites looking for clean fill. The excavator must also determine how much earth should remain around the perimeter of the excavation providing sufficient material to backfill around the foundation for proper grade slope. It is also essential to leave at least one opening at the excavation for foundation and concrete trucks to gain access to the perimeter of the hole. That does take some experience and skill.

Note: Every full basement addition will require a connecting access from the old basement to the new. When the excavator is digging the basement, have him over-excavate an area at the planned access doorway the length, width, and depth required (see Concrete Cutting on page 143 for a detailed explanation).

After the foundation waterproofing and weeping tile have been completely installed, inspected, and approved, the excavator will return to backfill the hole using a bobcat or small caterpillar. He must backfill on an angle to the house so the weeping tile will not be crushed. Also, if there are any large clay lumps they will be pushed in on an angle to the foundation rather than directly at the foundation. If not backfilled correctly, the clay could cause the still-fresh and curing concrete foundation to crack or cave in. The house is slowly and carefully backfilled first at each corner, and then, still on the angle, backfilled to the middle of the foundation walls.

The foundation must be totally backfilled with a proper slope to drain away from the house. With the settling of the new perimeter earth over the next 10 to 12 months, there will be some uneven soil settling. If possible ask the excavator to leave sufficient hard-packed clay or dirt for you or another operator to fill and tamp the areas that require additional dirt prior to final landscaping. This leftover fill will guarantee proper drainage of the lot as well as the required sloping grade away from the house foundation for effective water runoff.

Some excavation contractors offer the service of simultaneous excavation to replace or install sewer and water lines. If required for the renovation, ask each excavator as it will eliminate the need to search for an extra subcontractor's estimate. Make sure the subcontractor knows where the new garage and sidewalk supporting piles will be located so that he can keep the water and sewer lines away from these areas and prevent the lines being crushed or hit by the pile auger.

- **Engineering**

The financial institution or city inspection department may require soil tests before the footings can be formed. Footing sizes are usually determined by the designer as per the requirements of the local building codes. However, the city inspector will require an engineer's report should the soil on the property contain too much water which will affect the foundation structure, and be too unstable for the footing size specified on the blueprints. In these cases the engineer will have to be on the construction site near the end of the excavation to collect soil samples. If this has happened previously with other renovation projects in the area, the engineer will already know the subdivision's soil conditions, and be able to determine the appropriate size of footing for that specific soil type. Be prepared in advance by asking the city inspector, neighbors, or the developer/builder who built the existing house. The city/bank inspectors will usually accept the engineer's on-site verbal footing size so that construction may proceed but will require a written soil test and report for their files.

Many people live in areas where the sand/aggregates for the foundation concrete are not readily available, or the concrete must be trucked over long distances at premium rates; the builder must then resort to the construction of a preserved wood foundation to maintain a cost-effective renovation project (see Chapter 15, page 217). In order for the treated wood foundation to meet most municipalities' building codes, the foundation must be designed and/or approved by a structural engineer. To withstand the horizontal ground loads and vertical, structural-bearing weight that will be placed on the wood foundation, certain engineering requirements must be incorporated into the design. The engineer will provide sufficient detail in the drawing for the framer, and confirm that these details are followed; the local building inspector will require the engineer to inspect the foundation during specific stages of construction. This will assure the inspector and the client that the foundation will have sufficient strength and ability to stabilize against the shifting ground pressures for the normal life span of an average house.

• Foundation Contractor

Foundation contractors, or cribbers, like to be present prior to completion of the excavation in order to double-check the foundation footing-depth. If the footing depth is too deep, the excavator must refill the hole to the proper level with compacted clay material, and tamp the clay to an undisturbed soil condition. This fortunately does not happen too often. When it does, the excavator bears the expense unless the surveyor was in error, or someone moved the surveyor's stakes. There is no way to guarantee that the pegs will not get moved; however, scheduling the survey crew for the early morning of the excavation will reduce or eliminate added costs and delays for a restake. The surveyor will provide the same stake positions with different depth markings if the foundation was designed as a crawl space.

Once the excavation is completed, using the plot plan, peg markings, a surveyor's transit, and tape measure, the cribber determines the height and location of the foundation footings, pilings, walls, reinforcing, and structural pads for the addition. It is also the cribber's job to scrape and hose down the remaining earth attached to the wall where the new foundation will connect to the existing. Once completed he will drill three side-by-side horizontal holes approximately five inches deep at the top, middle, and bottom of the existing foundation to accept steel reinforcing dowels. In order for the dowels to be secured tightly, the hole diameter will be slightly smaller than that of the dowels, and a concrete adhesive placed in the holes. The dowels will have to be hammered into the holes, and should protrude out from the wall a minimum of 18 inches to ensure a secure fit where the old and new walls meet. If the existing wall has a rough surface, to ensure a waterproof bond apply a concrete adhesive and a waterproof mastic seal about eight inches wide for the full height of the new foundation wall where the two will connect (see Figure 12-12).

If the job is small most cribbers supply their own (2" x 4" or 2" x 6") footing forms because the forms can be reused several times; if the addition is substantial or he is a small contractor, expect to supply the forms. It is the responsibility of the owner to supply a box of coated nails and pegs for nailing the forms together. Sometimes bracing materials are required to hold some sections of the forms together. If the cribber has to cut his forms for this, ask during the price negotiations if you will be required to replace them. Also, when you review his estimate, ask if he requires a concrete pump. If so, ask him or the concrete supplier what size you need, get several estimates, then see if the cribber or supplier can negotiate a better price. Again, make sure you know in advance who is supplying what before selecting the contractor as prices will vary drastically depending on how much material you supply.

This type of misunderstanding happened to one of my clients. At the initial on-site meeting the subcontractor forgot his estimate sheet at home. The owner and subcontractor got along very well during this discussion, with the subcontractor being very agreeable about the owner's scheduling, and very helpful in suggesting names of concrete suppliers and excavators. After several hours and several coffees, the owner, convinced that this subcontractor was the best person to do the job, decided to forgo searching for more estimates. In lieu of an estimate sheet, the owner was given a price on the back of a business card with a verbal guarantee of satisfaction. The owner was indeed satisfied with the work as his schedule was met, but after the foundation was in, he received a final invoice that was more than twice the estimate. Asking how this was possible, the subcontractor replied, "I was sure that you understood my price quote was for labor only. Surely you didn't expect me to supply all the footings and foundation forms for free." The subcontractor also suggested that if he was not paid immediately he would place a builder's lien on the property the next day. The owner reluctantly paid the bill, but stopped the construction process to contact the other suppliers and subcontractors and verify in writing on a proper estimate sheet what was to be included and excluded. Even though the rest of the construction went well, this experience made the whole renovation project an effort, and less enjoyable than originally anticipated.

For your peace of mind get at least three price quotations from each supplier or subcontractor, and make sure all the pertinent details are written down.

The footings, as the lowest part of the house structure, evenly distribute the full weight of the upper dwelling over a large enough area of soil to minimize settling and movement. Because they support so much weight it is very important that the concrete footings' strength be a minimum of 3000 pounds per square inch (psi) and that the footings rest on undisturbed soil. This strength of concrete, unfortunately, is the most expensive, and many contractors pour the footings with 2000 or 2500 psi concrete, adding horizontal reinforcing rods to compensate for the reduced concrete strength. The number of horizontal reinforcing rods to be set into the footings will depend upon the soil conditions and the required footings' width suggested by the engineer. Typically, two or three reinforcing rods are required for a footings' width of 16 inches, and an additional rod for every 6-inch width of footing.The horizontally laid steel rods should be 3/8 to 1/2 inch thick, and elevated from the ground at midpoint of the footings or four inches from undisturbed soil (see Figure 12-2). The bars should also be covered by a minimum of three inches of concrete at all points with 12-inch overlaps wherever the bars meet.

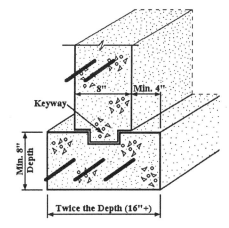

Figure 12-2. Footing size with keyway and reinforcing rods.

The day the footings are poured, ensure the cribber inserts a proper keyway into the footings. This keyway will eliminate any side movement of the foundation during and after backfill (see Figure 12-2). After the footings forms are removed, the cribber will install the vertical foundation forms which are held together with metal snap ties which he supplies. The owner/builder will supply the horizontal and vertical reinforcing rods, metal or wood window bucks (see Figure 12-15) and perimeter 2" x 4" nailers to be placed in the foundation forms prior to pouring. Prefabricated wood basement-window bucks can be supplied by the window manufacturer, but they have a reputation for poor construction. Usually put together with staples they occasionally fail when the concrete is poured. A better plan is to purchase the material from the lumberyard, and have the cribber construct the bucks on-site. He will charge you about the same price as the window manufacturer, but they will be made to his specifications, and he is ultimately responsible if they fail during the foundation pour. Another possibility is to have the window supplier quote on steel-framed basement windows, but this frame type is not often used due to its poor insulating properties.

To pour the concrete for the footings on small jobs, the cribber uses wheelbarrows, shovels and wooden chutes; for larger footing pours, a concrete pump is used especially where vehicle access is limited, or the chute of the concrete truck is too short. The length of the pump's boom is determined by the distance required to pour the concrete into the furthest part of the foundation. Concrete pumps have a very expensive hourly charge, therefore ask the cribber to order the pump so that he can schedule its arrival with the concrete supplier.

Basement walls can be poured without the floor joists; therefore, it is good practice to brace walls over 30 feet in length to eliminate movement. Many cribbers include the framing and placing of the structural basement beams, floor joists, structural walls, structural wood, and steel posts in their service. This helps to support the foundation, and eliminates movement when pouring the concrete. Most cribbers are not to be considered framers, but with more years of experience they become better at framing floor joists. The crew is only as good as the owner/supervisor; therefore if you find that he has been on his own less than three years, ask him to split the estimate into one price for the foundation with structural beams included, and a second with floor joists included. This way you have the option of having the cribber or framer placing your floor joists with full knowledge of costs involved. Regardless of who sets the joists, you will have to supply all the lumber, nails, sealants, etc. The cribber is responsible for making sure the foundation and grade beam are

square and level to accept the floor joists and wall studs. The leveling is usually done with the foundation forms in place just prior to pouring, and immediately after pouring the walls to confirm accuracy.

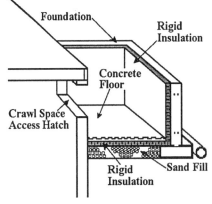

Figure 12-3. Crawl space requirements before enclosing.

When the concrete foundation and grade beam walls are being poured, in order for the new foundation wall to properly attach itself to the existing wall, a worker must vibrate the concrete. This will eliminate the chance of air pockets or 'coning' in the foundation around the reinforcing rods and window bucks. Air pockets reduce the strength of the concrete's structural capability, and if this happens the gaps must be patched and repaired by the cribber using a special hand-mix concrete and adhesive cement.

When the renovation project has a crawl space with a foundation and footings or grade beam and piles, it is essential that before it is enclosed by the floor joists and subfloor the *cribber* installs sand, wall and footing insulation, and a layer of rough concrete. You are responsible for ordering a load of sand that will allow for a six-inch thickness, or is sufficient to bring the sand flush with the top of the footings (see Figure 12-3).

After the sand has been evenly spread and tamped, the walls and floors are insulated *by the cribber* with 1-1/2 to 2 inch boards of rigid insulation (see Figure 12-3). If the finish of the foundation wall will not secure the insulation firmly in place, it will be glued to the walls using subfloor glue. Many rigid insulation products have a smooth finish which is designed to act as a vapor barrier, but if the insulation you choose does not have this property, the *cribber* will be required to apply an inner layer of 6 mil polyethylene to the floor and walls. The final step is a 1-1/2 to 2 inch rough layer of concrete that is poured by the *cribber* over the insulation or poly on the floor. If rodent or bug infestation is a concern it would be a good idea to spend the extra. Because these floor areas are so small you may be required to pay a partial load charge when ordering the concrete. Ask the concrete supplier to waive this charge, as they usually prefer to maintain customer satisfaction and positive

reputations. After the crawl space is enclosed by the joists and subfloor, access will be limited to a hatch/door (approx. 36" wide and 20" high) cut out of the existing foundation (see pages 143-44, Concrete Cutting; also see Figure 12-3).

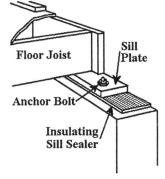

Figure 12-4. Joists sitting on wood sill plate.

Note: When constructing crawl spaces for home additions the scheduling of materials and supplies will differ. The cribber is used to doing these additional labor-intensive steps; however, in order to avoid unexpected costs make sure that they are included in the price estimate.

If the floor joists are not to be set into the concrete foundation, the cribber will be required to insert anchor bolts into the top of the concrete wall every four feet on center (see Figure 12-4). The bolts should be partially embedded into the wall and protrude out two inches, sufficient to secure the perimeter mastic or foam insulating seal under the wooden sill/sole plates. These plates are the wooden planks which are used to structurally tie the perimeter wooden rim/header joists and floor joists to the foundation wall (see Figure 12-4).

Schedule the cribber to return after the backfilling has been completed. At this time he will stake the areas stipulated on the drawings to be augured for the garage floor, garage grade beam, sidewalk and deck piles. Several holes will also be drilled in the new and/or old house foundation to accept reinforcing rods where the garage or any other structural grade beam will connect with the house foundation. Once the pile holes have been augured, the cribber will set up the forms for the grade beam, and place the required reinforcing rods in the piles, grade beam, and predrilled foundation holes. The concrete delivery should be scheduled directly after the forms have been installed and leveled, and the reinforcing completed. This way all the piles and grade beam can be poured at the same time (see Figure 12-5).

Note: The local building code may require an insulated Styrofoam void form under the grade beam between the concrete piles to eliminate frost penetration from the earth into the grade beam. The grade beam is poured after the void forms are placed in the wood forms (see Figure 12-5).

The location of the garage piles are carefully specified by the designer. Piles are positioned in areas underneath the floor where the automobile's weight can be transferred onto the supporting piles and grade beam rather than the garage floor to reduce the inevitable cracking caused by vehicles.

Note: Have the cribber do a total quantity estimate for

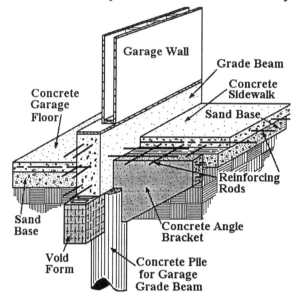

Figure 12-5. Grade beam, piles, and void form locations.

the concrete and separate the estimates into eight categories: footings, foundation, grade beam, piles, garage pad, basement floor, driveway and sidewalk. Front entrance stairs can be included in the sidewalk quantity. This way you can compare the cribber's and supplier's quantities. If they are way off, someone is wrong, but it can then be corrected and the price adjusted before building start. This quantity comparison will also confirm the square footage or lineal footage charged by the cribber for the foundation, piles, and grade beam is correct.

- **Lumber and Materials**

Lumber suppliers tend to treat the larger purchasers of complete house packages as their most important accounts, and customer satisfaction for those clients is higher on their value scale than someone who is purchasing materials for a small renovation project. If your renovation project is for the addition of a bay window, deck, or other small project, expect to be treated like any other retail client. However if you are planning an extensive addition and/or interior renovation, inform them up front that you are interested in purchasing the complete lumber and finishing package, and you expect to receive contractors' pricing. After the second lumber estimate, you will realize they are all in tight competition with other lumber suppliers, and require the business to move existing stock so they can order new. In order to offer the best prices they must order the lumber and hardware in bulk, and this requires customers ordering complete house or large addition packages to achieve effective material turnover.

Note, too, that many lumberyards charge for estimates. Every estimate from each lumber supplier will vary (sometimes drastically) both in lumber quantity and price; some estimates have more wall or roof material, and others more joists or plywood. For all sizes of renovations/additions an accurate estimate is the best estimate, i.e., where every stick and sheet is counted, and a 5 percent waste factor added on. This, however, is usually not calculated into the estimate. Estimates are actually best *guesstimates*. If they do a proper estimate they would lose customers: first, because the estimates would be so exact that the total cost of the package would be higher than their 'competitors', and second, the client could take the estimate to a competitor, and without lifting a finger the competitor would guarantee the same price. The first business then has only a 50-50 chance of getting the contract, but has invested 100 percent of the time and effort. Therefore, the lumberyards usually estimate low so that the price is low, and they have a better chance of getting the contract. Detailed estimates for a *complete material package* will require the lumberyard to provide you with a guarantee, and this is frowned upon especially when the potential customer is still shopping for other prices. When the final supplier selection has been made, many yards will provide an estimate for a complete material package at no additional cost upon request.

Many lumber suppliers are not used to providing accurate estimates for areas of the house that will require demolishing, or building up existing 2" x 4" walls to match the new 2" x 6" construction standard. Old construction methods had all walls built of 2" x 4" materials and layered with built-up plaster sometimes an inch thick. This difference will cause a problem for some estimators when calculating how much of the existing wall will be demolished, and then estimating how much exterior or interior strapping will be necessary

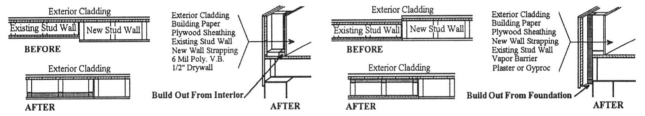

Figure 12-6. **Options for interior/exterior walls being built up to match new wall thickness.**

to build up the old wall to the level of the new (see Figure 12-6). To assist them, sit down with the framer and mark on two blueprints in different colors of pencil or felt-tip pens the walls that will be completely demolished, and those that will have the plaster removed and only require strapping. One of these marked drawings will be kept for your file. The other will enable the lumber estimator to accurately calculate a material list which will include the rebuilding of the demolished walls of the house.

The lumber and finishing packages in total are the most expensive items of the construction project, so shop smart. With blueprints in hand, go to the selected lumberyards and ask for the best *contractor's price* possible for lumber, finishing materials and finishing hardware. Then ask for their monthly price list. These price lists are calculated on a price per thousand board measure or per item. When the time comes, regardless of the lumberyard chosen, that is how you will be invoiced. Go to each lumber supplier and ask for the same price list. Review all the price lists, and compare the price per item or per thousand board measure for each individual material type, i.e., 2" x 4" and 6" studs, 2" x 10" and 12" floor joists, 4' x 8' by 1/2" and 3/8" sheets of plywood, etc., making sure you are comparing the same grades of materials, i.e., fir, spruce or pine.

Establish who has the lower all-around prices for most of the lumber and finishing materials, and especially the expensive items. This is most likely the company you want to buy from. Go back, and indicate you will be purchasing the full material package from them based on their price list, and you would like to open an account. Ask for a material estimate (it will most likely be free now that you are purchasing from them), and the length of time the price will be honored. After reviewing the detailed estimate and comparing it to the other suppliers' price lists, ask if they will give you a better price on the more expensive items (no harm in asking), and honor that price at the time you are building. Have all that written on the estimate.

Note: If a contractor is doing the renovation, make sure the contract reads that he is to provide you with copies of all estimates, and you will review them for cost approval prior to placing the order. This way you can compare his material price and those price lists you received by other suppliers and make an informed choice about the supplier and your budget.

Also when selecting lumber suppliers, check to make sure they carry the full line of construction materials needed. This will eliminate having to run around to purchase unstocked items at other stores which will waste your time, and usually incurs direct cash payments if you do not have an account with the other supplier. Also, lumberyards usually have a delivery fee per load, so try to keep the delivery trips down to those listed on page 133 under price summary.

Material estimates:

Over the past few years, and probably for the next few, the construction industry has been very competitive to attract the builder/contractor. Profit margins need to be justified to the smart shopper to a point where accurate price estimating will be the determining factor of who does or does not survive. Much of the success of the surviving contractors is due to providing the more educated home owner with a fair price. Doing this means limiting costly waste and depending more upon the estimator to provide a fair and accurate estimate and pricing.

An organized estimator will provide a detailed and complete material list which has been well thought out and is realistic. The estimator who has substantial residential construction knowledge will reduce the chance of error, and provide the purchaser with an accurate accounting of the actual cost of the material package.

The detail of the estimate provided will depend upon the accuracy of the working drawings, the thoroughness of the estimate requested, and an on-site visit. The purpose of the on-site visit is to get a feel for the extent of the renovation project. The final cost of the estimate can be affected by such things as matching existing materials or finishes, and how much of the existing material will have to be replaced once the demolition work has been completed.

The layperson does not need to be able to estimate the amount of material that will be required in the home renovation/construction project, but it is important to know what materials the supplier will be required to provide, what those materials will be used for, and when they will be required during the construction sequence. This information will protect the selfcontractor against duplication of orders or over-ordering of materials by the subtrade and/or home owner during the project.

Many of the subcontractors will require the owner to provide the materials for them to complete their work. Supplying the correct amount of materials to the subtrades is the responsibility of the chosen building supply company. Too much material will result in additional expense; too little will cause costly construction delays.

Many building supply companies will have a standard estimate form to be completed by the estimator. To depend entirely on the single estimate provided by a material suppler might not be to your advantage. There is always a chance of human error. Quantities may differ greatly due to varying building practices, the experience of the estimator and the construction details provided by the designer. Review the other suppliers' estimates and cross reference each with the best quotation for similar material content. Remember the building supply company is not interested in providing a detailed **material list** that you might give to their competitors, but rather one with sufficient information and a bottom-line price to close the deal on your construction project. Quantities are not always exact which may cause costly purchases during the construction project enough to send your budget out of control; therefore, the cross-checking will point out major gaps and inaccuracies.

Using the following material list for all the building supply companies, and cross-referencing the package prices with each estimate will be invaluable when calculating your construction budget for the selected financial institution.

MATERIAL LIST

Name: _____ Date: _____

Mailing Address: _____ Phone (bus.) _____

Project Address: _____ Phone (res.) _____

City/Town: _____ State/Province: _____ Zip/Postal Code: _____

Estimator's Name: _____ F.O.B. Point: _____

Delivery Instructions: _____
_____

Payment Schedule:

Supplier's Name: _____ 1) $_____ on completion of _____

Address: _____ 2) $_____ on completion of _____

Zip/Postal Code: _____ State/Province: _____ 3) $_____ on completion of _____

Phone Number: _____ 4) $_____ on completion of _____

Fax Number: _____ 5) $_____ on completion of _____

Mobile Number: _____ **Final Payment** $_____ on completion of _____

Price Summary:

1) Sub-grade & Main Floor Joist Package	$_____
2) Main Floor Framing Package	$_____
3) Garage Framing Package	$_____
4) Second Floor Joist Package	$_____
4) Second Floor Framing Package	$_____
5) Roof Framing Package	$_____
6) Exterior Finishing Package	$_____
7) Interior Finishing Package	$_____
8) Delivery Charges	$_____
A) Material Total	$_____

Optional Material Packages:

9) Manufactured Truss Package	$_____
10) Manufactured Joist Package (silent floor)	$_____
11) Manufactured Beam Package	$_____
12) Manufactured Window Package	$_____
B) Material Total	$_____
Total Materials (A+B)	$_____

Material List Price is firm for _____ days or until _____ ____, 19___.

Signature: _____

• **Equipment Rentals**

During many stages of the renovation project you will be required to rent equipment that normally would not be handy in your workshop or tool box. Pre-application for an account for equipment rentals such as pumps, vacuums, tarpaulins, etc., will assist in getting the equipment to the site quickly when needed. Choose a rental company that has a large selection of items and several store locations within easy access. Many rental companies purchase doubles of any one item; therefore, even if the store has already rented their stock to someone else, they will phone around to have one delivered to your job site usually within the hour. Many rental companies also have special pickup and delivery services for customers with a pre-approved account, which will allow a customer to phone for delivery and pickup. This will save many hours of driving around to several rental stores only to find that they do not stock the item required, or have already rented it out. Without an established account you will either have to pay a cash deposit, or give them a presigned credit card slip as collateral for their protection. They may also require a full day's rental fee for the item when it might be cheaper to rent for only a few hours. Again, remember that phoning around to several different rental stores will allow you to pre-apply for an account at one of the larger and better stocked stores which will generally mean lower rental costs.

Sometimes when a subtrade forgets to bring some equipment, or his equipment breaks down due to parts wearing out or poor maintenance, the account with the rental store will save hundreds of dollars in waiting time, and allow you to complete that day's work. Once while supervising a house renovation for a client I was on-site inspecting the concrete finishing for the garage floor reinforcing and concrete. Everything had been completed on schedule in a good workmanlike manner, and the workers, having completed the leveling and hand troweling, were ready to power trowel. Two men were removing the power trowel from the back of their rusted half-ton truck when one of the workers put his foot through the metal floor of the truck. The weight of the trowel was more than one worker could handle, and it slipped off the truck, falling sideways onto the foot of the other worker and breaking it in several places. My client was very quick witted and always enjoyed joking around, so when he heard the noise and commotion he came running around the corner of the garage and yelled out, "I hope you guys have paid up your Workers' Compensation because I didn't." Once he found out what had happened, he realized the situation was not all that funny. It was however a valid question to ask. The concrete finisher did have his insurance paid up; however, the power trowel had broken into several pieces and would require a major repair job. After the injured worker was taken to the hospital, the concrete finisher was ready to call it a day as he did not have another power trowel, nor did he have an account with a rental company. I looked at the owner who had listened to all my suggestions when we were working on the design, and felt sure he would have an account with one of the local rental companies. He looked at me very sheepishly, and with half a smile said, "Guess what I forgot to do?" I smiled and said that we could phone one of my contacts and have them deliver a power trowel, but he would have to pay C.O.D. I called the rental company and arranged for it to be delivered to the job site within half an hour with pickup when we were finished. My client went to the bank and returned before the power trowel arrived. Although he had to pay the daily rental fee, the garage floor was completed, and the trowel picked up at the end of the day. The next day he called to thank me, and report that he had now opened an account with a rental company.

Examples of some of the equipment that might be required during the renovation project:

      Pumps and hoses to remove groundwater

      Commercial vacuum for dirt and drywall dust from ducts and floors

      Ladders, shovels, wheelbarrow, rakes, sludge hammer, crow bar, etc.

Tarpaulins to protect the house against bad weather conditions

Ground tampers and vibrators

Post hole augers for decks and landscaping

Propane heaters for drywall and concrete curing

Other equipment such as large commercial propane tanks, scaffolds, trucks, and heavy-duty items might not be available through small rental companies. Request a list of the products in stock before opening an account.

• Weeping Tile Installation

Weeping tile suppliers have probably the dirtiest job during the construction period. It is their responsibility to make sure that any existing groundwater is directed away from the foundation through perforated six-inch diameter plastic pipes leading to either the sanitary sewer line or a sump pit. What they connect to depends on the local building code, but with either connection the basement walls and floor should remain dry. The standard building code requires that weeping tile be placed around the outside perimeter of the footings with washed gravel around the tile to prevent sand and silt from blocking the water flow inside the tile and the sump drain lines (see Figure 12-7).

Check with the city engineering department for building

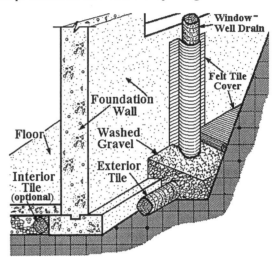

Figure 12-7. Felt cover and perimeter weeping tile around exterior and interior of footing.

code changes such as sump pit installations. When collecting estimates for the weeping tile, have them include the sump pit, window-well drains and replacement of old/ineffective tile in the quote if indicated. Discuss the location of the sump pit with the designer, so that one of the future rooms in the developed basement will not have a sump access hole in the floor. Suggested locations are in a basement laundry area, furnace room, or underneath the stairs as these areas are generally used as storage and will not have carpeting. The weeping tile

suppliers do not connect the footing pipe to the sump pit; that is the job of the plumber when he installs the basement drains and water lines. The sump pit can also be installed by the plumber; however, they prefer someone else do it.

Note: If you are planning to put the sump in or near the center of the basement, it is a good idea to have the plumber install a check valve in the sump's drain line. This will stop the backflow of water and the gurgling noise that goes along with it when the water in the line flushes back into the collection pit. This will be especially appreciated at 3:00 in the morning when you want to sleep and not listen to running water.

Window-well drains remove the collection of water around the foundation wall at the frost level, thus

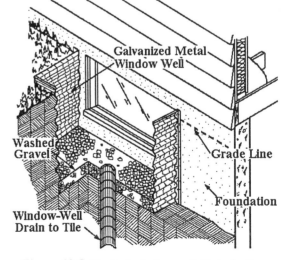

Figure 12-8. Vertical window-well tile to footing.

eliminating the potential problem of ice and frost shifting and cracking the foundation walls (see Figure 12-8). Prior to backfill these vertical pipes are placed at the bottom of the window well, attached to the foundation, and connected to the weeping tiles around the footing. Washed rock is placed over the drain tile at the bottom of the well. All basement windows within three inches of grade or below grade level should have window wells and/or drains to facilitate groundwater removal.

Since the tile installer supplies products that eliminate water problems he will also apply the waterproofing (dampproofing) to the foundation walls. This waterproofing is a brushed and sprayed coat of tar to the face of the foundation, i.e., brushed where the cribber's snap ties remain to eliminate seepage, and sprayed to approximately one foot above the level any backfilled earth will be in contact with the foundation wall. Some building codes and mortgage companies require that this waterproofing also be applied to the interior walls of the foundation. Check with the city inspector to see if this is required in your area before collecting estimates.

Many homes built before the late 1950s were not required to install perimeter weeping-tile systems, and many tile systems that were installed are no longer working. After many years of the earth and house shifting, and the rain collecting around the perimeter of the building, small particles of sand find their way into the tiles and sump system, causing them to fail. If the existing weeping tiles have not been performing properly, and you suspect they might be filled with sediment or sand, have the excavator expose some or all of the exterior footings to replace the tiles. This same problem may occur sometime in the future with the new tile system if some precautions are not taken. An innovative idea that has been used to reduce the collection of silt in and around the tile is placing landscapers' felt over the tile and rocks after the application of the tar dampproofing on the foundation wall and before backfilling. The backfill material can be very sandy or silty so it is also a good idea to wrap the material around the vertical window-well drain pipes, or adhere the material to the sticky surface of the foundation tar (see Figure 12-7). Ensure the material will not slip during backfilling as this will defeat its purpose. The material available in widths of one yard and lengths of 25 to 100 feet will be able to fully cover the tile bed. It will extend the life of the tile system by at least seven years and virtually eliminate the problem of silt entering the sump drain lines which will prevent the clogging and burnout of the sump motor. This initial, inexpensive procedure will reduce or eliminate spending several hundreds of dollars years later. This is usually not included in the price of the weeping tiles, and should therefore be considered an extra.

Check with the city building inspector for recent groundwater problems as additional precautions should be taken if the groundwater is high. As mentioned previously you will know this problem exists when the cribber tries to pour the footings and the excavation has pools of water, or the floor has become very muddy and too sloppy to work in. This major problem requires additional weeping tile placed around the inside perimeter of the footings, and depending on your local building code, a line directed toward the sewer or sump. Your plumber or subcontractor installing the line should know if the code will allow direct flow of the groundwater into the sewer system. It is an extra expense, but it will eliminate future water damage and very costly repairs especially if you are considering under-slab or in-slab heating.

- **Concrete Selection**

Concrete suppliers differ very slightly in their selections of concrete available, and are all able to supply the different concrete strengths and custom aggregates required. The difference would be in the aggregate size and color which is dependent on the gravel yard supplying their raw materials.

Prices will vary within two to eight dollars per cubic metre or yard of concrete which does not make a significant difference for small renovations. The important difference will be the delivery times available as suppliers prefer to service their larger contractor clients first unless booked a day in advance. Some suppliers will not deliver before 7:00 a.m., after 5:00 p.m., or on Saturdays. When collecting estimates, find out which supplier will provide the best service and the best price. Have the supplier quote the price and strengths available for each different aggregate type as discussed with the cribber and concrete finisher. Also provide the supplier with the required set of blueprints for a quantity estimate, and have him separate the estimates into the eight categories, i.e., footings and pads, foundation, grade beam, piles, garage pad, basement floor, driveway, and sidewalk (include the stair material in the sidewalk quantity).

There are five common types of concrete. Starting from Portland type 10 they increase by tens to the highest sulphur-resistant mix, type 50. Each mix is used during different seasons and for different weather conditions with heat, calcium, and air added selectively to improve strength and setting times. Calcium and heat are added to accelerate the setting time of concrete during cold weather. The amounts to be added are determined by the concrete supplier, who considers use and current temperature. During weather around the freezing point, scaffolds with tarpaulins and rpropane-powered heaters will be required to cover and heat the concrete during the pouring and curing process. These extra costs will have to be considered, and discussed with the cribber when pouring in cold weather. It is not necessary to match the type and strength of new concrete with existing. The more important factors are leveling to provide proper drainage and sufficient reinforcing dowels to secure the joining.

Air is added to concrete where foundations and floors will be in contact with water. It creates a medium that acts as a sponge, allowing the mix to contain more water, and then allowing it to evaporate without destroying the structural integrity of the concrete. A garage floor, even though protected by a polyethylene vapor barrier, reinforcing rods, and a roof, still requires air as it is exposed to water dripping from cars. The surface of the garage floor has a slight back-to-front slope, and has to be power troweled to a smooth and shiny surface which allows for proper water drainage without pooling. Water collection on a garage floor will cause frost damage during the cold months of winter.

Basement floors do not require air as the vapor barrier will not allow water to penetrate. The basement is also heated, and therefore any water that might come in contact with it will quickly evaporate. The surface requires a slight slope to a basement drain, and has to be power troweled for proper water drainage in the event of a water pipe bursting.

For different areas of the renovation, you might require three concrete strengths, and their selection will depend upon the amount of reinforcing, present weather conditions, and structural requirements of the area to be poured. In general, 2000 psi (15.0 mpa), 2500 psi (17.5 mpa), or 3000 psi (20.7 mpa) are used for the following areas of house construction:

Garage pad	3000 psi (20.7 mpa)
Footings, pads, piles, driveway and walkway	2500 psi (17.5 mpa)
Foundation, grade beam and basement floor	2000 psi (15.0 mpa)

If you have already chosen a cribber, ask for the name of his preferred supplier. Ask if he has an account with them, or has any connections before you open an account. If you have already opened an account, but the cribber likes to deal with a different supplier, phone that company to see if they will honor or better your supplier's price. If they can, open an account with them because they are all so similar it does not matter who you purchase from as long as the price is right, and your cribber is satisfied with the one chosen.

Because the concrete pour depends so much on weather conditions, have the cribber organize the orders and deliveries to the site. This could eliminate costly delays or truck sitting charges. To put the importance of scheduling into perspective, here is a story about a neighbor who decided to replace his old heaved, crumbling asphalt driveway with a permanent concrete one. I did not feel I knew him well enough to offer advice. When he started talking about contracting the project himself, I told him that I often went to the library if I was about to handle a new project. He said that as he had organized the subtrades when placing the asphalt driveway, he thought his expertise was sufficient for scheduling the labor and materials for this small project. As an added precaution he decided to take my suggestion and read up on forming, reinforcing and placing concrete.

A few mornings later I noticed a bobcat and a gravel truck sitting in front of his house. When I returned that evening all the asphalt had been removed, sand had been delivered ready for spreading, reinforcing rods and wire mesh was sitting on his front sidewalk, and he was forming the driveway in preparation for the concrete pour. I was very impressed. I wandered over that evening to check on further progress, and found he and his brother already laying out the reinforcing and wire mesh. He said that it had gone so well he had ordered six yards of concrete for Saturday at 8:00 a.m., and scheduled his concrete finisher for 8:30 a.m. When I said I would wander over about mid morning to see how things were progressing, he said with a smile, "By the time you get here the finisher should be cleaning off his tools ready to go home." The Saturday weather reports predicted about an 80° temperature and sunny all day. A perfect day for pouring concrete. Around 10:00 a.m. I had completed my yard work and decided to check on my neighbor. There were no trucks of any type at the front of his house so I figured he was already finished, but as I got closer I could see only a 10' x 10' very rough slab of concrete. He and his brother were sitting at the front landing and their facial expressions told me that something was not right.

They told me the truck had arrived 15 minutes early, and at 5 minutes to 8:00 the concrete finisher called to say he was just completing another job and would be about 30 minutes late. The concrete supplier was not pleased, but admitted it was partly his fault because he was early. He felt it would not be a problem for the next 30 or 40 minutes and he would reduce the rotation of the concrete, and add water to the mix to keep it from setting, but they would have to pay for the additional waiting time. After an hour had gone by, the neighbor called the finisher's house to see if his wife could reach him, but she did not know the job site and could not get hold of him. The concrete supplier was getting very anxious when an hour and 20 minutes had passed. If he put more water into the mix, the concrete would lose its strength, and if the concrete was not removed soon, it would start to set in the drum. Just as this discussion was finishing, the concrete finisher showed up. They started to pour, but as the first yard of concrete came down the shute, it was obvious that some of the concrete had already set. The supplier was very angry, emptied the shute, filled the rotating drum with water, and said he hoped that he could get to his company's dump site before the concrete had set too much.

My neighbor said by that time he and the concrete finisher were just staring at each other, and he was ready to kill him until the finisher said, "I told you that I should handle the ordering, but you said no, so this is all your fault, not mine." The neighbor could not say a thing because the finisher was right. The finisher started to pack up his tools, but before leaving said that he would not charge for his time. If the neighbor still wanted him to do the job he would get his concrete chipper to remove the existing slab, order the concrete, and get the job done in the next few days, but he would bill for all the extra work. One morning the following week, I saw the concrete finisher chipping away at the rough slab on the driveway, and when I returned that evening they were just about completed and ready to go home.

Several months went by and I heard from another neighbor that the concrete supplier sent a bill for several hundred dollars for waiting charges, dumping charges, and a portion of the cost of the concrete. After that experience, it has always been my practice that the concrete finisher and cribber include scheduling the concrete delivery in their contract.

Most cribbers and finishers like to pour concrete early in the morning, the earlier the better. If the concrete was ordered for 7:30 a.m., and at 6:00 it is raining very hard, chances are they will not pour concrete that morning. They will then phone the order desk of the supplier, cancel the order, and request another time in the day just in case the weather changes. If the weather remains poor they can always cancel the order again. Concrete suppliers are used to this happening, and do not mind as long as they have 90 minutes or more notice. Check with the supplier for their cancellation policy which usually depends on the time it will take the trucks to travel to the job site.

- **Sand and Gravel Supplier**

Provide suppliers with the square footage of the floor area where the sand will be spread and average depth of sand required for each area, and they will calculate the number of square metres or yards of sand required. Because they charge per metre/yard of sand delivered with a surcharge for partial loads, have the basement and garage sand delivered at one time.

The basement and garage work areas are protected from the elements by the roof structures. Water is the worst enemy of sand. If not protected from rain, the sand could wash away or become too wet, making it impossible to spread and level by hand. Several days might be wasted before the sand dries and is spreadable. Also double-check the amounts to be delivered with the supplier and the finisher, as it is better to have extra sand than not enough. Any excess sand can be mixed into your existing flower beds or spread around the children's play area.

Timing the delivery of sand for the driveways and walkways is very crucial. Have the concrete finisher order the sand for you as he will make sure the weather conditions are favorable, and the sand will arrive when he is at the job site. Suppliers who specialize in the delivery of sand for basements and garage floors use a conveyor belt attached to the end of their truck to toss the sand through specified window and door openings. Request the supplier to place more than the required amount of sand in hard-to-reach areas to minimize the amount the finisher will have to use the wheelbarrow. He and his helpers will appreciate it.

- **The Concrete Finisher**

Concrete finishers pour and place flat concrete surfaces, i.e., the basement floors, garage floors, driveways, sidewalks, and specialty items such as exposed aggregate steps. They perform an extremely valuable service. They are a special breed requiring the patience of Job, and the ability to discuss all the qualities of concrete, the weather and politics for many hours without stopping. When it comes time to pour or power trowel the concrete, get out of their way as they work like nobody else I have ever seen. Really good finishers who care about their work are worth having on your team.

Concrete finishers do not supply the sand, reinforcing rods, wire mesh, vapor barrier, pegs, or forms. They provide only the labor for cutting the reinforcing and wire mesh; spreading and tamping the sand; cutting and placing the poly vapor barriers; drilling the holes in the foundation to accept the dowels which tie the floor to the foundation; installing the stair, walkway and driveway forms; and finally, placing and finishing the concrete. The only items supplied other than the required nails and operating equipment are the chemical retarder and sealer which are used when placing and finishing exposed aggregate finishes. The charge for the finisher's labor is based on a cost per square foot for placing and finishing the concrete, and a flat rate for spreading and tamping the sand.

Before ordering sand for the basement, make sure that all the rough-in plumbing, floor drains, sump pit, sewer and water lines, and under-slab heating are completed and inspected by the mortgage/city inspectors, and all the subcontractors have removed their debris from the basement (as included in their contracts).

The following are four important parts of placing concrete, and points to remember when working with concrete finishing.

Basement floor:

After the sand has been delivered by the supplier (through the basement windows), the finisher spreads it evenly so that when compacted it will be the same thickness as the footings and structural pads. A string and level are used to make sure the sand is uniform after being compacted with a power vibrator. A 6 mil polyethylene vapor barrier is laid over the sand, structural pads, and footings, overlapping each sheet about 12 inches to eliminate water penetration into the concrete. Narrow sheets of waste plywood are laid on top of the poly to protect it from tears by the wheelbarrows used to transport the concrete. A surveyor's level and measure are used to make sure the concrete floor around the perimeter will be approximately four inches thick, and a minimum three inches thick at the drain which allows for a proper slope to the drain. Because the

existing basement of the house already has a slope to a floor drain, have a floor drain installed in the addition with its own slope. This will eliminate any existing basement water problems affecting the addition or vice versa. Unlike the sidewalk, driveway, and garage floor, the basement floor of a house does not require reinforcing or a connection to the basement walls or footing (see Figure 12-9). The basement floor floats on top of the sand and footings with sometimes only a perimeter expansion joint in areas where the soil has potential for movement. The expansion joint will eliminate rubbing between the two concrete surfaces which could cause powdering or cracking. This expansion joint should also be placed where the old basement floor meets the new, eliminating the need for reinforcing.

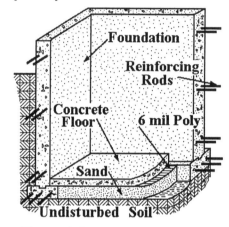

Figure 12-9. Basement floor drawing.

To level the newly poured concrete, the finisher uses a very long-handled, wide trowel, called a bull float, which forces the water in the concrete to the surface to create a smooth and even finish. Once this process has been completed, he must wait until the concrete has set sufficiently before using the power trowel which makes the concrete hard, smooth and shiny. Because the power trowel is unable to reach into corners, around structural posts, or under stairs the finisher has to smooth these areas with a hand trowel, blending these areas in to match the appearance created by the power trowel. Because the basement has little air movement, is

shaded, and has a cool inside temperature, the concrete sometimes requires a 1 or 2 percent calcium content to speed setting.

Garage floor:

The finisher marks the top of the concrete floor which is determined from the level of all the rough garage door accesses. Measuring for a three to four inch concrete floor, the finisher drills holes approximately 1-1/2 inches below the chalk line and at 24 inches apart all around the interior perimeter of the garage grade beam. Steel dowels approximately 24 inches long are then hammered into these perimeter holes to which the floors 6" x 6" 10/10

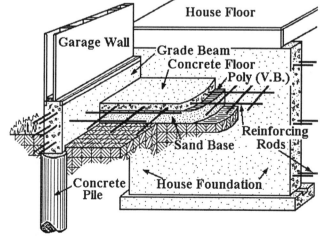

Figure 12-10. Garage floor slab connected to the grade beam.

wire mesh reinforcing will be connected later by wire ties (see Figure 12-10).

After the sand has been delivered and spread by the finisher, a string and level are used to ensure the sand is uniformly spread and allows for a proper slope to the floor drain before being compacted with a power vibrator. If possible, the sand should be sprinkled with water to achieve its maximum compression in order to stabilize the weight of the garage floor. This will provide a hard base and eliminate potential sinkholes caused by water seepage after the concrete is poured.

A 6 mil polyethylene vapor barrier is laid over the sand to eliminate water penetration into the concrete floor. Concrete, stone or brick spacers approximately 1-1/2 inches thick are placed on top of the poly to ensure that the mesh or reinforcing rods will be buried at half the garage floor thickness. If additional strength is required, wire mesh and reinforcing rods are laid every 24 inches on top of the spacers, taking care not to puncture the vapor barrier, and then connected to the perimeter reinforcing dowels which tie the floor to the foundation. As the concrete is being spread over the poly, the finisher will pull up the wire mesh and the rebar at unsupported lengths; vertical rods from the piles will be straightened or repositioned to make sure they are contained within the middle of the concrete floor to increase its structural stability. As with the basement floor, the finisher will use a bull float, and then wait until the concrete has set before using the power trowel. The concrete is troweled until hard, smooth, and shiny. Depending on the wind, weather, and finisher, the concrete sometimes contains 1 percent calcium to speed setting and is ordered with air to speed up curing and the evaporation of water. Many people who wish to keep the winter dirt and liquids dripping from the car from penetrating into the finished concrete will apply a floor paint to the surface. This paint application should be done after the concrete floor has had sufficient evaporation time to deal with any remaining water. To prepare the floor for paint, first remove any concrete powder, dirt, paint or drywall that has accumulated on the floor during the construction process with an acid wash. This 50/50 mixture of muriatic acid and water when broomed over the concrete will cause foaming and bubbling on the surface, and lift unwanted particles. After that, hose-wash and broom all the acid off the surface, and after a thorough drying, brush or roll the paint onto the concrete to seal.

Driveway and walkways:

The finisher uses chalk lines to measure the sidewalk from the front garage floor height to the entry steps, and allows a 3/4 to 1 inch slope for a distance of 20 feet. This will allow for a proper slope to drain and will determine the number of steps required for the front entry steps. The driveway is measured from the front garage floor height to the top of the city curb or sidewalk with a slope predetermined by the surveyor's plot plan, and should not be deviated from without consultation (see Figure 2-3). If the concrete finisher or owner changes the finished height of the garage floor, the driveway slope might exceed the 10 to 12 percent maximum desired slope and cause problems when driving in and out of the garage during some winter conditions. This will also increase the property's slope to drain, causing potential water problems for neighboring properties for which the city engineering department will require the installation of retaining walls down the length of the property.

Walkways attached to the garage and house should be supported every eight feet on the outside perimeter by concrete piles to eliminate sinking. Where the soil has been disturbed, or drilling piles might break or damage water or sewer lines, an alternative method is to pour supporting concrete brackets, or use the same brackets supplied for a prefabricated concrete stair and bolt them to the pile and grade beam. The brackets, if poured in place, are eight inches wide, and set directly over and connected to every grade beam and pile by the same reinforcing dowels used to attach the garage floor to the grade beam which ensures structural strength (see Figure 12-5).

The concrete finisher sets the height of the sidewalk and driveway pegs and support forms sufficient to allow for at least 5 inches of compacted sand, and an additional 4 to 5 inch concrete walkway and a 4 to 6 inch concrete driveway (see Figure 12-11). If applicable the finisher drills holes approximately 2 inches down from the chalk line and 24 inches apart around the exterior, adjacent perimeter walls of the garage grade beam and house foundation. Steel dowels approximately 24 inches long will be hammered into the perimeter holes and connected to the driveway and walkway reinforcing rods after the sand has been compacted.

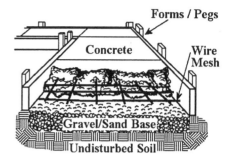

Figure 12-11. Typical support forms for driveway and walkway.

After the sand delivery, the finisher uses a string and level to make sure the sand has been uniformly spread and allows for the required concrete thickness. The sand, as for the basement and garage floors, is compacted with a power vibrator and sprinkled with water for maximum compression. A polyethylene vapor barrier is not required for any exterior concrete as water should be allowed to penetrate the concrete and flow through the sand to undisturbed soil. This will carry any water away from the foundation.

As with the garage floor installation, stone or brick spacers approximately 1-1/2 inches thick are placed on top of the sand to ensure that the mesh or reinforcing rods will be buried at half the driveway thickness. Steel reinforcing rods, or rebar, 20 feet in length and 3/8 to 1/2 inch in diameter are laid on top of the sand, and connected to the perimeter dowels with wire ties which structurally secure the driveway and walkway to the grade beam and foundation. Steel dowels 24 inches in length must always be used to attach the driveway, garage pad and walkway to the grade beam; however, wire mesh can replace the 20-foot reinforcing rods for the sidewalk pad. Adding wire mesh to the rebar in areas where the driveway and sidewalk connect will structurally strengthen these usually weak areas, and reduce substantially the future chance of cracking.

As the concrete is being spread over the sand, the reinforcing rods at unsupported lengths are pulled up to make sure they will be contained in the middle of the concrete, thus increasing its structural stability. The finisher, as with all floors, uses the short back-and-forth motions of the bull float to smooth and level the concrete. Depending on current weather conditions, the finisher will patiently wait for hours until the concrete has sufficiently set before roughening the surface with a broom to produce a nonskid surface.

The finisher's last task is to place a finished edge around the perimeter of the walkway and driveway, and their expansion joints located every ten feet. Additional expansion joints on the walkway are located where there might be potential cracking, eg., where the driveway and city sidewalk connect. The city sidewalk and your driveway are usually compacted using different equipment, and will move differently with freezing and thawing. The expansion joint will absorb the difference in expansion and contraction rates, and eliminate potential powdering or cracking caused by friction.

Exposed aggregate:

The concrete supplier has a special size and color of gravel that is used to produce the rough and colorful exposed rock surface. The finish requires special care, accurate timing, and additional work by the concrete finisher to achieve the desired result, therefore expect him to charge more for the job. If the budget can afford it, it is well worth the investment and gives the streetscape of the house a real touch of class.

Pouring this concrete follows the same process as for a standard driveway or walkway. However, once finished with the bull float, a retarder solution is evenly sprayed over the concrete to stop the top layer of concrete from curing and allow the coarse, colored gravel to stand out after washing. The finisher cannot spray too much or too little. Too much retarder will penetrate too deep, stopping the curing of the lower layers of the concrete; too little will not stop enough of the top layer of concrete, leaving the colorful stones buried. Once sprayed the concrete must be watched closely for three to eight hours, or until the retarder is ready for removal and the concrete base has cured enough to be walked on. Clouds, sun, or even shade from an overhang will vary the curing time of the concrete, and the time required for the retarder to work. When the finisher sees that the concrete is ready, the retarder must be washed off as quickly as possible. A water tap, hose, and broom must be available for the finisher to wash down, and then sweep the retarder and the uncured concrete skim.

Note: If the finisher returns too late to apply the retarder, or the weather does not cooperate before, during, or after the spraying of the retarder, the delayed curing will not occur. Under these unusual and undesirable circumstances, the concrete finisher must then search down a sandblaster at an additional cost to expose the colorful gravel. The price the finisher charges for the retarder and wash down is about one-fifth the cost to have the driveway, sidewalk, and/or entry steps sandblasted.

Because all the exposed aggregate should be poured at one time for proper consistency, expansion joints are placed only at the connection of the city sidewalk and driveway. Other expansion joints must be saw-cut into the concrete (see the next section on concrete cutting). The exposed aggregate is also considered the final product so the finisher does not use a trowel to provide a finished edge as for a brushed concrete finish.

After the expansion joints have been cut and the powder washed off to avoid rehardening, the concrete is left to cure over three to seven days before the finisher gives the surface a final diluted acid wash. The brushed-on muriatic acid cleans the rocks and removes any remaining excess concrete powder. It is then brushed and hosed off to expose a clean and porous rock surface. This surface should be protected from the elements by sealing it with an epoxy or plastic-like finish which is brushed or rolled on. Once completed it brings out the natural colors of the exposed aggregate, and protects the concrete surface with an almost shiny, acrylic polish. Depending on the amount of traffic, this protective finish will wear off after a few years; therefore repeat the acid wash and sealant application every few years as part of the home's maintenance program.

The finishing processes described are similar for each construction area, but may change based on variables such as the concrete aggregate type, air and water content, and reinforcing and final sealing requirements. For all jobs, include in the estimate that the finisher is responsible for stripping the forms once the concrete has completely set. You can give the forms to the finisher, have him purchase them for a cheap price, or have him throw them on the material trash pile.

- **Concrete Cutting**

    As discussed earlier, when excavating a full or partial basement for an addition, have an access door or arch cut between the existing basement and new basement or crawl space. Rather than renting a bulky, expensive, and time-consuming concrete chipper to hammer out small pieces of concrete, hire a concrete cutter to complete the job in less time and provide a smooth-finished access hole. The excavator must have the wall completely exposed so the cutter can saw from the outside of the foundation wall which will eliminate any interference of side walls, basement floors, or floor joists.

    When the concrete cutting is completed, the question will be, "What to do with the concrete slab?" Options include hiring a crane to remove the slab and truck it to the dump, or renting a concrete chipper to break it up into more manageable pieces to be trucked away to the dump. Once when renovating a house I found the estimated cost of hauling the slab away to the dump was much more than I wanted to pay, so I had the excavator dig a hole for it to fall into. The hole was dug eight inches wider and taller than the proposed slab approximately four inches deeper than the foundation thickness, and located directly in front of the proposed access doorway (see Figure 12-12). A long crowbar was used to slowly maneuver the slab out and away from its position, and force it to fall directly into the excavated hole. The excess water from the cutting process (see next paragraph) made the base of the hole soft, so when the slab fell into the hole it sank in deeper, and its weight plus the compression force of the falling slab shot the remaining water all around the excavated hole, allowing it to evaporate more quickly. The rationale for digging the hole four inches deeper was to have a margin of safety in case the slab fell on a slight angle, causing it to protrude out more on one side, and force me to pour concrete onto concrete. After the basement sand was delivered and tamped, the sand created a buffer between the concrete floor and the slab, eliminating any potential heaving. Problem solved at minimal expense.

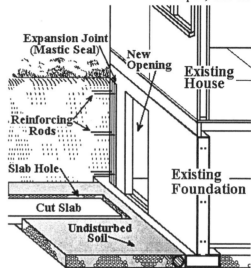

Figure 12-12. Door access cut into existing foundation wall.

The access requires straight and square walls, and in order to achieve this the cutter uses a water-cooled, diamond-tip saw blade capable of cutting through the full eight-inch thickness of the wall, the reinforcing contained in the wall, and the foundation's concrete strength. The straight cuts are accomplished by bolting a metal straight edge horizontally and then vertically to the saw. Following a preset gear system contained inside the straight edge, the saw cuts through the wall at a rate that will not chip or burn the saw blades. A 3' x 7' doorway will take several hours to complete, and will require a substantial amount of water to cool the blade; therefore, the foundation weeping tile should be checked and cleared if necessary to remove the water. Be prepared to rent a small pump as the remaining water trapped in the excavation must be pumped out prior to proceeding with foundation work.

Exposed aggregate requires expansion joints every ten feet on the driveway surface, every five feet on the walkway, and anywhere potential cracking might occur. A high-speed, self-moving, concrete saw is needed to cut the expansion joints in the driveway. Closely following the chalk lines marked on the concrete by the finisher, the concrete cutter uses a water-cooled cutting blade to penetrate about 1-1/2 inches into the concrete. This cut depth will force the expanding and contracting concrete to crack along the cut line rather than in uncontrolled or undesirable directions. The worker directing this machine takes his time to make sure the line being cut into the concrete is straight. This machine is used only to cut expansion joints on large surfaces such as driveways as it is too long and bulky to cut sidewalk expansion joints.

For sidewalks, tight corners, and areas of limited access, a hand-held concrete cutter is used. The hand cutter does not have its own water supply so the operator frequently waters down the concrete to control the dust. This does not prevent the dust from blowing all over the concrete surface; therefore, he immediately hoses down the entire concrete surface to remove these dust particles. He needs ready access to a water tap because if the expansion joints and concrete surfaces are not thoroughly washed out, the concrete dust particles will clog the cut lines and rebond with the finished concrete surface. This unsightly bonding will require careful chipping by hand before the concrete finisher can complete his job. As previously discussed the concrete finisher's estimate should indicate an acid wash about 72 hours *after* the concrete sawing procedure is finished.

Concrete cutters charge by the lineal foot for all expansion joints, so for budget planning, count on about 200 lineal feet of expansion joints for a regular driveway and sidewalk.

• **Framing the House**

When renovating, word of mouth is the best way to find a good framer, but the final choice should be made knowing (a) years of experience with renovation projects; (b) completion price; (c) number of crew; and (d) conscientiousness about clients' needs. Once you find a good framer, be honest about the renovation budget, and he will try to be flexible within reason with his price.

The more work experience someone has, the better the quality of work, and also the less time it will take to finish. The downside is the more experienced the framer, the more he will cost; however, do not let the price difference scare you too much. Most framers know what their competition is charging, especially if working for general contractors who will pay only so much to a framer. (If a final price for the project has been contracted by a builder for the client, he will expect the framer to be more flexible in his pricing.) Competition for work is usually in the builder's favor as a framer who wishes to keep his crew must keep them busy. Even during boom economies you will find a good selection of framing crews who tend to migrate around the country to find the jobs.

Framers charge by the hour when there is a substantial amount of demolition work for the existing structure, and by the square foot for new framing walls. Extra charges will be incurred for demolition, a fireplace chase, bay windows, decks and balconies, strapping to match existing and new wall thicknesses (see Figure 12-6), or other items that require on-site framing. Before signing the contract for the renovation, review the estimate and the blueprints, and make sure the following has been included: "that he will return as needed to move or add any floor joists, bracing, backing and wall studs for the electrician, drywaller, finisher, plumber or heating contractor."

Discuss with the framer which walls or portions of the house are to be removed, partially demolished or rebuilt; the type, location and installation of vapor barriers for existing walls; and the insulation requirements for corners and hard-to-get-at areas that might be inaccessible to the insulator once framing has been completed. Mark the walls/roof areas that are to be demolished and rebuilt on two sets of blueprints with different colored magic markers and have him sign your set for the file. Some areas of the renovation will be harder for the framer to estimate, as the older the home the more unexpected or unforeseen items will crop up during demolition, eg., supporting walls or beams which have to be replaced because they do not meet the present building code requirements. Having to replace walls which have had years of water seepage within their structures is another additional framing cost. If the inspection fails to reveal signs of this dryrot, the framer will still have to replace the areas affected. The total finished price will then vary with the subsequent labor costs to upgrade or relocate that wall's electrical, plumbing, drywall, painting, etc. These costs will be absorbed by the contingency factor calculated into the initial cost projection. If the framer has sufficient experience with renovations, he should be able to spot these problem areas during his initial inspection and allow you at that time to adjust the completed renovation cost. He should expect the unexpected and be able to quote you a price within 5 percent of the actual demolition cost; the labor cost for framing the new house structure should be exact. With the help of sledge hammers, crowbars and chain saws the demolition and removal of sections of walls can be done very quickly by an experienced crew, and within the first day much of the house as you once knew it will be gone. This phase of the renovation project requires the rental of a garbage container for the old plaster, wood, and nonrecyclable materials. If sinks, toilets, bathtubs, light fixtures, kitchen cabinets, and carpets are to be replaced, assess their condition and place an ad in one of the local newspapers or bargain finders to see if anyone can use them for a cottage or basement development project. You might be pleasantly surprised to find many people are willing to purchase and recycle these items, and you can use the money collected to reduce the cash outlay for rental equipment or other items. Don't neglect to consider protecting the areas undergoing demolition from rainy or snowy conditions. Consider the

need to rent tarpaulins during the estimating process as the size of tarp required to protect that area of the roof against inclement weather will determine the final cost. Weather conditions on the day of demolition can never be second-guessed. If these areas are not properly protected, the rain or snow will soak the materials and gradually saturate the ceiling finish, causing these areas to fall down and resulting in more unexpected damage and repair work. Protect your schedule with the necessary rental applications so you can rent any equipment as and when required.

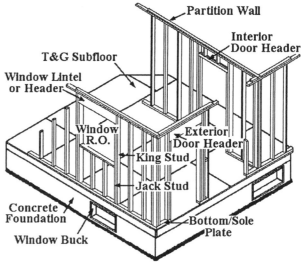

Figure 12-13. Typical exterior and interior framed walls.

Placing the joists:

As discussed earlier, either the cribber or the framer can place the floor joists, but before making

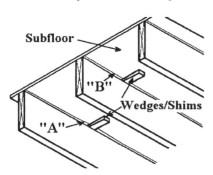

Figure 12-14. Wedges and shims to level the existing floor. (A) Joist crown up, (B) Joist crown down.

that choice, make sure the cribber has the experience. A cleaner job results if the framer places the joists, because he knows exactly where the main floor structural walls are and will place the joists directly below (see Figure 12-13). Because he will be doing the demolition and new construction for the house, he will have access to the proper tools to adjust the finished height of the new and old floors when installing the joist package. Some adjustment of the new and old floor joists might be required to maintain the same floor level throughout. Installing shims to the perimeter sole plate of the addition or adjusting the existing floor height using wood wedges/shims will accomplish this. These wedges can also be used to eliminate existing floor squeaks caused by loosening of

the seal and nail/screws resulting in separation of the subfloor from the floor joists (see Figure 12-14).

Assume that the framer was chosen to lay out the joists and the cribber has already installed the structural

beams and posts as per plan (see Figure 12-15). After reviewing the floor plans, the framer will start selecting the lumber to be used for the joisting. Request him to use only the joists that are not twisted, split or damaged when delivered, and provide a lumber count of the material to be returned to the lumberyard for credit and exchange for better material. Give the lumberyard a copy of the framer's count so they can deliver the new floor joists when they pick up the unusable lumber. It is a good idea to have the framer inspect all deliveries, and reject any lumber or materials not up to specified standard.

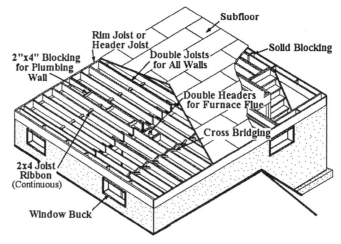

Figure 12-15. Floor joist framing with subfloor.

Many builders are using premanufactured floor truss systems which are made by combining long lengths of layered plywood which when attached to a top and bottom cord provide superior strength and the ability to span lengths longer than 2" x 10" or 12" solid lumber (see Figure 12-16). The second type of silent floor system, called the open-web joist, is used most for commercial projects, but has found its way into

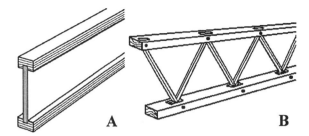

Figure 12-16. (A) Floor truss, (B) Open web.

residential construction because it simplifies the installation of associated electrical, plumbing, and mechanical systems (see Figure 12-16). The difference between the two floor systems is that the open-web has angular metal or wood bridging between the upper and lower cords, and the plywood system is closed between the two cords. Predetermined hole sizes can be drilled for the electrical and mechanical lines in the closed web system.

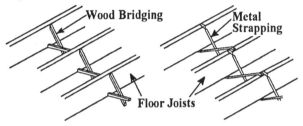

Figure 12-17. Wood cross bridging and metal strapping between floor joists.

Both these silent floor systems offer savings to the home builder in several ways. Because the trusses are delivered to the site ready for erection construction, time is reduced. Their high strength and rigidity over long spans reduce the need for basement and main floor bearing walls. The ability to span longer unsupported distances provides more flexibility in design by not limiting the size of potential rooms.

On completion of the floor joist layout, and prior to cross bridging and subfloor installation, do a quick walk-through with the framer. Make sure that there will be sufficient headroom created at any new stairwells (see Figure 12-21), and sufficient insulation placed in all foundation floor-joist voids that will not be accessible after the subfloor is in place and the vapor barrier/insulation installed. Once these items have been visually inspected and approved, the top supports of the cross bridging (see Figure 12-17) will be permanently nailed, leaving the bottom supports free to be completed (nailed) once the addition has been completely framed. At this stage of construction have the framer adjust and level any new teleposts to match the existing floor level of the house. The 3 inch structural steel teleposts are supported by a concrete base pad and at the top is bolted to the basement beam and having a vertical adjustable screw, when turned allows for the horizontal leveling of the beams and floor joists.

Renovations that consist of bay, bow, and box windows are usually cantilevered because it is much cheaper to extend the floor joists beyond the house foundation than build the more costly concrete footing and foundation. The distance the joists can project beyond the foundation may vary in every state or province. It depends on the building structure and snowloads it can safely support. The designer will know the cantilever requirements for your specific area (see Figure 12-18). Most cantilevers are framed using a 2" x 10" header/rim joist

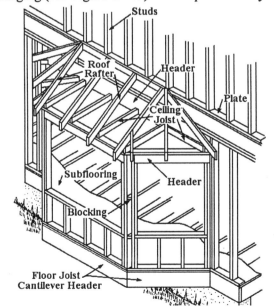

Figure 12-18. Framing of a typical cantilever for a bay window.

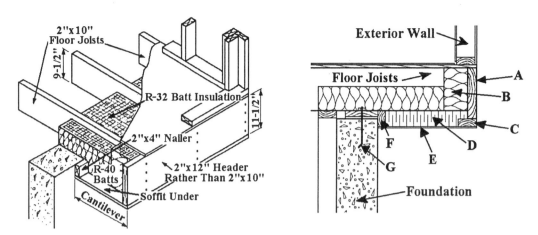

Figure 12-19. Typical framing and insulating of cantilevers. (A) Header, (B) R-28 Insulation, (C) 2" x4 " header nailer, (D) Rigid insulation, (E) Soffit, (F) 2" x 4" foundation nailer, (G) Anchor bolts @ 4'-0" on center.

around the perimeter of the cantilever with the more energy-wise builders use 12-inch headers. The former will not allow sufficient insulation in the joist area to keep the cantilever properly heated and warm during winter months. To maintain a warm floor it will be necessary to eliminate air infiltration on the underside of the bay where the soffit is attached (see Figure 12-19). The amount and type of insulation as well as the header joist construction required will depend on the location's winter chill factors. The typical 2" x 10" floor joist extending beyond the foundation is deep enough to hold an R-24 insulation value with a minimum two-inch air space for warm air to circulate. This is insufficient in colder climates that need at least an R-32 insulation value and a minimum three inches of air space between the top of the insulation and the underside of the subfloor. This can be achieved by installing a larger 2" x 12" header joist to the perimeter of the cantilever, and adding a 2" x 2" nailer strip under the header for an additional 1-1/2 inch depth. The framer will install an R-32 batt value into the header space, and fit a sheet of rigid insulation with an R-8 insulation value into the 1-1/2 inch nailer's space. A perimeter sealer of caulking placed around the underside of the rigid insulation and the nailer prior to the soffit being installed will keep this area airtight.

The addition of a cantilevered bay or box window may be more costly than first anticipated, especially if the floor area is to carry some supporting weight. In an existing structure, to cantilever beyond the foundation, the floor joists must be structurally supported by a length inside the structure at least three times the distance it protrudes beyond the foundation, i.e., for every foot the cantilever protrudes beyond the foundation, the joists must be set three feet into the house structure. The expense involved to remove the affected perimeter header, finished basement ceiling, and sometimes the existing floor joists is sometimes too costly, and the cantilever idea is discarded.

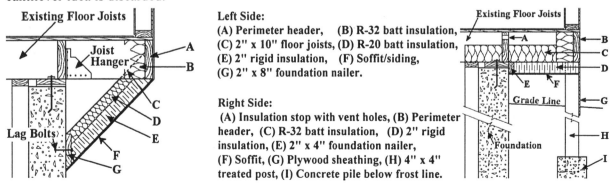

Left Side:
(A) Perimeter header,   (B) R-32 batt insulation,
(C) 2" x 10" floor joists, (D) R-20 batt insulation,
(E) 2" rigid insulation,   (F) Soffit/siding,
(G) 2" x 8" foundation nailer.

Right Side:
(A) Insulation stop with vent holes, (B) Perimeter header, (C) R-32 batt insulation,   (D) 2" rigid insulation, (E) 2" x 4" foundation nailer, (F) Soffit, (G) Plywood sheathing, (H) 4" x 4" treated post, (I) Concrete pile below frost line.

Figure 12-20. Framing options for attaching a bay/box window to an existing structure.

As a designer I have had to come up with some less expensive alternatives to reduce the cost of construction especially when the client requested several cantilevers and it was necessary to remove part of the finished basement. The alternative method would also have to structurally support interior weight and satisfy the local building codes. After several trial designs and discussions with the city inspector and a structural engineer, I found that a structural supporting bracket under the cantilever and treated vertical 4" x 4" timbers sunk below the frost line with a concrete pile/base would be approved by the city and the engineer (see Figure 12-20).

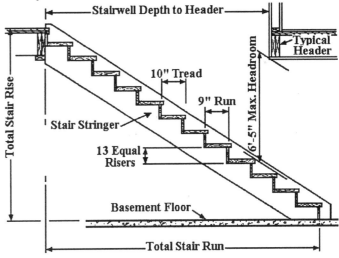

Figure 12-21. Typical stair construction.

Laying the subfloor:

The framer applies elastomeric glue to the top of the floor joists prior to laying the subfloor and screwing the sheets at the corners to secure them in place. Remind him to place enough glue to ensure a good bond. The most common subfloor material comes in 5/8 inch or 3/4 inch thickness in 4' x 8' plywood sheets with tongue and groove ends for a continuous, tight fit. The eight foot lengths of the sheets are laid perpendicular to the joists so the four foot joint ends of the subfloor are directly over a joist to minimize waste when cutting the sheets. The ends of the sheets are staggered to the connecting sheet to provide additional strength to the floor's structure (see Figure 12-15). The tongue and groove plywood will stabilize the floor joists, making the floor more structurally rigid for the walls. After a few of the subfloor sheets have been placed, the framer will anchor the sheets in place with additional screws before the flexibility of the glue is lost. Request him to place the screws no more than six inches apart and staggered to the opposing sheet.

It is important that the upper floor framing be completed and roofed as quickly as possible to eliminate warping in the existing or new house structure. Once the roof, windows, and doors are completed, the rain and snow will have little effect on the lumber. Some lumber will have to be replaced or braced by the framer as some twisting will occur as the lumber dries.

Stair installation:

Today, the parts for the main stairways to basement or upper floors are usually prefabricated in a stair shop or millwork plant, and then installed at the job site by the framer after he has completed framing the addition. The framer will build temporary stair ladders from framing lumber to provide easy access to the different levels of the house. Doing this eliminates any damage to the finished stairs during the framing and rough-in plumbing, heating and electrical stages. Basement stairs should be installed after the basement floor has been poured and has a few days to cure.

Stairs consist primarily of risers and treads supported by stringers. The height of the riser is called the unit rise, and the width of tread (nosing included) is called the unit run. The sum of all the risers is the distance from a given floor to the next floor up or down, and the sum of the total tread is the

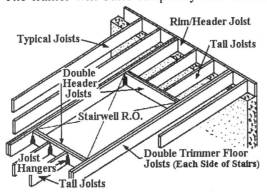

Figure 12-22. Typical stair framing.

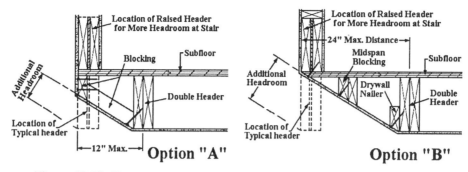

Figure 12-23. Optional framing procedures to gain more headroom at stairwells.

total run (see Figure 12-21).

Framing of stairs requires that trimmers and headers in the rough framing of the floor joists be doubled especially when the span is greater than four feet. Headers more than six feet in length should be installed with joist hangers unless supported by a beam, post, or partition (see Figure 12-22). Providing adequate headroom where a wall crosses the stairs often constitutes a problem especially in smaller house structures. Installing an auxiliary header within a maximum of 24 inches to the main header will permit additional headroom above the stair. An alternative solution is to contain the header within the wall itself (see Figure 12-23). The width of the main stair should allow two people to pass without contact, and also provide sufficient space so furniture can be moved up or down. A minimum width of 36 inches is recommended. When walking up or down a stairwell a person must have the opportunity for support which is provided by a continuous handrail along one side.

The complete set of working drawings for both existing and addition plans will include detailed drawings, in section, of the stair system, especially if the stair layout has a landing at any level. All the stairs will also be shown on the floor plans showing the correct number of risers and treads.

Wall framing:

The wall framing of a house is standard throughout the industry, and the city inspector makes sure everything complies with the building code. Here are some things to look for when walking through the house:

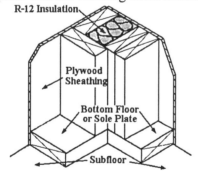

Figure 12-24. The meeting of two framing corners

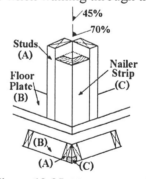

Figure 12-25. More than a 90° corner with nailer strip.

1) Use a carpenter's level to make sure all walls are level and vertical especially where any two corners meet (see Figure 12-24).

2) Check that the framer has installed a drywall nailer strip where walls meet at more than 90° (see Figure 12-25).

3) Check to ensure sufficient insulation has been placed where interior walls meet exterior walls, and two exterior walls meet at corners (see Figure 12-26 on the following page).

4) Check for insulation of a continuous strip of 6 mil polyethylene vapor barrier and a drywall nailer on all top plates, and at the connection of interior and exterior perpendicular walls (see Figures 12-26 and 12-27 on the following page).

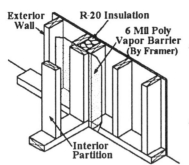

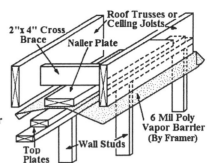

Left: **Figure 12-26. Insulation and vapor barrier at all exterior wall connections.**

Right: **Figure 12-27. Vapor barrier and nailer at top wall plates.**

5) Discuss with the framer the rough opening of the windows and doors, and make sure that no more than 3/4 of an inch is added to the total width and height of each window when the rough openings are framed (see Figure 12-28). Have the framer include in his estimate that, if the windows are on back order or if they have been broken and have to be returned, he will return to install them. In the meantime he will cover the openings with a polyethylene vapor barrier.

Note: Windows are usually placed on back order if they are out of the ordinary, or if the window manufacturers are backlogged because they have taken on too many job contracts.

6) Check that the framer has stapled a strip of tar paper around the exterior rough opening of the windows. Before actual installation of the windows and doors, have him put a bead of flexible silicone around the perimeter of the tar paper where the window frame will be nailed to the exterior wall. This will eliminate wind drafts especially if the intended exterior finish is stucco (see Figure 12-29). There may be an additional charge for this service; however, this amount will be repaid as reduced heating costs during the first year.

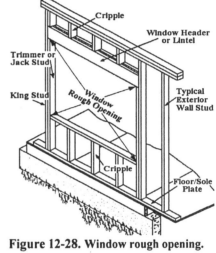

Figure 12-28. Window rough opening.

7) Do a visual walk around the house, making sure that all the attic insulation stops and baffles have been installed where required. If not completed correctly, there will be potential heat loss or water damage by the wind blowing attic insulation away, and snow melting at the roof perimeter (see Figure 12-30).

Roof installation:

Unless agreed otherwise in writing, it is the responsibility of the framer to provide the necessary equipment, eg., a crane, and/or manpower to place the trusses on the structure for proper roof installation. Confirm with the framer the type of roofing material to be installed, and ensure installation of the proper type of outlooker

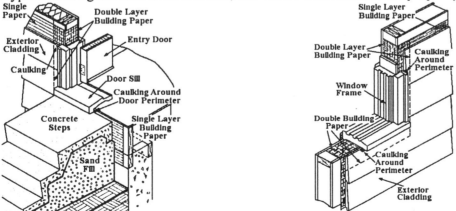

Figure 12-29. Caulking locations around the perimeter of door and window frames.

for the roof structure. Adequate roof outlooker strength must be in place to carry the roof load set by the local building code. The truss supplier will supply all the necessary engineered roof trusses except for those areas that require stick framing, i.e., fascia boards, outlookers, saddles, braces, and furred/dropped down ceilings, etc.

Note: In order to utilize as much of the on-site materials as possible, the framer will use the wall bracing lumber to construct the outlookers (see Figure 12-31).

The installation of roof sheathing provides the protection needed to keep inclement weather from warping the framing material, and allows the material to properly air-dry. The material selection for roof

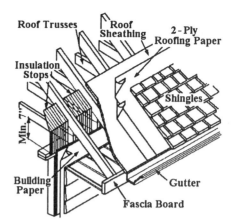

Figure 12-30. Baffle location drawing.

sheathing depends on factors such as quality of material, affordability, life span of the home, roof finish selection, and truss spacing. The choice is usually very simple if cost is an important factor. The cheaper chip/strand board is composed of wood chips and chemical rosins which when placed under pressure and

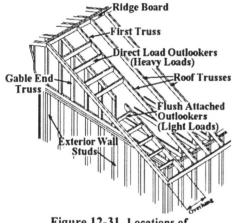

Figure 12-31. Locations of gable overhang outlookers.

cured provides a very rigid sheet. These sheets when placed in contact with water/moisture have a tendency to swell and become very brittle; however when properly protected with roofing paper and a finished roof, they can last for the life of the house. The most common roof sheathing used throughout North America is plywood which is manufactured by layering thin sheets of wood in opposing directions with layers of chemical rosins sandwiched between, and then cured under pressure. The thickness of the roof sheathing will depend on the finished roof material and the chosen spacing of the trusses. Normally for asphalt roofing, the trusses are framed at 16 inches on center (o.c.) to accommodate the installation of 3/8-inch roof sheathing; for a wood or tiled roof a 1/2-inch sheathing should be used with the roof trusses at 16

inches o.c. Depending on the region and the building code for the area, some builders will attempt to reduce the truss costs by installing them 24 inches o.c. This method of cost reduction sometimes backfires in areas that receive heavy snowloads, as the weight of the snow compresses the sheathing between the trusses and over a period of years will cause the sheathing to sag. Using minimum building code standards to reduce the construction costs usually passes on potentially costly repairs or undesirable visual streetscapes to the next owner.

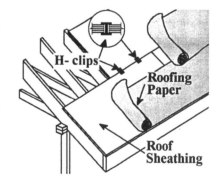

Figure 12-32. Location of H-clips on the plywood roof sheathing.

The 4' x 8' roof sheathing is applied very much like the subfloor with the eight foot length of the sheet being laid perpendicular to the truss direction. The four foot joint ends of the sheet are placed directly over a truss to minimize waste when cutting the sheets, and the ends of the sheets are staggered to the connecting sheet to increase the strength of the roof structure. The sheathing rows must have sufficient space to expand and contract, and are therefore spaced approximately 1/8 inch apart. As a result of many builders cutting costs and installing the roof trusses at 24 inches o.c., many city engineering departments require the use of H-clips when installing the roof sheathing. The H-clips are installed onto the sheathing between the truss span to increase its horizontal strength and eliminate sagging between the spans (see Figure 12-32).

Miscellaneous framing:

After completing the roof sheathing, have the framer level the addition to the existing floor height of the house by adjusting the basement steel teleposts, and bolting the posts to the structural beams with two-inch lag bolts. Then he will complete nailing the cross bridging in the basement and second floor, if applicable, which provides the lateral strength for the floor joists. The full bearing weight of the renovated portion on the newly installed floor joists will allow them to settle into their final position so there will be little or no further adjustment required after the cross bridging is nailed in place.

An important item to remember is to have the bathtubs and shower stall units delivered by the plumber during the framing of the bathroom areas (see Figure 12-33). Due to the size and shape of these one-piece units it will be impossible for them to be installed at a later date without having to remove walls at great expense. Select the models and colors well in advance so the plumber can order and receive them in time to be installed when the framing crew is ready.

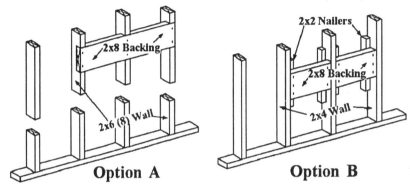

Figure 12-33. Plumbing wall backing locations.
(A) 2 x 6 wall,   (B) 2 x 4 wall.

Review the locations of any framing and backing requirements for any new wall fixtures such as towel bars, grab bars, toilet paper holders, soap dishes, medicine cabinets, wall and attic access hatches, spa pump service hatch, and other heavy wall and ceiling light fixtures or fans that might be required now or in the future. If you have a pet, should you provide an access hatch so it can enter and exit the basement as required? Have all these jobs completed before the framer leaves the job site, because there will be little or no chance of getting him and his crew back before the house is ready for insulating and drywalling. If these items were not included in the estimate, it will be very hard to get them to return especially if they have been paid in full. You may have to do the job yourself, or hire someone else to do it.

At the same time, check to see if he has made provisions at the attic and roof for the attachment of sheet-metal tie straps and metal firestops which are required by code for furnace and fireplace flues. The framing for heat lamp boxes, snow and water saddles for chimney chases, and the roof cut outs for plumbing stacks or attic vents should be visually checked and approved by the city inspector before the framer leaves for another job.

Note: The framer when on-site cuts any holes for dryer, basement fans, and cooktop or furnace vents that go through the outside wall or floor joist. Have him cut the hole as close as possible to the duct size indicated by the heating contractor.

As a result of the earth's ozone depletion and subsequent weather pattern changes, additional precautions need to be taken during construction for wind, snow and water protection. After completing the application of building paper around all exterior rough openings for windows and doors, and prior to the actual installation of the windows and doors, supply the framer with a quantity of flexible caulking compound. This will be applied on top of the building paper around the window and door openings, as well as on all exterior vertical inside wall corners. This is an additional cost, but a very important item which will eliminate any water and air leaking into the house and significantly reduce heating costs. This caulking application is usually not done by the framer, but if you supply the materials it would be simple for him to do the caulking while installing the windows and doors so have him include this application in his estimate.

To illustrate the importance of this item, I was constructing a multi-angled house, and was so involved with the completion schedule that I forgot to have the windows, doors, and inside plywood corners caulked. The house was completed, and no problems encountered until a very rainy and windy spring a year later. It rained continuously with high driving winds for several days which forced the rain up and underneath the flashing over some of the windows and doors, and caused the water to travel down the sides of the frames, under the door sills, and onto the floors. Normally, the flashing would have been sufficient to stop the rain from getting in, but the high driving winds were just too much. Once the bad weather ended and the house dried up, the finisher was contacted to remove all the exterior door and window casings and add the caulking that should have been applied during construction. The casings were replaced and repainted. The remainder of that year was off-and-on wind and rain, but no water leaks.

At the beginning of the construction, establish with the framer and other subcontractors an area set aside for lumber scraps and garbage collection. This way the framing crew will throw any lumber scraps on one pile, and not scatter them all around the house. It should be the responsibility of the framer to remove any debris, and sweep the house floor when he has completed his contract.

Walk-through inspection:
- Has the framer double-checked the headroom to see that it conforms to code?
- Are the stairs securely attached to the walls to eliminate squeaking?
- Have all the backing boards been installed for bathroom fixtures and electrical fixtures?
- Are all basement joist blocking, cross bridging, continuous strapping, and joist hangers installed?
- Has the framer installed all nailers for firestop insulation as per code requirements?
- Has he completed all the service work and framing requirements indicated by both the city and mortgage inspectors?

Construction hint:
Many people when renovating cannot immediately afford luxuries such as a deck, and will wait until the savings account allows further expenses. Sometimes it is not financially practical to include the cost of the deck in the mortgage or loan payments; however, prepare the structure for the deck's future installation by having the framer install the 2" x 10" wall header to the house where the deck will be attached. This way the exterior cladding installers will flash the top of the header and install the cladding to the header. You will then have the header waterproofed in preparation for the deck to be attached later. If not done by the framer during construction, the cladding installers will apply the exterior finish to the underside of the exterior sheathing. Then when you are ready for the deck, the exterior finish will have to be removed, the header installed

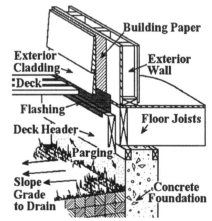

Figure 12-34. Deck header installation.

with the flashing strip, and the exterior finish replaced to the top of the deck header sometimes at great expense. If stucco was removed it could become very costly and difficult to match the existing color. This preplanning will eliminate unnecessary future expenses and duplication of work (see Figure 12-34).

● **Settling Disputes**
There are very few areas where the subcontractors' jobs overlap. If they do, you will have to make a decision, i.e., which subcontractor is responsible to complete or repair what, and then stick with it. A good rule

to follow when this problem occurs is anything to do with plumbing the plumber will do, anything with electrical the electrician will do, and the same for heating, painting, finishing, etc. The same stand should be taken when damage is done, i.e., cross bridging, studs, or backing being removed and not replaced. Whoever broke or removed the item should replace it, or put in some other structural material to support or take its place. If he does not honor your decision, tell his boss, and write a note informing him that you will determine who is responsible, have someone else fix it, and charge it back to the guilty party. Send them a photocopy of the repair invoice when it is taken off their final invoice. If repair work is completed by yourself or another subtrade, photograph these problem areas for the record until payment is received from the responsible party.

● **Roof Truss Selection**

Most of the roof structure is constructed with premanufactured roof trusses designed to the specifications shown on the house plan blueprints. The simpler the roof-line the cheaper the overall truss costs; therefore try to design the house with as many standardized roof trusses as possible. The more trusses that are the same, the fewer times the manufacturer has to change his truss template, and hence the cheaper cost. When more roof-lines are added to the inside or outside, or the roof slope increased above a normal 4/12 slope, the more difficult the trusses are to build. There will also be extra costs incurred as a result of having each different truss

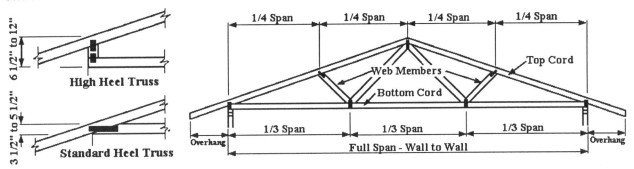

Figure 12-35. A typical Fink or "W" truss with standard and optional high heel heights.

engineered (see Figure 12-35). Many homes built in the 40s to 60s were constructed with roofs built on-site with varying slopes. The slopes of premanufactured trusses will generally not match these stick-framed roofs, and will have to be built up to accommodate some of the roofing materials used to upgrade existing homes. A roof initially constructed as a 3/12 pitch with asphalt shingles has probably been reroofed many times because improper slopes will accelerate the aging process of roofing materials. Over the years a leaking roof may have caused unseen material dryrot and water damage which will require replacement. If this is the case, and especially if planning an addition with premanufactured trusses, consider matching the roof-lines by building up the existing roof (see Figure 12-36). To ensure that the existing house structure and roof will support the new roof, the city engineering department will require an engineer to approve the design.

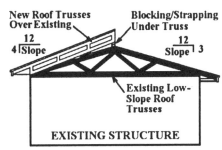

Figure 12-36. A built-up roof over an existing low slope roof.

Just as there are different roof types, there are different roof trusses available to create the different roof-lines (see Figure 12-37). Any one truss style may have many design and structural variations. The structural capacity, design, and cost will vary with different truss spans, roof slopes, roof snowload, truss spacing, end heel height, grade of material, and weight bearing function, eg., carrying other truss loads. There are also many names used for different parts of a truss such as heel height, gussets, cords, etc.

Trusses in the past were designed to be supported by a central bearing wall with a structural wall at each end. Given more complicated roof lines and current house styles, they have been adapted to allow clear spans without any central support and cantilevers. The design of the cantilevered length of truss will be determined by the local ground snowloads, size of the top and bottom cords, roof slope, and bracing location or size (see Figure 12-38).

When collecting the estimates, ensure the package price includes on-site delivery, repair of any damaged trusses up to the delivery date, all connecting devices, and a list of all the individual trusses detailing their span lengths, slopes and number to be delivered. The manufacturer must provide engineered drawings for each individual truss with the engineer's seal, or a covering letter stating that all the trusses have been engineered. These authorized drawings and/or covering letter will be required by the city engineering department for their files before you get your final building permit. This paperwork is for your own

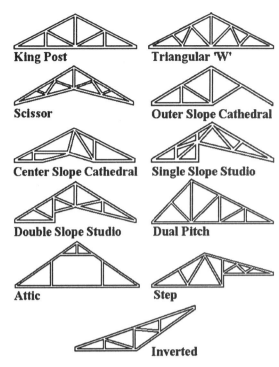

Figure 12-37. Different truss types.

protection against poor workmanship or poor lumber quality causing potential truss failure, and is required even though you have already received approval to start the construction.

To illustrate the importance of damaged product, a careless delivery of trusses unfortunately caused one of my clients a week delay in the framing of their house. It had been raining for a few days prior to the delivery date, and the construction site was still muddy. The trusses were to be delivered at 8:30 in the morning, so my client arranged for his father-in-law to wait at the job site to show the supplier where the framer wanted them placed, i.e., at the front of the house where the ground was relatively dry. The father-in-law waited until 10:00, then decided to drive over to a local convenience store to phone the truss supplier. The supplier apologized, and said that the delivery had been delayed for an hour or so, but the driver should have been there and gone. When the father-in-law arrived back at the site, the driver of the delivery truck had somehow driven to the back of the lot, and was proceeding to unload in the muddiest area. Unloading consisted of reversing the truck and

quickly braking so the trusses would slide off the rollers of the flat bed of the truck. The trusses did slide off the truck, but rather than sliding off gently, the metal strap that was holding them together broke and some of the trusses slid into the foundation and through the exterior wall of the house, resulting in considerable breakage.

Luckily, it was witnessed, and the driver of the truck and owner of the company were verbally and colorfully informed of damages and responsibilities. The next day the owner sent one of his sales representatives out to inspect the damage, and take a truss count for replacement. Four days later the new trusses were delivered and the damaged trusses removed. This unfortunate problem, however, cost my client

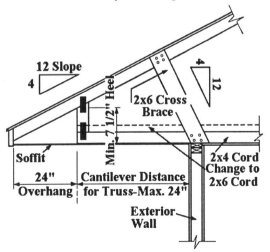

Figure 12-38. A truss cantilever at exterior wall.

five days of delay and interest payments to the bank, and required the framer to rebuild the damaged wall. My client asked me what he should do. I told him to record it in his diary, have his father-in-law immediately write down exactly what he saw, send a letter of intent for nonpayment to the truss supplier with an invoice for property and structural damages, deduct that amount from his estimate, and try to settle out of court. The end result was rather favorable, because the owner of the truss company agreed to pay for all damages, and had the property regraded once the ground had dried up. The only irretrievable thing was the five days lost in construction time, but all construction will incur some delay caused by this type of damage or poor weather.

Note: A cellular phone would have been an invaluable item on this job site.

The truss manufacturer must also supply the framer with a detailed truss drawing showing the layout and location of each individual truss, and their connection to each other. This way there will not be any mistakes with extra trusses left over or trusses not

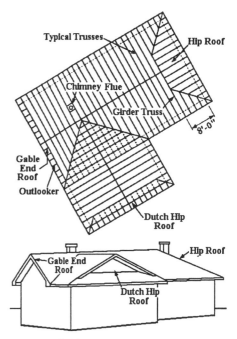

Figure 12-39. Different roof types shown from overhead and as in an elevation view.

delivered (see Figure 12-39). Framers get exasperated with truss manufacturers that do not include the location of *all* valley, gable end, hip jack, girder, king post, and extension trusses in their layout. The designer will usually register only the size and direction of roof rafters and ceiling joists for stick-framed areas that will not be supplied by the truss manufacturer. The framer should provide in the estimate a detailed list of all work to be done, and include all stick framing and gable end "lookout" soffit framing based on the working drawings, and the truss manufacturer should do the same.

For clients to better understand the many truss applications for any one house, ask the designer for a truss chart showing the different possible types of trusses, and have him explain the functions for each truss type. It becomes much easier for the layperson to understand what the room or roof slope will be with a visual presentation. The truss drawings (see Figure 12-37) and the assistance of your designer will help you to better understand and select the most appropriate truss styles for your renovation project.

- **Selecting Proper Roofing Materials**

It is the responsibility of the roofer to protect a home from the sun, snow, wind, dust, and rain via the installation of a weather-tight roof with high durability. It is essential to roof the home as soon as the framer has installed the roof sheathing in order to protect the existing and newly renovated portions of the home, and provide a cover so that further construction can proceed despite inclement weather. Due to the large amount of surface that is usually visible, the roofing material significantly contributes to the attractiveness of the building.

The selection of roofing materials is influenced by such factors as the age and condition of the existing roof, the installation cost, maintenance, durability, and final appearance. Before purchasing there are many good reasons to explore the various types of roofing materials available, and the selection may be influenced by the following:

- Certain roofing materials hold up better in certain climates.
- Due to increasing labor costs, it is very expensive to replace a roof. Choose a material that will last more than 10 years, and preferably one that has a warranty for 20 to 30 years.

- For a house style with a large expanse of sloping roof that is visible from the street, choose a material that will contribute to its overall appearance.

- The budget designated for the exterior finishing materials may affect the selection. Many people cut back on the roof to reduce the budget or balance the costs after choosing an expensive exterior brick finish. Try not to downgrade the finished appearance with a cheap roof.

- The insurance rates increase substantially for roofing products with a high flammability rating, especially if the home's location is a distance from the nearest fire hydrant. You may wish to select a material more fire resistant than wood.

The slope of the existing roof may limit your selection of materials; a low slope requires a heavy-duty material for a weather-tight seal. If the slope of the existing roof is less than the new, consider building it up (as discussed in the truss section) to match the new roof slope (see Figure 12-36); however before building-up, first determine the cost to install low-sloped shingles or a multi-layered membrane roof versus a false roof. Increasing the slope generally increases the final budget. The roofing installer estimates and charges his labor and materials by the "square" (the amount of a given type of material needed to provide 100 square feet of finished roof coverage), but having the

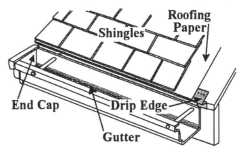

Figure12-40. Location of a metal drip edge at roof overhang.

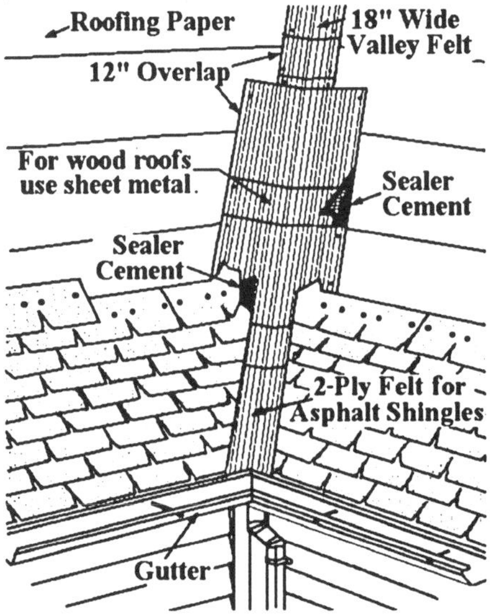

existing material removed and replaced will be at extra cost. The reasons for removing the existing roof may vary, ranging from the exposure of the roof to the elements, differing dye colors of the new and old material, pre-existing roof problems, or the different aging stages of the new and the old roof forcing a staggered maintenance schedule.

In order to make the roof weather tight with all material installations, the contractor must make sure the roof material is installed directly after the framer has completed the sheathing. Before the roofer starts to install the selected material, the plumbing and heating subcontractors must supply their weatherproof materials for venting, furnace flue, flashing, and metal collars. (At this time he will do his plumbing rough-in for the basement and main floor drains, and the venting stacks to the roof.) As this is being done the roofer schedules his material to be delivered and placed directly on the roof the same day. He does this for ease of access when installing, and to protect the materials against theft and water damage.

Figure 12-41. Valley flashing requirements at roof connections.

The second step of the roof preparation is the installation of the metal drip edge. In existing homes it was installed where the roof sheathing protrudes over the fascia board to protect against backwashing of water under the roof sheathing (see Figure 12-40). In the renovated portion of the home these drip edges are manufactured on-site as part of the metal fascia which is slid under the starter strip of roofing paper or polyethylene roof strip. The roofer will staple the roofing paper or underlay to the roof sheathing in overlapping layers to protect against wind-driven rain or snow that might penetrate the roofing material. It also prevents direct contact between the roofing material and resins contained in the roof sheathing.

Areas where two roof-lines connect, called valleys, or where a vertical wall connects with the roof (see Figure 12-41) must be waterproofed with metal flashing. These are the least protected areas of the roof, and moisture driven by wind will gradually work its way into the roof cavity, causing dryrot and structural failure if the cavity is not caulked and flashed properly. Galvanized metal flashing being a nonporous material is installed in these areas to direct water away from areas of the roof affected by accumulations of water, snow, and ice. The roof is then ready for installation of the selected material.

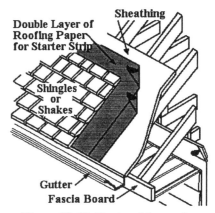

Figure 12-42. Starter strip overlap and application at overhang.

Asphalt shingles are the most common roofing material used by contractors for several reasons. They come in a variety of colors; provide a good weatherproof seal; are easy to service; are light weight, which eliminates excessive roof loads; and are the most cost-effective roofing material made. Asphalt shingles do not require any special structural changes to the roof trusses, and require only 3/8 inch roof sheathing for their nailing base.

A 30-pound starter strip of roofing paper is laid over the sheathing material where the overhang and the fascia board meet. A 36-inch starter strip of roofing paper or polyethylene should be (but is not always) used along the eaves followed by a reversed starter strip of full-length shingle laid directly on top of the paper. Both roofing paper/polyethylene and starter strip overhang the roof sheathing at the eaves by 1/4 to 3/8 inch to act as a drip edge for water runoff going into the gutter. A 24-inch roll of roofing paper is lapped over each strip with an 8 to 12 inch stagger as it repeats itself up the roof to the peak (see Figure 12-42). Asphalt shingles are usually packaged in bundles containing 100 square feet of material.

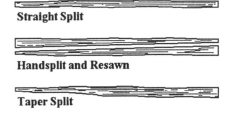

Figure 12-43. Wood shake split options.

Wood shakes have been used for many years in residential construction, and are often called the aristocrat of roofing materials. Wood shakes weather to the soft, mellow, silver grey color after a year's exposure, an appearance desired by many home owners. When properly installed, they also provide a very durable roof potentially outlasting the building structure itself. Shakes can be applied to roofs with a minimum slope of 4 inch rise to a 12 inch run (4/12) and up. The main drawback to wood shakes is the increased cost of the home insurance fire policy because of their flammable nature.

Wood shakes made from red cedar or redwood are highly decay resistant. They are generally cut as straight split, handsplit/resawn, or taper split, then graded as No. 1, No. 2, or No. 3 utility, and available in random

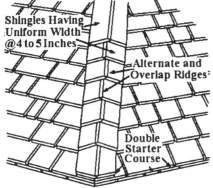

Figure 12-44. Hip and starter course application.

widths, lengths and thicknesses (see Figure 12-43). The ends of the shakes, called butt ends, vary in width and thickness from 1/2 to about 3/4 inch, and taper down to 1/4 inch or less at the opposite end with lengths of 18 or 24 inches. They are packaged in bundles, and four bundles contain sufficient shakes to cover one square (100 sq. ft.) of normal installation. Pine shakes are now added to the selection of roofing materials with their application being the same as cedar.

The application starts much like that for to asphalt shingles, i.e., placing a 36-inch strip of 30-pound roofing felt or polyethylene along the eaves edge. The beginning or starter course of the shakes is doubled. After each subsequent course-length of shake is applied, an

18-inch strip of roofing paper may be applied over the top portion of the shake. This application is not always done if overlapping roofing paper had already been stapled to the roof sheathing. Individual shakes should be spaced from 1/4 to 3/8 inch apart to allow for expansion, and these spaces offset by at least 1-1/2 inches with each previous and adjacent course (see Figure 12-44).

Use rust-resistant nails or staples, preferably a hot-dipped and zinc-coated type, that are long enough for adequate penetration through the roof sheathing. Two nails or staples should be used for each shake, and driven at least one inch from each edge, and about one or two inches above the butt line determined for the next course.

Concrete roofing until recently had been used in only a few locations across North America with the product never gaining general popularity. Concrete roof-tiles are now readily available throughout the United States and Canada at prices competitive with other roofing materials (see Figure 12-45). Concrete roof-tiles conserve energy far better than most roofing materials. Due to the mass of the roofing tile, the sun takes longer to heat it, but then it retains the heat longer, producing temperatures in the attic and the rest of the building that will maintain cooling in the summer and heat in the winter. Based on appearance, low maintenance, and energy efficiency, a building with a concrete-tiled roof has a greater resale value than one with conventional roofing, and a lower fire insurance rate.

Figure 12-45. Ridge, end and face tiles.

Tiles come in a variety of colors and shapes from the traditional Spanish style to ones that look like wood shakes. Compared to other materials which deteriorate and grow weaker with age, concrete actually grows stronger with the passing years. From the standpoint of longevity, roof tile is considered a lifetime roofing material. No one really knows how long concrete roof-tiles will last in North America because they have not been used that long, but in Europe they have been on some buildings since before the turn of the century and are still functioning well.

In areas where a heavy snowload is the norm, the supporting trusses should not be less than a 4/12 slope, and must be engineered to support the additional weight of the tiles plus the local calculation of roof load. The roof sheathing for concrete-tiled roofs need only be 5/16 inch because the tiles require horizontal strapping as a nailing base. The strapping is nailed to the structural roofing trusses over roofing felt laid in both vertical and horizontal directions with a four-inch overlap.

The outlookers for all roof installations are located at the gable ends of the house. They provide the roof overhangs in these areas with the structural strength to support the weight of the roof sheathing, roof finish, fascia boards, and soffits. In

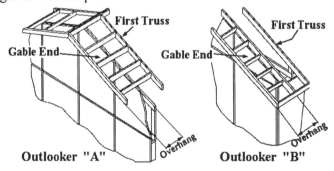

Figure 12-46. Outlooker A directs heavier roof loads to exterior walls. Outlooker B supports typical loads for asphalt roofing.

order to support concrete roof tiles the outlookers must be fastened to the first roof truss after the gable-end framing structure. The gable end, now located at the mid-point of the outlookers, will be able to carry a greater amount of the direct load of the roof tiles (see Figure 12-46). For the lightweight asphalt or wood roof, the outlooker will carry much less actual load, and can therefore be attached directly to the gable-end framing structure.

Note: It is the responsibility of the roofer to remove any debris from the roof and around the house, and place it in the designated area for scraps and garbage when he has completed his contract.

Roof ventilation is the single most important item when it comes to protecting the home's structure against condensation in the walls, roof, floor, and window/door openings. Improper ventilation of the roof and soffit areas in older homes has led to structural failure in portions of the walls and roof. This failure is due to the inability of the existing venting system to properly remove the accumulation of water vapor from appliances such as showers, toilets, clothes washers and dryers, dishwashers, jetted spas, and stoves that add humidity to the house. In coastal areas or during seasons of high humidity, i.e., winter, if the house is also too airtight and not properly vented this accumulated moisture will cause the house to sweat.

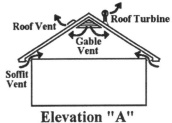

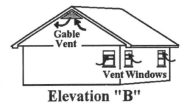

Figure 12-47.
(A) Showing proper ventilation,
(B) Showing poor ventilation.

To better explain this unhealthy environment, compare the house to an airplane which is purposely designed to be airtight and contain a few hundred passengers. Have you ever noticed that after a few hours you become more uncomfortable and irritable? That is due to the moisture which has been building up in the recycled air from the flushing of toilets, from the passengers' bodies and breath, and from the galley cooking. This combination causes the air to become stale and heavy.

Have you ever wondered why there are paper bags by the mushrooms in the grocery store? The moisture contained in the mushrooms must have some means of escape, and putting mushrooms in a plastic bag in the refrigerator will invite spoilage. The air in the plastic bag cannot freely circulate around the mushrooms to remove the evaporating moisture so that after a while that moisture condenses onto the mushrooms causing them to rot. When this happens in a house, it is called dryrot, i.e., wood will rot, mildew will form on the insulation and drywall, and moisture will penetrate the sheathing of the roof, causing the deterioration of the asphalt or wood shingles.

By today's standards, homes built in the 1940s and 1950s were constructed without adequate roof or soffit vents. Instead, contractors relied upon louvres in the gable ends (see Figure 12-47) and double-hung windows which were opened when a crossbreeze was required. When these homes are closed during the winter months and rainy periods, the humidity in the house accumulates in and around areas not allowed to properly ventilate, i.e., attics and exterior wall cavities. Many older homes exhibit mildewed and rotting window sills and frames, and roof areas which have sagged because of accumulated dryrot.

Over the last 20 years home builders have new methods to ensure proper attic and roof ventilation, and

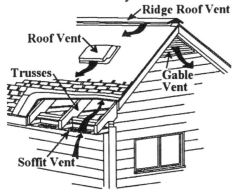

Figure 12-48. Proper venting with different roof-vent units.

there are ventilation standards set out for the better insulated homes now being constructed throughout North America. Your builder, knowing the direction of the prevailing winds, number of trees sheltering the home from the sun, and the proximity of the neighboring houses, should be able to determine the number of roof vents and the style of vent that will provide proper ventilation. There are many types, colors and styles of mechanical and natural venting systems that can be used in new homes (see Figure 12-48).

These vents also allow the home to expel built-up heat and dangerous gases that accumulate during the summer, and draw in cooler outside air to circulate throughout the attic area which keeps the living areas of the house cooler. Venting toxic fumes outside also eliminates any potential combustion that might occur should they mix in hot attic spaces. Proper ventilation is especially important for homes that are exposed to sunlight all day and have been equipped with air-conditioning units.

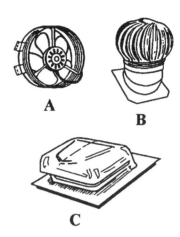

Figure 12-49. (A) Power vent fan, (B) Turbine, (C) Ridge vent.

Gable vents are common and the most widely used venting system throughout the construction industry. Made of metal or wood they are located at the highest point of the gable-end ridge (see Figure 12-48). Depending upon the size of the vents and orientation of the home to the prevailing winds, this venting system can create a very strong crossbreeze which in extreme cases may blow the attic insulation around, causing it to collect in unwanted areas of the attic.

Turbines and fans are becoming very popular as they can quickly exchange the hot attic air and allow the home to maintain a cooler constant temperature throughout the day. They can be electronically powered with thermostats to control the length of time they are on. This will assist in extending the life and boosting the efficiency of any air-conditioning system. The turbines are installed at a high point of a roof slope so that the naturally heated air inside the attic rising to the vertical vent pipe causes the turbine to rotate at a very high speed (see Figure 12-49). This constant high-speed rotation very efficiently sucks the remainder of the heat out of the attic area, and in the cooler evening periods becomes a natural airflow system.

Ridge vents made from plastic or painted metal are positioned at the highest part of the roof peak, and offer an efficient method of natural venting. A continuous roof vent consists of a metal cap which prevents rain from entering and two continuous vent cracks running along both sides, permitting attic air to escape from the house (see Figure 12-49).

Soffit vents in all colors of the rainbow are being installed on new homes. Premanufactured from sheet metal, they are easily installed under the soffit areas and provide a continuous, attractive and effective venting system. They provide natural side-to-side venting of the attic space, but are only effective when roof vents are also used. Hot attic air rising out of the roof vents acts as a suction mechanism to pull cooler air under the soffits through the soffit vents and into the attic. When a power roof vent or turbine is used in conjunction with the soffit vents, they become the most efficient method to exchange air in the attic (see Figure 12-47).

- **Scheduling Concurrent Suppliers and Subtrades**

Before you go into detail about heating, plumbing and electrical in house construction, it is important to establish a schedule so that these trades are not getting in each other's way. Starting at the design phase with the main floor beams, upper floor bearing walls and floor joist layout, try, if possible, to accommodate and separate the heating and plumbing lines. Early planning will help to reduce the heating and plumbing contractors cutting and removing each other's lines, and thereby stop many disputes about who is responsible for fix-ups and unnecessary service calls.

If the designer allocated joists for each subcontractor, or the silent or open-web floor systems are being installed in the addition, always call the plumber in first, i.e., just after the framer and before the roofer so he can complete his rough-in for basement drains and water lines before the basement floor is poured. At that time he will also run the gas line for the furnace, lines for the drains, and plumbing stacks to the roof for the upper floor venting. If the plumber is still using copper lines, have him complete his rough-in before the heating contractor. This way the plumber would have first selection of joist spaces not required by the heating contractor drawings, i.e., joist spaces for the main plenum or the return air ducting. With the introduction of flexible water lines, plumbers can now be scheduled after the heating contractors. Schedule the electrician after the plumbing and heating contractors as their wiring is flexible and can be worked around heating and plumbing lines. This will eliminate any unreported cuts or torched electrical wires.

- **Plumbing Installation**

It is a dirty job, but someone has to do it, and they get paid very well so do not feel too bad about them getting dirty while removing the old water lines and appliances from the home. The decision to install more modern or energy-efficient plumbing fixtures in the home will be based upon the age of the pipes and their appearance, and the ability of the mechanical parts of the fixtures to function properly. Over the years the pipes, welds, and solders might have corroded, or an accumulation of deposits may have reduced the effectiveness of the copper water and cast steel drain lines. Although many renovation and new home projects are using plastic pipes which are simple to install and more economical, cast iron has two major advantages. First, it muffles the transport noise, and secondly is more durable and able to withstand the destructive effects of chemical drain cleaners and mechanical cleaning units like the "Roto-Rooter." Copper hot and cold lines have been replaced by plastic because, unlike copper, plastic does not require special pressure chambers and brackets to muffle or prevent "pipe hammering," a loud, banging noise created by the sudden turning on (or off) of water pressure in the lines.

Note: It is a good idea to have the existing fixtures and other recyclable materials such as hot and cold copper water-lines removed and set aside for resale. They can be advertised in the local newspaper or bargain finder press for cottage or basement renovation projects. The copper lines can be sold to scrap iron dealers or shops that recycle products for construction projects. Monies received can be used for cash payments, or loan reduction on future payments to the suppliers or subtrades, and you will have the satisfaction of helping to keep nondegradable items out of landfill sites.

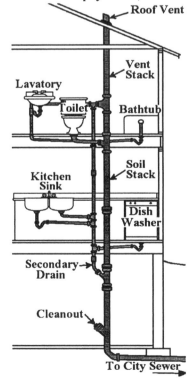

Plastic pipe does not require soldering or threading of the ends in order to attach straight lines to elbows. The plumber works with premanufactured elbows and fittings, easy-to-cut plastic pipes, a can of plastic cement, and a brush. Because of its light weight the plumbing can be done by one person with access to an easy-to-follow, do-it-yourself book on plumbing, some time, and a willingness to get a little dirty. The advantages of plastic over cast iron include its chemical inertness, minimal reaction to corrosive materials, and smooth inside surface, which aids the movement of liquids and materials through the lines, reducing the potential buildup of chemical, iron, or lime deposits and future blockage.

When initially used in home construction, the plastic lines did not have bending capability, and therefore could not be used under heavy loads such as concrete due to constant cracking. With the advent of more flexible and durable plastics, its use has increased. Now more than 98 percent of home construction will use plastic lines throughout. The only major complaint with plastic drain lines is the noise created when water and waste run through the lines. This can be a serious source of irritation and embarrassment if the walls and pipes are improperly insulated for sound, especially

Figure12-50. Drain and
vent requirements.

above the first-floor living areas in multi-level homes.

The plumber is scheduled to be on the job site on several occasions, the initial visit on the same day the footings are completed and formed. He will install the new plastic water and sewer lines just before the footings are poured so there will be no need to excavate or further disturb ground under the footings.

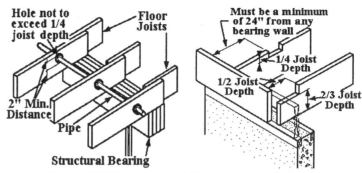

Figure 12-51. Notch and drill requirements for joists.

He will return after the framer has completed the demolition in the existing portion of the home to remove and replace water lines and stacks. Before roof installation and basement sand-delivery for the addition, he will run the rough-in lines for any under-slab sump line(s), city water lines, storm-sewer floor drains, basement and main/upper drains, hot/cold water lines, and all cleanouts with vent stacks to the roof (see Figure 12-50).

When requesting rough-in plumbing for a future basement bathroom, it is important to understand the plumber's estimate and what he will include as a "rough-in." Many plumbers will state in the price quote that they will provide a three or four piece rough-in for a future bathroom, but this does not mean they will include the installation of the actual floor drains for the toilet or tub in the concrete floor. It might mean that they will provide the vertical pipes which will be contained in the walls for the fixtures, but not install the drains. This is not necessarily a false statement because they will provide a "rough-in," however it will be the owner's responsibility and future expense to have the concrete cut and the floor drains installed. To eliminate this confusion, make sure the quotation states that the floor drains for the toilet, sink, and tub/shower will also be installed with a protective cap for the basement fixtures. The actual location of the bathroom fixtures must be registered in the blueprint so the plumber can correctly locate the drain holes. A notation on the blueprints stating the floor drains are to be installed for the basement rough-in would also eliminate this problem.

Most of the plumbing pipes will run parallel to the joists hidden between the joist spaces. Sometimes it is necessary for the plumber to change the direction of some water or drain lines which will result in the drilling and cutting of studs, plates, and/or joists in order to properly line up the pipes. Where cutting and drilling is done in dimensional lumber, the structural strength of that piece of lumber is reduced. In floor joists that are touching a bearing member, these notches or holes should be made only at the top of the joist, and measure in depth not more than one-third the depth of the joist, and in width not more than one-half the depth of the joist. If holes or notches are required at or about midspan of a joist, the hole should again be placed no more than

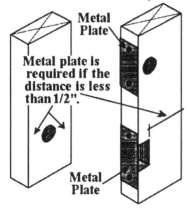

Figure 12-52. Notch and drill requirements for stud walls.

two inches from the top of the joist, and measure no larger than one-quarter the depth of the joist (see Figure 12-51). The tongue and grooved plywood subfloor when glued and screwed properly substantially eliminates the floor joist splitting or deflecting where the notches and holes are made.

All plumbers are aware of these standards, but sometimes get carried away with their chain saw when cutting joists in order to have water/drain lines change direction. If this happens the joist will have to be structurally reinforced with plywood or joist support nailers. The plumber will be able to do simple framing work; however, if floor joists or studs have to be moved or added, the framer must return to do this work. If the depth of a load-bearing stud is reduced by more than one-third, it will require a metal stud-bracket or a 2" x 4" stud nailed perpendicular to it to return the member to its load-bearing structural capacity. Where a non-load bearing wall has been notched or drilled and has only 1-3/4 inch total depth remaining, the stud will require a metal stud-bracket or a 2" x 4" stud nailed perpendicular to it (see Figure 12-52). The plumber should be held responsible for fixing these structural discrepancies, or be charged back on his final draw if the framer is called back to repair these mistakes.

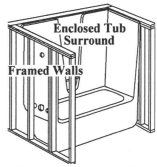

Figure 12-53. A one-piece tub enclosure.

Note: Where any vent stacks, water-line holes, or notches are cut into any top/bottom wall plates or exterior wall studs, they should be sealed with a flexible caulking or scab material to prevent air leakage from the attic, basement or outside walls. Make sure the drywall estimate includes this in his price (see Figure 12-54).

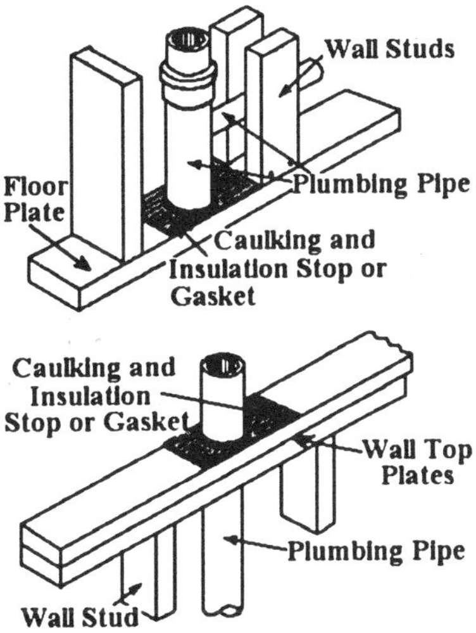

Figure 12-54. Location of potential air leakage around plumbing pipes.

While installing the plumbing lines, the enclosed bathtub, shower, and spa units must be placed (see Figure 12-53). *On or before the day the tubs are placed, the insulator must first insulate and then place the vapor barrier behind the tub and spa.* Once the units are in place, it will be impossible to install the poly.

Note: Protect the spa and tub units by completely covering and wrapping them with the same packing cardboard they arrived in. Make sure the cardboard remains wrapped around the corners so that the subtrades when working around them do not scratch or mark the surfaces. If scratched it is very expensive to match the original color, and refinish the surface to original status.

The plumber is responsible for installing the plywood gusset to which the toilet-floor flange is secured. Be sure to ask the plumber doing the rough-in whether he has verified that the gusset thickness is correct for the subfloor overlay and the selected finished floor thickness. For a linoleum floor a 1/4-inch good-one-side (G1S) plywood overlay should be sufficient; a tile flooring requires a more solid base so a 3/8-inch G1S overlay would be installed. If the plumber has not verified the gusset size, when the finisher installs the overlay and the supplier tries to lay the lino or tile, the gusset thickness could be too thin or thick (see Figure 7-1). The actual plumbing fixtures and accessories are not required until the cabinets, flooring, and finishing have been completed, and these items are delivered and installed at that time. The overall subcontractor scheduling must be coordinated properly.

Most local and federal building codes now require that all under-cabinet, vanity, and toilet water lines have shut-off valves located for easy access in the event of a water leak. Such a valve shuts off the water supply to the unit so an overflow will probably be limited to a quick mop up. These valves also provide the plumber or service person access to the unit for repairs without having to shut off the

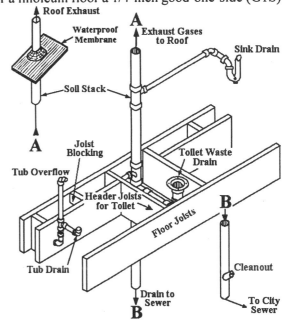

Figure 12-55. Schematic of framing/plumbing requirements for a typical three-piece bathroom.

main water valve and affect the whole house (see Figure 12-56). It is also a very good idea to have the plumber's estimate include shut-off valves in several water lines in the basement close to the main hot and cold feeder panel. These valves can shut off lines in the basement that might weaken with age, and cause costly water damage to the developed basement ceiling, walls and floors. These valves can be turned off for holiday periods, and limit any water damage to the area of the main-feeder water line rather than the entire basement. The main-feeder line is or should be located above or near the sanitary floor drain.

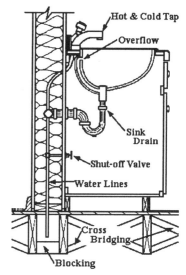

Figure 26-56. Typical location of sink shut-off valve.

The plumber must have direct access to all drains and water lines for servicing and repair; therefore the framer installs the floor joists for all plumbing walls the same way. All lines are hidden in the plumbing walls, and run vertically down through the bottom wall plate and subfloor into the basement floor to the sewer. The building code requires that all bearing and nonbearing walls that run parallel to the joist and are more than four feet in length have double floor joists directly underneath. This, however, is not possible with plumbing walls as the floor joists under the plumbing walls must be separated to allow vertical access for the pipes contained within the plumbing walls (see Figure 12-57). The framer must also allow space for the soil stacks or large pipes

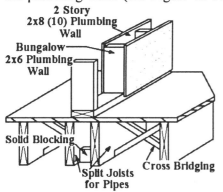

Figure 12-57. Floor joist framing under plumbing walls.

which will be running perpendicular to the washroom plumbing wall and at right angles to the joists. To allow for these stacks the framer will provide headers where necessary to frame out any joists (see Figure 12-55).

The plumber's contract includes installation of the gas lines once the furnaces are installed in the house. However, before he can install the interior gas lines, the outside meter must be installed by the utility company. The meter must be located a specific distance from any opening windows and fresh air intakes. This distance will vary from region to region so contact your utility company to find out their meter location requirements. The exterior siding, stucco, or brick should also be completed. If not, the cladding installers might not be able to install the cladding under the gas pipes and meter attached to the house.

Note: When the utility company is called for a site inspection, they will request that you mark the location of the gas meter with spray paint, and clean and remove all of the lumber and debris away from the working area. If you do not do this to their satisfaction, you will be asked to make an appointment for another inspection, and this will continue until they are satisfied. Lack of compliance could cause several days or weeks of delay depending on when another site inspection can be scheduled. Once the utility company is satisfied, they will make an appointment to install the meter and the exterior gas line in anywhere from 7 to 21 days depending on how heavily they are booked. The plumber will request a city inspection prior to installation of the interior gas lines. Once approved, the plumber's gas fitter will connect the meter to the furnace(s) and water tank or boiler via rigid pipe and flexible hose, and then request a final city inspection.

It is critical to discuss with the plumber the style, brand name, size and color of fixture he has included in your price estimate. Here are some questions to ask to confirm your plumbing needs:

- Will he remove the fixtures and copper lines in the house and set them aside for recycling?

- Are all the fixtures and colors going to match, and are all the washrooms going to have the same fixtures and colors?
- Will there be rough-in plumbing located in the basement? Should it be for a three or four piece bath, and will he include the installation of the floor drains in the quote?
- Does the area require a sump pump? If so, does his quote include intake and exhaust water lines, and installation of the sump pit and pump? Will it have a reverse back-water valve to eliminate back wash?
- Is an in-line back-water valve required for the basement floor drain to prevent backups and flooding?
- Will he provide a sufficient number of cleanouts and where are they located?
- Are there shut-off valves for gas and water lines in the basement?
- What size should the hot water tank(s) be, and should there be more than one?
- If you have two furnaces and are planning a fireplace for future basement development, does that change the size of the gas line into the house? Should you rough-in that fireplace gas line now?
- Where is the best location for the gas line and meter to enter the house? Have him mark the best and most effective meter location.
- How many compartments should the kitchen sink have? Should it have a vegetable sprayer and a garburator, and on what side?
- On which side of the sink should the dishwasher be located?
- Are the showerheads fixed to the wall, or should there be an adjustable telephone showerhead or both?
- Will the molded shower stall or tub include the glass enclosure? Will he supply and install the waterproof membrane for the shower which holds a concrete base to set the shower tiles?
- Will the spa or whirlpool tub have grab bars and sufficient jets correctly located?
- Will he deliver the standard or single-unit fiberglass shower, spa, and tub enclosures prior to the framing of the bathroom walls?
- Will the main floor fireplace, garage space heater, deck barbecue, kitchen appliances, or clothes dryer require a gas line?
- Should there be a small bar sink placed somewhere for children?
- Does the refrigerator require a water line for ice or water?
- Should the laundry area or garage have a sink or tub for clean up?
- Does the laundry room require a floor drain?
- Are taps for the clothes washer included in the estimate?
- If planning for a sprinkler system at a later date, should the provisions for a 3/4 inch water line in the basement be made now?
- How many outside, nonfreeze water taps should there be for proper coverage?
- Should there be a water line to the garage or basement? Should it be hot and cold?
- Are there provisions for future water lines for a steam shower or sauna?
- Will a water softener be required to save on water consumption and minimize cleaning of the humidifier?
- Is a floor drain required in the garage, and will the installation of the pipe and grill be included?
- Will the plumber insulate and caulk around all exterior pipes and holes to stop air infiltration and freeze ups? (See Figure 12-70 on page 184.)

Floor drain specifications:
- Toilets: 3 inches
- Shower stall and clothes washer: 2 inches
- Tub, shower, sinks, and dishwasher: 1-1/2 inches

• Heating Systems

Will the present heating system be adequate or will it be necessary to replace or add another furnace to the existing unit? When a major renovation/addition project is planned, it is generally necessary to increase the size of the furnace to provide adequate heat to the new areas of the house. If the furnace unit is old, has never been upgraded, is just providing sufficient heat, and is not energy efficient, consider replacing it. Installing one high-efficiency furnace will dramatically reduce the heating bills especially if the wall and ceiling insulation is also upgraded. These furnaces are very pricy, so for the same cost consider upgrading the insulation values and installing two mid-efficiency furnaces to create a two-zone heating system. Request that one furnace heat the living environment and the other heat the bedroom areas to produce a more comfortable home with a substantial reduction in heating costs. You can still reduce or increase the amount of warm air entering each room by adjusting the floor vents. When these units are also installed with electronic thermostats, the furnaces can be set to turn on and off at desired times, i.e., heat on when getting ready for work, but heat off after leaving for work. Discuss all heating questions with the designer who will provide drawings which will locate the furnace(s) and accommodate the installation of the main heating plenum, the room ducting, and return air for the basement, main, and upper floor joist cavities.

The heating contractor's first contact with the house is when he drops off the premeasured furnace-flue flashing, chimney collar, and bathroom fan venting for the roofer to install. You will see them nailed to the front wall of the garage or house to be seen easily by the roofer.

Have the heating contractor include in his estimate the supply and installation of the sheet metal cap for any stick-framed chimney chase. This metal cap is made with a slope to shed any water away from the furnace or fireplace flue pipes. The heating contractor is generally responsible for the installation and waterproofing of the storm collar for the furnace flue; the fireplace installer will install the collar for the fireplace flue.

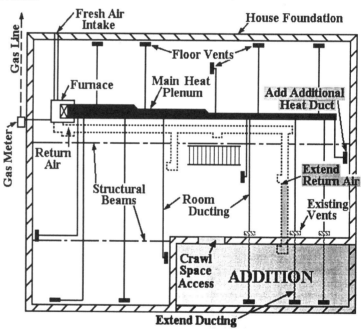

Figure 12-58. Plan view of a typical home heat/return air ducting.

Note: Unless clearly stated the furnace contractor may not supply and install the metal chase cap. He will assume the fireplace contractor is responsible, and the fireplace installer will assume the reverse is true. Also, find out the fireplace flue diameter so that the furnace contractor can cut the correct hole size for a proper fit. As you can see, you must control this overlapping area.

The heating contractor provides the bathroom exhaust vents for the bathroom fans, but there are alternative venting methods. To believe that a house is energy efficient, you first have to be satisfied that as little heat as possible is radiating up fan ducts to the roof. With fewer holes in the roof there is also less chance of water leakage especially when the house gets older. If no heat is rising or no drafts are blowing down through a bathroom fan with a bad damper, there will be less indirect loss of heat through the roof. If no roof vents are sticking out, the roof-lines look cleaner, and you save about 15 dollars worth of sheet metal and a few dollars in the heating contract. How is this done? Very simply. Have the heating trades reroute the flexible fan vent to the soffits. This way the exhaust air blows out the soffit, and any outside wind is stopped by the soffit before it hits the vent. This will reduce the amount of heat escaping as the ducts are positioned horizontally, not vertically, and cool wind blowing into the bathroom is virtually eliminated.

The heating contractor should supply and install any sheet metal work or venting ducts required for items such as the cooktop fan, laundry dryer, and hot water tank.

All types of heating systems can be safely and easily installed in a wood-framed house. There are, however, certain fire separation devices that have to be used, and clearances that must be maintained between parts of the heating system and combustible wood materials. The heating contractor will know these building regulations, but for safety's sake, request that the city building inspector check these areas of concern after the heating contractor has completed putting in the furnace flue, and prior to installation of the insulation. When doing visual inspections, there should be a minimum two-inch clearance provided by metal spacers, shields or strapping between any flammable material and hot surfaces.

Forced air heating:

A good heating contractor should be able to supply a B.T.U. loss calculation and a schematic drawing of the heating and return-air ducts for your house, but get it in writing when you accept the estimate. This B.T.U. loss calculation and schematic drawing is required by some financial institutions as part of their mortgage package and should be kept as a record for the house (see Figure 12-58). It will also tell you that the heating contractor knows how to read the blueprints, and is up-to-date with his heating systems.

Note: When calculating the heating specifications, have the subcontractor make allowances for future basement development by running ducts to the windows for each room that will require heat. Until the basement is fully developed the loss of heat through these ducts can be reduced by closing off the dampers located inside and adjacent to the main plenum. Also make sure the heating contractor includes the basement dampers in his estimate.

When reviewing the schematic drawing with your heating contractor, make sure that return-air ducts are provided for all hallways and rooms. Return-air ducts are not required in areas where people do not spend much time, such as bedroom walk-in closets, bathrooms, and storage closets. These areas are always considered when calculating the total return-air requirements for adjacent rooms or halls (see Figure 12-59).

Whether heating with oil or natural gas, the energy efficiency of furnaces will vary from low to mid to high. The more efficient the furnace, the more complicated and the more expensive it will be. Mid-efficiency furnaces with electronic ignitions are the most common, more economical, and rated from 64 to 68 percent efficient. These furnaces require a vertical, metal chimney flue to exhaust the heat and furnace gases to the roof. These metal flues become very hot, and must be separated by at

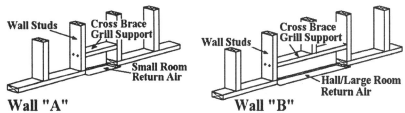

Figure 12-59. Return air wall framing requirements.
(A) - Small room.   (B) - Large room.

least two inches from any wood structure by using a sheet metal flue shield. These shields should be installed by the heating contractor during instal-lation of the furnace ducting, and prior to installation of the wall insulation and vapor barrier (see Figure 12-60).

The high-efficiency furnaces, which can be from 96 to 98 percent efficient when located by an outside wall, require only a side-vent system to exhaust the furnace gases. These two or three inch exhaust pipes are made of a heat-resistant plastic and will not interfere with any house floor space. One 120,000 B.T.U. high-efficiency furnace will heat an average 1,200 to 1,700 square foot house without any problems. However, this creates a single control or zone which heats the entire house at the same time. In order to best divide the heat equally throughout the house, the furnace needs to be centrally located; however, this is not always possible depending on planned basement development (see Figure 12-58). To accommodate for different family lifestyles, heat in a room can be reduced or increased by adjusting the floor vents. After living in a house for one year, you will know which rooms to adjust, and how much to reduce or increase the venting.

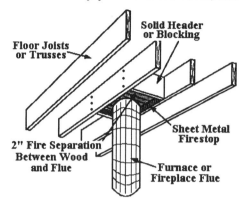

There are a few convenient options to consider installing on the furnace to reduce ongoing maintenance functions. Most furnaces come equipped with small, inadequate humidifier units, which have to be upgraded in order to allow for sufficient humidity in the house.

Figure 12-60. Location of the metal flue shield at floor joist or roof truss area.

The most common upgrade is to the drum humidifier which will provide sufficient humidity, but has to be maintained every six months by dismantling and cleaning the sponge rotation drum. The buildup of mineral deposits left by chemicals added to the water must be routinely removed as too much residue will strain the motor, causing burn out. Many home owners are selecting the more expensive but efficient drip humidifier which supplies humidity directly into the house via a constant water drip into the main heating plenum. Maintenance will depend on the degree of mineral deposit buildup in the plenum from the hard water. With all humidifiers almost all the mineral deposits are eliminated with the installation of a water softener.

Another good option designed to keep down dust, particularly for people with allergies to animal fur or pollen, is an electronic dust zapper. This unit, when added to the furnace, electrically zaps dust particles that are circulating in the air, or brought into the house via the furnace fresh air intake or open doors.

A garage space heater, if required, can be hung about 12 inches below the ceiling at the back of the garage, and faces the front garage doors. This direction is selected to prevent overheating the fire-rated wall separating the garage and the house. Space heaters are manufactured in several sizes varying from a 40,000 B.T.U. unit suitable for a well-insulated, double garage to a 75,000 B.T.U. unit capable of heating a well-insulated, triple car garage. There are other sizes available, and the selection will depend on the type of work you will be doing in the garage. Discuss this with the heating contractor so he can best determine your heating requirements. He will install the unit heater and its vent flue prior to the plumber connecting the gas line.

Note: The framer, when on-site, cuts any holes for vents that go to an outside wall. Have him cut the hole as close as possible to the duct size as indicated by the heating contractor. Once the vents are installed, the heating contractor will seal around the vent perimeter with insulation and caulking to eliminate potential air leaks or rodent entry.

Hot water heating:

This heating system has been around for many years, but only recently have sufficient changes been made for it to be more affordable and practical. The basic principle of heating water and sending the heated water through pipes remains the same; however, the use of old steel wall radiators is outdated. The most common is the under-the-window, low profile baseboard style. This system provides good outside wall coverage and is generally favored because it allows for in-front furniture placement. This baseboard style may run the full length of a wall where a window is located, and stands about six to eight inches high. The water is transported in copper piping, and the heating coils are often made with copper or aluminum for proper, even heat distribution (see Figure 12-61).

The most modern and efficient hot-water heating system uses flexible plastic tubing capable of handling the necessary hot water temperature to heat the total floor area of a room with each individual room having its own zone control. These flexible tubes can also be placed within concrete floors, or under wood-floor structures by having them run parallel along the floor joists and secured with brackets to the underside of the subfloor. This will provide sufficient heat to warm the floor, and keep the radiant water temperature comfortable to the touch without

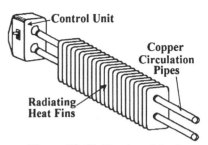

Figure 12-61. Baseboard heat distribution coils.

causing damage to any adjoining wood materials. A separate ducting system for air circulation will be required to eliminate high humidity levels and the subsequent condensation on windows resulting from radiant heat. Hot-water heating systems are initially more expensive to install, but are very energy efficient. They will justify themselves with cheaper monthly heating bills, and provide your family with years of comfort.

Hot water/forced air heating:

A hot-water heating system can be combined with a forced air system to bring the benefits of both heating systems together. Hot water is circulated in coils contained within the boiler, and air is blown over the coils, heated, and then sent through a duct system to each individual room similar to the forced air system. The design of the heating system allows each room to have its own thermostat, therefore letting each family member control their own living environment.

Electrical heating:

Since electrical wires are easily hidden behind stud walls and under floor joists, the planning and design specifications for electrical heating systems are negligible compared to that of forced air and hot water heating. Electrical heating units are located around the perimeter walls of rooms and under the windows to allow heat to radiate evenly throughout the rooms using convection principles. Because the heating units are mounted against the inside walls, there is no need for cutting and blocking the floor joists and wall studs. The more energy-efficient houses require an additional source of fresh air to the rooms using a separate ducting system. This added air helps to eliminate the condensation usually created by slow, electrical radiant convection.

Electrical heating in areas where natural gas and oil are abundant is not economical, but where it is too expensive to run underground gas lines, electrical heating is usually the only alternative system. An electrical heating system combined with a forced air system will bring the benefits of both systems together. The air is heated when blown over hot coils, then circulated through a duct system similar to a forced air system. The design of this system allows each room to have its own thermostat.

● **Lighting Solutions**

There are three important considerations when selecting lighting: decor, energy costs and lighting needs. Good lighting brings a room to life. Lighting systems should provide a visually comfortable and safe level of light for the family's activities, and accentuate the elements of your decor using general lighting, local lighting, and accent lighting techniques.

General lighting encompasses the total light available in a room which must be sufficient to ensure safety and allow the performance of simple tasks. It must minimize eye fatigue by reducing the contrasts between selective lighting and all-around lighting. In order to adequately light an entire area, space recessed fixtures evenly so that the distance between them is not more than the distance from the top of the work area to the ceiling. Around the room perimeter fixtures should not be more than 36 inches away from the walls, or 18 inches away from the edge of any furniture placed against the walls. Recessed fixtures use a substantial amount of bulb wattage which can be minimized by using sliding dimmer switches to save energy, extend the bulb life, and allow adjusted lighting levels in the room for various occasions.

Local lighting is provided by lamps or small fixtures. Local lighting raises the level of the room's general lighting requirements to fill specific needs for selected areas, eg., a reading lamp next to a bed.

Accent lighting focuses on an interesting object in a room and enhances the colors in the furniture and artwork, or the texture of the walls themselves. Tracklights, potlights, and eyeball lights are examples of lighting used to gain this effect.

The balance of these three types of lighting, their interaction with natural light, and the selection of fixtures and lamps determine the total effect of any lighting system. Efficient and effective lighting requires careful planning. In order to achieve this, make a daytime and nighttime inventory of all the rooms' available natural lighting, identify both day and nighttime activities in each room, and then select the lighting required for visual comfort. The lighting sales representative should be able to assist with lighting selections given the positioning of the house on the lot and relation to the north/south sun exposures.

Task lighting is the amount of lighting required to comfortably perform specific activities, such as cooking, reading, sewing, shaving, make-up application, studying, and hobbies, to prevent eye strain and accidents. Direct the light to the applicable work, play and study areas, and install fixtures to the sides or back edge of work surfaces to avoid shadows or glaring reflections.

Bedrooms. Each bedroom can be a study, sewing room, television room, sickroom, or games room. Plan for adequate lighting for seeing in drawers and closets. For reading in bed, consider a "hanging lamp" which saves table space, tracklights, or wall lights. Young children often play, study, or read at a desk, on the bed, or on the floor of their bedrooms. These areas therefore need high-level lighting.

Kitchens. Fixtures should be located directly over kitchen work areas to avoid shadows on the work surface. Mount fixtures as close to the center of the sink or island as possible. Dropped fluorescent island or complete sunshine ceiling units are used for high-level, nonglare lighting. For work areas florescent lighting under the front edge of the upper cabinets is effective and economical.

Living/family areas. Many designers and custom home builders favor recessed lighting for the look of clean, contemporary ceilings, but will use it with traditional furnishings too. Recessed fixtures are especially useful for low-ceiling areas, such as basement recreation rooms. There are many styles and sizes of recessed fixtures available. The open potlight generally gives the most illumination; eyeballs project below the ceiling line and can be directed at any area or object.

Lighting can be an important part of your decorating scheme. For example, use potlights or eyeball lights to make a small room seem larger by accenting the walls with light. Use dimmer controls to make a large room seem cozier, or softly light a conversation area. Use eyeballs to dramatize the texture of brick, stone, wood and draperies, or spotlight bookshelves, sculpture, prize prints and wall hangings. Choose potlights or eyeballs according to the style, wattage and the area or space to be lit. Eyeballs tend to give a reflective lighting effect at the ceiling line which can be reduced by either placing the eyeballs closer together, or requesting a non-reflecting inner baffle with the trim kit selected.

To accent the dimensions of textured walls and draperies, install recessed fixtures closer to the wall; to mininize reflected glare from glass covered artwork, install an adjustable eyeball slightly to the side of the picture. Adjustable eyeballs are also excellent for lighting sculpture and plants. These objects are often best displayed with back, side or front lighting rather than direct overhead fixtures (see Figure 12-62).

Built-in lighting is expensive, which may make it too costly and impractical. The effect of built-in eyeballs and potlights can be simulated with spotlights attached to tracks mounted on walls or ceilings. A track light system can have different styles, and any number of lights that swivel at selected angles for either general illumination or spotlighting specific areas or objects. Create interesting effects by using different types of bulbs on two or more tracks set in a parallel, perpendicular, U-shape, or rectangular arrangement on the ceiling. The new halogen bulbs available for tracklight units can also create a very pleasing visual effect and design on their own through the selection of different styles and types of tracklight cannisters.

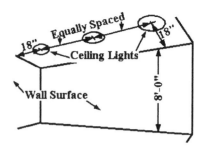

Figure 12-62. Location of some ceiling pot/eyeball lights.

Decorative lighting is usually provided by chandeliers as the centerpiece of an area, and its size will depend on the ceiling height and wall width of that particular area. In a dining area the chandelier should be approximately 12 inches smaller than the width of the table. The bottom of the chandelier should be about 30 to 36 inches above the table for proper lighting and placement out of the direct line of vision when seated. For a chandelier centered in an open foyer the bottom of the chandelier should not be less than seven feet from the floor. Ask the lighting supplier for assistance when selecting these items.

Bath and vanity areas. Broadway lighting is one of the many ways to beautify the bath or vanity. It can be mounted individually, horizontally, vertically or joined together around a mirror as seen in dressing rooms. Broadway lighting strips have knockouts at the ends so they can be connected in a continuous run, and have as few as 3 or as many as 12 lights. This lighting system uses more wattage, and creates more heat as the number of lights increases. It is therefore the least energy efficient. Overhead fluorescent strips are more economical, but require a valance or cover to hide their appearance.

• **Saving Energy Dollars**

Although lighting accounts for only 15 to 25 percent of the electricity used in a home, this energy cost can be reduced substantially. One way is by using fluorescent lighting which gives more light per watt of electricity than incandescent bulbs, i.e., the same amount of light but using up to 65 percent less energy (see below). A ceiling fixture that uses two 60 watt bulbs can be replaced with two 20 watt fluorescent tubes. The saving is about 80 watts for approximately the same amount of light. To further illustrate this point:

Figure 12-63. A Wattage Comparison.

Incandescent	VS	Fluorescent
4 - 40 watt light bulbs	=	2 - 20 watt fluorescent tubes
2 - 60 watt light bulbs	=	2 - 20 watt fluorescent tubes
1 - 1000 watt light bulbs	=	2 - 20 watt fluorescent tubes
3 - 60 watt light bulbs	=	4 - 20 watt fluorescent tubes
2 - 75 watt light bulbs	=	4 - 20 watt fluorescent tubes

In addition to saving energy, fluorescent bulbs are excellent in areas where a high level of evenly distributed light is required such as the kitchen, hobby room, workshop, laundry and bathroom.

Other ways to conserve energy:

✓ Turn off lights when not in use.

✓ Put lights only where needed.

✓ Use dimmers to reduce the amount of electricity used and to extend the life of bulbs.

✓ Finish the house with light-colored, flat latex paint on the walls and ceilings.

✓ Keep all bulbs dust-free. Dust and dirt can reduce the efficiency of fixtures up to 25 percent.

✓ Replace old incandescent 60 watt bulbs with 40 watt energy-efficient fluorescent bulbs. The initial replacement cost is expensive, but they pay for themselves within the first eight months.

✓ Clean dust and insects from fluorescent plastic diffusers regularly and replace burnt-out bulbs.

● **Security and Low Voltage Lighting**

Safety and security are important reasons for installing good exterior lighting. Police recommend outdoor lighting and lighting with motion sensors as security measures that can easily be combined with interior lights on automatic timers.

The use of low voltage lighting in conjunction with exterior flood or walkway lights will add to the night appearance and security of the house, and save energy dollars. Floodlights or area lighting that shine on a shrub or the house can create an impressive nighttime display of shape, color, and shadow around the entrance or walkway. Low voltage outdoor lighting allows guests to see where they are walking, and family members to see who is coming to the door at night. These lighting units can be on ground level, or set on various lengths of poles with a main, light-sensitive sensor mounted on or by the house to turn the lighting on at dusk and off at dawn. Many of the low voltage systems use 12 volt light bulbs, similar to the ones used in automobile brake lights, which cost less to replace than floodlights or wall-mounted walkway lighting. During the warmer weather, cost-effective outdoor lighting can extend the amount of time spent outdoors in the evening.

● **Electrical Installation**

Most homes have an insufficient number of switches, plugs, and lights which are usually in the most inconvenient or inaccessible locations. Minimum requirements in the building code allowed the builder to provide only one electrical outlet per 12 lineal feet of wall distance; therefore, the renovation project will allow for correction of these deficiencies by installing additional plugs, switches, and lights where needed. In order for additional outlets to be accepted into the home's power supply, the electrician will add another electrical panel or replace the existing with a panel that has sufficient circuits.

For some years the building code allowed aluminum wiring in residential construction. Many of these homes are now not-to-code, and are considered fire traps. If an owner renovates and finds this wiring he is usually required to have it removed and replaced with copper wiring; where the appliances require a higher amperage line, as for stoves, ovens, and cooktops, the wiring must be replaced with an approved wire cable. Because this can be a costly item, have the electrician inspect the house prior to giving an estimate, and include the removal and replacement of the wire in his estimate so there will be no surprises half way through the renovation project.

The electrician is first called to remove the existing panel and wiring that is not-to-code and during this renovation phase the power is disconnected. If he does not have portable power generators, or approved access to a neighbor's outside plug, he will be required to supply temporary power from the meter to the house. This can usually be accomplished within a few hours; however, prior to connecting the temporary power from the meter, he must have the underground or above-ground power line and meter inspected by the city. Underground cable installation can be done before or after backfilling the foundation, and some electrical contractors are able to supply the trenching and laying of underground service if requested. If not, get another contractor to supply these services, and the electrician should be able to supply some names. If the meter and the subfloor are installed at this point of the construction, the electrician can install the main electrical panel. Make sure that the location of the main panel is clearly marked on the blueprints, and accurately defined with paint sprayed on the house wall to ensure the panel is not installed in an area blocking future development.

The electrical wiring is usually started after strapping/building out the existing walls and the house is watertight, i.e., the roof completed, windows installed, and plumbing and heating rough-in completed. This phase of wiring, usually called rough-in, includes drilling holes in the studs for the wires, and connecting the wires to electrical boxes for wall switches and plugs, and octagonal boxes in walls or ceilings for light fixtures. The design and installation requirements are usually controlled by the local or federal building codes, and are inspected by the city building inspector to ensure compliance with the electrical codes.

Because the location of switches, plugs, and lights is so important, discuss with the designer in detail all the planned locations of the appliances, televisions, telephones, table lamps, etc. As new products become available and existing products have more features added to them, it will be necessary to consider alternatives for the electrical design of your house. Home computers, portable rechargeable vacuums, and built-in vacuum power heads all require special considerations. Computers require several wall plugs in close proximity to each other to accommodate the computer terminal, printer, and modems without an extension power bar. A rechargeable vacuum on a wall location requires a wall plug of its own to provide constant recharging after use. Power heads for built-in vacuum systems require a power source within a few inches of the suction vent.

To determine the electrical requirements for your home, walk through the house with the designer room by room and visualize living in it day to day. Identify where switches should be located in conjunction to door swings, and picture furniture arrangements to determine the best locations for wall plugs and ceiling light fixtures. Will some switches control any outside security lighting or interior wall plugs for table or floor lamps? Should there be three or four way switches located in different areas of the house controlling one light fixture? An example of a "multiple switch" is a single hall ceiling-light which is controlled by a centrally located wall switch and another switch located near an exit door. This three-way switch can be converted to a four-way simply by placing another switch somewhere else that controls that same hall light. All stairways should be controlled by three-way switches. Also, discuss with your electrician the color and style of switch and plug plates as they should match or coordinate with the interior color selections.

Electrical requirements for special lighting, such as exterior Christmas lighting, should be considered at the design phase. To string lights on the eavestrough, consider installing soffit plugs at several corners of the house with interior control switches. Special waterproof plugs for exterior spotlights and tree lights can also be installed and controlled from inside the house. The designer can make recommendations for their locations so that all electrical requirements are incorporated into the design, and registered on the blueprints with notations. These details will help to ensure an all-inclusive estimate by the electrical contractor. Consider a dimmer switch to control the amount of light required for different occasions. If you are considering ceiling fans in some rooms, ask the electrician to install a rheostat to control the low, medium, and high speeds of the fan. This eliminates pulling the fan's chain each time the speed is changed, or dragging out the ladder if the fan is located on a high ceiling.

Once the number of switches, plugs, and lights has been determined, make sure that the electrician has provided a large enough service panel with sufficient breakers for present needs as well as additional empty breakers for future basement development or renovations. This prevents later having to add an expensive and poorly located sub-panel. It is illegal to double up on any existing breakers: this practice will potentially overload that circuit and possibly cause a fire. Most underground city services are capable of providing a 100 amp/240 volt service to the house permitting a 48 to 64 circuit main panel which will handle all present and future electrical needs. Locate it in the basement, garage, or on the main floor based on ease of access. Consider splitting the panels by placing the main panel of 48 circuits in the basement, and a secondary sub-panel of 32 circuits in the garage or on the main floor. The sub-panel could contain the heavy-duty circuits, such as range, washer, dryer, spa tub pump, cooktop, etc., and provide easier access to a circuit which needs resetting.

As discussed earlier, when scheduling concurrent suppliers and subtrades try to regulate when the electrician, plumber, and heating contractor are in the house as they work in the same areas of the basement and will require their own spaces to install their equipment. One way to reduce potential conflict and damage to the electrical system caused when other subtrades cut, burn, or pull out lines is to have the electrical contractor feed his wiring through the roof area of the home. For bungalows and upper stories of multi-level homes he will need to pull more wire through; however, there they will be protected, which will reduce the number of times he must return to repair the wiring. This is also a perfect location for wiring the security system. Since most of the motion detectors and door pads are located close to the ceiling, it is logical for the wiring to be run there. The only problem encountered with running all the electrical lines in the attic space is when there is an intercom system. When the electrical lines of the intercom run parallel to or overlap too many other wires, the electromagnetic force of the lines will cause static on the intercom speakers. Have the electrician run the intercom lines separate from the house wiring and security systems.

Select from the following information the list of detailed specifications to be included in the electrician's estimate for the house.

- Remove and replace all wiring that is not approved by the present building code.
- Total number of light, plug and switch outlets: ___ .
- Underground service provided: No. of amps ___ and No. of volts ___ .
- Wiring for a 220 volt plug in the garage for power tools.
- Underground trenching and wiring if needed.
- Number of circuits in the main panel to be 48 or 64. Specify location.
- Installation of a sub-panel in the garage or on main floor. Specify size.
- Wire, install the oven, and connect the power supply to the oven(s) (30 amp/240 volt).
- Wire, install the cooktop, and connect the power supply to the built-in cooktop (30 amp/240 volt).
- Install dryer plug (30 amp/240 volt).
- Wire and connect furnace(s).
- Wire and connect heat exchanger.
- Wire and connect humidifier(s)/dehumidifiers(s).
- Supply, wire, and install smoke detector(s).
- Wire and connect dishwasher, garburator, and trash compactor.
- Wiring for water meter and gas meter.
- Supply and install perimeter motion sensor lights with interior control switches.
- Wiring for telephone outlets with jacks in the kitchen, living areas, bedrooms, basement, and garage.
- Wiring for cable television outlets complete with jacks.
- Supply power for intercom.
- Supply power and install doorbell chime.
- Wiring for garage door opener(s) and push-buttons.
- Install exterior ground-fault-protected waterproof plugs/plates.
- Supply, wire, and connect bathroom fan(s) No. _____ .
- Supply all ground-fault-protected bathroom plugs.

- Wire and connect spa tub pump (15 amp/120 volt).
- Wire and connect hot tub and pump switches, steam shower unit, sauna heater, etc.
- Install plug for main vacuum supply unit.
- Set thermostats and connect power to attic ventilation fans.
- Supply and install standard (color) plugs and switches.
- Supply and install sliding dimmer switches - # single pole and # three-way sliding dimmer switches.
- Wire and install front-yard light standard, trenching included (light unit supplied by owner).
- Wiring for garage space-heater unit.
- Hang # owner-supplied ceiling fans, and supply and install # rheostats.
- Wire and connect heat-circulating fan built into fireplace.
- Wire and connect water-circulating pumps for boiler (15 amp/220 volt).
- Supply and install # insulated potlight cans.
- Supply and install # standard potlight cans.
- Supply and install # - ? watt (color) open potlight trims.
- Supply and install # - ? watt (color) eyeball trims.
- Supply and install # heatlamp cans complete with trim.
- Build # attic boxes around heatlamps or as per code.
- Install sump pump plug.
- Supply and install # - # tube fluorescent trim/wrap units.
- Supply and install # - under cabinet, # tube, # foot, side-mounted fluorescent(s).
- Supply and install # - # tube, # foot fluorescent strips for sunshine ceiling.
- Supply and install 15 amp/220 volt plug(s) in garage.
- Supply and install poly vapor hats around electrical outlets on all outside walls and cold ceilings.
- Hang and assemble all fixtures.

It is important to provide as much information as possible to the electrician when selecting electrical needs. When the electrician is ready, have the built-in ovens, cooktop and dishwasher delivered to the job site a.s.a.p. so they can be wired and installed into their positions. The rough openings in the kitchen countertop, shelves, floor, and cabinet base for the cooktop and down draft venting are precut by the kitchen cabinet installer. Supply the cabinet installer with the correct measurements or templates to properly cut the correct rough opening size. The dishwasher's flexible water lines are connected by the plumber before the electrician connects the power; therefore, the plumber must allow sufficient play in the lines for the electrician to move the dishwasher in and out.

Depending upon the electrical contractor, you can also get an estimate for wiring and installing vacuum, intercom, and security systems. However, get additional estimates from other suppliers who deal specifically with these products for a price comparison as they might be cheaper.

• Built-in Vacuum Systems

Many homes built before the 1970s did not have central vacuum systems installed because of cost, incomplete technology, and unavailability of the plastic tubing now used to feed the lint and dirt through to the cannister. Now more than 80 percent of the homes built today will have the system installed or roughed in.

The vacuum installer will require access to the house after the heating and plumbing contractors have completed their rough-ins, but prior to the electrician running his rough-in lines. The vacuum system selected will vary depending on the size/length of hose, number of service inlet locations, total length of the main collection lines, and the options available with the unit.

When collecting estimates for the system ask the following questions:

1) Are there quick release fasteners for easy access to the collection cannister containing the dust?

2) Is there an automatic shut-off switch in case of overheating?

3) Does the vacuum option include service inlets in the basement, garage, or workshop?

4) Will the proposed hose length be sufficient to reach all house corners from the selected inlets on the plans without moving furniture, over-stretching the hose line or loosening the inlet panels?

5) Is the motor's suction strong enough to pick up soil and dirt from deep in the pile of the carpet using either the standard or the power vacuum head?

Discuss and confirm the cannister and service inlet locations shown on the working drawings with the supplier prior to installing the system. You must first know where the cannister is to be placed so that the installer can run his main collection line to it, and the electrician can install the power plug. If located in the basement will it interfere with any future development, or be too noisy to carry on a conversation? Most importantly will there be easy access for cleaning and servicing? Because of these potential problems, many home builders suggest that it be located in the garage, where the common wall between the house the garage acts as a noise buffer during operation. The garage location is usually more accessible for servicing, and closer to the garbage area for emptying.

After installation of the cannister the lightweight plastic pipes are installed between the floor joists from all the separate service inlet locations, and connected to a main collection line running alongside a structural basement beam or bearing wall. Power heads are usually considered an option; however, in order for deep seated dirt to be removed the power head may be necessary. Finally, the color of the face plate for each service area should match or complement the color of the face plates for the switches and wall plugs.

- **Selecting the Intercom System**

The technology for intercom speakers has not changed all that much in the last ten years, but the options and features have advanced with the times. In addition to the usual AM and FM radio, and the interaction between the rooms, they can also include a tape cassette, CD laser disk, hands-free operation, and on/off timer features. If money is no object, consider having a television monitor for the front door, but remember, the more features and speaker controls the greater the expense involved.

Rough-in for the intercom system can be done at the same time the vacuum and security systems are being installed because the electrician can ensure none of the electrical lines will interfere with the intercom speaker wiring. Once again the locations of each individual speaker and main control panel are pre-determined by the home owner and shown on the working drawings by the designer. When discussing the placement of the speakers and master control panel, be sure that you have considered where the electrical switches, plugs, and most importantly furniture will be located in each room.

The location of the master panel should be central to the house, in an area of frequent use by most of the family, and not visible from the front door. When locating the speakers, avoid having the wiring for speakers, switches, and wall plugs on the same wall within four feet of each other, and/or on the back side of the opposing wall. Such wiring will cause static in the lines and result in poor quality sound. Sometimes, optimum spacing is not always possible so try to separate them as far as possible on different walls.

Consider the following locations for individual intercom units: bedrooms, bathrooms, dining/living room, family room, garage work area, outside deck or patio, basement, laundry room, front door, and office or den areas are all good locations for music and monitoring the front door. If you have considered placing a speaker in a bathroom, review your local building code, or ask the city building inspector for its possible location with respect to any water hazards. You might need an exterior waterproof speaker for this area.

Light switches are usually located as close to the opening side of a doorway as possible with the speaker beside it. Because the studs are framed 16 inches apart, placing the light switches on the closest stud to the door and the speaker on the next closest stud might be locating it too far from the door or too far into the room. You might have to consider placing the speaker on another wall, or above or below the light switch. Depending on the room, locate the speaker where it would be convenient to reach, eg., in a bedroom it could be over an end table, or on an otherwise unusable wall.

- **Security Systems**

A house is the single largest investment that a person or family will make in their lifetime, so it seems appropriate to protect the investment by a good security system. The system selected will depend on the degree of comfort and safety you wish to feel in addition to the locking devices installed on the doors and windows.

Is your neighborhood considered high risk because it is a new subdivision without fences? Does it have poor street lighting, back alleys, or is it just a subdivision which brands itself as "quality pickings" for the break-and-enter types? Do members of your family have regular daily routines, do you go out frequently, or do you have electronic gadgets, jewelry, or limited edition prints? If you answered yes to any or all of the above, then you should consider a security system to protect your property.

The best, noisiest, and least complex, however less economical or maintenance-free protection option, is a dog. The most practical and least expensive electronic security system can be as simple as lamps plugged into timers, and perimeter, motion-sensitive floodlighting; the more high-tech, micro-chip, master panel controlled systems comprised of pressure-sensitive floor plates, glass break and motion detectors, and door contacts depend directly on the allocated budget.

To choose the type of system best suited to you, discuss your fears or concerns with the security sales representative, and review the house blueprints and proposed landscape plans. Try to visualize the potential traffic pattern of the burglar, and protect those areas with the correct type of detector. Take into consideration either the family being away, or someone being alone in the house. Burglars like to select break-in areas that are dark and hidden by a fence, tree, garden shed, or object to avoid being seen. If glass is broken to gain access, the smaller the area of glass the less noise. Consider the following patterns of movement through the house.

1) Basement windows are usually the most accessible, low to the ground, and dark. Basement access muffles noise to the upper floor(s).

2) The basement provides direct access to the upper floor(s) via the stairs.

3) A main floor break-in would probably be in an area that is dark, and hidden by a tree or part of the house. Do any of these areas have easily accessible windows, or French or patio doors with poor locking devices? Check for quick entrance and exit possibilities.

4) Main floor hallways provide direct routes to the rooms with the valuables.

Having identified the areas of concern, the representative will help select and locate the keypads and best sensors. Security keypads are usually located near the door most frequently used by family members such as the mandoor from the garage to the house, back door, or front entry. Another possibility is the master bedroom or bedroom hallway for quick access to arm the security system. All security systems can be installed so that a family member alone in the house can roam about without setting the system off; however, once a secured door is opened the security will be activated, and the sirens will sound.

Security systems and smoke detectors can be directly linked to the local fire and police stations in addition to being monitored by a security company. Monitored systems increase the sense of security when family members are alone at home, or away on business or holidays.

Install the system at the correct time during the construction period to ensure that workers cannot mistakenly disconnect, cut, or cause damage to the wiring. The security installation should be after the electrician has completed his wiring, and just before the insulator/drywaller starts. Or, if you are constrained by budget, many installers will provide the rough-in wiring at a reasonable price, allowing you to complete the system later.

- **Walk-through Inspection**

Before the electrician, vacuum, intercom, and security installers leave the job site, it is a good idea to inspect their work for the following:

- Are the light switches, wall plugs, intercom speakers, master control panel, and vacuum receptacles located correctly and within reach?
- Are there light switches at the top and bottom of the stairwell(s), and is the light properly located for lumination of the stairs?
- Are the wall plugs in the kitchen, laundry room, and bathrooms properly located so the plugs will be immediately adjacent to the appliances used and not covered by the upper/lower cabinets?
- Will the ceiling fixtures be properly centered in the rooms, for example, over the table in the dining room? The breakfast room light should also be positioned over the table center.
- Is there an electrical plug within 18 inches of the hose receptacle for the vacuum power head?
- Will the chosen vacuum hose reach all corners of the rooms, and extend the full length of the stairs?
- Are there poly vapor hats around electrical outlets on all outside walls and cold ceilings?

- **Fireplaces and Energy Efficiency**

The fireplace has to be an item given initial consideration because it must be installed when the framer is on-site. Once the rough opening for the fireplace has been framed, the fireplace supplier will install the unit by bolting it to the floor or platform provided. The installer will measure and set the face of the fireplace flush with what will be the finished face of the drywall. The selected fireplace finish may be flush or protruding from the face of the fireplace, depending on preference, but make sure the fireplace installer has been informed of these distances before he installs the unit permanently in place.

With energy efficiency having such a high priority, fewer masonry fireplaces are being installed these days. A gas or wood-burning, premanufactured, "O" clearance, metal fireplace is the most common choice (see Figure 12-64). There are many options available with these types of fireplaces, however the most common for a wood-burning unit is a gas log-lighter. The plumber can install the gas unit during his rough-in so make sure the unit chosen has a log-lighter capability, and the plumber has included the gas supply line and installation in his estimate. Gas fireplaces come with the gas insert, and need only be connected by the plumber to the gas line. Most fireplaces are considered an extravagance and are not energy efficient at all. They can remove more heat than they put into the room, because they require combustion air to burn, and in doing so draw the interior air from the house up and out the flue. This air loss must be replaced as quickly as it is removed for proper combustion to continue. If the fireplace does not have its own fresh-air supply system, the air will have to be drawn in through cracks around the doors and windows, clothes dryer vents, bathroom or kitchen exhaust vents, and leaks between the house walls and foundations. The air removed by the fireplace is usually at room temperature before it reaches the unit, and many people consider throwing this warm air up the chimney a waste of heat and money. As a consequence, when the fireplace is on, the heating system must work overtime to heat the outside air being drawn into the house.

Many houses are being constructed so airtight that a standard built-in fireplace would not be able to provide sufficient draw-air for the fire to continue burning. This results in a fire that smokes rather than burns, and sends smoke into the room rather than up the flue. To rectify this problem, fireplace manufacturers now may provide the fireplace with its own fresh air intake, and recommend the installation of airtight doors to the face of the fireplace which eliminates the removal of warm air from the house during operation. The fireplace becomes truly energy efficient when circulating fans are installed to take the heat

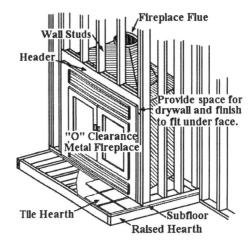

Figure 12-64. Typical framing for a "O" clearance fireplace.

from the super-heated metal walls and throat of the fireplace, and blow it into the room rather than send it up the chimney flue.

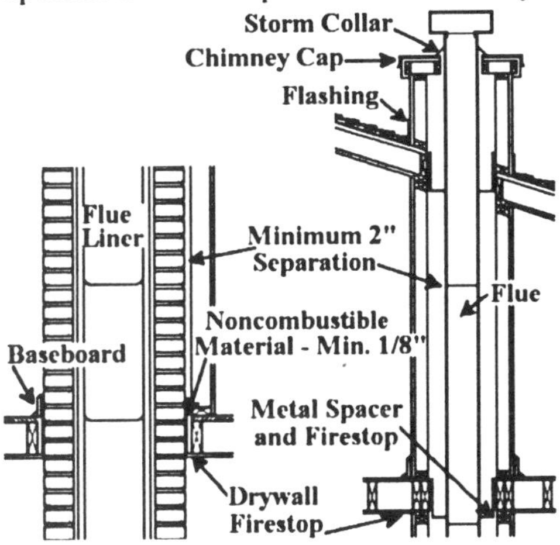

Note: Contact the fireplace installer for the diameter of the fireplace flue. Provide this information to the heating contractor as soon as you order the fireplace to allow sufficient time for the heating contractor to cut the correct size of opening into the sheet-metal chimney chase cap to properly accept the fireplace flue. It is the responsibility of the fireplace installer to connect and seal the fireplace chimney collar after the metal cap has been installed (see Figure 12-65).

Gas or wood-burning fireplaces installed close to the center of the house or room require a vertical, fire-rated chimney flue to the roof for exhaust gases. If a gas fireplace is selected and located on

Figure 12-65. Fire separation and chimney chase framing requirements.

an outside wall or within six feet of an outside wall, a direct-vent fireplace unit can be considered.

The hearth of a wood-burning fireplace is simply a fire precaution against flying sparks, and may be set even with the floor or raised above the floor level. Gas fireplaces do not require a hearth, but usually have one for the cosmetic effect. The front fireplace hearth should extend from 16 to 18 inches out from the finished face

of the fireplace, and is used as a display area or as a comfortable place to sit on chilly winter nights. Confirm with the city building inspector the required hearth extension for your area as local fire regulations may vary.

When planning a fireplace, locate it away from the flow of normal traffic. Placing it on an inside wall will not block an outside view; outside wall placements allow cold air to be conducted into a room (see Figure 12-66). It is a good idea to have at least 42 inches of wall length on either side of the hearth to allow comfortable furniture grouping.

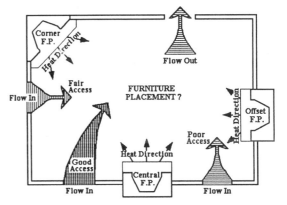

Figure 12-66. Different fireplace locations.

Wood stoves:

People have become so energy conscious in the last ten years that they have forced the fireplace manufacturers to convert the old and traditional cast iron stove into a new technology. These stoves have become visually more appealing with new heat-resistant, glass doors that allow a view of the fire. They are more energy efficient than their former models, and are capable of burning coal, wood chips, gas, or logs. There are many types and sizes of stoves on the market these days, and selection depends on personal heating requirements and tastes.

● **Installing Proper Insulation**

A common renovation project is upgrading the existing insulation to the R values required by present day construction techniques. Insulation is expressed as an "R-value," which is the ability of a material to resist the passage of heat. The greater the R-value of a material, the greater the material's resistance to heat loss. The R-value required in older homes was less due to the cheap cost of heating fuels, however, today's heating costs have substantially increased the need for additional insulating factors.

Increasing the R-value of the existing home is not easily done because the framing requirements of the older home's 2" x 4" walls do not match the 2" x 6" wall standard of today. In order to decide which walls have to be upgraded, first determine where the addition will be attached, if the new wall structure is to be flush (even) with the outside or inside of the existing wall, and how it will be built out. Usually the completed cost will determine whether the framer builds up the inside structure with strapping and adds insulation and new drywall, or straps the exterior wall and adds insulation, sheathing, building paper and finally new exterior cladding (see Figure 12-6). If a window is located on the wall in question, the framer needs to install brick mold to the window frame until it is flush with the plane of the built-up wall.

Over the last decade of increasing energy costs, many home owners decided to increase the insulation values of their existing walls by having urea-formaldehyde foam placed into the wall cavities. Backed by consumer demand, companies and the government rushed to approve the installation of this type of foam for upgrading projects. However, after completing safety tests they found that when burned, urea-formaldehyde gives off toxic gases, and it was quickly banned from residential construction. If your home contains urea-formaldehyde product you may be eligible for some government assistance to remove it especially if it was installed during the period of government approval. Check with the local city engineering department to see if this assistance is available for your area.

Although the insulator and vapor barrier installers are usually the same company, it will be more useful and easier to understand their uniqueness if discussed separately. Think of insulation as a cover or blanket. In order to keep the house comfortable and warm, you must insulate all perimeter walls, attics, floors, inside ceiling joists, and beneath wood or concrete floors exposed to exterior climate changes to prevent heat loss and cold air infiltration. Every area or level of the house is insulated with different amounts or thicknesses of insulation because different areas lose heat at different rates.

Basement:

The greatest outside area of a basement is generally below ground level. Since the earth retains a good percentage of its heat year round, it is necessary to apply insulation to that level of foundation that is affected by the winter cold. Each area in North America has a designated frost level, which is a depth below the surface that is affected by cold, and has a certain amount of winter freezing. Warm climates might have little or no frost, while other areas further north will have deeper frost levels. Basement foundations affected by frost levels must be insulated to stop the cold from radiating through the foundation and perimeter floor-joist cavities into the basement and eventually throughout the house (see Figure 12-67).

Building codes require insulation only to the level of the frost, however this is not practical if you plan on any basement development. Most builders recommend a full-height, framed, frost wall around the interior perimeter of the basement foundation. The framer installs the frost wall, usually a 2" x 4" framed stud wall, spaced approximately 24 inches on center, and checked for a vertical level with sufficient space between the foundation wall and the face of the frost wall to fit the R-12 or R-20 fiberglass insulation (see Figure 12-68). The insulator will then place R-20 or R-32 batt insulation between the floor joists around the perimeter, and R-40 insulation, or R-32 plus the required rigid insulation underneath all cantilevers (see Figure 12-19).

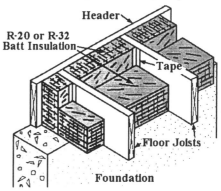

Figure 12-67. Insulation requirements between floor joists.

Note: Make sure the framer provides a perimeter strip of acoustical sealant and vapor barrier under the bottom plate of the frost wall,.or on the basement floor before he lifts and nails the wall in place. Also, while the framer is on-site constructing the frost walls, have him add, brace, replace and/or support any main floor wall studs or floor joists that have dried or twisted. The framer will use a crowbar or slug hammer to remove the bad wall studs, and hammer the exposed nails into the floor or ceiling plates. When installing the new studs the framer will toe-nail the studs into the plates; (see Figure 12-69) any replaced joists must be attached with metal hangers to pass inspection.

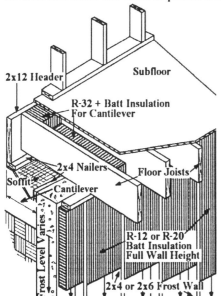

Figure 12-68. Insulation requirements for cantilevers and frost walls.

Main floor:

Insulation of the main floor is very important in maintaining all areas of the house at a comfortable temperature year round. Because this area is totally exposed to the elements, have all perimeter walls, corners, windows, doors and exterior drill holes insulated to eliminate cold air infiltration as much as possible.

When inspecting the electrician's and plumber's rough-in work you may be inclined to think that 50 woodpeckers tried to help but got out of control. There are holes drilled in the exterior and interior wall studs, top and bottom wall plates, exterior plywood sheathing, and through the subfloor of the house. These areas totalled are potentially equal in size to an uninsulated 4" x 3" hole in a wall of the house year round.

All the inaccessible corners of the exterior walls in the house should have been insulated by the framer during the framing stage. The insulator then seals all other potential air leaks in the house with insulation and acoustical sealant to prevent blowing air entering the walls from the attic and basement. This should include the sealing of all holes around electrical wires on interior and exterior stud walls, as well as all holes left by the plumber and electrician in the upper and lower wall plates (see Figure 12-70). This additional labor is usually not included in their estimate, so be prepared to pay an additional charge for a very beneficial option. Air spaces that are too large to be sealed with

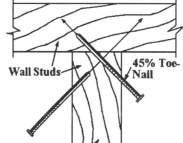

Figure 12-69. Toe-nailing detail.

acoustical caulking, such as oversized holes around the plumbing vent stacks and basement drain lines, should be sealed with a thick rubber gasket supplied and installed by the plumber. If this is unavailable, the insulator can pack the hole with insulation, cut a leftover insulation stop to fit on the face of the wall's top plate which will fit tightly around the pipe, and then caulk and staple it to the plates (see Figure 12-71). Make sure that your estimate from the insulator includes this service.

Once this has been completed the insulator will place friction-fit, fiberglass batt or other approved types of insulation between all the studs, around all window and door frames, and in all roof areas not accessible to standard blown-in or loose fill insulation after the vapor barrier and drywall are in place. These are the narrow spaces usually created by cathedral or open-beam ceiling requirements where the contractor is using narrow trusses, or 2" x 12" roof/ceiling joists (see Figure 12-72). Discuss these areas with the insulation installer so he can install the proper amount of batt or fiber insulation (usually a minimum of R-32 insulation) prior to application of the vapor barrier. Remember, these areas will

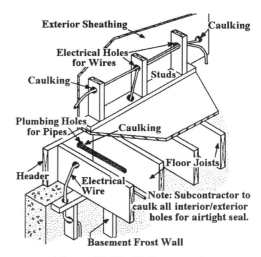

Figure 12-70. Wall areas to be caulked and sealed.

require a minimum three-inch air space between the insulation and roof sheathing for adequate air circulation. If this air space is not provided, the lack will cause winter freezing followed by warm weather thawing, resulting in major water damage to the adjacent structures. Proper soffit and roof ventilation in these joist spaces can be achieved by using premanufactured plastic sheets that fit between the roof joists. A roof-joist vent insert is usually not quoted in material packages from the lumber supplier as it is not always required in home renovation projects, but if your project needs it, be sure the supplier has been informed.

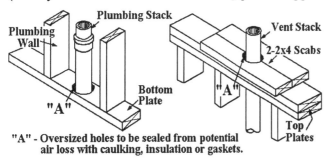

Figure 12-71. Caulking requirements for top and bottom plates at plumbing walls.

As discussed earlier, certain interior walls, such as plumbing walls and walls between bedrooms and other areas of the house, may require soundproofing using batt insulation. The thickness of insulation will depend on the wall. Most bathroom plumbing walls are from 5-1/2 to 7-1/2 inches thick so an R-20 batt should be used. Have the insulators place the insulation so that all sides of the plumbing pipes are covered with batts. Most other walls are 3-1/2 inches thick and would therefore require R-12 batt insulation as soundproofing (see Figure 12-73).

Make sure that at the end of the job, the insulation installer cleans up and removes all leftover insulation containers from the house and takes them to a disposal site.

To ensure you have a well-insulated house, it is necessary to inspect the job daily to see that it is being done correctly. If a contractor is spending most of his time running around trying to keep everybody happy, or has too many other houses on the go, he will not be able to provide proper supervision for jobs such as this. Omissions and discrepancies will show

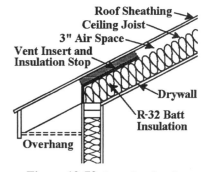

Figure 12-72. Location for the ceiling joist vent insert.

up after occupancy. Our personal experience relates to drafts that seemed to be located in the family, kitchen, and breakfast nook areas. After checking the furnace vents to see if they were blowing adequate air, the windows for drafts, and the walls to see if they felt cold, I decided to do the old smoke test. This simply involves lighting a match or an incense stick, blowing it out, and seeing where the smoke goes. After lighting half a package of matches, all the smoke seemed to be going rather quickly toward the ceiling. Time to check the attic insulation. There was none!!! No wonder it was drafty. All the heat was being sucked out though the ceiling. Good thing we had not yet had -10° to -20° winter weather. I contacted my own insulator, and had him install the required R-40 (10-1/2 inch) loose fill insulation throughout the attic area that same day. Earlier we discussed occupancy and lien holdbacks,

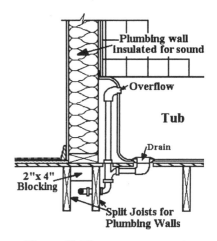

Figure 12-73. Insulated plumbing wall for soundproofing.

and the above story is a good example. Holding back the 15 percent for 45 days will pay off only if the discrepancy is caught during that time period, so remember to do your own inspections even if a contractor is building the house.

Why caulk?:

If there are any air spaces or holes in the floor joists or headers that have not been closed or sealed with caulking by the other subcontractors, have the insulator fill these gaps with insulation and seal them with acoustical sealant. This will prevent any rodents from entering, or winter winds from blowing into the joist spaces and potentially freezing the water lines.

In our present house, I thought that I had double-checked all the problem areas. One very cold evening our first winter in the house, my wife and I were sitting in the kitchen enjoying a coffee when I spotted movement under our refrigerator. At first I thought it was my imagination until I saw our 17-year-old cat streak across the floor and turn around, showing us a brown, string-like object hanging from his mouth. I did not think that cat could still move so fast! On closer inspection the string had fur on it, and was moving. The cat reluctantly gave up his prize, but the mouse by that time had expired so we put it into the garbage and thought the matter settled. We assumed the mouse had gotten into the house through an open door from the garage, and planned to set out traps the next day. About 3:30 that morning, we heard a banging noise and sounds of the cat running around the house. After what had happened earlier that evening, we knew what was going on. The cat was throwing a dead mouse into the air with his paws, and banging it into the walls. When this same scenario repeated itself the next two mornings, I knew that mice were getting in around a pipe or duct going to the outside that someone must have missed during insulating and caulking.

The next morning I had a handyman walk around the house and basement looking for an access hole, including the area underneath the deck as that is where the built-in cooktop vent and basement fan exhaust vents are located. The only way to access those areas was from the basement, so he removed some joist insulation from several areas, and found mouse droppings by one vent unit. Reaching in, he found that the furnace installer had forgotten to seal around one of the exhaust vents, so I had him do a quick patch job by packing insulation around the vent to temporarily seal the access. I had to wait to seal the exterior with caulking until the weather was warmer, and someone could get underneath the deck. Even after years of being in the design and construction industry, one can still miss something that appears to be minor, but resulted in the loss of several nights sleep, and most likely a fair amount of heat.

Vapor barrier:

The vapor barrier stops the interior humidity caused by normal use of household appliances, such as the dishwasher, clothes washer, bath and shower, from passing into the building structure. If the vapor barrier is not installed as is the case in many older homes, or installed improperly at the junction of the existing and new structure, the moisture contained in the house would transfer into the cavity of the wood structure where there is sufficient wind and cold to cause condensation and freezing on the studs and walls. This moisture would repeatedly freeze and thaw, and in time eventually cause rotting and decay (dryrot) of the structure, reducing its life span considerably. The most important feature of a vapor barrier is its continuity as it acts as an air barrier between the warm interior and the cold blowing winds on the exterior of the house. The vapor barrier must be strong enough to withstand the wind pressures which can occasionally reach very high velocities within the roof and walls. In many older homes there is no continuity of the vapor barrier from the ceiling to the basement floor, and in areas of the home that have a vapor barrier, the barrier is only 2 or 4 mil gauge sheets. In most homes built in the 80s and 90s, a 6 mil polyethylene vapor barrier is a standard: it is thick enough to stop the radiating vapor pressure and strong enough to resist the wind pressures (see Figure 12-74).

To ensure a continuous vapor barrier throughout the house, the electrician, during the rough-in, will have supplied and installed poly vapor hats around electrical outlets on all main and basement outside walls and ceilings to eliminate air leaks; the framer will have provided all the necessary vapor blankets at the top and bottom plates. When installing a vapor barrier over the vapor hats and blankets a thick layer of acoustical caulking is applied around the perimeter prior to placing the main vapor barrier on top, or a strip of tape is applied around the perimeter where the vapor barrier and vapor hats meet. This securely seals the house vapor barrier to the hats and blankets. The area where the electrician's wires enter the poly vapor hats is sealed with tape or caulking to eliminate air infiltration.

The 6 mil polyethylene film is available in large, room-height sheets to allow for a continuous application with a limited number of joints which further reduces the chance of air infiltration. Where

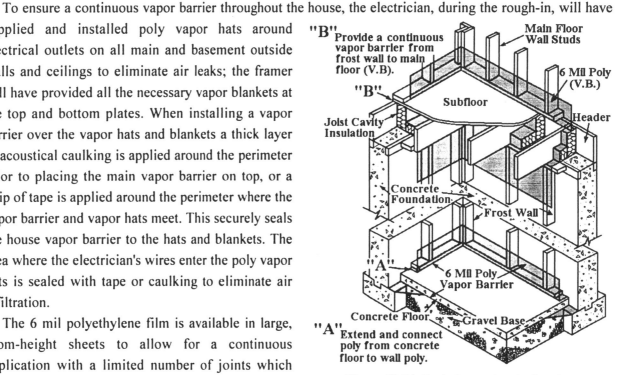

Figure 12-74. Typical vapor barrier location.

one sheet ends and another starts, the two sheets must be sealed with acoustical caulking or tape and then stapled at two adjacent studs. This method creates an overlap of poly for at least one adjacent vertical stud, and the stapling on top of the caulking or tape further seals the joints.

The ceiling vapor barrier should also overlap the wall vapor barrier, and be sealed with acoustical caulking at the intersection of the wall and the ceiling. In addition, the vapor barrier is stapled over the roof truss caulking to maintain the joint seal. Although the interior partitions are framed before the vapor barrier is installed, this continuity problem is resolved by the framer covering the top and ends of the interior walls with a strip of vapor barrier that is wide enough to allow sufficient overlapping with the ceiling and wall vapor barriers. The framer walks on the top nailers of the interior partitions when installing the roof trusses in order to avoid damaging the vapor barrier strips; to provide safer footing for the framer's crew, the vapor strips are installed between the top plate and the nailer (see Figure 12-75).

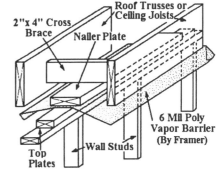

The single most consistent error made by builders is not stopping the air from blowing in around door and window frames. Most frames are constructed so that when installed by the framer they will protrude into the room the thickness of the drywall. This gives the finisher a base on which to nail the door and window trim, but leaves an unprotected crack around the frame. Vapor barriers are usually overlapped and stapled, but not caulked to the door and window frames by the installer. When the drywall board is applied later, the vapor barrier is inevitably torn or pulled from the frames, and this unprotected crack can prove costly.

Figure 12-75. Vapor barrier to be applied on all interior wall plates.

Have the drywaller's estimate, which usually includes the installation of the vapor barrier, state that the vapor barrier installer "will return to apply a bead of caulking in the gap between the drywall and door/window frames, and add a strip of cellophane sealing tape to the frame and the drywall." This will all be covered when the finisher nails his trim in place (see Figure 12-76). Note too that the vapor barrier installer should clean and remove all leftover polyethylene and empty caulking tubes from the house.

Renovating is a good time to install a vapor barrier protection to the insulation between the floor joists if missed during the initial construction of the home. This area is very difficult to protect because the vapor barrier must be cut to fit between the joists, and the installer must sufficiently caulk the joists and subfloor so that when the poly is stapled it will provide an airtight seal all-around. When floor joists in 2-story homes require a vapor barrier, the caulking around any batt insulation becomes very difficult; therefore a hard-surfaced, rigid insulation is better suited. A double thickness of two-inch rigid insulation fitted tightly between the joists with acoustical caulking around the perimeter allows the installer to press and better secure the vapor barrier in these tight areas. Extra care should be taken at the exterior header area between the basement foundation and the main floor joist area, and between the main and upper floor joist connections to prevent tearing of the vapor barrier. An exterior double layer of building paper or a tyvek paper wrap can be installed around the full perimeter of the house in these areas to further minimize air infiltration.

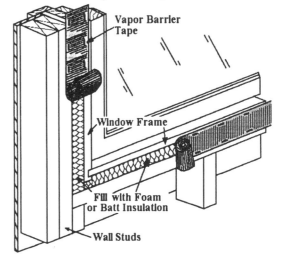

The weakest point in any vapor barrier of a house is the attic or hatch access. The plan may require only one access inside the house, but it should be properly weatherstripped, preferably located where it will cause the least air loss, eg., in an attached garage, or an outside gable wall.

Figure 12-76. Vapor barrier requirements around all door and window openings.

and preferably located where it will cause the least air loss, eg., in an attached garage, or an outside gable wall.

Note: The exterior finish on the house should be completed before the drywall is installed. The pounding of nails when applying the building paper and exterior finish will loosen the nails or screws from the drywall. Timing of the subtrades and installers is very important to the quality of the finished product.

● **Drywall Installation**

Progression to installation of the drywall brings the realization that the house is finally moving to the finishing stage where the actual room sizes can be seen, and not just visualized from working drawings. Drywall, or "gypsum board," which is basically a gypsum filler sandwiched between two sheets of paper, is the most widely used wall finish due to its speed in application, low fire-rating, low cost, flexibility, variation in size, and consistent quality of finished surface. The edges on one face along the length of the board are slightly tapered so a joint filler can be used without causing a ridge. The thickness of the board application depends on the spacing of the wall studs, or the required fire-rating. Many contractors building the lower-end or starter homes use 3/8-inch drywall for wall stud spacing of 16 inches on center to take advantage of the lesser cost. The 1/2-inch drywall board is more commonly used in construction because of its additional strength. In some energy-efficient homes where the wall studs are 24 inches on center, the minimum thickness used has been from a 1/2 to 5/8 inch drywall board. Where the house has an attached garage, the common wall between the garage and the house must have a one-hour fire-rating; therefore a fire-rated 5/8 inch gypsum board is used. In areas of high humidity and water, eg., tubs and showers, the drywaller installs a green-colored waterproof aqua board which resists moisture penetration and provides a proper surface for the tiles to adhere.

If the existing home was constructed with a plaster lath wall finish, it might be necessary in some adjoining wall to apply several different layers and thicknesses of drywall to provide a smooth and finished wall surface. The plaster lath process consisted of an initial layer of metal lath being nailed to lath board or the wall studs, then a base coat, scratch coat, and finish coat of plaster were added and troweled to a smooth surface for the paint application. The thickness of the plaster lath applied varied from 3/4 to 1-1/4 inches or more, and depended upon the climate of the area and the standard set by the owner and the installer.

The drywaller measures the house from the working blueprints, and calculates the longest length of board to be used with minimum cutting for each wall or ceiling area. The drywall is applied directly to the framing member with the minimum number of ringed nails and screws. If nailing is quoted on the estimate, ensure that the nails are driven into the drywall in pairs at intervals of about 12 inches along the studs, joists or trusses. This double nailing procedure will help to reduce nail popping. Pricing for drywall screws should be equal to the double nailing method. The main differences are that the screws will fasten themselves more tightly to the wood structure, eliminating popping almost entirely, and they can be fastened every 16 inches rather than the 12 inches required for nails. Drywall can be attached with ringed nails, screws, or a combination of the two. For an additional labor cost, have the drywaller apply glue in a continuous bead to the vapor barrier along the wall stud member to help seal the nails/screws against the poly, making the house more energy efficient.

The drywaller usually installs the ceiling board first, placing the long dimension at right angles to the joists or roof trusses. He should stagger the ceiling boards so that the butted ends of the boards do not all attach to the same joist or truss. This produces a stronger roof structure when nailed or screwed, and eliminates the possibility of a continuous running ceiling crack. Drywall is most commonly applied to walls in the longest lengths possible, and set horizontally rather than vertically to reduce the amount of cutting and number of nails or screws required, and allow for staggering of the joints. The drywaller should later remove all leftover material from the house and take it to a disposal site.

The drywall contractor is required to provide a warranty service call after one year to repair all the cracks and nail pops at no cost. Make sure this item has been included on his estimate. The drywaller at that time is responsible for only the repairs to the drywall, so the wall areas repaired with drywall cement will have to be painted at your expense. Choose this ideal time to have the painter return to apply the second coat of paint to the house and include a double application of paint in the areas of drywall restoration. You will gain a more uniform paint surface throughout the house.

Taping:

The taper removes all loose paper from the drywall board, and cleans all the joints of mud or loose dirt which could cause discoloration of the joint cement, or prevent the cement from adhering to the drywall. For the first step of the process, all joints and nail or screw heads are covered with joint cement and allowed to dry. All external corners are protected with corrosion-resistant metal or plastic corner beads. For all interior corners the tape is folded in half and applied with joint cement; for all horizontal and vertical joints the tape is applied full width with joint cement. In areas where there is a greater potential for crackage resulting from the foundation settling the taper will apply several graduated widths over the drywall joint. If the interior temperature is less than 68°F or 20°C the furnaces must be connected and running to provide sufficient heat to dry the joint cement.

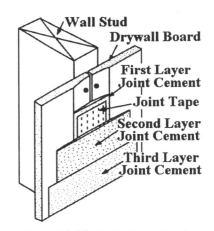

Figure 12-77. Typical board taping application at joint.

Note: If at this time during construction the gas line to the furnace(s) has not been installed, supply the taper with alternative heat to dry the drywall joint cement. Propane blowers are most commonly used, and the propane cylinders and blowers can be rented weekly or monthly. Propane is a moist heat and will therefore require more time to dry the joint cement. If building during the fall and winter, this type of alternative heat can be extremely expensive; therefore try to schedule the installation of the meter, interior gas line, and connection of the furnaces as soon as possible.

After the first layer has dried, usually within 24 to 48 hours, the taper will apply the second layer of joint cement to the corners, horizontal and vertical joints, and the nail or screw heads. The edges of the joint cement strips are feathered so that a bulge at the joint is eliminated (see Figure 12-77). Once again sufficient heat must be available for the cement to properly dry.

A third layer of cement will then be applied to all corners, joints, and if required, any nail or screw heads. This third and final layer of joint cement is applied and tapered wider and smoother than the first two layers so that one light sanding is required to achieve a smooth, flat look to the cemented areas of the drywall. The final application must not have any bumps, bulges, or rough edges in preparation for painting.

Many custom home builders request the drywall corners be finished with a rounded plastic corner bead. The application of cement is similar, except more care must be taken when adding the cement to the corners. The cement must be feathered out further to give the rounded corner a smoother appearance. Rounded corners are more expensive, but they produce a cleaner look and increase resale value.

Note: The taper should clean the floor with a scraper to remove all the dropped cement and remove all the leftover tape from the house, put it into boxes, and throw it on the designated scrap pile for removal. The cleaning is not always done as well as is should be, so be prepared to rent a commercial vacuum cleaner to thoroughly remove drywall dust from the floor, walls and floor ducts.

Textured ceilings:

Ceilings in some older homes had plaster lath ceilings with round coved corners and a sponged plaster design and paint finish. You will have to decide whether to continue the cove design into the addition which will be very expensive because the drywaller must match the arch by wetting and bending the drywall board, or remove the cove and have the taper smooth the wall and ceiling surface in preparation for painting and texturing. Some ceilings are discolored and coated with a film of grease and/or smoke which will require cleaning in order to allow the texture to adhere. Once the walls and ceilings are ready the texture will be evenly applied so the old and new ceiling areas visually blend.

Note: In homes built prior to the 1970s the paints used contained lead; therefore old walls and ceilings require some preparation prior to the application of texture. Due to potential health risks all lead-painted surfaces should be removed, and some building codes and federal laws require it to be removed, placed in plastic bags, and sent to an approved waste treatment plant for incineration. Many paint contractors can be hired to provide this service, or the cost to remove the lead paint can be included in the painting estimate. To better evaluate the costs for removal and repainting, have the painting contractor separate the two costs in the estimate. The price will depend on the number of coats of paint on the walls and ceilings, and the size of the area to be stripped.

A textured ceiling is commonly used throughout the house because of its speedy application, cost effectiveness, and the consistent high quality of the finished surface. A textured ceiling eliminates the cost and time for the taping and sanding steps in preparation for painting. To prepare the ceiling drywall board to accept the texture, the joints, nails and/or screws are covered twice with drywall cement and smoothed with a hand trowel. Usually, only light sanding of the ceiling at corners and questionable surfaces will eliminate any rough or bumpy areas which might show through the texture. Once the rough sanding has been completed, the walls are draped with sheets of polyethylene so that when the texture is applied to the ceiling, any overspray will stick to the poly rather than the painted walls. The ceiling is then machine-sprayed with a thick, even compound of drywall cement which, once dried, is called texture.

Note: Before the ceiling is textured the primer coat of paint must first be applied to the walls as this primer is usually applied very quickly with a paint sprayer or roller. Texture when dry is very white, and even a white paint is not as white as a finished textured ceiling. If the ceiling was already textured the paint from the sprayer or roller would discolor the texture, and result in expensive re-application to all involved areas. This preventative measure is important to remember when arranging the schedule for suppliers and subtrades.

More custom home builders are leaning toward a more expensive and fashionable style of ceiling texture called "California knock down." To prepare the ceiling for this style of texture, the taper must smooth and sand the ceiling to allow the drywall to accept a colored coat of paint. If not properly taped and sanded, the drywall joints will show through this texture style. When the painters apply the primer coat of paint to the walls, the ceiling is also painted. Usually a soft pastel color is chosen for the ceiling, so when the texture is sprayed in a more random pattern, the paint will show through the texture. The sprayed cement is then lightly troweled to flatten the finished appearance. The stylish effect of the completed ceiling is very hard to explain: if a background blue pastel paint color is selected, a white foreground paint will appear like white, billowing clouds passing over a blue sky background. In my opinion it looks fantastic, but is overrated for the price.

Once the textured ceilings are completely covered, the tape and polyethylene covers are removed from the walls, leaving a relatively clean house except for the floor. Because of the spray technique, the floor will be pitted with small, ballbearing-sized, white particles which are very hard to remove when dry, and impossible when wet. Include in the price estimate scraping the texture particles from the subfloor, and throwing any materials outside on the trash pile. In order to get all the texture particles off the floor, you may need to rent a commercial cannister vacuum cleaner designed to pick up this small, fine material. Also vacuum the furnace filter, heat vents, and return air registers as the texture particles and drywall can easily clog furnace filters, causing damage to the furnace fan.

- **Soffits, Fascia, and Eavestroughs**

The soffits, fascia, and eavestroughs of the house can be installed after the roof shingles or shakes have been installed, and before the exterior finish is applied. The downspouts for the eavestroughs should be added after the exterior finish is completed because they must be attached with screws and strapping to the exterior walls.

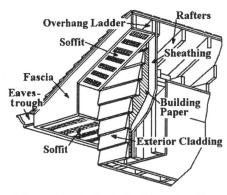

Figure 12-78. Typical gable end, soffit, and fascia projection.

Many suppliers of soffits, fascia, and eavestroughs also install the siding, thereby reducing the running around to collect estimates, and making the installation scheduling much easier. However, if stucco, cedar, brick, or any product other than siding has been selected, it will be necessary to have three estimates from suppliers that also do soffit, fascia, and eavestrough installations. These installers are not hard to find, but scheduling the different subcontractors must be coordinated correctly, so as not to cause any construction delays or installer callbacks.

Soffits allow the circulation of air through the attic via perforated ventilation holes to prevent condensation. They are maintenance-free, and come from the manufacturer in cardboard boxes cut to specific lengths that allow for quick and simple installation by the contractor. A starter strip of building paper must first be placed on the wall of the house at the level where the installer will staple the soffit sheet. The fascia manufactured on-site will have a ledge to hold the soffit section in place so that once the soffit is fitted on top of the fascia ledge, they are both nailed together to the underside of the wood rafter, truss projection, or overhang ladder (see Figure 12-78). Soffits must be placed under any protrusion or cantilever of bay or box windows in order to provide a finished and waterproof surface, and hold the insulation in place.

Fascia material comes in long flat rolls of prefinished sheet metal, and a wide variety of different colors. These prefinished sheets are bent by machine on the site, and molded into long lengths of six-inch fascia, which can be easily handled and installed by two men. Shorter lengths can be made if one person is installing the material; however, the fewer the number of joints the better the fascia looks, and the less the chance of water seepage. The fascia installation is as simple as taking the premanufactured length, sliding it up and under the finished roofing material, and nailing or stapling it to the rafter or truss projection board (see Figure 12-79).

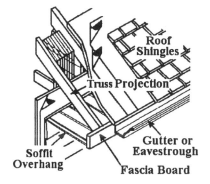

Figure 12-79. Typical eavestrough projection at overhang.

Eavestrough and fascia material are manufactured by the same company so that the color and product finishes will match. They both arrive on-site as long rolls of flat, prefinished sheet metal which are then cut to a specific width to fit into a portable shaper installed on the contractor's truck. The shaping machine can be adjusted to make several different eavestrough widths, and is capable of molding the sheet metal into single lengths of troughs that will fit almost any distance required.

The most common width for gutters and downspouts is five inches (see Figure 12-80). For roof areas no greater than 750 square feet, installers can use the minimum four-inch gutter; however, in heavy rains the gutters sometimes overflow, which may cause future water damage to the fascia and overhang area. The gutter and downspouts come in varying thicknesses of 26 or 28 gauge galvanized steel. The thinner 28 gauge is most commonly used by the installers who use prefinished materials as it is more flexible and less expensive.

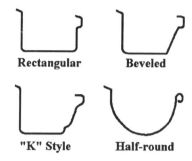

Figure 12-80. Different gutter types.

Eavestroughs are secured in place with long aluminum spikes randomly nailed through the fascia into the wood rafter or truss projection header board (see Figure 12-40). Gutters and downspouts work together to collect runoff and divert it away from the foundation, eliminating any direct water seepage (see Figure 7-3).

It is the responsibility of the fascia, soffit, and eavestrough installer to pick up and remove all sheet metal debris from the roof and perimeter of the house, and place that material on the trash pile.

● **Exterior Claddings**

The exterior finish will significantly affect the streetscape impression and resale value of the house. Select with care the color, style, type, and quality of cladding as this choice will directly affect your amount of personal leisure time, as opposed to putting in time maintaining the cladding and exterior finishes. The most common and economical types of cladding are: metal, vinyl and hardboard sidings, stucco, and masonry (brick or stone).

Beyond the cosmetic appearance, the exterior cladding acts as a protective layer between the occupants and seasonal climatic conditions. All exterior cladding or sheathing that can be affected by moisture must be kept a minimum distance of eight inches from the ground or finished grade of the house. Check with the local building inspector about the area's height requirement (see Figure 12-81).

Make a final inspection of the house before the exterior cladding installers leave the site. With working blueprints in hand, review the exterior electrical plug and light locations to make sure they have not been covered up with cladding. The electricians, when installing the fixtures and plugs, might assume they have been covered on purpose, decide to find them by punching poles in the cladding, or say that they will not return until the cladding installers return to find the buried electrical boxes. Either way, it becomes very inconvenient, and a final inspection can eliminate many potential problems and ensure a quality finished product.

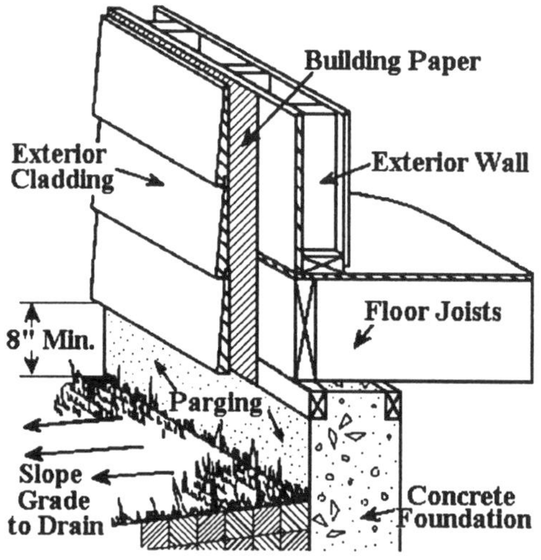

Figure 12-81. Typical grade to cladding height requirement.

As previously discussed in vapor barrier installation, it is critical that exterior cladding requiring any nailing be completely installed prior to nailing or screwing the drywall. The hammering vibration on the exterior of the house will loosen the interior drywall nails, causing them to pop and require premature servicing which adds extra cost for the house builder.

Note: When reviewing the cladding installer's estimate, check for the statement that he will supply all necessary labor and materials to complete the job, including scaffolds, flashing, and caulking.

Before any work is started on the existing walls, any wood surfaces that will remain exposed must first be protected from moisture with a sealer, and a finished coat of stain or paint. The painter will clean the wood, and then apply the wood sealer on both face and side surfaces for maximum penetration into the pours of the wood. Once dry, the finish coat of oil base stain or paint is applied. If the exterior cladding is applied first, the painter cannot protect the side surfaces of the trims, and may apply paint smudges to the siding.

Before selecting the exterior cladding, evaluate the different material types against these possible features:

- ☐ The cost of the material and labor
- ☐ Appearance: color and texture
- ☐ Resistance to weathering and pollution
- ☐ Accessibility for future renovations
- ☐ Expansion and contraction due to temperature and moisture changes
- ☐ Potential bleeding or staining when weathering

- ☐ Ease of handling, weight, and shape
- ☐ Resistance to scratching and impact
- ☐ Sound insulation and absorption
- ☐ Load bearing capacity

- ☐ Combustibility
- ☐ Insulating value
- ☐ Insect residency
- ☐ Maintenance

Exterior membrane:

Before the exterior cladding can be attached to the new walls, the studded wall cavity and exterior sheathing must be protected with a water-resistant, but vapor-permeable building paper or tyvec wrap which is stapled to the exterior sheathing every six inches. Its main function is to stop any wind or rain from passing through the exterior finish. It must be vapor permeable to allow the escape of any water vapor that may enter the stud cavity from the interior or exterior, and allow the house to breathe through the cracks or building imperfections. The building paper or tyvec wrap should cover the entire face of the exterior wall with four-inch laps for building paper and eight-inch laps for tyvec wrap, and taping at all end joints. Protect all cantilevers, corners, and edges of windows and door openings with double layers of this membrane. For optimal protection insist that the membrane be installed on all wood surfaces to the bottom of the exterior cladding and within eight inches of the finished grade.

Promoters of super-insulated homes recommend rigid insulation and strapping be attached to the exterior sheathing of the house. The rigid insulation is first covered with a wind-resistant, but vapor-permeable house wrap, and the exterior cladding is then attached to the wood strapping which is spaced approximately 24 inches apart in a vertical pattern. This added insulation is best suited for the north where the heating costs are very expensive, and winter temperatures reach well below the freezing point for many months. Weighing the additional costs against the payback term might not deem this step cost effective for all regions.

Flashing:

The protection of the house against blowing snow and driving rain is paramount especially in those areas that are poorly designed to protect themselves against moisture infiltration, i.e., chimneys, vents, roof valleys, plumbing stacks, window and door openings (see Figure 12-82). Any area that projects out from the surface of a house, whether it be the roof or a wall, must be protected with flashing. It will also be required where a roof and wall joins, such as a dormer, or where an attached garage meets a wall of a 2-story house. The installer will provide full-width metal flashing over the tops of all window and door openings prior to the installation of the exterior cladding (see Figure 12-83). This will stop water from infiltrating the trim through the

Figure 12-82. The many locations requiring waterproof metal flashing.

exterior membrane and sheathing, and possibly end up sitting between the door and window jams to eventually damage structural walls and drywall.

Note: Remember to have the framer install the 2" x 10" wall header to the future deck attachment so that the exterior cladding installers can add the waterproof flashing to the top of the header.

Metal and vinyl sidings are the most commonly used cladding, and are considered a maintenance-free product because the finish is heat-baked at the factory. They can be used alone or in combination with other exterior cladding. Manufactured for simple installation, the boards interlock together, and are nailed or stapled from the top of the siding board into the exterior sheathing of the house. The manufacturer sends the siding out prepackaged in virtually every color and tone of the rainbow with names such as "double 4 or 5."

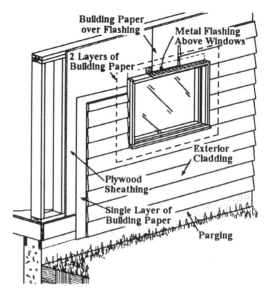

Figure 12-83. Protective flashing required over all window openings.

When these materials are installed in long lengths on continuous walls with a direct south or west exposure, the sun will cause substantial expansion and contraction which sometimes causes the siding to permanently warp. To limit this warping, *lightly* nail or staple the siding, allowing for more movement in these areas versus hammering it tightly to the wall. These materials are very easy to replace, and the potential warping should not be a major concern when receiving estimates.

For horizontal application of the siding, the first board will be fastened at a corner six to eight inches above the finished grade of the house, or for a high basement the starter strip will be fastened about three to four inches below the exterior sheathing level. The same rules apply to vertical installation of the siding.

When installing the siding, special trim pieces are manufactured to cover the end cuts and rough corners in such places as the perimeter of windows and doors, the intersections of siding and soffits at the gables, and all interior and exterior corners (see Figure 12-84). The trim pieces around the windows and doors are installed before the siding; the starting point is at a corner with the application of the first board and trim together. When finished the work, the siding installer should pick up and remove all debris from the roof and perimeter of the house, and place that material on the trash pile.

There are drawbacks to all siding applications, eg., metal siding if abused will dent, scratch, and will have a negative reaction to airborne chemicals. Vinyl, on the other hand, if not installed correctly will buckle or ripple when exposed to direct western or southern sun.

Stucco cladding is being more widely used as a feature material on the current California style homes with finishing styles of arches and built outs. Homes of the 1950s mixed crushed glass, washed rocks, stones, and even marbles into the usually bland, grey base to give it some color. Now with the many different additives and pigments the choice of color is

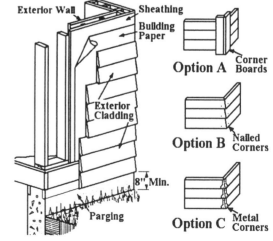

Figure 12-84. Different corner siding applications.

almost infinite. The stucco installer must mix the right proportion of cement, sand, and lime with the correct amount of pigment to match the brochure sample, but once he knows the specific proportions he will be able to produce it in sufficient quantities to finish the entire house. The cheapest and most standard stucco is white, and there is an extra charge for a color additive mixture.

The application of the water-resistant, vapor-permeable building paper or tyvec wrap as the first step is the same. Stucco, however, is not able to directly adhere or stick to paper; therefore, the stucco installer must next apply a galvanized wire stucco mesh to the wall. The mesh is stretched and nailed horizontally into the wall sheathing over the building paper, and all wall joints in the mesh are nailed and lapped over each other by at least four inches. The corners, and door and window perimeters are all reinforced with a special, tighter knit metal mesh to allow the base coat to adhere better in areas where potential cracking and water penetration might occur. Where stucco is applied over a large, uninterrupted wall area, control joints should be installed to permit expansion and contraction. Without these control joints the stucco will crack.

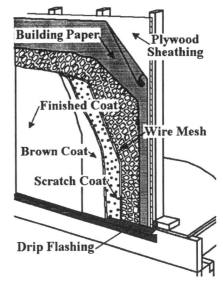

Figure 12-85. The different layers for stucco application.

After the windows, doors, and exposed wood areas are flashed and caulked, the first coat, or scratch coat, is forced into the reinforcing mesh with a hand trowel so that when completed the wire mesh will be completely covered. Before it dries completely the stucco surface is scored with a wire or hard bristle brush to provide a bonding key for the second coat. The installers will allow the scratch coat to set for a minimum of 48 hours, or until dry, before applying the second, or brown coat.

Before this second coat is applied, the scratch coat must be dampened with water to guarantee a proper bond between the two. Usually premixed with the color pigment, it is thickly applied with a hand trowel to completely cover the scratch coat. In addition, it is usually more fluid in consistency, so when added to the scratch coat, it will allow a slower curing process to occur over the next several days. This will provide a better consistent adhesion to the scratch coat.

The third and final coat is called the finished coat. As before, the second coat must be dampened with water to also ensure a proper bond. The finished coat is then applied with a smaller hand trowel to give the stucco the desired textured finish, and the house its California-troweled appearance (see Figure 12-85).

In warm, dry weather the stucco should be kept damp with a light sprinkling of water for several days to ensure proper slow curing. During cold weather it will be necessary to provide propane heat, i.e., a consistent, warm temperature for a period of three to seven days. If cracking or spider web striations appear, the stucco was not allowed to cure properly, eg., too much or too little water in the mix, too cool in the evenings, or too many dry, windy or sunny days during the curing. If this happens, recall the stucco installer for servicing the next year during better weather. Having this service included in his estimate may save a few heated

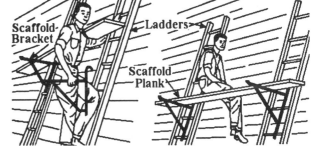

Figure 12-86. Scaffolds used as working platforms.

arguments, and several hundreds of dollars in extra charges.

For a 2-story house, the stucco workers will provide scaffolds to work from as this saves time by eliminating the climb up and down the ladder to collect and mix their materials (see Figure 12-86).

When finished they should remove all debris from the roof, eavestrough gutters, and perimeter of the house, and place that material on your trash pile.

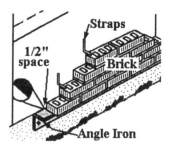

Figure 12-87. Angle iron supporting brick ledge.

Masonry/stone cladding has always held a certain attraction for individuals who appreciate the beauty and feel of brick or stone construction. Masonry and stone finishes also enjoy an intangible prestige that wood, vinyl, metal, and stucco claddings seem to lack. Due to the cost of installation, masonry and stone are the most expensive exterior finish, but they also require zero maintenance.

The application of the water-resistant, vapor-permeable building paper or tyvec wrap is the same as for other exterior claddings. The brick or stone veneer requires the foundation to carry a substantial amount of its weight. If the veneer height is one story or less, the builder can use a steel angle iron bolted directly into the concrete foundation as a structural supporting ledge (see Figure 12-87). If the veneer exceeds the single story height, it is suggested that the foundation be cribbed and poured to incorporate a structural supporting ledge wide enough to allow the width of the veneer plus 1/2 to 1 inch air space between the brick or stone and the building paper. A galvanized strip of flashing placed on the supporting ledge should cover the full surface of the ledge, and extend horizontally beyond the ledge to act

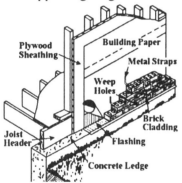

Figure 12-88. A concrete brick support ledge.

as a drip cap, and vertically six inches up the exterior wall behind the building paper (see Figure 12-88).

Regardless of whether the angle iron or the foundation ledge is used, the brick must be fastened to the exterior structural wall of the house with L-shaped, galvanized-metal tie straps. The straps are nailed vertically every 24 inches to the wall studs over the paper wrap, and the angled section embedded into the mortared section of the brick layers every second stud width, or 32 inches depending on the stud spacing. These straps tied to the structure of the house assist in keeping the brick or stone veneer vertical to the walls, and prevent the veneer wall from bowing out and collapsing (see Figure 12-87).

Door and window openings require special attention when installing brick or stone cladding. Special supports made of steel or self supporting curved/flat arches made of the same exterior cladding are installed above the opening, and bolted into place (see Figure 12-89). The steel lintel is the cheapest and simplest to install. It consists of steel angle iron attached to the full width of the opening with flanges 3-1/2 inches wide and a thickness of 3/16 or 1/4 inch. The lintel should overlap each side of the opening, by at least eight inches, so the weight of the cladding can be distributed across the adjacent cladding. A curved/flat arch is constructed on top of a temporary wood support which is removed once the mortar has cured. The arch is made of the same materials used on the wall application and installed to span approximately 3-1/2 inches beyond the width of the opening.

Because mortar and brick are porous, water is allowed to enter the

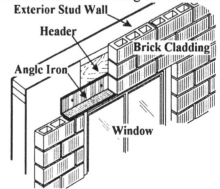

Figure 12-89. Angle iron requirement at window header used as brick support.

air space provided between the veneer and house wall. This water must not be allowed to accumulate to cause potential water and frost damage to the house structure. The brick or stone mason provides weep holes to ventilate the cavity and allow any water to drain out from behind the veneer. He does this by eliminating some mortar from the vertical joint every third to fifth brick, or at 32-inch intervals along the bottom course (see Figure 12-88). The outside mortar joints of the brick should be scored to a smooth finish to provide protection against the penetration of water and blowing snow.

If a brick veneer has been selected, it should be locally manufactured, or reclaimed from a building within the weather zone. This will ensure that the brick will withstand the climate changes for your building location. Many local manufacturers have a large selection of styles, shapes, and colors, and they can even reproduce the appearance and color of 50-year-old reclaimed brick. Stone veneers as well should be selected from local materials and quarries that supply several contractors within the area.

For two stories of brick veneer, the brick layers will provide scaffolds as a safety ledge to work from as well as a storage and mixing area to limit climbs to collect their materials. It is their responsibility later on to pick up and remove all debris from the perimeter of the house, and place that material on the trash pile.

During cold weather it will be necessary to provide heat to the brick face to allow the mortar to slowly cure and set properly. The temperature must be kept constant and above 40°F or 10°C by using propane and propane heaters, and covering the working area with a tarpaulin or cover. The heat required to keep this area at a constant temperature cannot be provided by the house heat as it would be too costly. As scaffolds, tarpaulins, and heat are all considered extra costs, try to schedule construction so that all the exterior work can be accomplished during the warmer summer months.

- **Finishing the House**

The lumber supplier usually delivers all the finishing materials to the job site on the day it will be required, and it is the finisher's job to cut and install the materials which give the house a more livable, completed look. Some of the most commonly used finishing materials are fir, spruce, pine, and basswood. The wood selected for finishing should match as closely as possible the cabinet style and finish already selected. A painted cabinet allows finishing materials to be selected from paint grade lumber such as pine or basswood; stained cabinets limit selection to the finishing materials that will, when stained, match the color and grain of the cabinets. Oak is the most widely selected finishing material for the pleasing appearance of the grain, and its ability to hold many colors of stain.

After a thorough sweeping and vacuuming the finisher will first install the plywood overlay over the rough tongue and groove subfloor in the areas that will need a smooth, finished surface. In areas where ceramic or quarry tile will be laid, the finisher will install 3/8-inch good one side (G1S) plywood overlay, and in areas where linoleum tile or sheets will be placed the finisher will install 1/4-inch G1S plywood overlay. These areas must have a clean, smooth, flat surface for proper adherence of the glue and cement. Bubbles or knots can cause future lifting and cracking of the tile, or unsightly blemishes which will be visible through the linoleum flooring.

Note: If the plumber has installed the gasket for the toilet flange, make sure that the top of the gasket is no higher or lower than the surface of the finished overlay. If higher, once the flange is attached to the toilet it will be higher than the finished surface causing it to rock when any weight is applied, or if lower, it will not allow the seal to make proper contact with the drain, resulting in water overflowing into the floor potentially causing warpage. The toilet fixture must always be level with the floor's finished surface.

For speed of installation most finishers use power staple guns to fasten the overlay onto the subfloor. The staples are approximately 3/4 inch long and will penetrate only halfway into the subfloor; therefore this method will not guarantee a permanent bond between the wood sheets. The movement of the house when settling, along with expansion and contraction of the materials, will cause the staples to loosen, causing air gaps between the wood sheets. These gaps after constant walking pressure will cause the sealant and grout in tiled areas to separate from the overlay and powder after a period of time. To eliminate this costly problem, have all plywood overlay screwed down through the subfloor and into the floor joists with 1-1/2 inch subfloor screws. This will guarantee a structural bond between the overlay, subfloor and floor joists for the life of the house.

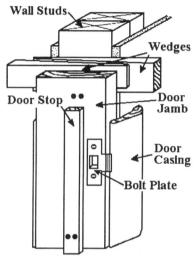

Figure 12-90. Door jamb assembly.

The finisher will also install the door jambs to the rough openings of the doors. One door jamb consists of two side jambs and a head or toe jamb which when assembled will hold the door, the door casings, and the door stops in place. The jambs have already been routered by the finisher to fit the doors hinges, and are usually precut for the wall thickness and door height. Some jambs may come pre-assembled with the door hinged and mounted to the casing, but without the door stop installed. If so, ask for a credit from the finisher because he does not have to do any of the assembly work. Before installing the door jambs, the finisher must make sure the jamb is set square in the rough opening, and in order to do this, wedges and spacers are used around the rough opening until the jamb is square and fits the finished door size. Nails are driven into the jamb through the spacers and wedges, and into the wall studs along the line where the door stop will be nailed. The door stops, once in place, will hide the nail heads (see Figure 12-90).

Door installations:

Interior swing doors are usually delivered with a predrilled hole for the door knob, and side mounts preroutered for the hinges. When ordering the doors, make sure that the door jamb and the door have been routered to accept the same number of hinges. Depending on personal preference, order the doors and jambs with two or three hinges. Review the blueprints and make sure the swing and hinge location of each door is discussed with the lumber sales representative. This will eliminate having a door swing the wrong way, hit another door, or cover up the room wall switches.

Hollow-core swing doors are the most common interior doors because of their cost, light weight, and multiple options for stain or paint finish. A hollow-core door is constructed with a perimeter frame carefully sized to fit the specific door opening, and an allowance for only a slight amount of on-site cutting and adjusting. The perimeter frame can also be ordered with a wood grain finish that will closely match the door face should you decide to stain and lacquer the doors. Overcutting the perimeter frame will reduce the structural integrity of the door, and result in warping due to the inability of the inner core of softer and less expensive wood materials to withstand the pressures applied. The interior is composed of cardboard or soft wood baffles which support the wood veneers on the face of the door. Hollow-core doors with designer panels are constructed by mixing the hollow-core sections with molded plastic or wood fiber components to produce a very nice wood grain finish.

Note: When the door is installed onto the jamb, check the floor-to-door distance. If the room does not have its own return-air duct the finisher must provide sufficient space between the door and the *finished* floor for proper air circulation, and adequate clearance for door swing. The proper space from the finished floor to the underside of the door for air circulation is no less than 3/8 inch, and no more than 5/8 inch.

When the finisher has installed the hinges to the jamb and set the door in place, he will then install the door casing making sure the entire door jamb is rigid. The next step is installation of the perimeter door stop to ensure the door will close comfortably, but not too snugly to the door stop. This step will allow a proper alignment of the door knob and strike plate to the hole drilled to accept the door latch. When closing the door the latch should catch the strike plate easily without requiring force to close the door. When the casing is installed to the jamb, the bottom of the casing is cut to accept the thickness of the finished floor under it (see Figures 12-91 and 12-92).

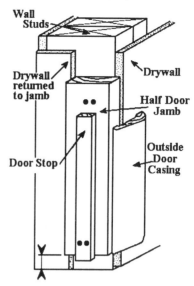

Figure 12-91. Half jamb with casing cut to accept the finished floor.

Bi-fold doors commonly used for interior linen and closet doors consist of two narrow pairs of hollow-core doors hinged together. The bi-fold doors are pre-assembled, and manufactured the same as a swing door to visually match the selected pattern and style. A variety of door sizes can be selected. Two-door units generally range from two to three feet wide while four-door units are variable in total widths of three to six feet. When the door width is wider than six feet, sliding door units with heavier hardware are suggested.

The folding action is guided by an overhead track hidden and screwed into place beside a half jamb. Unlike a swing door which requires a full jamb because it will be seen when entering and exiting the room, a bi-fold door only requires a half jamb (see Figure 12-91), as it is only seen when the closet door unit is closed. The bi-fold tracks hold and direct the center guides which have self-lubricating nylon bushings that ensure smooth, quiet operation. The weight of the doors is supported by pivot brackets and hinges between the doors, not by the overhead track and guide.

Baseboard installation: For this next step, the cutting of the casing to accept the finished floor thickness determines the height of the baseboard to be attached to the walls around the perimeter of each room. The baseboards are usually the same style as the door casings, but taller to give a more finished look between the walls and the floor. The finisher cuts the baseboards to fit, and leaves them in the house for the painter to stain or paint. In carpeted rooms the baseboards are attached to the walls before the carpets are installed; carpets are cut to be stretched and fitted under the baseboard. After the tile, wood, or lino has been installed, he will return to install that baseboard so it can be nailed tight to the lino, wood, or tile, and eliminate any unsightly gaps. The thickness at the bottom of the baseboard must be wide enough to cover any gaps or floor undercutting caused by the installer. These gaps can become more obvious if the floor joists are set into place with the

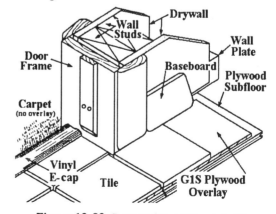

Figure 12-92. Door casing and jamb to fit the floor level material heights.

crowns arranged in different directions resulting over time in a wave in the floor's finish. When the baseboard is nailed level with the door casing, there will be obvious spaces visible between the finished floor and the bottom of the baseboard. This cannot always be corrected, but is usually not too unsightly. As previously mentioned, one way to minimize this problem is by making sure the finisher allows for the proper door casing adjustments, i.e., when one doorway has two different floor heights, the bottom of the casing must then be cut at different heights to accept the different floor levels (see Figure 12-92).

Note: Make sure that your finisher has been informed of the floor's finished thickness, i.e., lino, tile, or carpet. This way the casings or doors are not overcut, possibly leaving a large gap between the finished flooring and the underside of the casing or door.

Special framing:

Any opening that requires covering with a frame and a finished casing is installed by the finisher. The casing for the windows should match the style of nearby doors. Service access hatches at the backs of tubs or spas and attic access hatch boxes which should be insulated and weatherstripped also require special framing.

Because of their detailed work, finishers tend to be temperamental and finicky. They work their own schedule, and like to complain to anyone who will listen about the quality of the framing, drywall finishing, etc. As a general rule I always suggest that the owner show the builder and subtrade in question the problem area, and have them prove that they are unable to work around or repair it themselves. After that discussion it usually gets completed without any more verbal complaints. I believe that everybody usually tries to do their best to make you, the owner, happy, and if not they can usually expect to receive some repair back charges, and not be hired again.

It is in your best interest to get estimates from several finishers, and keep in touch with a few of them during the early phases of the house renovation. Keep asking them how their schedule is going, and if it will coincide with your construction schedule. This way, if one of the finishers cannot show when you are ready, you will have the option of hiring another.

The finisher, as his name states, must provide in his price estimate all the necessary labor, nails, staples, and glue to install all the materials that give the house a finished look ready for occupancy. His price will depend on the amount of work he will be required to do. The following list will assist you when requesting price estimates.

The finisher should do the following:
- sweep, vacuum, and prepare the subfloor for the overlay installation (vacuum supplied by owner);
- screw the plywood overlay in all areas where linoleum, tile, marble, or any other flooring requires a smooth and finished surface for glues or cement to bond;
- build and install all attic access boxes with rigid and batt insulation, perimeter weather seal and casings;
- cut material and install with perimeter casing all plumbing service access hatches;
- square and install door casings for all exterior doors, and caulk around the exterior and interior of all such casings for weather-tightness;
- square, cut, and install all interior swing, folding, and by-pass door jambs, doors and casings;
- cut, drill, mount, and install all hinges, strike plates, door tracks, doorknob hardware and locking devices for all interior and exterior doors;
- cut to fit and install all baseboards and door casings as required after paint or stain finish to the required

height to accept the selected floor finish;

- sand all joints, corners, and nail holes, filling them with sealer ready for stain or paint;

- install all window casings;

- build a custom or install a prefabricated wood fireplace mantel;

- install all spring door stops to baseboards for swing doors;

- measure, cut, and install all linen, pantry and closet shelves, brackets and clothes rods;

- install all brackets, posts, balustrades, and stair handrails to the basement, main, and upper floors;

- measure and install all bathroom towel bars, paper holders, soap dishes, or grab bars as required;

- install all built-in units such as medicine cabinets, ironing boards;

- install all garage closure devices required by building code;

- measure, cut, and install additional weatherstripping as required for exterior house and garage doors;

- install additional storm or screen doors to house;

- build and/or install any custom shelves, window features, or hardware as required;

- cut and fit material for wood feature walls;

- sweep, pick up and remove all debris from the house.

Walk-through inspection:

Here are some special points to consider.

- If the railings have spindles are they close enough together so a child's head will not get caught?

- Should there be a keyed lock for the basement door as security or child safety?

- If you have a pet, should you provide an access hatch so it can enter and exit the basement as required?

- Is the handrail to the basement or upper floor well attached directly to the wall framing studs?

• Painting Inside and Out

The painting contractor will be required at the job site at different times during the construction period in order to prepare and finish his work. It is his job to protect from moisture and enhance the appearance of the interior and exterior surfaces of the house. Most painters suggest a flat latex paint for the walls because it hides many faults and blemishes that would normally be visible in the drywall, and it provides a nonglare, low-maintenance finish to the walls. The doors, trims, baseboards, and casings require a higher maintenance finish than the walls, so an oil-base paint is often used. When the wood surface is properly cleaned, sealed, and painted the better quality paints or stains will last a good 4 to 7 years on exterior applications and 5 to 10 years on the interior.

The quality of the paint selected by the builder and the painting contractor will determine how easily it can be cleaned and maintained by the family. A simple soap and water mixture will remove most stains and finger prints from oil base-painted wood surfaces. Try to choose good quality paints and stains, especially since the cost of the materials is usually only 10 to 15 percent of the total cost of painting labor. The painting contractor's price estimate is usually determined by the quality of the paint or stain selected, and the amount of time required for painting or staining the walls, trim, and woodwork. Most painting contractors charge a cost per square foot of wall area to be painted once they know your requirements.

A common mistake made when collecting estimates from painting contractors is to forget to include the proviso "to clean all surfaces to be painted by removing any dust or chemicals that will interfere with the adherence of the paint or stain." If someone is a good painter and cares about his work, he will do the cleaning automatically. However, just in case it is overlooked, have the surface cleaning put down in writing as a part of the estimate.

The painter will apply the primer coat to the interior walls quickly by using a sprayer or roller after the drywall taper has completed sanding, and before the ceiling texture has been applied. The subcontractors are used to this scheduling, so you should not have any problems keeping the texturer out of the house while the painter is priming the walls. In fact, the person in charge of drywalling or texturing may remind you to schedule the painter.

After the primer application many suppliers and subcontractors will go through the house dinting, marking, and scratching the walls with tools and other items. Under your supervision they will keep the damage to a minimum, but before the painter can apply the first finished coat, these defects must be repaired using a filler. Once the filler is dry and sanded he can apply the first thick coat of paint to the walls and woodwork, i.e., a brush coat to all the door casings, trim, and wall and ceiling corners. Rollers are not able to reach those hard-to-get areas, so when the painter rolls the paint on the walls these corners are already covered. On the day the painter arrives at the house, remind him to be extra careful not to spatter or paint any part of the textured ceiling. Paint marks are easily noticed on textured ceilings, even when it is white paint.

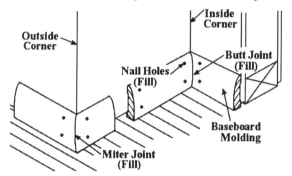

Figure 12-93. Holes and corners to be filled and sanded prior to painting.

The electrician when installing all the lighting and switch plates will be working on painted surfaces, and will most likely scratch or mark some of these surfaces. When the painter returns to the job site to paint the baseboards, he will patch any scratches or marks on the wall, and apply touch-up paint to those areas. This is the last time the painter will repair any damage done by other subcontractors so make sure they touch up every wall, trim, or door blemish before leaving.

The baseboard that has been cut and set aside by the finisher is painted and left to dry in an area or room of the house that will not be worked in until the paint has dried (about 24 hours). The baseboard installed over carpet will have a bead of caulking applied by the painter at the junction of the baseboard and wall to produce a smooth and finished look. Upper caulking to the remaining baseboards will be applied later when the finished flooring has been completed throughout the house. Once all the baseboards have been installed, the painter will apply caulking and filler to all nail holes, interior/exterior corner joints, and cover them with a coat of paint (see Figure 12-93).

For two consecutive applications of paint, the second coat can be applied after a full 24 hours of drying time at a constant 68°F or 20°C. Some clients ask if an immediate second coat of paint is really necessary. Usually during the first winter and spring, the basement structural teleposts will have to be adjusted to match the settling of the home's foundation, and the structural wood members in the walls, floors, and ceilings will also dry out and shrink due to the winter heating requirements. This settling may cause the drywall nails to pop and joint tape to crack. Sometimes the corners for the door and window casings separate during settling, and these gaps require filling and sanding with repainting. Therefore, I recommend a delay on the second and final paint coat although it will involve moving the furniture, and removing all the electrical wall plates and pictures a year down the road.

Exterior wood surfaces must be protected from potential moisture with a good quality primer oil base stain or paint. Special care must be taken to clean the surfaces, and remove any dirt or oil so that the sealer can penetrate into the pours of the wood, and eliminate any moisture penetration which consequently reduces the chance of blistering or pealing. The sealer is usually an oil-base paint or stain that will provide maximum protection. The sealer color is usually tinted the same as the finished coat, and once dry, the finished coat of stain or paint is applied. If there are any exterior touch-ups required, the painting contractor will do this at the same time he returns to complete the interior touch-ups. He is responsible for picking up and removing all paint cans, used brushes, and solvents from the house and taking them to the dump or city chemical and waste recycling center too.

Note: In order to get the job some painting contractors will provide a low cost estimate, quoting on two coats of quality latex paint on all exterior door casing and trims. However, this does not necessarily mean that one of the coats will be a primer or sealer coat. Some painters will say that it is not necessary to apply an oil-base sealer as the first paint coat on exterior wood, and it is better to have a double coat of latex stain. But latex stain is intended to allow the wood to breath, and therefore does *not* act as a sealer. Unless it is an oil-base stain you will only be applying paint to an unprotected surface.

During the life of the house the owner will be involved in some repainting of rooms, or touch-ups. Have the painting contractor leave at least one gallon of each type and color of paint used in the house marking the containers with the re-order numbers for future reference, and the room location for that particular color. Make sure the painters tightly seal the marked containers so the paint will not be dry when reopened.

- **Finished Flooring**

A happy discovery may be finding that the finished floor under the existing tile or carpet is hardwood. Hardwood as flooring has been used by builders for centuries and comes in many types and styles. The most popular species are white and red oak which are well known for their ability to withstand wear in high-traffic areas of the home.

If hardwood floors have not been abused by the applications of glues and tar to secure the carpet or linoleum, it should be a very simple and inexpensive process to restore the natural wood appearance. The floors may have been protected with many layers of wax buildup, but do not have the stain or scuff resistant covering that today's technology can provide. It is usually necessary to power sand the wood to remove the wax and stain to expose the grain of the wood so that it can be properly refinished and sealed with a polyurethane. Polyurethane provides the floor with a protective finish and attractive appearance which requires no waxing, but note that in areas of high-volume traffic it will eventually need to be reapplied.

The term "finished flooring" applies to the material used as the final wearing surface of the floor. A wide selection of materials are prefabricated for this purpose, and selecting floor finishes is strictly a matter of personal taste. Choose from elegant plush carpets; multi-colored, sculptured designer carpets; artwork area rugs; decorative resilient sheet flooring; or natural materials such as prefinished woods, tile, stone, slate, or brick. Keep in mind that patterns, tweeds, and small floral patterns will conceal dirt and footprints better than one-tone light or dark colored carpets, but if you wish the latter, relegate them to areas of least traffic such as bedrooms. Before making the final decision on the floor covering, consider the requirements given the traffic patterns and use of that area of the house, eg., a high resistance to water, soil or dirt, and easy maintenance.

Note that when selecting the flooring for each area it is not only price, appearance, and wear, but also the type, density, preparation, and installation of the underlay material that will determine how the floor will look, and how long it will last. The flooring installers must sweep and prepare the subfloor or plywood overlay by nailing, filling any cracks or gauges, sanding, and thoroughly vacuuming the floor area before they install the finished flooring. (The owner is to supply the vacuum.) The installers will supply all the materials necessary to install the finished floorings; however plywood overlays are firmly secured to the floor and floor joists by the finisher. It is also important to have included in the estimate that the carpet installers will return to restretch the carpet after one year without charge.

In addition, consider the following when making floor covering choices:

- Cushioned, resilient flooring or carpeting is a foot saver.
- Avoid hard-surfaced flooring in areas that require a lot of standing such as the kitchen and laundry.
- Avoid area rugs in areas of the house used most by children or the elderly.
- Carpets and cushioned flooring increase the insulation factor.
- Carpets help to muffle the noise between floors.
- Many carpets and resilient coverings are manufactured specifically to resist the moisture and molds present in the more humid areas of North America.
- To unite rooms or expand small areas, use the same floor covering throughout. A floor covering in a solid color creates an illusion of space while a pattern gives a feeling of intimacy. Geometric designs give architectural elegance to rectangular rooms while random designs disguise irregular room shapes.
- Take along color and fabric samples of furniture, draperies, and venetians to the show room.

Carpeting:

Wall-to-wall carpeting provides comfort under foot, works well with traditional and modern furnishings, and is found in every color imaginable at almost every price. Sophisticated dyeing techniques make colors fast. There are carpets manufactured to solve a wide variety of problem situations: fibers designed to control the static electricity that draws dust or gives a shock on cold, dry days; carpets with soil resistance built right into the fibers; industrial grade carpeting designed to take any punishment imagined; and textured carpet that will camouflage most stains.

The key to quality is the way the carpet is manufactured, fiber content, and pile density. The wear and quality characteristics of a good carpet are determined by the balanced combination of pile height, pile density (closeness of yarns), and ply (number of strands) of the individual yarns. High-density lessens abrasion on the sides of the yarns, produces a richer, fuller look, and reduces the depth of footprints. For very heavy-traffic areas, choose carpeting made of tight twist, high-ply yarns. Test the density of the carpet by bending the fiber side of the carpet toward you.

Carpet warranties against defects, such as excessive separation of carpet strands from the carpet backing during normal vacuuming, or color bleaching with shampoo cleaning, come directly from the manufacturer. Make sure that this warranty is in writing from the sales agent or the installer. Never even consider buying a carpet that is not warranted against manufacturer's defects.

Underpad cushioning:

Regardless of the quality or luxuriousness of the carpeting or rug, you must select the proper underpad to ensure a long life for the carpeting. In addition it helps to protect your feet, insulate, and muffle sound transmission.

When selecting the undercushion, keep the following points in mind. Thick, lush cushioning is best left to low-traffic areas in the home as the thicker the cushion the more the wear to the carpets. Waffled construction in buoyant foam rubber gives a rich, luxurious feeling; sponge rubber is resilient and soft under foot, but will hold moisture; urethane cushioning is resistant to heat and dampness. Firm underpadding is best for high-traffic areas. The synthetic material will resist mildew and make carpets last longer which makes this type of cushioning the choice for most commercial sales areas such as the show room of the supplier. The carpet supplier should be able to recommend the best underlay for the carpet selected.

Sheet flooring:

This type of linoleum, better known as vinyl flooring, is installed by cementing it to the smooth plywood overlay. The 6, 9 and 12 foot widths create a smooth, seamless, wall-to-wall effect which provides an ideal answer for areas exposed to surface moisture, such as laundries, washrooms, mudroom entrances, and kitchens. The cushion resilient goods are especially effective in areas where you stand for relatively long periods of time, eg., the kitchen and laundry. Vinyl flooring offers wide selections of patterns, colors, quality, textures and widths.

Care of resilient flooring is important. Use only the prescribed cleaning agents, or a vinegar and water mixture as some resiliences can be damaged beyond repair with harsh, strong cleaners. Dust daily and wipe up spots immediately, or for the ultimate in convenience, try the no-wax resilient which needs only regular wet-mopping to keep it maintained.

Hard-surface flooring:

As discussed earlier, hard-surface flooring can be wood, ceramic, brick, marble, or slate. When used in very high-traffic areas, such as foyers, they will require special care, but the beauty will more than compensate.

- *Sliced brick* can be country or contemporary, and lends itself to indoor/outdoor areas as spa or pool decks.
- *Ceramic tile* comes in many glazes, patterns, colors, and shapes, and is easily mixed and matched. The grouting is also available in a variety of colors.
- *Marble* is very elegant, and comes in many sizes and colors. It stains very easily, costs a lot, and is hard to maintain so therefore used sparingly.
- *Quarry tile* is fired from clay, comes in a wide selection of surface textures, and is available in their natural colors, i.e., brown, rose, and slate blue.
- *Slate* arrives precut in many colors and thicknesses. Commonly seen along mountain highways the color variations of slate include black, purple, blue-grey, charcoal, rust, green, and several brown tones.
- *Terrazzo* is marble or stone chips set in mortar, then polished to a smooth, shiny finish in a multi-colored, multi-shaded blending. This style of marble flooring is usually found in entrances of commercial high rises with a very high traffic flow.
- *Wood flooring*, especially hardwood, has the strength and durability to withstand wear, provides a highly attractive appearance, and offers selections from oak, maple, birch, beech, to name a few. There are three general types of residential wood flooring: strip, plank, and block. Wood flooring must be the last in the the sequence of the interior finishing steps. Manufacturers recommend that wood flooring be delivered four to seven days before installation and piled loosely throughout the house. This permits the wood to equalize its moisture content to that of the house.

- **House Cleaning and Garbage Removal**

This job however dirty must be done regularly during the demolition and construction of the house. The dirt, bent and rusty nails, soiled papers or rags, partially eaten lunches, half-full pop cans, lumber, and other scraps will accumulate in the house, or be spilled and ground into the subfloor. This material can potentially work its way up through the underlay to stain or discolor the finished carpet or floor caulking. There are certain times during the construction period when you will find it advisable to thoroughly clean out the garbage and dirt that accumulate with each subcontractor. The questions are, how often should this be done? and, should you do the cleaning yourself or hire someone on a contract basis to sweep and clean the interior of the house and take the debris to the dump?

The house should be swept out weekly as regular maintenance. If this can be done personally in a few hours on the weekend, it will keep the interior relatively clean as well as the interior sweeping and trash removal costs down. This leaves the exterior container or trash pile removal as the only expense.

The house should have at least four thorough sweepings: after the framers, after the drywall tapers, after the texturers, and after the finisher. The fourth cleaning after the finisher but prior to the application of the final coat of paint is the time to rent a commercial vacuum unit capable of picking up small dust particles from between the subfloor and overlay joints. Its suction motor should be powerful enough to pick up small nails, wires, staples, papers, and wood chips from the floor and heating ducts. Experience convinced me that the residential shop vacuum units are not built to do this job without the hose and filters constantly obstructing and burning out the motor, and are without suction power sufficient to pick up small nails and staples.

There are companies in business exclusively to clean the interior and exterior of houses by sweeping and picking up the garbage, and taking it to the dump. They will contract to come to the job site three or four times during construction to clean and remove the trash from the house for a fixed price. They will also contract to do this work only on request, and the rate will be determined by the amount of trash they remove each time, eg., a full load, three-quarter load, half load, etc., with an added charge for sweeping and cleaning large pieces of lumber from the furnace ducts.

Subcontractors are constantly running in and out of the house, and the floors will accumulate dirt very quickly. During rainy periods especially, mud tracked in will become layered which can only be removed with a scraper. If this is the case, it would become too costly to have a cleaning crew regularly remove the accumulation of dirt and trash. The best way of keeping this expense to a minimum is to have each contractor include the cleaning of his materials and mess in his estimate. If after each day they pick up their trash and unwanted material, and throw it outside on a designated spot or in a trash container, the dirt and trash collected inside the house will be kept to a minimum.

Note: Trash piles should be removed after the framers are finished, after the taper has finished, after the finisher has completed, and after all the appliances have been installed and the cartons thrown out.

An alternative system for garbage collection, as long as there is available room on the property, is a trash container rented on a monthly basis. Companies will provide a container that will be automatically picked up and emptied every month, or as required. These companies charge by the container size and the number of times required to empty the container during the construction period. One negative aspect to this method of collection is that some of the materials, such as sheet metal, some plastics, and other trash that does not decompose quickly, will not be accepted by a dump site. If these materials are thrown in, they will have to be removed before the container can be emptied. The subcontractors should be warned of this stipulation if you choose this method of garbage removal. The other negative side of this service is the ease of access for cheating by other trades and subcontractors working on someone else's house. A tradesperson with a half ton pickup truck can easily dump his garbage into your container after dark rather than take it out to the dump. You may end up paying for someone else's trash pickup as well as your own. This ease of access can be minimized by placing the container in a highly visible traffic area, or by having the electrician wire a temporary floodlight with a motion detector aimed at the container.

PART V: AFTER THE RENOVATION

CHAPTER 13

◆ HOUSE MAINTENANCE

• Post-Construction Issues

The impact of a good or bad maintenance program will have been evident in any extensive renovation, and a continuing program should start even before the final walk-through inspection. That is when all the structural, mechanical, electrical, plumbing, and heating components are fresh in your mind, and you are aware of how things should appear and operate. At the time of delivery of the equipment and at different periods of the construction, it is a good idea to open a file and record all the serial numbers of the appliances, and mechanical and electrical equipment that have been installed. Store this information along with your mortgage information, diary, contracts, etc., in a safe and easy-to-access file.

As the products installed in the home have become more energy efficient and maintenance-free, there is less weekend and summer holiday time spent caulking, scraping, sanding, and painting the house from top to bottom. Regardless of all the limited maintenance products, i.e., vinyl or aluminum clad windows, vinyl sidings, and metal doors, it is still necessary for the home owner to develop a program of preventative maintenance and fine tuning to prevent long-range problems from occurring. A preventative maintenance program cannot guarantee that breakdowns will never occur, but it will limit the time and money spent on major repairs, and increase the life of the structure and property value.

Follow-up after the resettlement date is an extremely important step of the building project. Active house maintenance requires only a few hours every third or fourth month and includes an inspection walk around the interior and exterior of the entire house to check for changes in the walls, trims, basement walls, structural posts, and perimeter settling of earth against the foundation. All these items can be easily noticed, and should be serviced as quickly as possible. If experienced and good subcontractors or suppliers have been hired, have provided quality materials, and have paid special attention to the construction details and building code requirements, the house will require minimal maintenance compared to a house that is not well constructed and contains poor materials.

It is common during the first year after construction for interior walls to develop cracks, for nails or screws to pop, and doors to shift so they do not close properly. A smart home owner knows his or her house intimately and routinely listens to the home's growing pains. When settling, the floors may creak, and walls will make loud snapping sounds during the day and night. When this happens, by knowing where things are located and the construction process, you are far less likely to feel something dreadful is about to happen. As discussed earlier on drywalling, these problems are usually first noticed during and after the winter heating of the house. Wood members will shrink or shift because of the moisture evaporating with the heat; foundation bearing walls and structural posts sometimes settle at different rates. When these sounds or visual cracks first occur, take it as a warning that it is time for maintenance and service work. The drywall cracks, and nail or screw pops are under warranty, and should be serviced one year from the work being completed by the drywall contractor. Quarterly adjustments of all the structural teleposts will reduce the damage to the drywall caused by the shrinking wood members and structural settling.

Inspections of the backfill material around the new perimeter during the first year will show settling. This is due to the weight of rain and snow moisture in the earth which forces the backfill to compact downward. If not corrected within the first year by tamping and filling the voids, water could pond and possibly freeze against the foundation wall, putting unwanted pressure against the foundation and causing the concrete to crack or the perimeter backfill to settle too quickly. Providing a grade with a good slope to drain will eliminate much unnecessary service work in the future.

A good seasonal checklist can be conscientiously followed during the entire life of the home. It can become a very important document, especially if sometime in the future you decide to sell. The potential new owners would be delighted to know their new home was well maintained. The following preventative maintenance checklist can be used and altered to suit individual needs and concerns.

- **Spring Maintenance**

The purpose will be to check for any winter damage caused by ice and condensation. Spring is also the time to prepare your property for the required lawn and garden projects.

☐ Remove storm windows, install screens, and check operating units.

☐ Test circuit breakers and groundfault wall plugs.

☐ Check sump pump.

☐ Check and test floor drains.

☐ Clean and repair garage parking pad and test floor drain if required.

☐ For the first few years check and adjust all structural teleposts to level.

☐ Bleed any air from hot water tank.

☐ Turn on water valve for sprinkler system and test.

☐ Clean or replace furnace and humidifier filters.

☐ During spring cleaning, check walls for nail pops, scratches, dents, and cracks.

☐ Wash windows and check for winter frost or water damage.

☐ Service water well pump and check septic system.

☐ Clean eavestrough gutter and downspout.

☐ Give visual check to roof, chimneys, and plumbing stacks and service if required.

☐ Clean out debris from basement window wells.

☐ Service and clean air-conditioning unit's drainage tubes and check Freon.

☐ Walk around perimeter fence line for winter damage and repair if required.

☐ Repair asphalt, concrete, and masonry damage.

☐ Inspect shrubs and trees for winter kill and trim if necessary.

☐ Fertilize lawn and evergreens and pull all visible weeds.

☐ Check perimeter security and sidewalk lights and replace blown bulbs.

- **Summer Maintenance**

☐ Inspect, spray, and repair basement and crawl spaces for bugs or water damage.

☐ Vacuum and clean all exhaust fans and filters.

☐ Clean or replace air-conditioning filters every four weeks.

☐ Fertilize and spray lawn with weed kill every four weeks.

☐ Clean, repair, caulk, and renail any damaged siding.

☐ Clean any winter-stained stucco.

☐ Give visual check to roof flashing and service if required.

☐ Inspect and spray shrubs, yards, and gardens for insects, weeds, and other pests.

☐ Adjust sprinkler system pop-up heads for proper lawn coverage.

☐ Inspect and spray the perimeter of the house monthly, looking for ants, termites, and other pests.

- **Fall Maintenance**

Fall is the least understood season for maintenance, and should be the busiest. The house has had only minimum maintenance all summer, and the property should now be protected from impending winter damage.

☐ Install storm windows and/or remove screens for proper window air circulation.

☐ Check and service all attic, door, window, and garage overhead door weatherstripping.

☐ For the first few years, check and adjust all structural teleposts to level.

☐ Inspect and clean all wood-burning fireplaces and stoves.

☐ Clean clothes dryer filters and vent.

☐ Test circuit breakers and groundfault wall plugs.

☐ Service furnace fan, vacuum ducts if dirty, change air filter, and check all thermostats.

☐ Turn on furnace fans for proper air circulation and moisture reduction around window openings.

☐ Inspect, test, and clean humidifier and filter.

☐ Test all household fire extinguishers and smoke detectors.

☐ Check sump pump and remove any accumulated silt.

☐ Bleed any air from hot water tank and drain about five gallons of water.

☐ Service water well pump and check septic system.

☐ Give visual check to roof, flashing, chimneys, and plumbing stacks and service if required.

☐ Clean out debris from basement window wells.

☐ Inspect and spray house and basement perimeter for ant and termite damage.

☐ Winterize and clean air-conditioning unit.

☐ Clean eavestrough gutter and downspout.

☐ Remove all hoses from exterior taps, drain lines, and check shut-off valves.

☐ Service sprinkler system, blow out all water from lines, and turn off supply water tap.

☐ Inspect, prune, and cover shrubs, trees, and plants as required.

☐ Check perimeter security and sidewalk lights and replace blown bulbs.

☐ Repair and paint deck, windows, doors, and perimeter fences as required.

☐ Repair asphalt, concrete, and masonry damage.

- **Winter Maintenance**

In cold-climate areas winter is the best season to make all interior repairs and find any energy-wasting air leaks. Check with the local utilities companies to see if they offer inspection services, eg., furnace safety.

☐ Inspect attic hatches and perimeter of basement for air leaks.

☐ Inspect and service door and window frames, electrical outlets, and vent fans for air leaks.

☐ Service and clean tub, shower, and floor tile grout.

☐ Clean or replace furnace and humidifier filters monthly.

☐ Inspect, clean, and service all appliances as required by warranty.

☐ Repair, caulk, and paint any nail pops or door/window casing cracks.

☐ Inspect fireplace flue bi-monthly and furnace flue monthly.

☐ Give visual check and service roof and eavestroughs against ice damage.

Especially over the first few years, a regular, preventative maintenance program is the best defence against the elements and time. Once you have completed your seasonal maintenance schedule, try to keep up with the repairs. Whether you chose to supervise the construction yourself or hired a general contractor, do not be afraid to contact the suppliers, subcontractors, and/or contractor to service any problem areas. Choosing to ignore or wait for the next year could end up being a very serious and costly mistake.

CHAPTER 14

◆ LANDSCAPING

● The Importance of Planning

The landscaping of the property after the addition/renovation project should take as much thought as did the design and layout of the house. Indeed, the home's renovation project and lot landscaping should be planned in conjunction with each other. The removal of existing trees for the renovation does not require identical replacement, and is an opportunity to enhance and beautify the entire yard plan. New shrubs and trees must be properly located with careful consideration of their growth over the next ten years or until maturity. A professional landscaper can assist by putting ideas for area use and visual presentation of the property on paper. This service may be limited to just the design, or extended to complete the entire landscaping project, including supply and installation of all the trees, shrubs, plants, terracing, lighting, sidewalks, sod, and irrigation systems.

The land value usually represents between 15 to 30 percent of the total investment so balance the values of the property and landscaping into their appropriate percentages of expenditure. To do this effectively, be prepared to spend about 20 to 35 percent of the present property value, or 10 percent of the completed house value, on landscaping. This percentage should include the rough and finished grading, the walks, driveways, trees, shrubs, sod, and fence package as well as the sculpting and earth burming (see Figure 14-1) required for the lot to conform to the family's outdoor living requirements. The final value, enjoyment, and cost to maintain the property will depend upon the placement, design, and quality of work and materials in its visual features. If the quality of materials and construction is poor, their maintenance will become costly and time consuming. Structural and visual deterioration will eventually result in real property devaluation.

Landscape planning may involve the following:

1) preparing a detailed design for progressive development of the landscaping over a period of months or years to accommodate a budge;

2) hiring a bobcat or small grader to shape the land for proper drainage in relation to the house and to take advantage of the contours and different yard landscapes possible from each window location;

3) taking into consideration the installation and location of features such as retaining walls, driveway, sidewalks, lawn areas, terraced decks or land, and fences or hedges;

4) selecting the proper seasonal trees, shrubs, and plants to complement the landscape shaping and the house's streetscape;

5) estimating weekly and seasonal maintenance requirements for lawns, garden, and permanent features.

● Planning Factors to Consider

The following factors may affect landscape planning and should be considered.

Existing grades. Wherever possible take advantage of the natural features of the property such as rocks, tree stumps, existing trees, uneven grades, etc. It is much easier and cheaper to build and develop a flat or level property; however, a sloping lot or variable grade will offer the owner or landscape contractor a greater challenge for different and more interesting visual effects. Land that lies above street grade is preferable and easier to work with than low-lying ground where water can pool, creating major drainage problems.

Existing features. Assess the property or adjoining properties for focal features, such as a well-treed backyard, a view, or an open field or utility corridor. Remember if you have a corner lot that there are two streetscapes to consider.

Climate. Many northern states and provinces are limited to about four months of warm temperatures or outdoor enjoyment. To make the best of a short season, plan decks or patios in sunny areas of the property sheltered from the wind. This way their use can be extended to include the early spring and late fall. These sunny areas are well suited for early growth of spring flowers and extended growth during the fall. Shrubs and plants located in these sunny areas will have their blooming periods extended two or three weeks more than those located on a northern exposure. Alternatively southern areas have factors such as water supply, severe climatic changes, and weed control to contend with.

House orientation. The view and door access from each room will determine the special needs and location of decks, play areas, and vegetable/flower gardens. The smaller the lot and house, the greater the need for careful house and landscape planning as each room should share in a pleasing view of the property.

Family considerations. The purpose and enjoyment of the outdoors will depend on taking into consideration each family member's hobbies, lifestyle and personality in order to develop a personal landscape design.

● **Grade Preparation**

During construction the rough grading is completed by the excavator or bobcat service. Consult with the city inspector, house designer, landscaper or surveyor when the excavator backfills around the perimeter of the

house to determine if there is sufficient fill material against the foundation to allow for most settling situations. The first year of settling will result in different ground compaction conditions around the lot and house. It is essential to direct all surface water away from the house, and for this reason the finished grade at the base of the house must be high enough to

Figure 14-1. House and lot with proper drainage.

maintain over time a slope down and away from the house. During preparation of the finished grade, sufficient black dirt will be brought in by the landscaper to fill these grade variations and satisfy the landscape design. The black dirt is spread in various thicknesses to comply with the finished grade and ensure there will be no ponding or erosion problems created (see Figure 14-1).

If the lot's contour slopes at right angles or parallel to the street, it may require some terracing via different levels with retaining walls to hold back the earth. Terracing must be carefully done in order to allow the surface water to drain away from the house and lot, and not cause potential flooding in a neighbor's lot. Be considerate and select gutter downspout and driveway locations that prevent water runoff from causing

flooding or drainage problems for adjacent neighboring property (see Figure 14-2).

The finished height of the city road will determine the lot grade steepness and options for terracing. In subdivisions having extreme side grades, it is common for the grade of the house across the street to be at the same height or only

Figure 14-2. Extreme grades require retaining walls and terracing to reduce soil erosion.

slightly higher than the city road height. Whatever the site grading condition may be, the most important consideration in preparing the site is establishing finished grade levels at all corners of the lot in relation to the adjoining properties. The plot plan from the land surveyor will provide that information.

• Existing Topsoil and Trees

If the quality of the black dirt on the lot is good, have it scraped off and saved before starting the renovation. The excavation contractor will scrape the top five or six inches of topsoil off the area to be excavated, and pile it on a corner of the property. Stripping and replacing the topsoil will cost less than having that same amount of black dirt trucked in at a later date. If unsure of its quality, send a sample to the local government department of agriculture for analysis, and request recommendations for the type of fertilizer required to enrich it.

Some city planning departments require property owners to spare the young and healthy trees around the lot's perimeters that will not interfere with the house construction. If the lot has protected trees, thin them out by selecting the healthy ones, and removing any dead or scrub bushes that might slow or interfere with the trees' growth. Young healthy trees should be saved, but consider also their location and potential size when fully grown. Any trees that will be too close to the house foundation should be completely removed to eliminate future root damage to the house structure and drainage systems.

If the lot has been without trees, you may find it worth the investment to plant several full-grown trees to provide immediate shade and visual landscaping. These trees are relatively inexpensive; the tree spade that digs the hole and plants the tree is the expensive part of the process. Instant trees will be an immediate asset to the value of the house and property.

When selecting trees for planting, view and purchase them from a local and reputable tree farm, i.e., one which has a wide selection of full-grown trees and shrubs. Avoid those trees that tend to seed in quantity, such as chestnut and silver maple, or trees that sprout and support secondary ground growth as these seedlings will have to be constantly pulled and destroyed. Avoid planting types of trees such as poplars, willows, or elms too close to the house foundation: they have a heavy root system which can cause foundation damage, slow plant growth, and find their way into nearby drains.

Too many trees on a lot will produce too much shade which inhibits the growth of grass, and only a few shrubs survive in densely shaded areas. However, plant a reasonable number of shade trees around the house to protect against the summer's hot sun. Trees are well known as natural air conditioners because they absorb the sun's heat in the summer and prevent it from entering the house to cause overheating. In the winter after the leaves have shed, they allow the warmth of the sun to enter the house. Special attention should be paid to the planting location of coniferous trees. They provide shade, and also block the winter winds, perhaps lowering winter heating costs.

• The Backyard Development

The backyard deserves the most care and design time because it is this part of the lot that provides the privacy, the family outdoor environments, and frequently the garden. Have each member of the family write down on a piece of paper their requirements for the area. Some needs will be the same, and others might be too costly, but this should provide sufficient information for the family to determine the level of priority for price, placement and design of the backyard (see Figure 14-3).

Deck, patio or terrace areas should be open and located off the family's living areas, dinette and/or kitchen. To provide protection and privacy, this area may be screened off with a lattice fence or shrubs, and partially roofed. These areas require good drainage away from the house with level areas for the placement of patio furniture. They can be protected against the growth of unwanted weeds by placing a polyethylene vapor barrier under the structure to minimize maintenance.

Service and holding areas should be located close to the rear entrance, kitchen or garage. These areas should have sufficient space to hold items such as firewood, scrap lumber, and gardening supplies or equipment. The covered, holding area for the garbage cans should be easily accessible from the back or front yard, but hidden from sight and away from the main activity areas of the backyard.

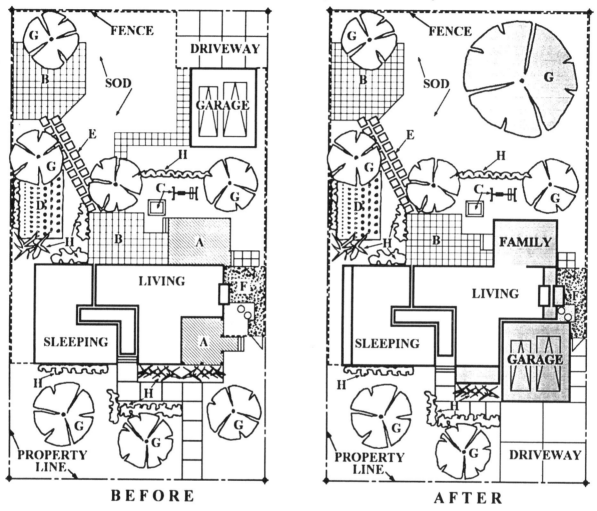

B E F O R E   **A F T E R**

Figure 14-3. Landscaped lot before and after renovations and additions.

(A) Raised deck, **(B)** Concrete patio, **(C)** Children's play area, **(D)** Vegetable garden, **(E)** Stone walkway, **(F)** Dog/trash holding area, **(G)** Large shade trees, **(H)** Low shrubs or hedges. Shaded areas on right side are new additions and trees.

Children's play areas should be located close to the house so that adults can keep an eye on the children when playing there. They should also be located fairly close to a door in case quick access in or out is required. A low wood or wire fence may help to isolate this area, and keep the children away from gardens or unsafe areas. A shade tree or structure located in close proximity will provide a cool and protected area to play in. Play areas should be designed with safety in mind, without any dangerous playground equipment.

Garden and lawn areas may have many different design requirements depending on the family's needs and lifestyles. These areas may consist of lawns, flower beds, or vegetable gardens. In order to obtain most benefit from these areas, the backyard should be divided in two or three parts separated by changes of grade levels, sidewalks, fences, or well-placed trees and shrubs. This segmentation will provide greater interest and individuality for each of the areas rather than leaving a single area cut up with small or scattered planting beds. These are often hard to maintain, and become obstacles when cutting the grass areas between. Simpler designs will provide a more effective and more organized impact on the backyard landscaping. Extra topsoil and peatmoss should be mixed and placed in the vegetable garden area with a small area set aside for composting. Compost material can be mixed into the garden in the fall to provide more natural nutrients to the soil for spring planting. A raised border of brick or treated wood should be used to keep the soil in these raised areas from washing onto the grass or sidewalk areas. Strategically placed fences will keep unwanted animals from wandering into the garden area.

- **Seeding or Sodding**

Budget, time, experience and need for an instant landscaped yard will answer the question of whether to seed or sod. In either instance, the rough grade must be prepared so that when the black dirt is placed over it any water will drain away from the house foundation. All shrubs, trees, flower beds and vegetable gardens should be in place, and sectioned off with borders, fences, sidewalks and shrubs before the black dirt is spread. The levels of these areas must also be considered before placing the black dirt and sod. Should these areas be raised or even with the sod, and will they be crossed with the lawnmower when the grass is cut?

Seeding should be done between June and September, or as soon as the spring frost has left the ground and the ground can be worked. The subgrade or finished rough grade should be superficially loosened up with a power cultivator, then at least four inches of black dirt spread evenly over the surface, and a commercial fertilizer spread on top. These materials are mixed together by raking the surface to a fine and even grade first in one direction, and then at right angles to the original direction. Before spreading the seed, use a hand roller to compress the dirt to a level and even grade without raised or sunken areas, and then lightly rake so the seed will fall into the loose grooves. When purchasing the seed, buy a mixture that has been known to grow successfully in the area, and is sold by the local greenhouse. It is to your benefit to purchase the better quality seed. In order to properly spread the seed, rent or purchase a push-type seed and fertilizer spreader to ensure an even spread over the areas without variations in the density of the grass growth.

Rake the seeded area gently, once again in two directions, so that the seeds and the fertilizer will mix properly and encourage the grass seed to germinate more quickly. If the soil is dry enough, use the hand roller to compress the seeds into the top soil. Then, lightly sprinkle the seeded area with water to a depth of about one inch. Keep the seeded area moist until the grass has reached a minimum height of two inches at which time the first cutting is done. When the lawn has been established, after about one month, give it a good watering only when the soil becomes dry, and then soak it thoroughly to a depth of four inches. Fertilize the lawn with a quality commercial fertilizer in the spring and fall to ensure a green and healthy lawn.

Sodding is usually done if you have an urgent need for a quick lawn. This method is more expensive than seeding, but it can be completed and ready for watering in a weekend. The area to be sodded is prepared in the same way as for seeding. Not less than four inches of black dirt should be used over the rough grade. Fertilizer is loosely mixed with the dirt in the same manner, but uses only a 25 percent proportion of the total amount. The remainder of the fertilizer is applied as follows: 50 percent after the black dirt has been rolled, leveled, and raked prior to laying the sod, and the remaining 25 percent spread over the snow in the winter, or in the late fall with the final watering. Sprinkle the black dirt and fertilizer lightly with water before laying the sod. Purchase the sod from a local sod farm or greenhouse, and check it for weeds, mushrooms, and other fungi. Each sod strip should be 1 to 1-1/2 inches thick, and evenly cut with the grass length being 1-1/2 to 2 inches long. When laying the sod, always stagger the joints with the next row. Handroll newly laid sod till the surface becomes uniform.

After laying the sod, water the grass immediately to ensure a five-inch penetration of moisture through the sod into the black dirt which allows the fertilizer to mix well into the black dirt under the sod. Then allow the grass to dry, but not to a point where the subsoil is dry to the touch. Keep the sodded area moist until the grass has reached a height of three to four inches at which time the first cutting can be done. Cut it initially to the two-inch level, and after two weeks of watering when the grass roots have had time to grow, cut the grass again to the desired level. Continue watering only when the soil becomes dry, and then soak it thoroughly to a depth of four inches. Fertilize the lawn with a quality commercial fertilizer in the spring and fall to ensure a green and healthy lawn.

- **Gardens**

Vegetable gardens are usually small in area, but can provide an interesting and productive hobby for family members. Locate gardens on the sunny side of the yard to obtain full exposure of afternoon and evening sun. Make sure that a vegetable garden has at least six inches of soil composed of black dirt, sand, and peat moss. The wet compost collected during the year from house waste should be added in the fall after all the vegetables have been picked to add rich nutrients to the soil for the next year's growing season.

Flower gardens are decorative components of landscaping, and add color to the visual streetscape of the house. Color becomes more appealing when similar varieties and colors are united rather than scattered throughout the flower bed. Plant flowers where they can be viewed and enjoyed through a window on the inside as well as from the outside of the house.

When selecting flowers from the local greenhouse for placement adjacent to walkways, terraces, or decks, choose five or six types of hardy perennial plants which flower at different times, and plant them in groups of eight to a dozen. Spring bulbs, like tulips and gladioli, can be added in random groupings between the perennials. Annual plants, such as petunias or snapdragons, will add color to the flower bed until it has developed and matured. Choose flowering plants and shrubs that have a high success and growth rate, and consult your local landscaper, greenhouse, and university or government department of horticulture for suggestions for plants suitable to your specific area.

PART VI: OTHER OPTIONS

CHAPTER 15

♦ PRESERVED WOOD FOUNDATIONS

• Advantages

There seem to be many basement/crawl space construction techniques available to choose from, i.e., concrete, concrete block, Styrofoam, and wood foundation. It will be up to the consumer to determine which method to use for the renovation project depending on personal preference, acceptance of the product, cost, and local building code restrictions. Diversion from the normal method of pouring concrete for the foundation structure will require some in-depth research into the selected alternative method.

Concrete and concrete block are a popular and proven construction method while Styrofoam and wood foundations are used by those contractors requiring an energy-efficient finished product. Styrofoam foundations require concrete to be poured between an outside and inside shell of Styrofoam held together with plastic or metal ties which eliminate the potential for separation when the concrete is forced into the central cavity. Styrofoam being relatively new on the market and expensive is seldom used by home renovators. Treated wood foundations, although not often used, are becoming more popular with home builders because of easier accessibility to the material, high insulating qualities, and increasing acceptance by engineers and many energy-conscious home builders. The abilities of a preserved wood foundation to hold back ground-water, structurally support heavy loads, and work well in conjunction with standard construction materials, such as concrete, drywall, and typical wall insulation products, make it a very attractive product to use for renovations.

A preserved wood foundation is a strong, durable building material that has unique advantages over other foundation systems for the contractors and framers that build them, and the home owners who have them. The energy-saving characteristics of a wood foundation is one of the major reasons for its dramatic rise to popularity in North America. A wood foundation is deemed energy efficient because the entire foundation wall below and above the finished grade is totally insulated at the time of construction. It is its own frost wall, whereas concrete foundations require the addition of a framed and insulated frost wall which adds cost to the construction, and reduces the actual living space in the basement. The exterior treated plywood and wall studs have natural thermal qualities (much higher than concrete) that are increased with the addition of R-20 to R-32 batt insulation between the studs, making the entire perimeter of the foundation an extremely efficient barrier to heat loss. The wood foundation will require less energy to heat or cool the living environment, so fuel costs will drop substantially especially during the cold winter months.

This construction choice has become very popular with the do-it-yourself builder. Easy to construct in all weather conditions, it provides a livable basement environment partly or entirely below grade level. The preserved wood foundation is a construction time saver compared to other foundation types because it goes together quickly in all types of weather, and uses only the framing crew to erect the structure. Wet, muddy, or frozen ground has little effect on the installation process: builders considering wood foundations will enjoy a longer building season without scheduling problems or weather shut-downs. All contractors considering an installation of the wood foundation system might first want to read the manuals provided by the local wood foundation council, and the government building standards branch to eliminate errors in material selection and construction practices. There is really nothing complicated or unusual about the preserved wood foundation system as it is just an innovative engineering adaptation of a proven frame construction technique. Pressure-treated wood has a long history of outstanding performance as a structural support material in residential and commercial structures.

Wood foundations have been used for about 25 years for single-family, and low-rise, multi-family dwellings. They can be built with a conventional concrete footing and floor, or entirely with treated wood (see Figures 15-1 and 15-2). The advantage of a treated-wood floor system is that the wood floor will give on weight bearing the same as the main floor joist system; therefore the special carpet

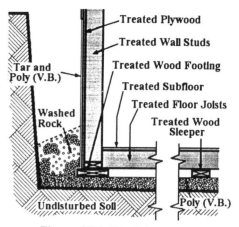

Figure 15-1. Wood foundation with a treated wood floor.

underlay for concrete floors will not be required. In the latter, the wood footing and wood floor on sleepers usually sit on a granular bed of washed rock. All materials used for the construction of wood foundations must

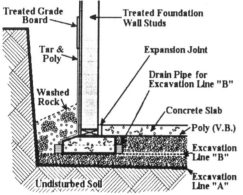

Figure 15-2. A wood foundation with a concrete footing and floor.

be treated under pressure with chemical preservatives to prevent decay. The high level of concentrated wood preservative makes the wood highly resistant to decay and insects that might destroy its structural integrity.

• **Construction Procedures**

The wall structure of the wood foundation must be engineered to carry the vertical loads of the house and roof as well as the horizontal pressures of the backfill material. The engineer, knowing the requested backfill height and the number of stories the structure will support, must determine the size of the supporting studs, thickness of the exterior plywood sheathing, and distance of the stud spacing for the perimeter foundation walls (see Figure 15-3).

The preserved wood foundations are constructed following the same procedure for framing a standard house. The treated wall studs are nailed to a treated top and bottom plate which rests on a concrete or treated wood footing. The exterior wall which will hold back the foundation backfill is made of treated plywood sheathing with a spray tar coating and a polyethylene cover that acts as a dampproofing material for the foundation sitting below the grade level. The space between the treated studs is filled with R-20 to R-32 batt insulation, and the interior walls are finished to provide a full and warm living environment. The method of attaching the wood foundation to the existing concrete is similar to connecting two concrete walls, as discussed earlier in Chapter 12. Holes are drilled into the existing concrete foundation as if to accept dowels, but for the wood foundation the dowels will be replaced by lag bolts. An expansion joint and waterproof strip must also be placed where the wood and concrete foundations meet, and the lag bolts when tightened will

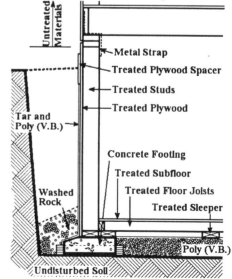

Figure 15-3. A concrete footing with a treated foundation.

compress the membrane to produce a waterproof, airtight seam (see Figure 15-4).

The manufacturer of treated wood materials provides a 30-year guarantee, although the wood material after this process will often have an even greater life expectancy. Pressure-treated wood is environmentally clean and safe. The chemicals used in preserved lumber and plywoods are permanently fixed in the wood fibers, and cannot be leached out even under conditions of extreme moisture. Air quality tests have also been conducted and indicate that the air quality in areas where preserved wood has been used is equal to air enclosed by other foundation systems.

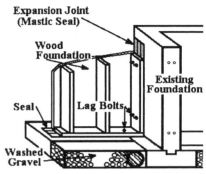

Figure 15-4. A typical wood/concrete foundation connection.

Many requirements for a wood foundation have been set by local building codes. However, depending on the local soil and groundwater conditions, there are advantages to using the standard concrete method. The following list will provide suggestions for the many options available when planning a wood foundation.

	Concrete with Treated Foundation	Treated Wood Foundation
Footing Base	Undisturbed soil	Washed rock 6" deep
Material Extension Beyond Footing	Undisturbed soil	Washed rock extends 24" beyond wood footing
Footing Materials	Typical - 16" x 8" concrete	2" x 8" treated lumber
Footing/Wall Sealant	Mastic gasket or elastomeric caulking	Not required
Structural Pads	Typical - 30" x 30" x 8"	2 layers of typical (5) 2" x 6" treated studs on flat. 2nd layer perpendicular to the first
Basement Floor Material	3-1/2" concrete	2" x 4" treated sleepers on flat with 2" x 4" treated joists + 1/2" treated plywood
Basement Floor Base	Washed rock 8" deep	Washed rock 6" deep
Foundation Wall	2" x 6" or 8" treated studs with 1/2" or 5/8" treated plywood	2" x 6" or 8" treated studs with 1/2" or 5/8" treated plywood
Additional Wall/Joist Supports	Hangers at all foundation openings, and metal strapping at all floor joists	Hangers at all foundation openings, and metal strapping at all floor joists
Waterproof Membrane Below Grade	Two coats spray tar plus 6 mil poly 8" above grade	Two coats spray tar plus 6 mil poly 8" above grade
Sump Pit	Treated wood or plastic	Treated wood or plastic
Wall-to-Footing Fastener Requirements	3-1/2" concrete nail every 48" o.c.	3-1/2" hot dip galvanized nails
Above Grade Fastener Requirements	Metal strapping at floor joists 3-1/2" hot dip galvanized nails and staples	Metal strapping at floor joists 3-1/2" hot dip galvanized nails and staples
Additional Requirements Above Foundation Wall	Typical untreated framing materials	Typical untreated framing materials

APPENDIX

♦ **METRIC CONVERSION CHART**

* Measurements *

Length	Hard Conversion	Soft Conversion	Length	Hard Conversion	Soft Conversion
1/4"	6.0 mm	6.4 mm	10"	250.0 mm	254.0 mm
5/16"	7.0 mm	7.9 mm	12"	300.0 mm	304.8 mm
3/8"	9.5 mm	9.5 mm	1'	300.0 mm	304.8 mm
1/2"	12.0 mm	12.7 mm	2'	600.0 mm	609.6 mm
5/8"	15.5 mm	15.9 mm	4'	1200.0 mm	1219.2 mm
11/16"	16.5 mm	17.5 mm	6'	1800.0 mm	1828.8 mm
3/4"	19.0 mm	19.1 mm	8'	2400.0 mm	2438.4 mm
1"	25.0 mm	25.4 mm	10'	3000.0 mm	3048.0 mm
2"	50.0 mm	50.8 mm	12'	3600.0 mm	3657.6 mm
4"	100.0 mm	101.6 mm	14'	4200.0 mm	4267.2 mm
6"	150.0 mm	152.4 mm	16'	4800.0 mm	4876.8 mm
8"	200.0 mm	203.2 mm	18'	5400.0 mm	5486.4 mm

* Lengths *

1 mm (millimetre)	=	0.3937 inch
1 m (metre)	=	3.28084 feet
1 m (metre)	=	1.09361 yards
1 km (kilometre)	=	0.621371 mile

1 inch	=	25.4 mm
1 foot	=	0.3048 m
1 yard	=	0.9144 m
1 mile	=	1.60934 km

* Area *

1 square centimetre	=	0.155000 sq. inch
1 square metre	=	10.7639 sq. feet
1 square metre	=	1.19599 sq. yards
1 ha (hectare)	=	2.47105 acres

1 square inch	=	6.4516 cm^2 (squared)
1 square foot	=	0.0929030 m^2 (squared)
1 square yard	=	0.836127 m^2 (squared)
1 acre	=	0.414686 ha

* Volume *

1 litre	=	0.219969 gallon
1 gallon	=	4.54609 litres

* Mass *

1 kilogram	=	2.20462 pounds
1 pound	=	0.453592 kilograms

* Insulation *

R-8	=	RSI 1.4	R-28	=	RSI 4.8
R-12	=	RSI 2.1	R-32	=	RSI 5.3
R-20	=	RSI 3.2	R-40	=	RSI 7.0

* Poly Vapor Barrier *

2 mil	=	2/1000 inch
4 mil	=	4/1000 inch
6 mil	=	6/1000 inch

GLOSSARY OF TERMS
****

AGGREGATE: Materials such as sand, rock, and gravel used to make concrete.

AIR-ENTRAINED CONCRETE: Concrete that has air in the form of minute bubbles mechanically mixed into the concrete to provide structural strength and quicker curing.

ANCHOR BOLTS: Bolts embedded in concrete used to hold a structural member in place.

ATTIC OR ROOF SPACE: The space between the top floor ceiling and roof.

BACKFILL: The replacement of earth after excavation.

BALUSTRADE: A railing consisting of a series of balusters resting on a base, usually the treads, which supports a continuous stair or handrail.

BASEBOARD: A molded board placed against a wall around a room next to the floor to conceal the joint between the finished floor and wall finish.

BASEMENT: The base story of a house, usually below grade.

BAY WINDOW: A rectangular, curved, or polygonal window, or group of windows usually supported on a foundation extending beyond the main wall of the building.

BEAM: A principal structural member used between posts, columns, or walls to support vertical loads.

BEARING PARTITION: A partition which supports a vertical load in addition to its own weight.

BEARING WALL: A wall which supports a vertical load in addition to its own weight.

BEVEL: To cut to an angle other than a right angle, such as the edge of a board or door.

BOARD FOOT: The equivalent of a board one foot square and one inch thick.

BRICK CONSTRUCTION: A type of construction in which the exterior walls are bearing walls made of brick.

BRICK MOLDING: A molding for windows and exterior door frames. Serves as the boundary molding for brick or other siding material, and forms a rabbet for the screens, and/or storm sash or combination door.

CABINET: Case or box-like assembly consisting of shelves, doors, and drawers used primarily for storage.

CABINET DRAWER GUIDE: A wood strip used to guide the drawer as it slides in and out of its opening.

CABINET DRAWER KICKER: Wood cabinet member placed immediately above, and generally at the center of a drawer to prevent tilting down when pulled out.

CASEMENT: A window in which the sash swings on its vertical edge, so it may be swung in or out.

CASING: The trimming around a door or window, either outside or inside, or the finished lumber around a post or beam.

CAULK: To seal and make waterproof cracks and joints, especially around window and exterior door frames.

COLUMN: Upright supporting member that is circular, square, or rectangular in shape.

CORNER BEAD: Molding used to protect corners. Also a metal or plastic reinforcement placed on corners before plastering.

COUNTERFLASHING: Flashing on chimneys at the roof-line to cover shingle flashing, and to prevent moisture entry.

DEAD LOAD: The weight of permanent, stationary construction included in a building.

DIMENSION LUMBER: Lumber 2 to 5 inches thick, and up to 12 inches wide.

DOOR FRAME: An assembly of wood or metal parts that form an enclosure and support for a door. Door frames are classified as interior or exterior.

DOOR STOP: A spring stopper screwed to a baseboard face or door frame to prevent the door from swinging through.

DORMER: A projecting structure built out from a sloping roof. Usually includes one or more windows.

DRIP CAP: A molding which directs water away from a structure to prevent seepage under the exterior facing material. Applied mainly over window and exterior door frames.

DRYROT: A term loosely applied to many types of decay, but especially to that which, when in an advanced stage, permits the wood to be easily crushed to a dry powder.

DRYWALL: Premanufactured materials for wall coverings which do not need to be mixed with water before application.

EAVES: The margin or lower part of a roof that projects over an exterior wall. Also called the overhang.

EFFLORESCENCE: Salty residues noted on surface of concrete structures

EXPANSION JOINT: A bituminous fiber strip used to separate units of concrete to prevent cracking due to dimensional change caused by shrinkage and variation in temperature.

FASCIA: A wood member used for the outer face of a box cornice where it is nailed to the ends of rafters and lookouts.

FLASHING: Sheet metal or other material used in roofing and wall construction (especially around chimneys and vents) to prevent rain or other water from entering.

FLOOR AREA: The gross floor area, less the area of the partitions, columns, and stairs and other openings.

FLUE: The space or passage in a chimney through which hot smoke, gas, or fumes rise. Each passage is called a flue, which, with the surrounding material, makes up the chimney.

FOOTING: The spreading course or courses at the base or bottom of a foundation wall or column.

FOUNDATION: The supporting portion of a structure below the first-floor construction, or grade, including the footings, which transfers the weight of the building load to the ground.

FRAMING: The timber structure of a building which gives it shape and strength, including interior and exterior walls, floor, roof and ceilings.

FURRING: Narrow strips of wood spaced to form a nailing base for another surface. Furring is used to level and form an air space between the two surfaces to give a thicker appearance to the base surface.

GABLE: That portion of a wall contained between the slopes of a double-sloped roof, or that portion contained between the slope of a single-sloped roof and a line projected horizontally through the lowest elevation of the roof construction.

GLAZING: The process of installing glass into sash and doors. Also refers to glass panes inserted in types of frames.

GUTTER OR EAVESTROUGH: Wood or metal trough attached to the edge of a roof or eaves to collect and conduct water from rain and melting snow away from the roof.

HEADER: Horizontal structural member that supports the load over an opening, such as a window or door. Also called a lintel.

HEADROOM: The clear space between floor line and ceiling contained in a stairway.

HIP ROOF: A roof which rises from all four sides of a building to meet at the roof peak.

HOSE BIB: A water faucet mounted on a wall that is threaded so a hose connection can be attached.

INSULATION: (Thermal) Any material high in resistance to heat transmission that is placed in structures to reduce the rate of heat loss.

JACK RAFTER: A short rafter framing between the wall plate and a hip rafter, or a hip or valley rafter and ridge board.

JAMB: The top and two sides of a door or window frame which contact the door or sash; top jamb and side jambs.

JOINT CEMENT: A powder mixed with water and applied to the joints between sheets of gypsum wallboard or drywall.

JOIST: One of a series of parallel framing members used to support floor and ceiling loads, and supported in turn by other beams, girders, or bearing walls.

JOIST HANGER: A steel section shaped like a saddle and bent so it can be fastened to a beam or structural member to provide end support for joists, headers, trusses, etc.

KILN DRIED: Wood seasoned by artificial heat in a mechanical kiln, with controlled humidity and air circulation.

LEADER OR DOWNSPOUT: A vertical pipe that carries rainwater from the gutter to the ground or drain.

LINEAL FOOT: Having length only. Pertaining to a line one-foot long, as distinguished from a square foot or cubic foot.

LINTEL: A horizontal structural member supporting the load over an opening such as a door or window.

LIVE LOAD: The total of all moving and variable loads that may be placed on a structure of a building.

LOOKOUT: Structural member running between the lower end of a rafter and the outside wall. Used on the underside of the roof sheathing at the overhang to support the soffit and fascia.

MASONRY: Stone, brick, hollow tile, concrete block, tile, and sometimes poured concrete, gypsum blocks, or other similar materials, or a combination of same, bonded together with mortar to form a wall, ledge, buttress, etc.

MECHANICAL EQUIPMENT: In architectural and engineering practice, this refers to all equipment under the general heading of plumbing, heating, air conditioning, gasfitting, and electrical work.

MESH: Expanded metal or woven wire used as a reinforcement for concrete, plaster, or stucco.

MOISTURE CONTENT: The amount of water contained in wood. Expressed as a percentage weight of even dry wood.

MOLDING: A relatively narrow strip of wood usually shaped to a curved profile throughout its length. Used to accent and emphasize the ornamentation of a structure and to conceal surface or angle joints.

MORTAR: A substance produced from prescribed proportions of cementing agents, aggregates, and water which gradually sets hard after mixing.

NONBEARING PARTITION: A partition extending from floor to ceiling supporting no load other than its own weight.

NOSING: The part of a stair tread which projects over the riser, or any similar projection. A term applied to the rounded edge of a board.

PARGING: A thin coat of plaster applied to stone, concrete, or brick to form a smooth or decorative surface.

PARTITION: A wall that subdivides space within any story of a building.

PARTY WALL: A wall used jointly by two parties under easement agreement, and erected at or upon a line separating two parcels of land that may be held under different ownership.

PILE: A heavy timber, or pillar of metal or concrete forced into the earth or cast in place to form a structural foundation member.

PITCH: Different variations of inclines or slopes, as of roofs or stairs. Rise divided by the span.

PITCHED ROOF: A roof with one or more angled surfaces sloping at an angle greater than that required for drainage.

PLAN: A drawing representing any one of the floors or horizontal cross sections of a building, or the horizontal plane of any other object or area.

PLASTER: A mixture of lime, cement, and sand used to cover outside and inside wall surfaces.

PLUMB: Exactly perpendicular or vertical; at right angles to the horizon or floor.

PLUMBING STACK: A general term for the vertical main of a system of soil, waste, or vent piping.

PRESERVATIVE: Substance that will prevent the development and action of wood-destroying fungi, borers of various kinds, and other harmful insects that deteriorate wood.

RABBET: A rectangular shape consisting of two surfaces cut along the edge or end of a board.

RADIANT HEATING: A method of heating usually consisting of coils, pipes, or electric heating elements placed in the floor, wall, or ceiling.

RAFTER: One of a series of structural members of a roof designed to support roof loads. The rafters of a flat roof are sometimes called roof joists.

RAIL: Cross or horizontal members of the framework of a sash, door, blind, or other assembly.

RELATIVE HUMIDITY: Ratio of amount of water vapor in air in terms of percentage to the total amount it could hold at the same temperature.

RESILIENT: The ability of a material to withstand temporary deformation with the original shape being assumed when the stresses are removed.

RETAINING WALL: Any wall subjected to lateral pressure other than wind pressure, e.g., a wall built to support a bank of earth.

RISER: The vertical stair member between two consecutive stair treads.

ROOFING: The materials applied to the structural parts of a roof to make it waterproof.

ROOF RIDGE: The horizontal line at the junction of the top edges of two roof surfaces where an external angle greater than 180 degrees is formed.

ROUGH-IN: The work of installing all pipes in the drainage system and all water pipes to the point where connections will be made with the plumbing fixtures. Also applies to partially completed electrical wiring, and other mechanical aspects of the structure.

ROUGH LUMBER: Lumber cut to rough size with saws, but which has not been dressed or surfaced.

ROUGH OPENING: The opening formed by the framing members.

SADDLE: A small gable-type roof placed on back of a chimney on a sloped roof to shed water or debris.

SASH: The framework which holds the glass in the window.

SCAFFOLD: A temporary structure and platform to support workers and materials during construction.

SEALER: A liquid applied directly over unfinished wood or concrete surfaces for the purpose of sealing the surface to prevent penetration of water or other chemicals.

SHAKES: Hand or machine-split shingles made of wood.

SHEATHING: The structural covering that consists of boards or prefabricated panels that are attached to the exterior studding or rafters of a structure.

SHEATHING PAPER: A building material used in wall, floor, and roof construction to resist air passage.

SHIM: A thin strip of wood, sometimes wedge-shaped, for plumbing or leveling wood members. Especially helpful when setting door and window frames.

SIDING: The finish cover of the outside wall of a frame building. Many different types are available.

SILL: The lowest member of the frame of a structure, usually horizontal, resting on the foundation and supporting the uprights of the frame. Also the lowest member of a window or outside door frame.

SMOKE ALARM: An electric device which sounds an alarm when sensing the presence of smoke or air carrying combustible products relating to fire.

SOFFIT: The underside of the members of a building, such as staircases, overhangs, cornices, beams, and arches. Also called drop ceiling and furred-down ceiling.

SOIL STACK: A general term for the vertical main of a system of soil, waste, or vent piping.

SOLAR ORIENTATION: Directional placement of a structure on a building site to obtain the maximum sunlight.

SPAN: The distance between structural supports such as walls, columns, piers, beams, girders, and trusses.

SPECIFICATION: A written document stipulating the kind, quality, and sometimes the quantity of materials and workmanship required for a construction job.

SQUARE: Unit of measure - - '100 square feet' - - applied to roofing material and some types of siding.

STAIR LANDING: A platform between two flights of stairs.

STAIRWAY, STAIR, OR STAIRS: A series of steps, with or without landings or platforms, usually between two or more floors of a building.

STAIRWELL: The framed opening which receives the stairs.

STEP FLASHING: Rectangular or square pieces of flashing used at the junction of shingled roof and walls. Also called shingle flashing.

STOOP: A small porch, veranda, platform, or stairway outside an entrance to a building.

STORM DOOR: An extra outside door for protection against inclement weather.

STORY: That part of a building compressed between any floor, and the floor or roof next above.

STUD: One of a series of vertical wood or metal structural members in walls and partitions.

SUBFLOOR: Boards or panels laid directly on the floor joists over which a finished floor will be laid.

TAPING: In gypsum board or drywall construction, the masking of joints between two sheets by means of paper tape which is smoothed over with joint cement.

TELEPOST: A metal, upright, vertically adjustable, supporting member, circular in shape, attached to a structural beam, and used to level floor joists to a horizontal position.

THERMOSTAT: An instrument that controls automatically the operation of heating or cooling devices by responding to changes in temperature.

THREE-WAY SWITCH: A switch designed to operate in conjunction with a similar switch, thereby controlling one outlet from two points.

THRESHOLD: A wood, plastic, or metal member that is beveled or tapered on each side, and used to close the space between the bottom of the door, and the sill or floor underneath. Sometimes called a saddle.

TOE KICK: A recessed space at the floor line of a base kitchen cabinet or other built-in units. Permits one to stand close without striking the vertical surface with the toe.

TOE NAILING: To drive a nail at a slant with the initial surface in order to permit it to penetrate into a second member.

TONGUE-AND-GROOVE LUMBER: Any lumber, such as boards or planks, machined in such a manner that there is a groove on one edge and a corresponding tongue on the other.

TOP PLATE: In construction, the horizontal member nailed to the top of the partition or wall studs.

TREAD: The horizontal part of a step onto which a foot is placed.

TRIM: The finish materials in a building, such as moldings applied around openings (window trim, door trim) or at the floor and ceiling levels of rooms (baseboard, cornice, picture molding).

TRUSS: A structural unit consisting beams, bars, and tie members usually arranged to form triangles. Provides rigid support over wide spans with a minimum amount of material.

VALLEY: The internal angle formed by the two slopes of a roof.

VALLEY RAFTER: A rafter which forms the intersection of an internal roof angle.

VAPOR BARRIER: A watertight material used to prevent the passage of moisture or water vapor into or through structural elements (floors, walls, ceilings).

VENEERED WALL: A wall with a masonry face, e.g., single brick. Veneered walls are nonload bearing.

VENT: A pipe installed to provide a flow of air to or from a drainage system, or a circulation of air within such a system to protect trap seals from siphonage and back pressure.

VENTILATION: The process of supplying and removing air by natural or mechanical means. Such air may or may not have been conditioned.

WALL PLATES: In wood frame construction, the horizontal members attached to the ends of studs. Also called top or bottom plates depending on their location.

WARP: Any variation from a true or plane surface. Warp includes bow, crook, cup, and twist, or any combination thereof.

WATER TABLE: A ledge or slight projection in the earth's structure which carries the water away or to a given point; the level below which the ground is saturated with water.

WEATHERING: The mechanical or chemical disintegration and discoloration of the surface due to the action of dust and sand carried by winds, and the alternate shrinking and swelling of the surface fibers caused by the continual variation in moisture content brought about by changes in weather. Weathering does not include decay.

WEATHERSTRIPPING: Strips of felt, rubber, metal, or other materials fixed along the edges of doors or windows to keep out drafts and reduce heat loss.

WEEPHOLE: A small hole, as in a retaining wall, to drain water to the outside. Commonly used at lower edges of masonry cavity walls.